LOOKING HOMEWARD
My Years On The Farm

Dennis Morgan

WESTBOW
PRESS®
A DIVISION OF THOMAS NELSON
& ZONDERVAN

WestBow Press books may be ordered through booksellers or by contacting:

WestBow Press
A Division of Thomas Nelson & Zondervan
1663 Liberty Drive
Bloomington, IN 47403
www.westbowpress.com
1 (866) 928-1240

Scripture quotations are from the ESV® Bible (The Holy Bible, English Standard Version®), copyright © 2001 by Crossway, a publishing ministry of Good News Publishers. Used by permission. All rights reserved.

ISBN: 978-1-9736-8815-0 (sc)
ISBN: 978-1-9736-8816-7 (e)

Library of Congress Control Number: 2020904458

Print information available on the last page.

WestBow Press rev. date: 6/20/2020

DEDICATION

◇◇◇◇◇◇◇◇◇◇◇◇◇◇◇◇◇◇◇◇◇◇◇◇◇

This book is for my family—immediate and extended. It is my hope that these pages have captured some essence of the past that will provide a deeper understanding and appreciation of the present and testify to our faith in an eternal future.

In a narrow sense it is a love letter—from the family of my past—the people who directly touched me: relatives, neighbors, brothers and sisters, grandparents, and especially Daddy and Mommy—to my present family and our posterity. Amid the complications and complexities of living, God sustains us through the love and care of family.

ACKNOWLEDGMENT

A debt of gratitude is owed my family for their help in creating this book. Tacitly or directly, parents, brothers and sisters, children and grandchildren have contributed. A few deserve special mention: my son Tim whose enthusiasm, loyalty, and love deserve more than a citation, conceived the idea; my brother Keith whose technical knowledge and graphic design assistance were requisite; my sister Susie whose recall corroborated events and substantiated portraits of life on the farm; my daughter Samantha whose love of language supplied artistic and aesthetic color, and whose critical and editing skills stood apart in her understanding, appreciation, and encouragement of this project; and my wife Suzie who willingly read and reread materials, argued for proper syntax, endured my impatience, waved the red flag when I was about to run aground, and lent expertise she gained from her own publications. Finally, it is my prayer that this book will testify to the role that Jesus Christ played in my life on the farm, and thus, it is in worship that I extend to Him the greatest acknowledgment.

Placing the chapters of this book into a coherent and meaningful order has been difficult. A chronological arrangement seemed obvious at the beginning, but several chapters are wrapped around two or three others, and a few chapters took place during events within chapters. As a result I have arbitrarily positioned them so that repetition is minimal, and events and circumstances clarify each other. "The Farm" was intended to be the first chapter, because the farm is cardinal in forming and understanding the ethos of my life. However, on an autumn night in 2015, as I listened to the recollections of my dying brother Joe at his home in West Virginia, it became plain that the farm meant as much to him as it did me. I then decided, as a kind of tribute, to write something of that night and include it in the book. Thus, the first two chapters are for Joe.

TABLE OF CONTENTS

INTRODUCTION
<><><><><><><><><><><><><><><><><><><><><><><><>

The past is never dead. It's not even past.

Requiem For a Nun
WILLIAM FAULKNER

*O*n Christmas day, 2006, my oldest son, Tim, had my name for our family gift exchange, and included with his present was a small booklet entitled "Grandfather's Memories." He asked if I would answer the questions in the book so that his daughters might have a brief biography of their grandfather. I was pleased to comply.

Sometime afterward I began answering: "Where were you born?" "Who were your parents?" "What is your earliest memory?" Etc. The more questions I answered, the more conscious I became of superficiality and cliché. Motivated by a desire to present material that was more thoughtful and comprehensive, and wishing to demonstrate my love for my family, I decided to provide greater depth and a more complete account of my life. This evolved into the essays, poems, and observations found in these pages.

*T*his book is memory. As such it is subject to the failings and impairments of recollection. Further, the chapters were written independent of each other, over a period of years, which resulted in a degree of repetition. Wishing to avoid error I have cross-referenced and corroborated timelines and events when possible, but I accept the reality that objectivity operates within the limitations of personal knowledge and private emotion. Thus, the portraits painted on these pages were brushed with an imperfect hand. The considerable skills of my editors have removed most of the miscolorations, but remaining blemishes are mine.

The perspective is essentially that of a grandfather writing to grandchildren who are sufficiently mature and able to appreciate and understand the circumstances of living and the consequences of behavior. The title "Looking Homeward" suggests a backward look to the people, places, and events that shaped my life, but it also connotes that which lies ahead and fills me with excitement and the hope of a glorious future. Jesus stated

> *"Let not your hearts be troubled. Believe in God; believe also in me. In my Father's house are many rooms. If it were not so, would I have told you that I go to prepare a place for you? And if I go and prepare a place for you, I will come again and will take you to myself, that where I am you may be also." John 14:1-3. (ESV)*

It occurred to me at the inception of this project that knowing a grandfather and knowing about a grandfather are distinctly different epistemologies, and that while the latter contributes richly to understanding and appreciation, it is secondary to an actual relationship. Knowing about an historic figure narrows the distance between two lives, but it never coalesces into a personal relationship. As Paul stated in 1 Corinthians 2:11, a relationship requires a willingness to reveal thoughts and feelings. For this reason I have tried to share with the reader, not only the people, places, and events that shaped me, but the thoughts and feelings that gave substance to my soul.

> *"No one can know a person's thoughts except that person's own spirit, ..."1 Corinthians 2:11. (ESV)*

My paternal grandfather died of tuberculosis in January 1937, nearly five years before my birth. I wish I could have known him. His family, most of whom later became an integral part of my life, spoke endearingly of him as a husband, father, and friend. He was, by all accounts, hard-working, honest, reliable. His untimely death created a void in the lives of his wife and children that was never filled.

William Cloyd Morgan
My paternal grandfather

My Aunt Mary kept in her possession several

letters that he wrote to his mother during his final days in the Cresson (PA) Sanatorium for tuberculosis. They reveal a spirit deeply sensitive to the circumstances of not only his own life, but to those of his loved ones as well. In the face of his tragedy, there is a philosophical bent to his view of life as he grappled with approaching death.

The introspective mind that penned those letters passed to his children and grandchildren a curiosity to inquire into the nature of things. I am indebted.

My maternal grandfather died in the winter of my fourteenth year. I have wonderful memories of him and am grateful for his imprint on my life. I was his first grand-child and was able to know him in ways denied most grandchildren—he and I lived in the same house for my first nine years. Afterward, when he moved into his retirement home a half mile down the road, I still saw him daily.

Charles L. "Pappy" Arnold
My maternal grandfather

He frequently took me with him—to the fields, to the barn, to the store. We were comfortable with each other. He loved to buy a stick of candy or a piece of gum for me, and in his latter years habitually coaxed me to "come down to the house." After telephone service was installed in 1956, he called so regularly in the evenings that whenever the phone rang, Mommy would say, "I'll bet Pappy wants some company."

At the end of a work day, he took delight in letting my brother Keith and me sit atop his Belgian work horses while he walked alongside from the fields back to the barn. Hundreds of times as a preschooler, I sat between his legs as he helped me steer one of our tractors to an outlying field and back. Being with Pappy was fun—unless he had serious work to do. He did not like distraction when there was exigency. Never a firm disciplinarian he would instead plead, "Now look, I'm busy. You have to play over there."

As a small child I sat on his lap while he rocked back and forth in his creaking rocking chair, positioned beside the wood-burning stove with the smell of burning chestnut, oak, or locust permeating the kitchen. Removing the heavy brogans which had that day trod miles of plowed ground or tramped untold acres where he had shocked wheat, he pushed them to the side, unhooked the straps of his bibbed overalls, lay back his head, and rocked methodically while contemplating the following workday.

The center of his attention was farm work. He took time for his grandchildren, but his focus was nearly always on cows and crops. Despite fatigue and the approaching toil of another work day, however, he never complained when we interrupted. In fact, he usually anticipated the interruptions by stuffing candy into one of his bib pockets inviting us to climb and search.

If he had a weakness it may have been his tendency to withdraw from confrontation, resulting in a failure to resolve disputes. During those times he retreated, not into submission but toward isolation. He seemed to believe that arguments and altercations dissolved if left alone.

His kindness was genuine but reserved. He was incapable of cruelty—either to people or animals but cautious in his display of affection. He did not caress or hug, but evidenced his love by rocking babies, carrying toddlers atop his shoulders, and permitting schoolboys to work beside him. He was my notion of the ideal grandfather.

I was born on September 22, 1942, at the Malta Home in Granville Township, Mifflin County, in the state of Pennsylvania, ten months after the bombing of Pearl Harbor and the nearly simultaneous US declaration of war against both Japan and Germany.[1] During my

---

1. The Malta Home was a one hundred thirty-one-acre project intended to be a self-sufficient care provider for the indigent and orphans, as well as for the old and enfeebled members of the Knights of the Order of Malta, an international organization whose roots can be traced to the 19th century Roman Catholic Church. Built around 1920, it included a farm and farmhouse. My step-grandfather, Irvin Philip Shawver, accepted a job as the resident farmer for the project about 1940. He married my widowed grandmother shortly thereafter and moved his new family into the farmhouse (six of Grandma's eight children were still living at home: Bill, Helen, Lolly, Mary, Dick, and Don). When my mother learned two years later that she was pregnant, Grandma introduced her to Dr. Brown, a Lewistown physician who had delivered some of Grandma's babies. It was decided that when it was time for my birth Mommy would come to the Malta Home where Grandma could act as midwife, and Dr. Brown would be nearby should he be needed. In his mid-sixties at the time and needing a less arduous job, my step-grandfather resigned that same winter to take a position as janitor at the Montgomery-Ward Department Store in Lewistown, resulting

Top: The Malta Home farmhouse.

Bottom: Standing in front of the farmhouse, front to back, L to R: Irv, Grandma holding me, Aunt Helen, Uncle Don, Aunt Mary, Uncle Dick, and Daddy.

earliest years, I saw uncles in uniform, wondered at my grandmother's tears as she read letters from the front, and heard table talk about faraway places. My consciousness, however, was that of a little boy growing up on a decidedly rural dairy farm in a remote sector of Decatur Township secluded from the reality of battlefields. My awareness of international events was limited to the staccato CBS news reports I heard on the radio each school day morning in Joe McKinley's General Store as my brother Keith and I awaited the school bus. In the ensuing years there were occasional suppertime comments about a relative or neighbor's war experiences in the Philippines or France, but my parents' and grandparents' greater interests remained parochial throughout my boyhood, and my personal concerns seldom extended beyond baseball. The young boy in the pages that follow was innocent, much like John Greenleaf Whittier's "barefoot boy with cheeks of tan."[2] Unlike that boy, however, I was introverted and introspective, characteristics that became more pronounced in my adolescent years and are evidenced within the recollections on these pages.

The great influence in my early life, my closest friend, the bastion to which I clung during the storms, was my mother. She was a safe, inviting harbor, never distant or preoccupied with self-interests. She wore her heart on her sleeve, was wholly devoid of affectation, and was incapable of camouflage.

Her impulse was irenic, conciliatory, many times submissive. This appeasing nature was often a weakness, since she craved reconcilia-

in another family move to the corner of Chestnut Street and Shaw Avenue in Lewistown.

2. See page 7.

tion at the cost of resolution. She fell wounded when pricked by the slightest thorns. She was incapable of vengeance or vindication but acquiesced *mea culpa*. Her reprimands and castigations were always conjoined with welcoming arms and a loving spirit. Simply, her door was always open. I never heard her voice raised either in joy or anger. She was reliable, warm, ever accessible, treating everyone as her superior.

Working tirelessly to provide for her family, she recognized the priority of spiritual needs. She read her Bible daily, making notations that reminded and advised. She knelt in morning prayer beseeching God for her children's salvation and protection. While she was not divine, she was a person of unusual virtue. Not perfect, nevertheless, a paragon. As a result she was admired throughout our community.

It is the ghost of my father, however, that hovers throughout the following pages. He was intelligent, ingenious, straightforward, honest. He cared about his family, his reputation, his theology. He loved learning, was a hard worker, and appreciated aesthetic and pragmatic beauty. He was a good man and a father for whom and to whom I am deeply grateful.

Despite these attributes, Daddy was often locked into his own world, with his own interests, his personal intrigues, and his private yearnings. He seldom was able to engage others within the framework of their affections and concerns, not that he disapproved of or impugned their worlds, but that he was unaware such worlds existed. He was not unkind, but his temper distanced loved ones and gave his relationships a precarious balance. He and I were not close in the way a boy hopes to be close to his father.

Curiously, in spite of his self-absorption, and at times, my self-pity, despite the wounds inflicted and suffered, he was the person I most wanted to please. I craved his attention and approval. Much of my disappointment, no doubt, resulted from my own immaturity, self-centeredness, and withdrawal, but regardless, even now there are

My relationship with Daddy was strained.

moments when I wish for his approbation, his encouragement, his delight.

I understand that just as I am a product of circumstance and choice, so Daddy faced life with extrinsic influences and unsolicited dispositions. His passions were familiar to most men. I could have been more understanding, less critical, more appreciative.

It must be acknowledged that he loved his family. I witnessed first-hand the long arduous days he worked without complaint for our welfare. I can vouch for the sacrifices he made and the discomforts he endured for our benefit, and I was there during the times he took extra work upon himself so that his children could experience conditions more comfortable than his own had been.

I will see him again. Daddy accepted Jesus as his Savior during my earliest years. He was faithful in his study of the Scriptures, in his worship, and in his willingness to share the Gospel. It is true that he made mistakes, behaved badly at times, and needed repentance. My own failures preclude criticism of him. God forgave Daddy and saved him in the same way He forgave and saved me. I praise God that he was my father, and I look forward to our day of reunion when the distance between us will be erased and both of us will experience and demonstrate our Heavenly Father's perfect love.

Thus, I write this book as a grandfather, a father, a son, a grandson, and a brother. Most important, I write for you—for you personally ... for you as an individual ... . I have thought much concerning you. You have made my life immeasurably sweeter. Whether you are a son, a daughter, a grandson, a granddaughter, a brother, a sister ... you have consumed my consciousness much more than you can know ... It is true that the reciprocity of love never seems equal, but it is my hope that my love for you can be found within these pages ... in the revelation of shared truths, exposed feelings, and admitted frailties. It is an unspeakable joy to look backward and be filled with gratitude ... to God, and to each of you ... for making my time here so special.

The Barefoot Boy
JOHN GREENLEAF WHITTIER

Blessings on thee, little man,
Barefoot boy, with cheek of tan!
With thy turned-up pantaloons,
And thy merry whistled tunes;
With thy red lip, redder still
Kissed by strawberries on the hill;
With the sunshine on thy face,
Through thy torn brim's jaunty grace;
From my heart I give thee joy, —
I was once a barefoot boy!
Prince thou art, —the grown-up man
Only is republican.
Let the million-dollared ride!
Barefoot, trudging at his side,
Thou hast more than he can buy
In the reach of ear and eye, —
Outward sunshine, inward joy:
Blessings on thee, barefoot boy![3]

---

3. There are additional stanzas to the poem.

JOE'S LAST REQUEST[1]

Joseph Edward Morgan

November 1, 1956 – October 6, 2015

Never let your brotherly love fail, nor refuse to extend your hospitality to strangers—sometimes men have entertained angels unawares. (Hebrews 13:2)

---

1. In mid-January 2015 Joe was diagnosed with brain cancer (Glioblastoma). Through several operations, radiation treatments, and various therapies, he never lost his sense of humor, burdened friends and family with his crisis, or felt sorry for himself. He found comfort, even joy, in his relationship with Christ, and was assured of eternal life. He did, however, experience concern for the physical well-being of his wife Cathy, and for the spiritual welfare of his loved ones. The nine months that stretched from January to his death in October were difficult for those of us who loved him; not just because he was suffering, but because we were losing the quintessential father, husband, brother, and friend.

After great pain, a formal feeling comes –
The Nerves sit ceremonious, like Tombs –
The stiff Heart questions 'was it He, that bore,'
And 'Yesterday, or Centuries before'?

The Feet, mechanical, go round –
A Wooden way
Of Ground, or Air, or Ought –
Regardless grown,
A Quartz contentment, like a stone –

This is the Hour of Lead –
Remembered, if outlived,
As Freezing persons, recollect the Snow –
First – Chill – then Stupor – then the letting go –

EMILY DICKINSON

PART ONE

Several nights before his death, my brother Joe and I sat in the darkness on the deck of his home in Charleston, West Virginia, enjoying the closing of a grand fall day. My sister Susie and her husband Ray had visited a few days earlier and brought with them some of Joe's favorite foods: pon haus, smoked ham, smoked sausage, dried beef, minced meat pies, Middleswarth potato chips, and Tastykakes.[2] Though I had made fried chicken for our evening meal, he was anxious for some of his favorites and requested that I make smoked ham gravy on toast for his supper. The few extra minutes that it took to prepare the food were well worth my time, because he really enjoyed it, even asking for an additional slice of bread to wipe the last bits of gravy from his plate. His wife Cathy and I

2. Pon Haus (scrapple) is a mush that is sliced, fried, and served with various toppings. My grandfather's (Pappy) recipe combined head meat, liver, cracklins (seasoned and fried pork skins), salt and pepper, corn meal, buckwheat and wheat flours, and pork broth. Tastykakes are a brand name of pies and cakes made in a Philadelphia bakery bearing the same name.

ate the chicken, and, after eating, she went inside, leaving Joe and I alone. He fell asleep in his favorite zero-gravity chair, a rolled-up pillow propping his head, resting under a heavy blanket against the October chill. In spite of the darkness, the screen of my laptop supplied ample light for me to occupy the interlude with research for my upcoming annual baseball trivia night. I enjoyed the diversion.

Joe fell asleep in his favorite chair.

Forty-five uninterrupted minutes passed. The tops of trees were black-silhouetted against an unclouded sky. In spite of ambient noises, the night was still. In the distance the sounds of retiring neighbors surged and faded while traffic on the road below the house was reduced to the day's final commuters arriving home. The drone of a large truck could be heard in the background, its empty bed clanging and rattling as it spiraled down the hilly mountain terrain, the driver gearing down until the sounds faded into the beyond. Night had descended before Joe stirred.

"How'er you feeling?" I asked quietly.

"Sleepy." He rejoined.

"You warm enough?"

He did not answer immediately. I had become accustomed to the lengthy suspensions of his conversation. In the beginning of his illness I repeated myself, but repetition elicited no response. Minutes would pass when, with no sense of interval, he would continue as though he had been struggling to process his response.

"Tell Cath I need the other blanket."

I arose, walked to the front of the enclosed porch, opened the screened door and lifted the blanket that Cathy kept folded for him, returned and draped it over his legs and torso.

"Do you want me to read to you?"

On several previous evenings, before helping him from the deck chair to his bedroom, he had listened to my written recollections of our common past on the farm where we had spent our formative years. It had sparked conversation and given him opportunity to wander back over the crucibles of his life: being the youngest child, struggling for identity during his teens, distressing over the barbs and tantrums of an unyielding and temperamental father. These recalls lasted but a few moments; each time he grew tired and asked to be returned to his bedroom.

The vitality that once marked his personality was gone. His face had become distorted from months of radiation and steroids. Sometimes I stared, incredulous that the once vibrant body was reduced to a torpid frame, ponderous, the muscles of his legs atrophied, skin shrunken against bone. When I changed his socks or bathed him, his thighs and calves evidenced huge black and blue discolorations. Further complicating his condition, he had fallen several times, leaving hematomas that encased his thighs, ribs, and portions of his arms. His body had become a stranger, struggling against time.

Ten minutes passed. When he spoke, I realized that his mind had wandered far from immediacy.

"I would like you to speak at the funeral." His tone was matter-of-fact, determined, his words measured and slowed by the disease that was fouling the circuitry of consciousness.

Raw emotion flooded over me as I choked back tears. The two of us were frozen in dumb abeyance.

"You were only four years old when I left for college." I paused, unable to talk. Looking away, I wiped my eyes with the back of my hand. "I can't tell you how hard it was to leave you and Dave."

He did not answer.

I had poured a tumbler of soda and placed it on the stand next to his chair. Without speaking he pointed to the tumbler. I arose and picked it up. Holding it so that he could drink through the straw resting in the cup, he took two long draughts.

"Cover my feet," he requested.

He already lay under two heavy blankets, but his body was calling on reserves in the wake of constant trauma. He was continually cold. Pulling the top blanket down over his stockinged feet I spoke into the night, abstracted, far away, lost in memory and time, aloud, but not conversing, "Whenever Mommy and Daddy went anywhere, I stayed home with you guys."

The silence became awkward. Amid undisturbed intervals, cold October winds rustled the trees below the slope that ran down behind the house. The specter of death hovered in the darkness.

Then abruptly, tearful, with perfect lucidity, not looking at me, as though a confession, "It was a big thing when you came home." An admission, private, uncomfortable, as though a burden. "You and Bill and Keith were my heroes. I wanted to be like you."

Dumb, I turned toward him, his form barely visible in the darkness. Then, a further revelation, confidential, "I thought April and Linda and Ann were the most beautiful girls in the world. They always talked to Dave and me and made us feel important." The young wives of his older brothers had doted on him, their attention and affection indelible in his memory.

Minutes passed. It was time to move him back inside the house, but the moment was inviolate. I waited.

"I'm really glad Dave came," he whispered.

Earlier in the week Dave and his wife Kathy had driven from their home in Lynchburg, Virginia. Joe had looked forward to their visit. He and Dave had grown up together, inseparable, Joe idolizing his big brother, though mutual introversion precluded overt expression. And then, eroded by quotidian circumstance, the relationship suffered protracted estrangement as each enrolled in college programs: Dave at the York campus of Penn State University, and a year later, Joe at East Stroudsburg University. Daily communication dissolved. A final breach was imposed a year later when Dave decided to attend Bible school in Virginia and Joe left East Stroudsburg to pursue a degree in physics at the University of Iowa. In the intervening years, they married, started families, and began careers: for both, a palpable void lingered.

As the circumstances of distance and time sequestered each from the other, doubts and sometimes misunderstandings of the other's desire to maintain a relationship encroached. Superventions moved each in their wake, though always in the recesses of his psyche, Joe felt the need for restoration. Dave offered something singular, apart from other brothers and sisters, apart from friends and new-found familiarity, something embedded in the soul, something vital that tied the past to the present and gave meaning to both. Reunion, however, had waited for an imperative, and now it had come on the wings of death. Dave had come to Charleston.

I knew they had been close. I had often listened to Joe's reminiscences of their days on the farm: the time Dave saved him from the ravages of the silo filler after his foot had caught in its conveyor chain and dragged him toward the great whirling knives; the occasion when Dave, broken by the

Dave and Joe grew up together.

abuse of a father's cruel criticism, walked away from home, leaving Joe to face the consequence of Daddy's temper; and always, the admiration he had for an older, stronger, more learned brother.

Finding his voice amid private nostalgia, he took long pauses to gather his thoughts, "When I started first grade at Decatur, ... there was a kid who picked on me. ... Alan Simonetti. ... He was bigger than me. ... A loud-mouth, ... I was afraid of him."

I heard Cathy moving inside the house, making a cup of tea while she waited to assist me in putting him to bed.

"His family lived up on the Old Stage Road... down from Sam Arnold," he continued. "He was crude. ... His older brothers were the same

Both were unassuming with a wonderful sense of humor.

way. ...The yard in front of their house always ... had a lot of garbage in it. ... They all cursed ... weren't too bright. ... Anyway, ... I was afraid of him. ... When we were at recess ... he ... sometimes pushed me or threw things at me."

He fell silent and it was obvious he was reliving the incident—one of those times rather ancillary to our youth that becomes swollen by memory and circumstance so that in retrospect it seems salient—a moment of high anxiety when ordinary behavior is transformed by memory into heroism. His mind had wandered to that time long ago. His description of Dave's intervention took on a tone of reverence. "One day ... Dave saw him wrestle me to the ground. ... Dave was only a second grader, ... but one of the biggest second graders, ... he came over and told Alan ... to leave me alone. ... Dave told him ... never to touch me again."

A prolonged pause suggested he was again falling asleep. As I leaned close to inspect, he reflected, "Alan never bothered me from that time on, ... so I always looked up to Dave. ... Even though we were just kids, ... as we grew up, ... I always asked him for advice."

His revelation was spent. He was fatigued and motioned toward the tumbler. I noiselessly got to my feet, now absorbed with my own past. Holding the container in position for him to drink, I ached to have him understand the depth of my affection for him, both when he was a boy and now that he was dying. I half-whispered, "I felt as though I was leaving you....and the farm.... behind .... abandoning everyone."

He raised his head on the pillow and pulled his blankets close. His eyes were open and in the light from the computer screen, I could see he was waiting for me to finish.

"It was especially hard to leave you and Dave," my voice was hushed, reflective. "I knew the two of you were forming a world apart from me, growing up in a place different than the farm I had known."

"Did you guys have a lot more cows then?" He had missed my intent.

"When Pappy sold half of the herd and some of the machinery in March of 1950 we had to rotate them into the barn for milking, and there were a couple tied up in one of the calf pens. I think we were milking a herd of about thirty with one or two standing dry."

He lay silent in the darkness. I could not discern if he was falling asleep or thinking about our conversation.

"That wasn't the difference I was referring to," I redirected. I paused, attempting to harmonize the discords of the past. "I was thinking about Daddy and Mommy . . . There were a lot of . . . changes . . . during the years I was home. After Pappy and Mammie moved away, it felt as though . . . we were on our own . . . kind of insecure. Daddy and Mommy were there . . . every hour, every day . . . but they had a strained relationship ... we didn't do things as a family ... there was continual talk of selling the farm ... part of the tension was financial ... part was the unending routine of the farm ... the pressures on Daddy choked any sense of . . . gratification . . . or joy in farm work ... after a while his only goal was to get things done ... to be finished and over with. He no longer looked forward to the next crop ... the next horizon ... never entertained notions of something larger . . . or grander ... he was boxed in ...."

Neither of us spoke, but I knew he had been listening, for he lifted one arm outside the blanket and pushed away a portion that had covered a bit of his face.

"I think Mommy actually loved it," I conjectured, "The work ... the continual cycles of old beginnings . . . and new endings. The farm and the work were her *raison d'etre*." Anyway, by the time I left, I felt Daddy had been defeated by life . . . that he had given up as a farmer . . . his chance for adventure had passed. I had a sense that . . . he had no energy for you or Dave."

It was true that the farm was not as vigorous after Daddy went to work at the Hallmark Cabinet Factory in McClure. For Dave and Joe, the farm became a province where the governor was gone most of the day. There was more freedom, but less certainty. There were fewer cows in the barn, eggs were no longer being sold, one side of the chicken house stood empty, and more time and greater energies were needed for repairs of buildings and implements.

Disposed to feelings of inferiority and oversensitive to criticism, Daddy's job away from the farm provoked paranoia. He suspected the pointing fingers of neighboring farmers' "I told you so's," sensed the gossip of a community who had collectively doubted his competence and commitment to farming, and felt the comparison to my grandfather who had seemed to welcome the same concerns and responsibilities that now burdened the younger man. Pappy experienced passion for farm labor in the same way Mommy looked forward to the next planting.

I sat lost in the moment, aware that for both of us something had fled that would not return; something intrinsic to the farm, to the people—

something unnamed, haunting, elusive—an affectation of the soul—inherent, not to farming and farm life, but to our farm, to the conjunction of particular people and particular conditions at a particular time. I was aware, too, that after all these years the farm had not relinquished its grip on me. Emotionally, I continued to be tied to long ago. I knew that, in reality, my boyhood was lost, never to be regained, and with it, the indulgent fantasies of adolescence. Gone were the sweet sanctums of solitary retreat, the places unknown and foreign even to brothers and sisters: evening fields of tall corn with the soft warm breath of zephyr drifting above, hay mows and corn cribs where summer rains drummed on close tin roofs, cloistered groves of pine fixed in dusky silence. Each offered seclusion that excited imagination and provoked introspection: sanctuaries where a book was read, a poem written, a tear shed.

I didn't get home frequently during Dave and Joe's boyhood years, though each time was a delicious reunion. My older siblings were out of the house, off to college. When I did visit, I brought Christmas gifts, helped with barn and field work, played the guitar and sang songs with them. I was, however, a visitor, a stranger to most of their activities and interests. In short, I was removed from the ethos of their lives—detached from the daily demands and concerns of their childhood. I was not the big brother I wanted to be, not part of the strategic and serious occasions when youth responds to encouragement and love.

The summer of 1966 had provided an opportunity to recover lost time. I packed my Volkswagen "Beetle" with a tent and four days' provisions, and with Daddy and the boys crammed into the little car, set out for sightseeing adventures in Kentucky, the birthplace of Lincoln, a trip that I hoped would recover something of the lost years. Daddy rode in the passenger seat while Dave and Joe nestled into

Joe, Dave, and I on the steps of the Lincoln Memorial in Hodgenville, Kentucky. Daddy took the picture, but his refusal to tour the memorial shows in the disappointment on our faces.

the crowded back seat. We were to visit Mammoth Cave, Stephen Foster's "Old Kentucky Home," Churchill Downs in Louisville, the horse farms at Lexington, and, most importantly, the Lincoln repositories.

While the boys and I joked, planned, and amused ourselves, the increasing miles produced a growing tension in Daddy. The strangeness and insecurity of a new experience, and my desire for him to be peripheral rather than central for three days, ran counter to his personality. As morning turned to afternoon and then evening he became a child, petulant and irascible, refusing to join in activities, sulking alone in the car when we stopped at a convenience store, and, later, when planning our evening meal, announcing that he wasn't hungry. Self-centered, he methodically began stealing the joy from our adventure. It was a pattern I had witnessed regularly while a boy, and realized it was continuing through Dave and Joe's boyhoods.

I learned that Daddy's unwillingness to engage with a world other than his own had been felt by each of his children. His refusal to empathize was especially painful on occasions when Joe received honors and recognition. During the summer of Joe's fifteenth year, he was named to the Mifflin County Babe Ruth All-Star team. The championship tournament was held at Morrisville, PA, a distant and foreign community for Daddy. For three consecutive days I drove to and from my home in northern New Jersey, increasingly aware of how important the games were to Joe, and how much he appreciated someone from his family being there. While I knew Daddy should have been there, I understood that he had no reliable transportation, and that he would have been extremely uncomfortable consorting with people whose circumstances he believed superior to his own. Still, I recoiled when my dying brother revealed that following the tournament, "Daddy never even asked me how I did."

The smell of wood smoke drifted in the night air. A neighbor sought to counter October's chill at his fireplace.

"I would like Cim to speak, too." Joe suddenly announced. The disclosure reawakened me to present realities.

My son Cim had become one of Joe's favorite people. The two of them shared a love for music and a skill for the guitar that distanced many of their friends. When he was informed of the cancer, Cim had twice driven long miles to Morgantown, initially visiting at the apartment of Joe's daughter, Shaun, and later, attending her graduation exercises, knowing how much it meant to Joe. On this night, in the midst of Joe's ordeal, it would mean much if Cim would agree to deliver a tribute at the funeral.

Joe's choice of Cim was some-what arresting. Cim was a generation younger than Joe. Nephews and uncles do not ordinarily become soul-mates, but a special bond was established between them, ostensibly because they shared a talent and appreciation for music, but also because both genuinely admired each other's character and acumen.

At that moment the love and gratitude I felt for both Joe and Cim overflowed. Speech was rendered ineffable. Tears dimmed the outline of

As testimony to their friendship, Joe requested that Cim speak at his funeral.

Joe as he lay waiting for me to respond. The profound love of a father for a child belies expression; but the love that flows out of the friendship of brotherhood is singularly precious as well. These are "the nameless feelings that course through our breast, ... for ever unexpressed."[3]

As though it were a private revelation, taking me into his confidence, Joe whispered, "He is one of the greatest people I have ever known. ... Your kids ... Your kids are the greatest people I have known. ... I don't worry about Shaun because she has Katie and Sam. I'm really happy they're so close."

The tenderness of that moment has never passed. Driving in the late afternoon or evening, walking mornings alone at the park, or lying in bed emptying myself for sleep, that night returns. Sometimes the memory is close and piercing, sometimes it is distant and surreal, and sometimes it is comforting. Holding onto the promises of our Savior, I envisage sitting again with him, in a place as lovely as he imagined his deck to be, sharing our love for all the wonders resplendent in God's world. The heaven we enjoyed intimates the heaven to come.

"I worry about Cath," he continued.

I got up and walked to where he lay propped in the gravity chair. In

---

3. Lines from The Buried Life, Matthew Arnold.

Joe and Cathy in earlier days. In his final days she selflessly attended to his needs.

the darkness, I knelt beside him. "Do you want me to pray?" I asked.

I placed my right hand on his right arm, my left on his shoulder and prayed. I prayed that he would immediately experience the "peace that passes all understanding," that God would give special attention and comfort to Cathy, and that he would one day be reunited with Cim.[4]

When the supplication was ended, he quietly directed, "Take me to bed."

I called for Cathy. She came as though she had been waiting, and the two of us helped him into his wheelchair. I wheeled him around the outside of the house to the front doorway which was wide enough to permit entrance and nearest to his bedroom and bath. Cathy and I helped with his toilette, then put him to bed. He asked Cathy to lay beside him, and with a tender demonstration of her love and devotion, she complied while I returned to the deck to fetch my computer. It was nearly 9 pm, when, the day completed, I fell to my knees in the darkness of my room and pleaded for strength to withstand what was imminent.

PART TWO

Joe died during the first hours of Tuesday, October 6, 2015. Because his death was anticipated, many of the necessary conventions and preferred proprieties that accompany death had been addressed by Joe himself in the days and weeks following his January diagnosis. His cremation was charged to a local mortuary, the placement of his effects was detailed, and the participants in his memorial service were notified. He compiled a set of his recorded music for each of his siblings and some of his nephews and nieces, chose a gravesite in the Samuel's Church Cemetery bordering the farm, and selected music for the funeral service. His attempt to create an autobiographical video, however, had to be abandoned by midsummer when his depleted condition vitiated the production. And, in his final days, he exhorted me to present a gospel message instead of a eulogy

---

4. *And the peace of God, which surpasses all understanding, will guard your hearts and your minds in Christ Jesus.* Phil. 4:7. (ESV)

at the memorial service.

The substance of Joe's charge was understood but giving it expression required considerable sensitivity and thought. Conveying concern for the salvation of loved ones had to be done without patronization or condescension.

Two days after our late-evening conversation on the deck of his house, in the late afternoon, Cathy and I decided it would be refreshing for him to go for a car ride. The suggestion was excitedly endorsed by Joe. Motion might temporarily obscure reality.

Moving his unresponsive body from a wheelchair to the rear seat of a compact car was, however, complicated and exhausting. He was heavier than I anticipated, and his small car precluded easy manipulation. I opened the rear driver-side door and parked the back of his wheelchair against the car trunk. Cathy and I then lifted him to a standing position by placing his arms across our shoulders. After he was standing, Cathy hurried to the other side of the car, opened that rear door and waited to help once he was inside. Straining against his two hundred plus pounds, I placed his left arm around my shoulders, took his full weight and began maneuvering him a few feet at a time toward the open door. I realized that if I lost my balance, I would not be able to break his fall, and worse, if he fell, his head could not be protected, and we would then need professional assistance. Just a few nights earlier as Cathy and I had attempted to move him from his bedroom, he had bumped against the bed rail and fallen because I had been unable to keep him upright. As a result, the three of us had spent seven hours in the emergency room of the Charleston Hospital. Perspiration beaded my forehead as I steeled myself against catastrophe. Gathering myself I lifted him backward against the seat. Relieved that he was now in position to sit, I started to lower him when my strength failed. Frightened that he might slide down off the seat and onto the stone driveway, I reflexively pushed him backward, his torso falling onto the seat surface, his legs hanging outside the car.

Joe's eyes were closed as I began apologizing for my failure. He did not speak. Cathy tried to raise him to a sitting position but could not since his legs were pinned outside the car. Simultaneously, his body began convulsing and both Cathy and I realized we needed help.

The trauma of the moment had triggered seizures, and he was no longer able to respond to either of us. Cathy immediately called the local hospice center that had been providing palliative care and advice since

The Hubbard Hospice Care House in West Virginia where Joe died

early September. Their medical expert, who was familiar with Joe and his condition, decided Joe could better be served at the center than at home. An ambulance was dispatched for the transport, and while Cathy and I waited for the help we knew was on the way, I leaned into the open door of the car, stroked his legs and tried to give a measure of comfort. Cathy opened the passenger side rear door, spoke reassuringly to him, and the three of us waited.

As soon as the emergency vehicle arrived, trained volunteers carefully reached into Joe's car and lifted him onto a stretcher, which was then transferred to the ambulance. Within twenty minutes, all was secured, the seizures were arrested, and the transport began. Cathy rode with him, and I followed in my car. Both of us reserved hope that the move was temporary, but I intuitively suspected that he was leaving home for the last time.

Cathy and I visited daily; I arrived at 7:30 am and stayed until he finished his dinner. When he slept, I worked at my computer, making notes and organizing material for the memorial service. Cathy arrived at about 11 am, and if he was awake, she sat on his bed, her presence a comfort. She fed him, helped wash him, and ministered to incidental needs. If he were asleep, she read, or the two of us sat quietly, our movement and conversation reverential. Oft times, when visitors stopped by, he slept undisturbed or else fell asleep during their visitation. Each day ended similarly. Around 6:00 pm Cathy loaded the DVD player in his room with a WWII movie, adjusted the volume to his liking, then, tenderly, held and caressed him before departing. The two of us then returned to 1615 Woodvale Drive in Charleston, where Cathy busied herself with customary housework while I prepared a late meal. Afterward, we retired to the quiet of our rooms until bedtime.

For several days his condition seemed to stabilize; there were periods when he was lucid, laughed, or reflected on present concerns. Most of the time, however, was lost to sleep induced by medications. The days began sliding by without discernible change in his condition.

On the afternoon of Monday, October 5, two nurses came to the room to wash him and freshen his bedclothes. Desiring to be unobtrusive, I excused myself and went out into the hallway until they completed their work. As they were departing I reticently approached and asked if they could estimate his remaining time. Among other concerns we wanted family members to have a final opportunity to see him. Beneficent both by character and design, neither nurse volunteered specific information.

Having been in the room since early morning I excused myself to go outside for some fresh air. As I passed the front desk, the senior nurse motioned me to the side and gently, standing directly in front of me, took both of my hands and confided, "I overheard your question concerning your brother. I'm going to tell you the truth. All the signs indicate he has, at the most, 48 hours. … but more probably, …less than that."

Personal motives, however praiseworthy, however principled, are never entirely pure. I had been granted the sacred task, the blessing, of caring for a dying brother and yet, upon being told of the finality of it all, my first reaction was inward. For a betraying moment the senior nurse's confidence resulted neither in pain nor in pathos; instead a gladdening, not that I was losing a brother, not that he would be released of suffering, but that I would be free from death's ordeal. Simultaneously, guilt flooded over me. I was conscience-stricken. The moment that most demanded selflessness had been compromised with egocentrism. The Apostle Paul's description of the human condition, "There is none good, no, not one," was apt.[5] Ashamed, I walked outside. The grounds of the hospice included a garden area where flowers decorated a walkway that led to an idyllic recessed porch, serene with white patio table and chairs, a bower of solitude. I retreated to one of the chairs, bowed my head, and prayed for forgiveness.

The garden outside the hospice

---

5. *"None is righteous, no, not one; no one understands; no one seeks for God. All have turned aside; together they have become worthless; no one does good, not even one."* Romans 3:10-12. (ESV)

Self-absorption dissolved, but I did not linger. Retracing my steps, a sense of duty and urgency compelled that I update Cathy with this latest news.

The entrance to the hospice opened to a large reception room. The nurses' station was on the left, behind a semi-circular counter that ran along the wall. To the right a corridor opened that led to Joe's room. Final valediction is laden with duties and is apperceptive of time. As I entered she was sitting quietly by Joe's left side, in a chair pulled close to his bed. He lay on his back, asleep from the stupor of drugs and fatigue. I sat to his right and tactfully shared the information. Cathy nodded that she understood.

Excusing myself, I withdrew to the corridor to call my sister Susie. She would want to come immediately, and I knew she would be willing to contact our brothers and sisters. I then called my youngest daughter Sammy, because she had made me promise that I would notify her of any change in his condition. For the next hour, I walked the grounds, raw emotion bending me to the earth. Praying, recalling Scripture, drifting into the past, I surrendered my spirit to the promises of my Savior. Gray evening light had begun to diffuse the brilliance of a beautiful fall afternoon. It was time to confront the reality that waited within his hospice room.

Somber and resigned, Cathy and I waited by the bedside throughout the late afternoon and evening. Joe's supper arrived, but he did not respond to Cathy's questions or tugs at his clothing asking if he was hungry. We set the dinner tray aside and let him sleep. Cathy asked me, "Do you want to eat it?" During his stays at the various hospitals to receive treatments, he had developed a craving for tomato soup. I had not eaten since breakfast, so with license from Cathy, I ate his soup. Within the hour a nurse poked her head into the room to see if he had eaten and to retrieve the tray. Not wishing to mislead her into thinking that he had awakened and been fed, I guiltily acknowledged that I had eaten the soup. "Good," she said, "Would you like something else?" Already contrite, I declined the offer.

The remainder of the afternoon and evening seemed protracted. Cathy and I read, checked his breathing, and awaited the inevitable. A WWII movie played on the television, but with Joe asleep, someone had turned off the audio, the muted images contributing to the impotence of the hour.

My sister Susie called at 10 pm to tell me that she and Ray were about 45 minutes from the hospice and that Beth was with them. Beth was a special blessing because she was a trained nurse with an immense capacity for compassion. As well, she was the youngest sibling and had a special bond with Joe. Both Cathy and I looked forward to their arrival.

A few minutes after 11 pm they walked into the room. Beth asked several questions about Joe's condition, and, when neither Cathy nor I could answer, she went to the front desk to find a nurse. In the meantime, Susie sat on Joe's bed, leaned against him, and cried.

My concern for Cathy, coupled with our mutual desire to be with Joe at the end, precluded our leaving the room. Beth returned and the next hours were spent in periodic reserved conversation and lingering silence.

It was after 1 am when I suggested that two or three of us take turns returning to the house to get some sleep while the others maintain the vigil. Although death might be only hours away, we understood the possibility that the watch could last through Wednesday. It was decided that Ray and I would be the first to leave.

It was nearly 1:30 am when we pulled into the driveway of Joe and Cathy's house. Neighboring homes were strangely dark, and the sounds of the night seemed dulled as though life was suspended. I asked Ray if he wished to eat something, but since the hour was late, he declined and went directly to bed. I showered and shaved and, shortly afterward, did the same. It was a few minutes past 2 am.

About 4:40 am Ray knocked on my bedroom door. I sat up and asked, "Yes?" He told me that Susie had just called to say that the end was near. We threw on our clothes and were about to leave when Ray's cell phone rang a second time. He listened for a moment, hung up, and, his voice slightly above a whisper, resignedly stated, "It's over." It was 5 am.

There was no longer a need to hurry. We drove cautiously back to the hospice, empty, inanimate. Inside the room his body lay supine on the bed. Cathy, Susie, and Beth sat leaden, emotions surrendered, desolation hanging oppressively like a miasma.

Cathy sat, head bowed, in a chair that had been pulled close to his bed. She looked up as we entered, her eyes reddened with the anguish that only love knows. Susie rested on the bed, caressing the body as though he were still alive. No one spoke until Beth turned to me, "Are you okay?" I nodded while simultaneously choking back the tears that made it impossible to speak. Susie motioned for me to sit with her and quietly began sobbing. Beth knelt beside us and the three of us hugged and cried. I then turned to Cathy. She stood and fell limp against me, the two of us holding each other against the grotesque reality that he was gone.

Impotent to change the finality of it all, we sat passively, looking at one another, lost in a foreign wilderness. As the minutes slowly passed, as though recovering from the stupor of anesthesia, we began to awaken, phlegmatic and fatigued, to life's continuum. Within minutes Shaun arrived, hugged Cathy, then sat in a chair at the foot of the bed and spoke quietly with her mother.

The conventions of another day descended. The morning shift of nurses and hospice personnel arrived and departed. The hospice chaplain, sincere and accommodating, came by to lend a hand and provide solace. Though exhausted by the anguish of the long night, the *sine qua non* of living stirred and impelled each of us to activity. Thus began a pervasive tedium as his effects were collected: clothes, to hang forgotten in a deserted closet, books to sit in the mildew of damp cellars, and toiletries, to be emptied into bathroom drains and waste baskets. Some were discarded. Others were folded into a cardboard box and carried to a car he would no longer drive. Reality benumbed us. He was gone, but the body that had been home to his spirit and with which he had been known to us remained. I walked to the bed where it lay, depleted and worn, pathetic. Its features were swollen and pallid, but it was all the moment afforded—one final attempt to claim what had been so special. My brother was dead. Momentarily, neither the hope of resurrection nor the unfailing promises of faith, afforded comfort. He was dead, … … and would not return. …My brother. I kissed the lifeless form, ran my hand over his hand, whispered to his departed spirit, and left the room, never again to have what had been so precious.

During the days following Joe's death, well-wishers and sympathizers mingled with family at his home. There were meals to serve, errands to run, and, of course, unanticipated interruptions and demands on time. Despite these duties, fulfilling my obligation to speak at the funeral dominated my consciousness. On Wednesday night, notes in hand, I sequestered myself and worked past midnight to give my remarks final form.

S aturday's service was memorable. Joe had been singular in the lives of dozens of friends who knew him as a roommate, co-worker, coach, or neighbor. His church family and business acquaintances were effusive in their accolades. But it was the tributes of immediate family: brothers and sisters, nephews and nieces, of the people who best knew him, that were especially poignant. His Christian testimony touched everyone. He had been faithful to Jesus's two commands: love God with all your being and love your neighbor as yourself.

G od's spirit is mysteriously wonderful in its capacity to assuage human suffering. Without His promise of renewal, the human soul is forced to grope in death's darkest hour in its attempt to rally, rationalize, and buffet the anguish of earthly terminus. Christ's assurances of ultimate purpose and eternal life, however, sufficiently and timeously displace this despondency and compel re-engagement in life's flow. For those who struggle against despair without the assurance of Christ's resurrection, hope is a house built upon sand. "Believing what we don't believe, does not exhilarate."[6] For we Christians, the suffering validates our hope, for it was in suffering that Christ proved the reality of our future reunion with Joe and Himself.

---

6. "That It Will Never Come Again," Emily Dickinson.

EULOGY
◇◇◇◇◇◇◇◇◇◇◇◇◇◇◇◇

Joseph Edward Morgan

November 1, 1956 – October 6, 2015

Stonewall Jackson, the southern Civil War general, carried several notes on his person throughout his military campaigns. One of them was a reminder never to appear more learned than anyone in his company, whether it was a family member, a guest, or a visitor. The implication was, of course, that everyone is repulsed by condescension and arrogance.

Jackson was one of Joe's heroes, and it is not ironic that Joe's life was a demonstration of the apothegm carried by the general. Joe was intelligent, insightful, perceptive, yet, he never permitted his erudition or achievements to discomfort or reduce his company. Although his family and friends knew he was bright and well-read, he was not regarded as bookish or an academe. In fact, his cultivation and sophistication were secondary to his willingness to engage in all sorts of social exchange and fun. He did not think of himself "more highly than he ought,"[1] but was self-effacing

---

1. *"For by the grace given to me I say to everyone among you not to think of himself more highly than he ought to think, but to think with sober judgment, each according to the measure of faith*

and self-deprecating to make others comfortable. He enjoyed intellectual engagement, but his assertions never carried an air of pedantry or narrow-mindedness. Rather, his convictions were presented with qualifiers as though he wished to defer should a correction or acknowledgment be necessary. His concern for others and his desire to avoid dogmatism resulted in a carriage that was a testimony to both humility and grace.

In spite of an age difference of fourteen years, there was a good-natured consonance to our relationship. We shared a common disposition as well as common interests, values, and senses of humor. The *joie de vivre* inherent in our Christian lives bonded us, drew us into easy confidence, and generated mutual blessing. When occasion found us together, we sang, reminisced, and exchanged ideas. Frequently he might say, "Tell me everything you know about Alexander the Great," or "What have you read that I should know about?" He loved to page through books in my library, read underscored passages of philosophy, theology, or history and comment on their applications. To the end, however, he was mystified by my love for poetry, and although he conceded the truths found in great poems and appreciated the music of lyrical verse, he saw no need to aureate truth with metrics and sentiment.

He loved conversation, and when the two of us traveled by car, he insisted that I ride in the passenger seat rather than drive, so that my part of the discourse would not be distracted. He asked questions, made associations with things he had read or heard (especially as it related to his Biblical studies), and drew parallels with contemporary times. He continually made notes, later copying them into his computer. After days or weeks passed, he might email or text commentary on our earlier discussion.

As a small child is grateful to be included in the activities of older brothers and sisters, so I was indebted to him for making me an integral part of his world, particularly his music. Truth was, that while he and Cim and my son-in-law Josh were slowed and inhibited by my participation in their musical get-togethers, they insisted that I tag along.[2] In fact, Joe always made certain that our occasions included songs that I loved, even when it restricted the group's creativity and minimized their skills. I am forever grateful, because being included in Joe's world afforded me one of my greatest joys.

Joe delighted in his rapport with young people. Shortly before his

---

that God has assigned." Romans 12:3 (ESV)
2. Cim Morgan, my son, and Josh Grissom, my son-in-law.

death, he recorded and produced a musical album for children that has proved to be a lasting contribution to our family. Within days of its distribution, grandnephews and grandnieces from ages two to eight had memorized every lyric and given voice to the ditties, rhymes, and stories that comprised the songs. Sometimes awkward with teens, he nevertheless listened to them, took them and their friends to breakfast, and showered their efforts and accomplishments with praise and celebration. In return, he reveled in the respect and admiration he received.

I suspect that recognition filled the void, real or imagined, he experienced as a teenager, being the youngest in a large family.[3] By the time he arrived in 1956, Mommy and Daddy were encumbered with a failing farm and associated financial concerns. Joe's well-being became largely the duty of siblings. During his teenage years, as both parents took jobs outside the home, he sometimes felt unnoticed and unappreciated, because six older children, each with individual needs and concerns also required attention. His diffidence was compounded when, at age eight, the birth of baby sister Beth eliminated any remaining attention he might have received.

Despite the insecurities and the lack of self-assurance he may have suffered as a teenager and young adult, he grew to be sanguine, enthusiastic, and compliant. He embraced life with alacrity. As a Christian, he was devoted to his Savior and God. Up at dawn, his day began with Scripture reading and prayer. Exegesis and hermeneutics were requisite studies, and his computer contained dozens of pages of resulting notes and commentary. As a Christian whose values were grounded in his relationship with the God of the universe, excitement was found in everything that vibrated from God's transcendent hand. The laws of physics, the chemistry of the material world, the beauties of mathematics and music, and the spiritual substance of the metaphysical world all filled him with intrigue and wonder. He was a modern Renaissance man.

Embedded in his love of learning and the variety of his experience was the richness of his conversation. Coupled with his humility and willingness to listen, everyone enjoyed his company. His admiration for the skills and achievements of friends and family was never tainted with envy. He was pleased to be associated with what he considered the talents and character of gifted and admirable brothers, sisters, nephews, nieces and in-laws.

---

3. Joe remained the youngest family member until October 28, 1964 when baby sister, Beth, arrived.

He was athletic and loved competition. During his high school years, the Chief Logan Joint School District dropped interscholastic baseball, forcing Joe to turn to the summer Babe Ruth League. He was named to the Mifflin County All-Star Team and played in the National Babe Ruth

Joe (first row, second from right) was the center fielder on the Mifflin County All-Star Team.

Tournament. Throughout high school he also performed as an all-around gymnast on the Chief Logan High School Gymnastics squad. After graduating, and continuing until his final days when he became ill, he played in pick-up basketball games and regularly shot in the 80s as a golfer. Whether he was playing with friends and family or competing in a recreational league, sports were fun for Joe. No more and no less. He was always able to laugh at himself and never boasted. More importantly, he embodied sportsmanship. The end never justified the means.

Friendship, wherever it appears, is the desired end of a relationship, whether it be with an acquaintance or with a blood brother. I loved him as my baby brother, but as the years passed, our relationship transcended blood. We became best friends, able to share our most personal feelings and thoughts, able to delight in each other's achievements and recognitions, able to suffer each other's grief, and able to look beyond death and separation to a final and lasting reunion. Joe's desire to please God, to do the right thing, and to be a "worker who has no need to be ashamed, rightly handling the word of truth,"[4] established a sweetness, an aroma, an understanding to our relationship that is reserved exclusively for the saints. Perhaps, that is the reason his daily absence is so visceral, so palpable, so near. One is not easily separated from a saint.

---

4. II Timothy 2:15 *"Do your best to present yourself to God as one approved, a worker who has no need to be ashamed, rightly handling the word of truth."* (ESV)

C.S. Lewis wrote of friendship:

"It is a relation between men at their highest level of individuality."

"Notice that Friendship thus repeats on a more individual and less socially necessary level the character of the Companionship which was its matrix. The Companionship was between people who were doing something together - hunting, studying, painting or what you will. The Friends will still be doing something together, but something more inward, less widely shared and less easily defined; still hunters, but of some immaterial quarry; still collaborating, but in some work the world does not, or not yet, take account of; still travelling companions, but on a different kind of journey. Hence we picture lovers face to face but Friends side by side; their eyes look ahead."

"THE FOUR LOVES,"

C.S. LEWIS

THE FARM

<small>◇◇◇◇◇◇◇◇◇◇◇◇◇◇◇◇</small>

These beauteous forms,
Through a long absence, have not been to me
As is a landscape to a blind man's eye:
But oft, in lonely rooms, and 'mid the din
Of towns and cities, I have owed to them,
In hours of weariness, sensations sweet,
Felt in the blood, and felt along the heart;
And passing even into my purer mind
With tranquil restoration:—feelings too
Of unremembered pleasure: such, perhaps,
As have no slight or trivial influence
On that best portion of a good man's life,

"LINES COMPOSED A FEW MILES ABOVE TINTERN ABBEY"
WILLIAM WORDSWORTH

Attachment to a person or place requires investment. If the attachment is to be meaningful, the investment must be both emotional and spiritual. Thus, it will remain ever visceral, felt in the soul. If the place is a dairy farm, with its relentless demands and ineffable beauties, if its time is the days of youth with their hyperbolic and indelible impression, then the attachment becomes a grip, enveloping the self, never to be trivialized or forgotten.

These biographical sketches of Daddy and Mommy, of brothers and sisters, of grandparents, of relatives and neighbors, are colored either directly or tacitly by experiences on the farm. Many of the ideas and ideals with which I was confronted as a young person resulted from the conflation of people, circumstances, and time encountered there. In time, many of the people who populate these pages and much of that world passed.

Grandparents, parents, relatives and acquaintances moved from this world to the next. The farm, as well, was sold in 1976 and is no longer recognizable amid the renovation, relocation, and removal of its appurtenances. As well, my brothers and sisters went separate ways, diverse in expression and circumstance. Yet something of a common kinship has remained, tying us inextricably to the farm and to each other. Though distant, phantasmal, elusive, those farm years continue to bind us as family.

1911 – 1976

The farmhouse as it looked in 1923-1924 when Pappy bought it

In 1911, on or about the occasion of their wedding, my grandparents, Charles L. Arnold and Carrie E. Arnold (Pappy and Mammie) leased and moved onto what was then known as "The Brower Farm."[1] It was located at the far eastern end of Decatur Township in Mifflin County, Pennsylvania. Twelve years later they purchased the farm outright. By that time, their family included four children: Marvin "Bud" (11), Beatrice (8), Iva (5), and Hazel (3).

In June 1939 Hazel, the youngest (my mother), married C. James

---

1. The date and circumstance of Charles (Pappy) and Carrie (Mammie) renting the farm in 1911 is somewhat speculative. Before her death, Mommy confirmed that her brother and sisters were born at the farm. Her parents were married on January 8, 1911, and Bud, the oldest, was born in May 1911. Thus, I use that date as a starting point for occupancy.

PAPPY, MAMMIE, AND THEIR FAMILY IN FRONT OF THE FARMHOUSE IN 1926.
Sitting atop horses, left to right, are their children: Bud, Beatty, Ivy, and Mommy.

"Jim" Morgan (my father), and after living in Lewistown for about a year, the couple, upon invitation of Pappy and Mammie, moved into one side of the farmhouse and began farming as a cooperative with the older couple. The farm house had become somewhat vacant after Pappy and Mammie's three older children moved to homes of their own, and Pappy needed help with his expanding farming operation.

In late 1949 Pappy and Mammie began building a retirement home at the eastern end of the farm and by the fall of 1951 left Daddy and Mommy and their four children, Dennis, Keith, Bill, and RuthAnn, as sole residents. In the ensuing years four additional children were born: Susie, Dave, Joe, and Beth.

THE LAND

In 1836 Simon Gratz, a merchant of Philadelphia, sold 479 acres of land to James Robb, a farmer of Lewistown for $2,400. James Robb in 1839 sold 196 acres of this plot to Samuel Barr, a Lewistown lawyer, and

THE FARM 1940
Mommy and Daddy had begun residence. Daddy's car is parked next to the barn. Note the absence of utility poles and wires, the garage, the smaller silo, the second milkhouse, the second corn crib, and the wire fence that later extended around the yard.

in 1840 sold another 190 acres to Samuel Brower for $1,600 at which time Samuel moved from Menno Township and began farming. There were already buildings on the land when Brower purchased it. These buildings were probably constructed between 1836 and 1840, with the house originally framed with logs.

At that time, the farm was part of Union County.[2] Demographic records show that it had earlier been a part of both Northumberland and Cumberland Counties. Neighboring farms in 1840, per the deed, belonged to Jacob Krick (now the Kenneth Loht farm), Peter Lehr, John Lawver, and Samuel Barr.

---

2. By 1860 newly aligned boundaries placed the farm within the eastern limits of Mifflin County.

LEGACY OF THE FARM

In the 1860 census of Decatur Township, Mifflin County, Samuel Brower's family consisted of Samuel (52), Margaret, his wife (46), and their four children: John, Samuel, Sarah, and Jacob. Also living with them were Samuel's father, Jacob, and his brother, James H. Brower. The farm was valued at $7,000, the highest assessment of any of the neighboring farms including those of Jacob Krick ($3,000) and David Yeater ($1,800).

For the next 41 years, until Samuel Brower's death in 1881, the farm was known as the Brower Homestead. The appellation continued long after Samuel's will partitioned the land into two separate farms: the upper farm bequeathed to his son, John L. Brower, and the lower farm handed down to the second son, Samuel L. Brower. The upper farm was subsequently owned by Jacob O. Dreese, Calvin S. Goss, John S. Goss, and Ronald Goss, the son of John S. Goss. Ronald passed away on September 11, 2019, and it is assumed that his son Tim, who lives on the property, will purchase and continue the farming operation.

The lower farm was leased for a brief period at the turn of the century, first to William Erb and in 1911 to Charles L. Arnold (Pappy). It continued to be owned by Samuel L. Brower until he sold it to my grandfather in 1923 for $5,500. Neighboring farms at that time were those of Jacob Krick, Calvin S. Goss, John Lawver, William Erb, and Isaiah Knepp.

Pappy farmed the land from 1911 until his retirement in the late fall of 1951 when he and Mammie moved into the house he built on a 3-acre plot at the eastern end of the farm. In order to finance the venture, a public sale was held on Saturday, March 11, 1950, at which time he sold half of the livestock and some of the machinery. The remaining animals and implements were retained for his son-in-law, C. James (Jim) Morgan (Daddy), who continued to farm the land. At that time Pappy designated his four children to receive equal shares of the $13,700 sale price as a portion of their inheritance at his death.[3]

Pappy built a house, chicken house, garage, and grain storage building

---

3. Pappy died on February 12, 1957, at which time the farm was formally sold to Daddy. The purchase was made feasible for Daddy when Mommy had her share applied as a payment, and her sister, Beatrice, to keep the farm within the family, magnanimously lent her share at no interest until Daddy could pay it back. Daddy borrowed the remaining money from the bank at McClure in order to pay Bud (Marvin) and Iva, the other siblings, their share.

on his three wooded acres. He died in February 1957, but Mammie continued to live on the property until her death in October 1972. The 3-acre property was then sold to Pappy's grand-nephew, Paul E. Arnold, Jr.

In 1972, following Mammie's death, Daddy sold 5 acres from the southeastern corner of the farm to Clarence Sheriff, a neighbor. A new road from the Krick School to Samuel's Church had divided off the 5 acres isolating it from the farm proper. Another piece of land, consisting of 28 acres at the far eastern edge of the farm, was sold to my brother Keith in 1972 as Daddy needed money to satisfy tax and mortgage payments. Finally, in 1976, struggling to meet financial demands and having lost the work force provided by his children who had moved on to colleges, Daddy sold the farm. Desiring that the land continue to be farmed rather than falling into the hands of a realtor who might subdivide it, he sold it to Daniel Yoder, an Amish farmer for $80,000.

SAMUEL'S CHURCH

In 1848 Samuel Barr donated land from his acreage for a church, thus named "Samuel's Church."[4] Prior to that time, the Evangelical Lutheran and German Reformed Christians in the area needed a place of worship closer in proximity to their homes than the church at St. John's, Black Oak Ridge, which was founded about 1790 and lay 8-10 miles eastward. The new church was built and was in operation by June 16, 1851.

---

4. "In 1848, Samuel Barr donated a plot of land to a board of trustees of the Lutheran and German Reformed congregation. This congregation was a considerable portion of the members of the church at Black Oak Ridge (St. John), living west of that place, some a great distance, who came to the conclusion to put up a church building more convenient for them. The corner-stone was laid November 3, 1849. It was finished and dedicated to the worship of the Triune God on the 16th of June 1851. It was built for the use of the Evangelical Lutheran and German Reformed denominations. The house is a log frame, and weather-boarded, painted white. The building is two stories high, with galleries on three sides. The seats are so arranged as to accommodate about five hundred individuals. At its dedication it was Samuel's Church, after the owner of the land. The dedicatory ceremonies were performed by Rev. J. P. Shindel in the presence of a very large concourse of people. On the 6th of November the Rev. J. R. Shindel commenced his labors among them as pastor of the Lutherans, and Rev. Hackman became the pastor of the German Reformed congregation. They preached alternately every four weeks, so that service was held regularly every two weeks. The first communion was held on the 1st day." (Ellis, 1886)

SAMUEL'S CHURCH

The surnames of Decatur Township inhabitants who attended Samuel's in 1815 were the same as those who attended during my years on the farm. They included: Baker, Bell, Bowersox, Criswell, Gill, Gross, Goss, Hoffman, Henry, Hauer, Krebbs, Kline, Lepley, Lawver, Knepp, McClintic, Price, Romich (Romig), Reigle, Rager, Ritter, Smith, Stroup, Stumpff, Ulsh, Thomas, and Wagner.

SCHOOL

Children in grades 1- 8, from the farthest eastern boundary of Mifflin County, attended the one-room Krick School, located one mile east of our farm house.[5] The eponym was for Jacob Krick, the farmer who donated the parcel of land. It existed as early as 1878 and operated without interruption until it closed, in conjunction with all township one-room schools, in May 1952.[6] Decatur Elementary, a regional school, was

5. "The schools prior to 1836 were pay or subscription-schools and were taught either in rooms in houses or some abandoned building fitted for that purpose. The directors appointed at the November term court, 1834, under the law of April preceding, were Samuel Bair and John H. Bell, who took charge of the schools of the township and formed them into districts. The first schoolhouse was known as Siglers' and stood near the old Parshall mill. Four districts were formed under the law, which were increased as occasion demanded, and at present there are seven districts. In the Bowersox schoolhouse the German language was taught until 1860. The largest house in the township is at Lilleyville and contains two schools. It was finished September 1, 1885, at a cost of ten hundred and forty-five dollars, Samuel Sterrett being the contractor. The present school directors are F. H. Miller, R. W. Ingram, Emanuel Oldt, Henry Goss, George Benfer and John S. Groff." (Ellis, 1886)

6. Edith Erb, who is further described in this book in the chapter *Edie Erb*, taught the 1928 class which included Mommy (Hazel Arnold Morgan), Aunt Beatty (Beatrice Arnold Boonie), and Aunt Ivy (Iva Arnold Brindle). She also taught the 1950 class that included my brother, Keith (6 years old), and myself (7 years old) as third graders. She then retired

opened at Shindle in the fall of 1953. Formerly, students seeking a high school education had traveled seven miles to McClure High School until after WWII, at which time the Decatur school district contracted to send grades 9-12 to Lewistown schools. Citizens of the township, long used to the convenience of a local one-room school, complained of both the increase in taxes and logistical problems associated with bus transportation. In the wake of this unrest, concern was compounded in 1954 when sending districts to Lewistown High School were notified of a tuition increase. The local Board of Education felt the ire of neighbors and began looking for solutions. A public meeting was held at the new Decatur school, and afterward, Lyman Guss, the board president, asked Daddy to serve on an *ad hoc* committee to investigate alternatives and encouraged him to run for a vacated board seat. He accepted the *ad hoc* appointment and a few months later won election to the Board of Education.

Concurrently, the soon-to-be Chief Logan School District was building a new high school at Highland Park, a suburb of Lewistown, and its Board of Education, needing extra money, offered Decatur Township reduced tuition costs to become part of their district. The Decatur committee submitted the proposal to a referendum that passed with the contingent compromise that students already enrolled in the Lewistown system would be grandfathered. Thus, by the fall of 1954, Decatur Township became part of the new Chief Logan school district. Daddy was instrumental in that change.

Chief Logan Joint High School did not open its doors until the spring of 1959. In the interim Decatur students were sent to Burnham Junior High (grades 7-9) and Yeagertown Senior High (grades 10-12).[7]

THE ROADS

after 45 years of teaching at Decatur Township schools. The Krick school bell, a two-seater desk, the teacher's desk, and the porcelain water crock were purchased by my uncle Bud when the school closed. Before his death he gifted all but the desk to my brother Keith, who, in turn, donated them to the Mifflin County Historical Society in Lewistown, PA in 2010.

7. Daddy continued to serve as a board member until after his sons, Keith and I, graduated in the spring of 1960. In fact, he was given the honor of presenting us our diplomas at the graduation exercise.

The earliest public road in eastern Decatur Township was an Indian path, later named "The Stage Road," that ran from Lewistown to Adamsburg (Beaver Springs). Sometime prior to Pappy's purchase of the farm in 1923, the portion of the artery that ran directly from Sam Arnold's farm to the Loht farm was closed and rerouted south to connect with what is now Ertley Road and Krick Road. The residence of Fern Loht, a quarter mile from the fields of the farm, was a stopover where the stage changed horses. To accommodate the stage passengers, a hotel was built close by in Bannerville and another west of Belltown. The artery that ran to the farm (now Decatur Road) connected what was the McKinley General Store to the west, to what is now Krick Road to the east.

FARM EQUIPMENT

The farming was done exclusively with horses until 1930 when Pappy purchased a gasoline operated, steel-wheeled Fordson tractor. In spite of the new mechanization, he continued to employ horses until after WWII, due in large part to the shortage of gasoline, but also because horses were his first love.[8] A 1938 Allis-Chalmers WC, bought in 1940 from Jim Herman, a dealer in Beaver Springs, replaced the Fordson.[9] In 1949, he traded the WC to Marvin 'Bud' Arnold, his son, an implement dealer in Lewisburg, in exchange for a new Allis-Chalmers WD. The last tractor used on the farm, introduced in 1950, was an Allis-Chalmers C.

Allis-Chalmers 1938 WC

As American farming became more mechanized, new machines appeared on the farmstead. By the late 1940s the dump rake, pulled by two horses, gave way to a tractor-pulled side-delivery rake. Fields were plowed with a two-bottom plow that was raised and lowered by the tractor's hydraulic system. By the 1950s hay and straw were no longer stored loose in

8. By 1944 most civilians were allotted two gallons per week, although farmers were less severely restricted.
9. See chapter *Tractor Accident*.

mows, and straw stacks had disappeared from barnyards. Hay loaders had become obsolete, replaced by power-take-off driven balers that compacted and tied hay into bales, at first with heavy gauge wire and later with twine. Concomitantly, the binder that had for many years cut and tied grain into sheaves was discarded in favor of a combine, so that grain no longer needed to be cut, tied, shocked, and threshed in separate processes. After WWII, as technology continued to provide farmers with faster, more efficient methods, and as the constraints of a war-time economy loosened, horse farming proved to be impractical, and Pappy divested the farm of its last horses about 1948.

As soon as electricity was installed, two Delaval milking machines were purchased.

Perhaps the most impacting of the new equipment, introduced in 1946-47, were two De Laval electric milking machines. Until their introduction, cows were milked by hand into a bucket, which had to be carried to the milkhouse where the milk was strained through a cloth filter and placed into a cooling tank. The older method was labor intensive and time consuming as the milking of each cow required 10-12 minutes. The new machines extracted milk from the cow by a pulsating vacuum that applied a periodic squeeze to the teat. This system permitted one person to milk two cows simultaneously in 5-7 minutes. By the 1950s the success of the farm depended almost entirely upon mechanization as sprayers, elevators, watering fountains, and other apparatus became commonplace.

In addition to the tractors, a three-quarter ton 1946 Chevrolet pickup truck that functioned both as a farm vehicle and a family car was bought in 1947. It saw considerable use hauling animals, grain, machinery, and produce. It transported our family to church each Sunday, made daily trips to market and mill, and was the vehicle I drove in September 1956 to take my state driver's test. It was the farm's *piece de resistance* until the engine seized up in 1966.

THE FIELDS

Most of the acreage on the farm was reserved for corn and wheat, the "money" crops, or for crops that provided provender for the cattle. Mills and granaries paid higher prices for corn and wheat, thus both Pappy and Daddy depended upon a surplus of these grains to supply the liquid cash needed for food and supplies not generated by the farm. For several summers in the mid-1950s Daddy planted barley as a money crop, but its bearded heads made harvesting tedious and the experiment was shortly abandoned.

There were several summer droughts during the late 1950s and early 1960s that resulted in a scarcity of hay and grain. This necessitated their purchase from outside sources and caused a downsizing of the cattle herd. The fear of penury forced Daddy to find work at a local steel cabinet factory and to place the bulk of farm responsibilities into the hands of his older children. While the new job generated stabilizing income, it also portended the demise of the farm.

Until around 1953 approximately 30 acres were sown annually with a mixture of clover and timothy grass that yielded winter feed for the cattle. Afterward alfalfa was preferred because it was easier to handle, produced a larger plant, and survived periods of aridity better than red clover. It also yielded two or three crops in one season.

ORCHARD AND GARDEN

While the fields produced staples for the animals, garden and orchard crops supplied fruits and vegetables for the family. The garden was originally located on the eastern side of the house enclosed with a six-foot high wire fence strung on whitewashed 4 x 4 wooden posts. Large plots of potatoes and sweet corn, long rows of string beans, wax beans, lima beans, peas, onions, carrots, cabbages, lettuce, endive, radishes, beds of rhubarb, patches of raspberries and blackberries, stakes of tomatoes, and arbors of grapes and currants occupied significant areas. An orchard of fruit

Pear trees in bloom in the orchard above our house

trees to the north of the house had been planted sometime prior to my grandfather's arrival in 1911. He added to it so that by the 1920s the variety of apples included Red and Yellow Delicious, Green Sweet and Northern Spy. The apples were spiced and canned, used for pies, pressed for cider, cooked into apple butter and applesauce, and eaten raw. Bartlett and Kieffer pear trees adjoined two varieties of plums: one purple and the other green. Taking advantage of all available space, turnips, pumpkins, watermelons, and cantaloupes were planted between corn rows.

Although not within the orchard, an assortment of other trees and plants scattered throughout the farm produced additional food. Chestnuts, black walnuts, hickory and hazel nuts were common. Red and black cherries, a potpourri of wild apples, sassafras roots, dandelion greens, and wild strawberries were plentiful. Catnip, spearmint, and teaberries were available for medicinal purposes.

Aesthetics were contributed by pine, hemlock, spruce, ash, locust, birch, pin oak, white oak, red oak, and maple trees. School children passing birch saplings on their way home from school on late afternoons routinely broke off flavorful twigs and chewed them as gum.

ANIMALS

Animals included cows, pigs, chickens, horses, and occasionally ducks and turkeys. Although cats and dogs were present, their value was restricted to utility. They were not pets in the traditional sense. Owing both to his affinity for horses and the milieu of the time, Pappy kept 4 to 6 draft horses (mostly if not entirely Belgians) and mules from the time he began farming until he neared retirement in 1948.

The number of cows fluctuated, peaking in Pappy's final years on the farm when approximately 30 were being milked, and plunging to 8 or 10 in the last years before the farm was sold. Most cows were bred to deliver their young in the fall, however, some had to calve at other times in order to balance the milk supply. As a result of this pattern, milk production was lowest in August when a greater percentage of cows were "standing dry," a 6 to 8-week condition that prepared them for their next lactation period. Bull calves were usually sold for veal while heifers were kept to replace and add to the milking herd.

In the mid-1950s artificial insemination of cattle became standard practice. Earlier, a bull had been housed and partitioned away from the herd, or else a neighbor's bull was rented for the period of rut. During my childhood years, while Pappy and Mammie were on the farm, the resident bull was a two thousand-pound Holstein named "Sammy." By 1950, however, he had become too large for service, required extra maintenance, acquired a cantankerous disposition, and was, in fact, a bit dangerous. He was sold at the salebarn in Belleville.

Pigs were requisite to the meat supply, although it was not infrequent that shoats were sold for cash. Three or four mature animals were slaughtered at Thanksgiving after the weather had cooled, the meat preserved by canning, salting, and smoking. To regenerate the drove two or three resident sows were bred in cycles, each yielding between 6 to 10 piglets on average.

Chickens played an important role on the farm both as egg producers and as a source of meat. Egg sales provided critical income, and chicken was a staple in the diet of a large family. To maintain a sizeable flock, 300 white leghorn baby chicks were ordered annually from the Montgomery Ward catalog in early spring. They arrived in boxes of 50 at the McClure post office, where they were picked up, placed within a closed truck or car, and transported to their new home. They progressed in stages; six weeks restricted to a heated area in the chicken house atop a layer of newspaper that absorbed their droppings, then, at about four weeks, as the spring weather warmed, loosed within the chicken house on a bed of straw. At ten weeks roosters began to be culled from the flock and eaten. The remaining males and the pullets were then transported in a portable coop pulled by horse or tractor to an open field where they had free range, their diet supplemented by finely ground grain and treated water. Finally, at 4 months, they were returned to the chicken house, where, shortly afterward, the pullets began to produce eggs.

A mélange of wild animals made their homes in the nearby fields and woods.: white-tailed deer, bear, foxes, opossum, skunk, raccoons, rabbits, squirrels, weasels, chipmunks, snakes, groundhogs, hawks, ringed-neck pheasants, killdeer, crows, and owls. Pigeons, barn swallows, sparrows, bats, and a variety of small birds frequented the buildings while turkey buzzards daily scavenged the fields for carrion. Salamanders, minnows, frogs, and water snakes were regular inhabitants of the creek that ran the length of the meadow. Crickets, cicada, and tree toads gave chorus to spring and summer nights. The creek at the far eastern boundary of the farm contained brown trout until the stream was diverted by a new roadway in the 1950s.

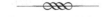

PROVISIONS

The farm table was supplied with meat from various sources. Beef, pork, and poultry were slaughtered from existing farm animals and hand processed in the garage and kitchen. When colder fall or winter weather arrived, beeves were shot with the family .22 rifle, hung by rope and tackle from a rafter in the upper barn, skinned, sawed into halves, and then quartered and laid on meat tables in the garage from where the men performed the cuts that yielded roasts, ribs, and ground meat.[10] Atypical cuts such as the stomach (tripe), lower shanks, tail, and soup bones were sometimes canned, but until refrigeration introduced freezers, many modern cuts, like steaks, were virtually unknown because uncured meat had to be used immediately. Canning was the most common method of preserving beef, although small portions were sometimes dried. These could later be boiled for stocks and soups. By the 1950s a refrigerator had replaced the earlier ice box in the kitchen, committing ice trucks and twice-weekly ice deliveries to the ages and introducing frozen foods. In the mid-fifties, Daddy rented a walk-in storage freezing facility at Lewistown. As a result, beef was more readily available, and became a staple at the farm.

Pork was consumed more frequently than beef because hams, shoulders, and large cuts could be more easily preserved through salting and smoking processes. On or around Thanksgiving Day, 3 or 4 hogs were shot with the same .22 rifle that killed the beeves.[11] One of the men (usu-

---

10. Electricity came to the farm in the late 1940s. It enabled the purchase of a refrigerator and rendered obsolete our ice box. It did not, however, permit the storage of quantities of frozen meats since the freezing compartments in refrigerators were extremely compact. Thus, large cuts of beef: roasts, steaks, ribs, etc. were rarely seen on tables. Change came in the early 1950s when entrepreneurs built frozen storage locker plants in Lewistown and McClure. This enabled our family to butcher our own beef and transport it to a rented locker where it was frozen. In spite of the ability to store steaks and roasts, cuisine clung tightly to the traditions of hundreds of years. It was not until I was in college that I tasted my first steak.

11. The .22 caliber Winchester pump rifle (model 62A) that became the family gun had been

ally Daddy) then climbed into the hog pen and "stuck" (cut the carotid vein) the dead animal, draining the blood. The hogs were then dragged by horse or tractor to the butchering area and scalded, one at a time, by lowering them briefly into a barrel containing a bath of about 150-degree water and pine tar.[12] The tar acted as an agent

Scrapers were used to remove hog bristles following the scalding process.

to loosen the hair from the follicles. Bristles were scraped from the hide, and each carcass was hung by its rear ankles from a rafter or tripod where it was sawed down the backbone into halves, in the same manner as beeves. The meat and fat were then cut, trimmed, and processed.

Butchering day began in the wee hours of the morning when fires were lit beneath large black cast iron kettles, and water was heated to boiling in preparation for the scalding process. This was usually a one-man task because the daily demands of morning milking and animal care required the other hands. Mammie started a fire in the house stove, dressed the younger children and began breakfast while Mommy and the older children helped at the barn, fed the pigs and chickens, and gathered eggs from the henhouse. At about 6:30 am the animals designated for meat were killed, bled, and dragged to the butchering area. By seven they were scalded, scraped and rinsed.[13] The heads were removed, and the entrails

---

the property of Daddy's brother, Uncle Bill, who had bought it as a target and groundhog gun in the late 1940s. After Uncle Bill was discharged from the army and living on Belle Avenue in Lewistown, he no longer found much time to use the gun. As a result, when Daddy asked to borrow the gun for fall butchering, Uncle Bill insisted that Daddy keep it. During the farm years, it is likely that every member of the family used it at one time or another. Although many times it was carried to the fields during the work day, normally Daddy kept it in his bedroom. Every family member knew its whereabouts and where in his bureau drawer he kept cartridges. On several occasions Daddy, who was an expert shot, used the gun to shoot rabbits and squirrels. After leaving the farm, Daddy kept the gun as an heirloom although it was probably not fired in his remaining years. After his death, Mommy sold the gun to me for $300.00. It is officially listed as an antique firearm.

12. The butchering area was located behind the smokehouse where two large black iron kettles with iron frames sat until Pappy built the garage in 1945. The garage was equipped with a two-kettle furnace, butchering tables and, in the earliest days of the farm, a coffin sized wooden scalding trough that was also used in the chicken house to hold mixed grain. By the 1950s metal barrels replaced the trough. Although the garage offered shelter from cold and inclement weather, the smokehouse area continued to be used for butchering on nice days because it was equipped with a ready water supply.

13. We scalded our hogs in a 50-gallon barrel. Using a rope and tackle the carcass was lowered

dragged to a remote place in the pasture or pig lot where they could de-compose without offensive odor. The brains were removed from the heads, pan-fried into a crisp, and served with eggs for breakfast.

The entire family took part in the butchering. The men handled the heavier jobs while the women cleaned the intestines to be used for sausage skins,[14] cooked the kettle meats (kidneys, hearts, livers, head meats, etc.) which were used for pon haus (scrapple), boiled the fats that were trimmed from different cuts to be rendered into cracklins and lard, and maintained a supply of boiling water.[15]

Boiling the fats required particular attention. To prevent the fat from burning, the fire was carefully tended, and the kettle was stirred constantly as the fat melted into liquid. Low heat was required, because a fire too hot caused the lard to turn brown as it hardened. Brown lard quickly became rancid.

The processes of making sausage and ren-dering lard took place after the large cuts (hams, shoulders, side meat, etc.) were completed. The remaining meat and trimmings were set on a separate table where sharp butchering knives re-moved skins from the fat and trimmed the meat that was to be used for sausage.

Sausage and lard press

The trimmed meat was then ground, sea-soned, and stuffed into a sausage press that forced the sausage meat into cleaned intestine skins. The sausage subsequently was cured by smoking.

Next, the fat was cut into one-inch cubes. After a small amount of water was poured into one of the hot cast iron kettles to prevent the fat from sticking to its surface (the water boiled out as the fat cooked), the cubes were thrown into the pot. Rendering lard was a long, slow, careful

---

into the boiling-hot water for just a few seconds then laid on planks and saw horses where several men quickly removed the bristles so that the next pig could be processed before the water cooled. Heating water was both time consuming and labor intensive.

14. Until she was no longer able, the tedium of scraping and cleaning these intestines fell upon Mammie. She carried several pans of heated water and a 3-legged stool to the isolated area of the pig lot where the innards had been dragged and began the wearying task.

15. Leaf lard is the highest grade of lard and comes from the visceral, or soft, fat around the kidneys and loin of the pig. As such, it has a very soft, super spreadable consistency at room temperature. It has less of a porky taste than other lards.

process. It could be ruined by cooking too rapidly, since the tallow required time to release its liquid fat. Older children fed the fires until eventually the pot was brought to a slow boil and the lard cooked for two or three hours. The procedure was taxing because it required constant and continual stirring with a lard paddle.

Sometimes while the lard was cooking, hungry bellies might sneak some tenderloin from the meat table and throw it into the lard pot. Fully cooked and beautifully browned, the loin could be skewered with a knife, sprinkled with salt and pepper, and eaten as the tastiest of treats. More frequently, however, pieces of liver or kidney were stolen from the stock pot, salted, and eaten, because the loin was intended to be saved for the evening meal.

The cubes of fat eventually turned a golden brown and floated to the top of the cast-iron pot. The appearance of these cracklins announced that it was time for the lard to be removed from the fire. Two men, each with a pot hook, lifted the heavy pot from its seat and set it where the boiling liquid could be strained through a white cloth and ladled into 5-gallon lard cans. Two workers held the cloth atop the lard tub while a third person used a metal dipper to ladle the lard and cracklings into the cloth where the solid matter was separated from the liquid. Finally, after the lard was emptied from the pot, the cracklins were run through a lard press to squeeze every last bit of liquid from the rinds. The resulting cakes of cracklings were saved to be later used in the pon haus. The lard was set aside to cool into a soft solid, white as snow, to be used for cooking and making soap. Normally, it was stored in the attic or cellar.

As the day drew to a close, butchering activities were suspended in favor of the evening meal and barn work. Men and boys milked and bedded the cattle, fed the stock, and tended the chickens and pigs. Women prepared supper. Traditionally, fresh loin or backbone was served with boiled potatoes, cabbage and perhaps, raw onion. Homemade breads, jellies, cakes and pies were routine trimmings.

My brother Keith provided this graphic illustration of the smokehouse. It sat between the wood house on left and the outhouse on right. The building in rear housed baby chicks.

The aftermath of butchering involved inordinate scrubbing, scouring, and washing. Following the evening meal, everyone returned a final time to the processing area and helped with the cleanup. Knives and cooking implements were degreased and stored, the great kettles were rinsed with soapy water and dried, debris was swept away and the area was restored to its earlier order.

Depending upon the temperatures, the curing process might begin a few hours afterward or the next day. Regardless, it was important that the meat remained cold to avoid spoiling.

Finally, bags of salt were emptied into one of the large pots and heated to temperatures nearly too hot to touch. Hams and shoulders, one at a time, were laid into the salt vat where one of the men packed them with the curing agent, being careful to force the salt into the area along the bone which was most susceptible to spoilage. The large cuts remained in the salt overnight, well after the pot and its contents were cooled.

For several days the meats hung in the cold butchering shop, stiffening for easier handling. Finally, along with the bacons, they were carried to the smoke house and hung from the rafters above a smoldering fire of hardwood. Hickory, maple, and even oak were common, and, in special cases, aromatic woods such as apple or sassafras were used. Depending upon individual recipes and traditions, the meat was smoked for several days. When sufficiently cured, it was carried to the cellar where it remained until used.

THE CELLAR

The spring cellar of the farmhouse had an earthen floor until Pappy poured cement in the mid to late 1940s. The walls were stone and mortar. The room was approximately 40' x 30' with a ceiling height of six and one-half feet. Twelve by eight-inch oak beams were laid across the ceiling and rested upon the stone walls of the foundation. Like most of the house it was unheated and during the spring months and periods of rain, underground springs emptied icy water across its floor to a corner drain that siphoned the contents to a leach field in the meadow below the house. The presence of the underground springs was by design. The spring cellar was originally constructed to permit water to flow through a trench around the perimeter of the floor. This water, at about 55 degrees, kept anything in the trough cold. The most common food product was raw milk, stored in crocks or kettles, set in the cold water. The flowing cold water also chilled the air that, in turn, extended the life of food items kept dry but cool on the shelves. The trench disappeared with the advent of the cement floor.

An open stairwell of perhaps ten steps descended from the living room to the cellar floor. Until a furnace was installed in the fall of 1961, at the top of the stairwell hung the hams, shoulders, and bacons that were currently in use. A butcher knife and a meat saw lay on an adjacent shelf for convenience. It was not uncommon that a trip to the cellar might include a brief stop where a thin slice of the salty smoked meat could be eaten or chewed. To the right and rear of the stairs Pappy erected a cement ledge to hold some of the canned goods that were too plentiful for the framed shelves that ran along the front wall. The jars of canned goods included meats, fruits, and vegetables that provided sustenance through the non-growing months. One-quart, two-quart, and pint jars of peas, lima beans, wax beans, green beans, beets, corn, mixed vegetables, slaw, sauerkraut, tomatoes, sweet pickles, dill pickles, apple butter, spiced apples, raspberries, blackberries, cherries, pears, peaches, and the jellies (apple, raspberry, blackberry, strawberry, peach) decorated the shelves. To the left rear sat the water pump and beside it, the barrel of vinegar, both raised on a cement platform for easy access. Facing the stairwell and against the southern wall sat the wringer washer that was pushed close to the water supply for its daily operation. On the immediate left against the eastern wall was an open shower.

In the early 1950s, Daddy served in Lewistown on a sequestered jury that deliberated the innocence or guilt of a man charged with killing his daughter. Housed in a hotel that featured conveniences alien to farm life, he took hot showers. His only other exposure to showers had been cold ones taken as a boy when he was a member of President Franklin D. Roosevelt's Civilian Conservation Corps. He found the heated accommodation so luxurious that he determined to build one in the cellar of our farmhouse. Punching nail-holes in one end of a Prestone antifreeze can, he suspended it from the ceiling. Mommy heated water on top of or in the belly of our wood stove, mixed it with cold tap water, then dumped the warm water into the antifreeze can. Daddy also laid a small wooden platform on the floor so that bathers could avoid standing in the cold water that flowed through the cellar. The shower was primal both in appearance and function, but it was efficient and gratifying.

At the bottom of the stairwell, crated eggs rested against the cool floor. An egg scale used to grade each egg sat beside a cardboard crate that held 24 dozen. When the day's eggs had been gathered, they were carried down into the cellar where, one at a time, they were graded as small, medium, large, or extra-large. Nearly all the eggs graded large and these were placed on a flat that held three dozen. When the flat was filled, it was inserted into the crate. The small, medium and extra-large eggs were set aside to be used by the family. In addition to the graded eggs, cracked eggs were common. These were kept in the ice box or refrigerator until there were enough to make noodles or a recipe that required multiple eggs. Our "egg man," who wholesaled his product to local area stores, collected our crates twice weekly and distributed them so that only 2-4 days was required for an egg to move from chicken to consumer.

Egg grader

HUNTING AND FISHING

A ll males hunted. State law required that hunters be twelve years of age, but 10-year-old farm boys hunting on their own land were common. Rabbits, squirrels, and ring-necked pheasants were shot in the fall, deer and turkeys in November. Small game was cleaned the same day and eaten the next. Deer carcasses were hung in a cold place to stiffen, perhaps the garage or barn, and butchered the following day. Until cold storage became available, the meat had to be canned or used within a few days.

Throughout Pappy's tenure small game was plentiful, and it was not uncommon for a hunting party of three or four men to bag a dozen rabbits and squirrels in one day. By the late 1950s, however, groundhog hunting had become increasingly popular, resulting in a disappearance of the holes that

Daddy, Keith, and I prepare to hunt rabbits on Opening Day. Uncle Don snapped the picture.

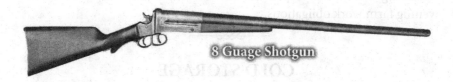

8 Guage Shotgun

I was the fourth generation to own this antique shotgun.

provided a haven for rabbits. As a result, finding small game became increasingly difficult. In addition, as grain harvesting became more thorough and efficient due to improved technology and machinery, less ground food was available for birds, rabbits, and squirrels.

Both Pappy and Daddy owned several guns. In addition to shotguns that were used for small game, and rifles for deer, Daddy owned the aforementioned .22 caliber rifle that was used to kill foxes, groundhogs, field snakes, rats, cats, weasels, and troublesome vermin. It utilized a pump-action and held 13 to 17 cartridges, depending upon their size. The gun was lightweight, making it unusually portable and popular, resulting in its ubiquitous presence on the farm. Daddy also owned an 8-gauge single barrel Shattuck "AMERICAN" shotgun, also known as a "punt gun."[16]

In the summertime, Daddy sometimes packed a lunch and took us boys fishing. These reprieves from long, hot summer days in the fields found us at mountain streams, Middleburg Creek, or the Juniata and Susquehanna Rivers. We fished for rainbow and brook trout, large and small mouthed bass, catfish and carp, blue-gills and sunfish, all the while

---

16. It was manufactured in Hatfield, Massachusetts around 1884 by C.S. Shattuck and weighed over 13 pounds with a 36-inch barrel. The barrel was Damascus twist with its original browned finish showing, along with the twist pattern in the steel. The back area of the barrel was sleeved inside a huge case-hardened breech or block, made of fluid steel, which hinged to the frame. The action looked as though it had 2 triggers: the forward one moved the hammer to half cock automatically and unlocked the breech; the rear one was the actual trigger. The buttplate was thick and made of iron. Designed as a commercial bird gun, the black powder weapon had fallen into disuse after hunting laws required steel shot. In addition, the stock had cracked years earlier, the metal had acquired some rust through disuse, and the danger in firing an old gun caused it to be retired as a relic. It had come to Daddy as an heirloom from his father and grandfather and was to be passed to each generation's oldest son. In 2014, concerned that the gun was deteriorating, I commissioned a West Virginia gunsmith to construct a new stock, remove rust, clean and restore the weapon so that it was again operable. In the spring of 2015 ten cartridges of ammunition were custom made, and the gun was safely fired that fall for the first time in over 100 years.

picnicking. Always the respite had to be fitted between the morning and evening farm work obligations.

COLD STORAGE

In the earliest years of Pappy's tenancy there was an icehouse in the meadow wherein blocks of ice, gathered from the frozen creek during winter, were kept packed in sawdust. By the beginning of WWII, however, ice delivery had become available, and until the advent of electricity on the farm, an ice truck made deliveries twice each week. It is uncertain just when or why the ice house disappeared, but by the 1940s the blocks of ice were instead stored in the wood house where Mommy or Mammie scored them with an ice pick and carried chunks to the kitchen icebox.

Shortly after electricity was installed, a refrigerator with a frozen food compartment was purchased, and by the mid-1950s Daddy rented a storage locker in Lewistown so that frozen foods could be kept for lengthy periods.

WATER

There were several springs on the farm that provided ample quantities of cold, clear, refreshing water for both house and barn. The water was free of sediment, needed no purification, and flowed regardless of drought or heavy usage. A springhouse in the meadow below the farm buildings protected the principal supply. The small building was a wood frame with a cement floor, half of which had been molded into two subterranean troughs. The deeper trough was about two feet deep and, prior to electricity and refrigeration, was primarily used as a depository for milk cans, although jugs of cider and watermelons could be lowered into the 50-degree water. The second dugout was shallower, perhaps 8-9 inches deep, and was used to store butter, cream, and other perishables. Originally a hand pump had been installed in the right rear corner, but it was removed after water was pumped directly into the house. An ever-present dipper hung from the back wall to ladle cool refreshment on summer days.

Water from the springhouse was pumped to the main house by a gasoline engine installed in the house cellar. Sometime in the early 1930s,

Beatrice, Pappy and Mammie's oldest daughter, dug the original trench into which the pipe was laid that conducted water to the house. The engine was later replaced by an electric pump.

A second channel carried water from the house to a hydrant behind the wood shed. This supplied water for the washing machine that stood adjacent to the smoke house during summer months. Until the garage was constructed, that area was also used in the fall for making soap and apple butter, and for butchering.

A well on the western side of the barn fed water via a hand pump to both the old milkhouse and a large trough in the barn shed. It was the sole water supply for the stock until Pappy added individual drinking fountains inside the barn in the early 1950s. At about the same time, a new milkhouse was constructed against the eastern side of the barn. Along its northern wall another hydrant was installed which connected to the existing water supply. At the same time, pipe was laid between the milkhouse and the chicken house where a third hydrant acted as a water source for the chickens. Until that time, water for the chickens was carried from the barn.

In addition to the springs, a creek snaked its way from the western boundary of the farm, through the pig lot, then under a cement bridge that Pappy built, flowing the entire length of the meadow, and exiting at the far eastern end of the farm. Since the meadow was the primary pasture, the creek was the principal water source for pasturing animals.

REFLECTION

A man saw a ball of gold in the sky;
He climbed for it,
And eventually he achieved it—
It was clay.

Now this is the strange part:
When the man went to the earth
And looked again,
Lo, there was the ball of gold.
Now this is the strange part:

It was a ball of gold.

Aye, by the heavens, it was a ball of gold.

"A MAN SAW A BALL OF GOLD"
STEPHEN CRANE

Whatever the land had been prior to my grandfather's purchase of the farm, whatever it has since become, it was, for a time, my home, and its influence upon my life cannot be overstated.

It was there that I enjoyed childhood innocence and suffered adolescent insecurities. It was there that I learned many of life's important lessons and made some of life's critical decisions.

When the last descriptive word is uttered, and the soul is exhausted in its attempt to define life's meaning, it will come to this—worship God and enjoy Him forever.

The farm was my locus—my venue—the place where I learned to worship. The sky and the fields, the days and the seasons were cathedrals where I celebrated my joys and cerebrated my miseries. Each was a boon. But more than these, more than the place and the time were the people. My father and my mother, my brothers and sisters, my grandparents, my relatives, my friends, and my neighbors—they were the farm. They were the personification of all that is beautiful, and true, and lovely, and secure—all that is romantic and absolute, unconditional and eternal. The farm was people.

Those relationships, wonderful beyond measure, were the image, the representation of the greatest relationship—for only in the worship of God—the Author of love, beauty, and truth is there ultimate meaning. The farm pointed to a relationship larger than parents, siblings, relatives, and neighbors—a relationship spiritual, transcendent, and eternal.

Time sometimes garnishes the past with splendors that are phantasmal, that seem golden, but under scrutiny never really existed. This I accept. Still, there was a farm—and there was a boy—and upon closest examination many years afterward—despite the realities of time and place, of trial and pain, it really was "a ball of gold."

MY EARLY YEARS

THE FARM 1964
By this time improvements included electricity, a second silo, a new corncrib built into the side of the wagon shed, and a three-bay garage in back of the barn.

I arrived into this world on September 22, 1942. It was a time of war, a time of anxiety, a time of sacrifice. It was a time to do the best you could with what you had, a time to cooperate with your neighbor by sharing both the workload and the worldly goods, and especially a time of self-restraint, when love for your neighbor also meant not making his burden greater by visiting your misfortune upon him. This meant each person did his share and more.

Farming in the early twentieth century in Decatur Township at the eastern end of Mifflin County, Pennsylvania was not the mechanized enterprise it has become in the twenty-first century. Rather, survival and success required a cooperative effort from both family members and neighbors. Income in the farm community centered on milk production. As a result men and women worked side by side, climbing the silos and mows, feeding and bedding the livestock, and milking the cows. My parents and grandparents arose daily at 5:00 am to finish the morning milking before the milkman arrived to load their ten-gallon cans onto a flatbed truck and transport them to the Dairyman's League processing plant twelve miles away at Beaver Springs. When milking was completed, Mommy and Mammie went to the house to make breakfast while the men harnessed

WEDDING DAY - JUNE 1, 1938
Less than two years later Daddy and Mommy moved to the farm.

the horses, greased the machinery, and prepared for the day's field work.

Mommy and Daddy had moved to the farm from Lewistown two years before I made my appearance. Daddy had become disenchanted with a series of temporary jobs, including selling life insurance and working at the Lewistown Foundry, and Mommy was homesick for the farm where she had been raised. Circumstances seemed fortuitous when Pappy, who wished to expand his farm operation, offered the young couple a permanent role. Although Daddy was inexperienced, he was fully capable, and the workload and exigency of the dairy farm endowed him with a sense of belonging, a place of significance, and a desire to be a good farmer. For Mommy the move was easier. She did not have to adapt to the new life, but simply resumed what she had done for years.

For my parents to live in the same house with my grandparents, the house had to be partitioned, each family having their own kitchen and bedrooms. Since all farmhouse kitchens served as dining and family rooms, and since there were no indoor bathrooms, the living space needed was significantly less than modern standards but altogether comfortable. A common living room situated between the kitchens was accessible to both families, but it was used sparingly. When Keith and I had the measles in second grade, Mommy and Mammie closed off that room, shut the blinds, and kept us confined there for a week. Most days, however, the room seemed impractical, because by the time Daddy and Pappy were finished with their work in the evening, it was time to go to bed. In addition, until electricity was introduced, at night the room had to be lit with kerosene lamps which meant either transferring a light source from one of the kitchens or lighting extra lamps. There was a wood stove in the room, but its firing was limited to occasional Saturday and Sunday nights when everyone listened to radio programs or when Mommy, Mammie, and the neighborhood ladies quilted.

Each kitchen featured a wood-burning cook stove, a table with chairs, an icebox, and a sink. In most cases cooking and preparing meals was a cooperative effort, usually done in our kitchen. It provided greater efficiency and gave Mammie opportunity to help Mommy in caring for the small children. The actual eating of meals, however, was separate. Mammie filled plates for Pappy and herself and carried the food to the older couple's kitchen.

When Pappy or Mammie entertained relatives or other visitors, Mammie cooked in her own kitchen. Likewise, when Daddy's family traveled to the farm, Mommy cooked the meals. Curiously, there was little intercourse between Daddy's and Mommy's families. It was an early indication of Daddy's lifelong refusal to countenance Mommy's relatives. The reasons are somewhat nebulous. Perhaps his insecurities as a farmer came into play, perhaps his conviction that the worldliness of some of Mommy's brothers and sisters was corrupting to his children, but most likely his coolness was the residue of the growing hostility between the two men. They spoke to each other but seldom conversed. In Daddy's defense, Pappy was proud of his achievements on the farm and coveted the attention they garnered. He seldom asked for input and failed to understand Daddy's needs. In that sense, Daddy was an outsider. As a result the families never coalesced. If Mommy wished to see her aunts and uncles when they called, she did so on her parent's side of the house. Fortunately, the converse did not apply. When Daddy's brothers and sisters came to the farm, Mammie and Pappy enjoyed their company, helped with preparations, and were welcomed by everyone.

Daddy and Pappy never resolved their conflict.

Three or four times each year farm activity required the help of neighbors. This was especially the case when wheat, corn, or oats was shocked, when the grain was thrashed, or when the silos were filled. On those occasions, Mommy's larger kitchen was utilized to feed the 10 to 12 men who volunteered their help. She and Mammie combined efforts to produce lavish meals. In fact, long after more modern mechanization rendered the shocking of grain and the need for cooperative farming obsolete, years after my childhood, those farmers, now grown old, reminisced to me about Mommy's meals. They remembered the succulent roasts of beef and pork, the slabs of fried ham, the rich gravies, the mounds of snowy-white mashed potatoes, the platters of creamed lettuce and bowls of creamed rice, the heavy slices of ripe tomatoes and cucumbers, the wedges of apple and peach pies, and the chocolate layered cakes washed down with multiple cups of coffee.

In spite of private disagreements between the men and the minor irritations that are endemic to two-family homes, open conflicts did not exist. Both Mammie and Pappy loved their grandchildren and were grateful to have them as part of their immediate lives.

As our family grew, clothing, diapers, bedware, kitchen towels, etc. increased as did the need for more frequent laundering. By the time I reached my sixth birthday, there were four small children and four adults. This initiated an almost daily ritual of carrying and heating extra water, for although by this time we had cold running water in the kitchen, there was no hot water heater. In the earliest days, the laundry consisted of a 30-gallon cast iron kettle, a clothes basket, two ten-gallon galvanized washtubs, a scrub board and a pot stick. The articles to be washed were dumped into the kettle of boiling water. Lye soap was peeled and placed in the water. Intermittently, Mommy or Mammie took the potstick and

stirred the kettle. The other sat astride a stool with one of the washtubs between her legs. To one side was the clothes basket, and on the other side was the second washtub filled with rinse water. After sufficient boiling, the potstick was used to lift the articles from the water to the first galvanized wash-tub. Each article was then dipped, scrubbed, rinsed, and wrung dry. Diapers and especially soiled cloth-ing were scrubbed on the scrub board before being

Galvanized washtub and scrub board

placed into the kettle. They were rinsed in clean lye water (it was believed that a lye rinse brightened wash) and hand wrung a second time. Finally, after a third rinse in clean water, the clothing was laid into the clothes bas-ket. When the basket was full, the laundry was carried to the clothesline and, piece by piece, hung to dry.

The advances of technology throughout the twentieth cen-tury brought continual changes to nearly every facet of farm life. This included washing laundry. Sometime in the early 1950s we purchased a washing machine with a crank-operated wringer. It was positioned near the hydrant next to our wood house in the summer and was moved to the cellar during winter months. A clothes basket of wet clothes (that had already been hand wrung) was set on one side of the wringer with a wash basket on the other. Mommy or Mammie fed each article into the wringer while one of us kids turned the crank. When electricity arrived, we bought an electric washer. Hand wringing the wet clothes passed into obsolescence (or near obsolescence; the parade of new babies into our lives demanded that diapers still be scrubbed on the wash board and wrung by hand as it permitted quicker recycling). Now, a wringer was engaged, and clothes were fed between two turning rollers to a second person, usually a child, who took hold of each article of clothing as it appeared on the other side to prevent it from wrapping itself around the rollers and clogging the operation. Despite the precaution, articles frequently became entangled so that the process seemed as much an ordeal as a convenience.

All our clothing was dried on outdoor clotheslines until winter weather forced the ladies to hang items indoors in the kitchen and living room. Every article was folded and placed into the wash basket. Later, the ladies spritzed and ironed each item with flat irons that were alternately heated atop the stove. Our underwear and socks, of course, were not ironed, but the ladies carefully folded them and placed them in drawers. Even after electric irons replaced flat irons and synthetic fibers competed with cotton, wool and denim, Mommy continued to press the T-shirts and jeans we wore to school.

Washing detergents appeared in the 1950s. This meant the end of "peeling" soap, which made wash day somewhat less toilsome. It also resulted in less demand for lard, an essential ingredient for the homemade lye soap and relegated it exclusively for cooking.

The process for making lye soap took place at the fireplace behind the wood house each November. My grandfather arose before daylight to start the fires and heat water in two large cast-iron kettles. He then dumped wood ashes into the boiling water and began the monotonous task of constantly stirring the mixture until it produced the lye necessary for making soap. The ashes were gathered from the residue of oak, chestnut, and maple that had been burned in the early portion of the week for the sole purpose of making the soap. As the contents boiled liquid lye rose to the surface. Pappy wore old clothes and gloves that covered his hands and arms and was careful not to splash the caustic liquid that burned exposed skin and could permanently blind the eyes. When a sufficient amount of the chemical was available, he scooped it into a bucket and set it aside.

Besides heating water for washing clothes, our 30-gallon cast iron kettles were used to make apple butter, soap, and pon haus.

As gray dawn approached Pappy washed and rinsed the kettles, added wood to the fires, and poured buckets of lard into the pots. Again he continually agitated the contents so that the lard would melt but not burn. He maintained that soap properly cooked should be white not brown. Once it was melted, the lye was mixed with the lard and stirred until a paste-like consistency appeared. The mixture was then ladled into pans and set aside to cool.

After the soap was cooled, it was cut into four or five-inch cubes and placed in a dark, dry cellar or attic. During my elementary years Mammie kept five-gallon containers of lye soap in the attic of our house so that whenever I went into the loft the smell of fresh soap was pungent. After Mammie and Pappy moved into their own home, Mommy stored our soap in the cellar where it was more accessible and also placed bars in the milkhouse, at each hydrant, and beside the kitchen sink. Ironically, even after less harsh detergents became commonplace in the mid-1950s, Mommy continued to use lye soap to wash singular items, especially diapers. Women believed that a bit of lye soap added to regular detergent whitened and brightened laundered clothes.

The soap had a myriad of other uses: dissolving grease, preventing dry skin, treating poison ivy, insect bites, and lice, clearing acne, eczema, and psoriasis. It also worked for mosquitoes, chiggers, ticks, sunburn, athlete's foot, and dandruff. Further, it was a deterrent for ants, termites, spiders, snakes, and roaches. Pets that became lousy were bathed in the soapy water. Hinges and axels stopped squeaking after a liberal application.

The usage with which farm boys and girls were most concerned, however, was the correction and prevention of vulgar language. Cursing, profanity, and rudeness disappeared from young vocabularies after tasting a bar of the lye soap that Mom, Dad, or schoolteacher inserted with the peremptory directive, "Now, keep your mouth closed."

The black kettles and the fireplace behind the wood house saw other usages. In October, after the apples were picked and the cider pressed, Pappy dumped bushels of apples and gallons of cider into the pots and began the procedure that resulted in copious quarts of aromatic apple butter stored on cellar shelves. At hog-butchering in late November, usually Thanksgiving Day, Pappy awakened long before daylight to move the heavy kettles from the fire pits behind the wood house to those Daddy had built inside the garage. He carried water from the hydrant at the chicken house to the kettles, brought wood from the wood house and started the fires that boiled the water for scalding the pigs. With Pappy thus occupied, Daddy tended to the barn work. Since milking was a two-person job, Mommy substituted for Pappy. Women were not yet permitted to wear slacks or jeans, so she managed farm chores wearing a dress, a warm sweater buttoned against her neck, a waist-length jacket, and a bandanna tied tightly over her ears. Her legs remained unprotected from the pricks and scratches of hay and straw as she fed the cows and calves, and they were exposed to the cold as she carried milk to the icy milkhouse. Mammie tended to us kids, diapered the newest baby, and made certain that breakfast was on the table at 7 am.

When these activities occurred on a Saturday or a school vacation day, Mammie bundled Keith and me in warm clothes and allowed us to "help" Pappy. Sometimes he let us stir the contents that steamed in the immense cast-iron kettles, but invariably Mammie would appear, reprimanding, "Charl, don't let those boys get near the fire."

Another special event was "raising" potatoes in late September. Each year in late April, Pappy filled burlap bags with potatoes that had seeded.[1] The evening before planting, neighbors helped cut them into half-dollar size pieces. Then, on planting day, either Pappy or Daddy drove a horse that pulled a single-bottom plow and made furrows in the two-acre plot into which the pieces were dropped. Only one horse was needed, because potatoes prefer shallow furrows that are mounded and well drained. As a result our potato patch was usually in the field above the road that ran uphill past the pig lot to John Goss's farm. Then, in late September, grandparents, parents, and children combined efforts to harvest the crop. Pappy drove the same horse that had pulled the single-bottom plow earlier in the spring, turning up the soil and unveiling the yield. Daddy followed with a

---

1. A seeded potato is one whose eyes have budded. An eye is a bud that grows into a new plant.

A potato fork. The multiple tines prevented smaller potatoes from falling to the ground.

potato fork, sifting the soil to expose potatoes hidden in the freshly plowed dirt. Mommy and Mammie, bonneted and aproned, picked up the potatoes, shaking loose soil from them and placing them into pails. Keith, Billy, RuthAnn and I were given lesser jobs, placing the smallest of the potatoes in containers which were kept apart, holding open burlap sacks as pails were emptied, carrying mason jars filled with cool water from the springhouse, or cutting lengths of twine so that bags could be tied. Somewhat regularly the tooth of the plow would cut a potato in half. Not to be wasted, these were placed to the side until the regular harvest was finished. They were then gathered, scrubbed, and used for the evening meal. The busy day had its respites. Young potatoes (just harvested) have tender skins, and harvesters found time to brush loose soil from small potatoes, polish them with apron or shirt, and eat them as snacks. Health habits of the twenty-first century now preclude such delights.

My very earliest memory of farm activity, however, is standing in the field next to the eastern side of the house as a preschooler and helping to spread lime with a child's green shovel. A dump truck appeared one early spring morning, and men, strange in white coveralls, dumped chalky white lime in random piles across the 30-acre field. Pappy and Daddy watched from our summer porch as they ate their seven o'clock breakfast of ham and gravy. An hour later shovels and a wheelbarrow were brought from the wagon shed next to the barn and the wearisome labor of spreading lime across 30 acres began. My green shovel undoubtedly got in the way, but their patience and indulgence must have prevailed since I have a most pleasant memory of that morning.

Endemic to the men who labored at farming was the smell of perspiration, even in the winter months, as they sweat-worked. The odor resulted, in part, from not having a ready supply of hot water with which to wash, but also contributing to the pervasive redolence was the large, red handkerchief most farmers carried in the rear pocket of their bib-overalls. Pappy regularly took a minute from his work to wipe his brow and the back of his neck with the handkerchief before stuffing the damp cloth back into his pocket and resuming his task. Afterward, he might drape the wet cloth over a barn gate or front porch banister to dry, then use it the following day.

Most adult farm people bathed but twice weekly: on Wednesday nights a washcloth bath and on Saturday, before retiring, a full bath in preparation for Sunday morning church. Water was heated atop the stove or in its belly. During cold weather months children's baths took place behind the kitchen stove because there were no other heated rooms. Youngest children were put to bed before older ones. Thus, the baby was cradled into the warm water first, then the toddler, etc., until the oldest was given op-

Keith, Bill, and I – Circa 1950

portunity. There were five of us children in the early fifties, and being the oldest, it meant that the bath water was four kids dirty by the time it was my turn. Mommy and Daddy waited to take their baths until we were in bed. Mammie and Pappy bathed on their side of the house. When warm weather permitted, Mommy placed our galvanized wash tub in the yard, drew cold water from the nearby hydrant, and scrubbed us clean with lye soap. On hot summer nights adults bathed in our enclosed summer porch.

This routine came to an abrupt end one autumn in the early 1950s after Daddy served five days on a sequestered jury in Lewistown. While secreted in a hotel room that week, he experienced his first hot shower. It was a luxury of indescribable proportion. Upon his return home, building a shower became one of life's highest priorities.

My brother Bill was a small boy the day my dad

Dave taking a bath in a galvanized wash tub.

punched nail-holes in the bottom of a Prestone antifreeze can and suspended it from the ceiling in our cellar. Water was heated in the belly of our wood stove, then diluted with cold tap water, and dumped into the anti-freeze can. Each "shower" consisted of two canfuls: one to get wet, then, after soaping, one to rinse. It worked beautifully for several weeks until one Saturday evening after supper, the weight from the filled can tore loose the metal straps that held it in place, and it fell and cut a sizeable gash in Bill's head. Never inclined to overreact, Daddy held a dishcloth against the cut until the bleeding stopped, taped Bill's head, reinforced the antifreeze can and announced that the shower was again safe. Bill carried a small scar for the rest of his life, but consistent with the virtue that eschews pusillanimity, he never complained.

By the 1950s we had hot "running" water in the house, but Daddy insisted that heating water in the stove belly was more economical than using the electric water heater, so Mommy continued to tap cold water into a pot and transfer it to the stove.

Until I started to school in the fall of 1948, I slept with Keith in the upstairs bedroom at the top of the staircase. Frequently, as children commonly do, I had difficulty falling asleep. I knew my grandmother stayed awake until a late hour, and that I could sneak down the stairs and into her kitchen without getting into trouble. She never scolded or criticized me for visiting her at that late hour. Many nights she seated me in Pappy's rocking chair, spoon-feed me half of an orange, and then put me to bed alongside Pappy. After I had fallen asleep, my mother would retrieve me and put me to bed a second time.

When one of us was sick or needed to go to the toilet during the night, we used the basin Mommy placed beneath our bed. In the summertime, when weather permitted us to go out-of-doors, she would get out of bed and wait in the dark doorway while we walked out on the lawn or went to the outhouse.

During this time there were occasions when I wet the bed, had nightmares of lions and tigers, and suffered at night from leg pains. Mommy addressed the first problem by laying a piece of plastic under my blanket, but never calling attention to it in the presence of relatives or brothers and sisters. The only other person who knew was Mammie, and neither she nor Mommy made me self-conscious by criticizing or teasing. The methodology for dealing with lions and tigers was of a different nature. Frightened in the middle of the night by these phantoms, I called for Mommy. Sometimes she softly assured me from her bed that I was safe, but if I persisted, she crawled from her warm covers, threw a housecoat about her shoulders, and came and sat on the side of my bed. When I had leg pains she massaged my calf muscles until I was able to sleep. On the other hand, if I disturbed Daddy, he would warn with somewhat less compassion, "You go back to sleep, mister, or I'll give you something to cry about!"

Being in school meant that I was old enough to have farm responsibilities. As a first grader I carried water in mason jars (cooled in the springhouse) to the men working in the fields. Keith and I walked a mile to Joe McKinley's country store with a note indicating what we were to bring home. When potatoes were harvested I helped Mommy and Mammie gather the small potatoes that fell through the potato fork. Mornings before breakfast it was my job to feed the chickens and gather eggs from the nests in the chicken house. The nests were elevated so that rats could not break and eat the eggs, so I had to reach above my head into each cubbyhole, feel for the eggs, and avoid the pecking of a protective hen.

During those years of elementary school I assisted Daddy and Pappy with numerous assignments and responsibilities: I picked blackberries, raspberries and strawberries; climbed fruit trees to gather apples, pears, plums, cherries, and black walnuts; husked corn in the field; shocked wheat and oats; drove the tractors during silo-filling; cleaned stables, the barnyard, and the chicken house; threw silage down from the silo into the entryway and then fed it to the cows; "chopped"[2] the pigs and cows and bedded the stalls; shelled corn for chicken feed; bagged grain for pig and cow feed; chopped Canadian thistles in the meadow; weeded the garden; chopped wood for the stove (our only heat source); churned butter, adding the orange coloring from a packet; "picked chickens

The wheat sheaves were shocked into a standing position to dry, then threshed to separate the straw from the grain.

---

2. Corn, wheat, oats, and sometimes barley were ground (chopped) into a coarse meal, enriched with molasses and other supplements and fed to the livestock.

(scalded, removed the feathers, and singed); laid papers for "peepies" (baby chicks); cleaned the granary; swept down cobwebs in the barn; cultivated corn; "made hay" with a dump-rake and hay loader; whitewashed the barn; sewed, weeded and harvested the beans, peas, cabbages, lettuce, onions, carrots, radishes, tomatoes, corn, cucumbers, beets, and other vegetables in our extensive garden; and of course, did the incessant barn work.

When I was eight I was taught to drive. Daddy instructed me to steer our blue 1946 three-quarter ton flat-bed pickup truck through the fields where we were making fence. He rode on the bed and dropped fence posts at regular intervals while I kept my eyes on the end of the row so that the posts lay in a straight line.

Concurrent with my increasing responsibilities, my brothers and I experienced another change. RuthAnn was now two and old enough to occupy the downstairs bedroom, and so Mommy moved us boys upstairs to the bedroom above the living room. Bill, being the youngest, slept between Keith and me. Just as before, our room was unheated, but during the winters Mommy covered our bed with two haps, and although each of us complained that someone else had all the covers, we not only survived, but were grateful for each other's company.[3]

When I turned twelve and began junior high school, Mommy moved each of us boys into our own bedroom. It marked a special time of spiritual growth for me as it initiated personal meditation, Bible reading and prayer. During these years, Mommy sometimes called me in the middle of the night to come downstairs and hold the baby while she heated milk, or made medicine, or cleaned up the diaper and vomit messes that babies make. It was during those nights that I gradually learned about having babies, menstruation, and the wonders of adult life. Some nights the emotional duress that Mommy suffered in her relationship with Daddy poured itself out in tears and self-condemnation. I learned that their relationship was a precarious balance between

From my earliest years baseball was an obsession.

---

3. A hap is similar to a quilt, except that it is made of heavier material, stuffed, and tied rather than quilted. Frequently, quilts were used as fillers for haps.

the tenderness of contrition and the callousness of insinuation and blame. Daddy's moodiness and quick temper were difficult mixes with Mommy's disposition of insecurity and hyper-sensitivity.

In addition to the joy of having the privacy afforded by my own room, Mommy permitted me, on nights the Phillies were playing, to take our Zenith shelf-radio and listen to games. Baseball was my greatest pleasure.

By the time I began school in September 1948 I was already playing baseball and listening to games. It is difficult to determine exactly how or why particular affinities originate. Perhaps they are circumstantial, perhaps they are dispositional, or perhaps they are designed, but clearly baseball had become epochal to me. I suspect several influences combined. Foremost of these may have been that baseball freed me from farm work. It became a diversion that allowed me to escape what might otherwise have been the boredom and drudgery of farm routine. Regardless, I became addicted.

Daddy took me along to Joe McKinley's store on summer evenings and permitted me to listen for a few minutes to Philadelphia Athletics and Phillies home games on Joe's radio (road games were seldom broadcast and only as re-creations). Men from the neighborhood farms and hamlets congregated at the general store on those evenings where they played cards and listened to games. It contained the stuff of romance.

There were other imprints. I was at the store on the evening of September 15, 1950, when Phillies' pitcher Bubba Church was struck in the face with a line drive from the bat of Cincinnati first baseman Ted Kluszewski. At the end of that inning Daddy took me home, but the residual excitement of the game — the men, the store, and the drama of the Phillies' pennant clinching game two weeks later, impassioned me with a love for baseball that has lasted all my adult life.

A year earlier, my second-grade teacher, Mertie Baker, began asking for scores of A's and Phillies games when I arrived at school each morning. It made me feel important and fed my interest in the game. Ball games during recesses and lunch breaks inculcated the notion that I was a good player and motivated me to practice and improve.

Mertie became an even more integral part of my baseball influence a short time afterward. Until I left for college in 1961, nearly every village and hamlet in central Pennsylvania had its own baseball team. It was not unusual for families to convene and visit each other during those evening games. Daddy sometimes took Keith and me to Belltown or Wagner or Alfarata or McClure to see games and, of course, I hoped that someday I would be able to play.

Mertie's husband, Max, was a local milkman whom everyone knew and liked.[4] He was one of the men playing cards in Joe's store, listening to the game the evening Bubba Church was hurt. He frequently umpired local games, receiving no fee, but accepting the contents of a hat that was passed among the patrons. Typically, he might receive $2 or $3 for his effort. Max endured the second-guessing and criticism that characteristically resulted because he enjoyed baseball. To my mind, he was a giant, a figure to be revered.

When Max umpired games at Belltown, Mertie came with him. Warm-hearted and congenial, she visited each family, holding newborn babies, and taking toddlers for walks. Everyone was fond of Mertie. I loved her too, because she always managed to make me feel special and sometimes played baseball with us at school.

On a particular summer evening at Belltown when I was in the third or fourth grade, Daddy, Keith and I were watching a game from behind the home plate screen where I always asked to sit. Max was umpiring and Mertie was visiting with families. In the midst of the game she came to where I was sitting and climbed up beside me. As she frequently did with kids, she placed her arm around me, leaned over and whispered, "Someday, you'll be the best player."

A sequel occurred four years later. The one-room school Billy, Keith and I had been attending closed. We now rode a big yellow bus to the new Decatur Township School. It was a difficult transition for a farm boy, because I had both a new classroom teacher and new classmates. There was, however, a familiar face at the school. During lunch period (at a country school it was called "dinner time") Mertie, who was now teaching fourth grade, organized and umpired baseball games.

I was small for my age and at these noontime ball games, older, bigger boys called me "half-pint." It bothered me because it implied

---

4.   In rural America a milkman was someone who owned or rented a flatbed truck, contracted with local dairies, and hauled farmers' ten gallon cans of raw milk from farm to processing plant.

that I was too small to be a good player. On this particular day Mertie waited until lunch was completed, and after we had returned to our studies, she quietly opened the door to my classroom, walked around behind my desk, knelt beside me and whispered, "You're no half-pint."

Thus, she fueled what had already become passion. In all that time I never spoke personally to her, never knew her except as my teacher, but for many years afterward I wished that Mertie could know about my baseball joys and accomplishments. She died of cancer while I was in college, so I lost any opportunity to express the gratitude that might have reciprocated a portion of her kindness and attention.

It seems that all of my childhood was directly associated with baseball: all of my free time playing imaginary games behind the barn

I waited from May until August for my Phillies Yearbook.

(almost exclusively by myself, although after Billy was old enough, he and I spent considerable time playing "pepper" and similar games), all of my school time dreaming of games to be played, all of my day time fantasizing about high school and college and the big leagues, all of my nights listening to the Phillies and A's and studying my baseball cards and yearbooks.

The yearbooks were a special treasure and I cannot adequately describe the despair I suffered every summer afternoon when, after placing my order in early May, I anxiously watched and waited for the noon mail, only to find that my copy had not yet arrived. I should have learned patience, but summer after summer, I let myself suffer daily disappointment until the precious package arrived in late August.

Special too, was my love affair with Phillies pitcher Robin Roberts.[5] I scored his games, saved his pictures and write-ups, and emu-

5. For many years I sent Roberts a birthday card on September 30. He would sometimes answer with a simple "Thanks for the card" or "Best Wishes." I was thrilled. After he was elected to the National Baseball Hall of Fame in 1976 he always signed, "Robin Roberts HOF." In the spring of 2006 I was coaching at Lehigh University when we had occasion to play at Jack Russell Stadium in Clearwater, Florida where the Phillies had trained for many years. I wrote to him sharing my excitement and recalling memories of his games at that site. He returned a note and an autographed photo thanking me for my kindness. A few years later, following the death of his wife Mary, I sent a letter of condolence. Several

lated his idiosyncrasies. His career provided me many special memories over the years.

I especially remember the summer evening of Thursday, May 13, 1954, when a weekly neighborhood prayer meeting was being held at our house. Those meetings began about 30 minutes after the start of Phillies games and, of course, Daddy expected me to attend. On this evening, however, I was excused. Since we were not allowed to be indoors unless we sat quietly with the adults, and considering that I was not permitted to take our kitchen radio to the barn where there were electrical outlets, my only recourse was to sneak the radio into Mommy and Daddy's bedroom. Their room, however, was off limits.

Regardless, I stealthily sneaked the Zenith from its shelf in the kitchen, covertly concealed it beneath a blanket, furtively plugged it into the only outlet in their bedroom, then cautiously lowered the volume. Roberts gave up a leadoff home run to Cincinnati third baseman Bobby Adams and then began retiring every batter (he would retire the final 27 batters in order). It became a dramatic game. As it went into the final innings I knew that the end of prayer meeting was imminent and uncomfortable consequences would result if I was discovered. The broadcast, however, seemed worth the risk. Fortunately, I was saved when supernumerary petitions to Providence caused the prayer meeting to run long.

I remember the season opener on April 13, 1955, when Roberts took a no-hitter into the ninth against the Giants, giving up a one-out single to Al Dark. It was a Wednesday, and I had stayed home from school to help Daddy. As we worked I casually shared the news that the Phillies' broadcast would be at 2:00. I suspect he configured my remaining work so that I would

Keith sowing fertilizer in the spring of 1955

months passed, but he found the time to compose a longer letter of gratitude. When he died in 2010 I wrote to the minister of his church who handled the funeral, asking about Robin's spiritual life. The reply was somewhat vague indicating that Robin and Mary attended services regularly but were not active within the fellowship. I have kept the correspondence with my other memorabilia.

be free at that time, because he announced just before game time that he had to pick up something in Lewistown.

I remember a game late in Roberts's career with the Phillies when I dared to "break the rules." He had stopped winning, and I feared he might be released or traded. Daddy was away. The broadcast was at 2:00 in the afternoon, and I was working by myself in one of the fields raking hay. As it neared game time, I made an excuse to come to the house for water, turned on the radio and listened as he pitched a 2-0 shutout against Cincinnati. The game lasted less than 2 hours. I was back to work when Daddy came home, so he either never realized or chose to ignore what I had done.

By my junior and senior high school years I was responsible to carry out more involved assignments when Daddy was absent or occupied on another part of the farm. I milked the cows; combined and threshed grain; cleaned the electric milkers; sealed the silo doors with clay in preparation for their filling with newly chopped corn; mowed, raked, tedded and filled the mows with new hay; killed and cut up chickens for both our own use and for market; butchered hogs and beeves; opened ditches in the springtime; pulled cockle from the wheat, wild mustard from the alfalfa, and milkweed from the oats; sowed grass seed; sowed fertilizer; made fences; put tar on the roofs of the house and barn; spread manure; mowed the lawn; cleaned the corn crib and granaries before harvest; etc.

Besides the work that centered on the animals and grain, I spent days organizing and maintaining our orchard and garden. The garden was an especially important part of our food supply. Daddy would plow, harrow, and cultipack a two-acre plot alongside the house in the late spring where we planted lettuce, white and red radishes, carrots, cabbage, endive, tomatoes, lima beans, beets, string beans, peas, sugar peas, cauliflower, celery, onions, and peppers. In a larger plot in one of the fields we planted sweet corn, potatoes, and turnips. There was a rhubarb patch and shrubs of red currants. In the spring we picked and ate dandelion greens with a hot bacon dressing.

In addition to plowing, planting, cultivating, watering, dusting, and harvesting, Mommy was always after me to work in the garden. Many summer evenings after the barn and house work were done, I reluctantly went with her to the plot alongside our yard. With one hand I pulled weeds and with the other drove away the gnats. She was her father's daughter. The point of daylight was to work.

An essential part of gardening was preserving food to be eaten during the cold-weather months. One of my jobs was helping Mommy can. I peeled apples for spicing, removed the stones from peaches, shredded cabbage, shelled lima beans and peas, snapped string beans, and cut corn from the cobs. By autumn our cellar was piquant with the pungency of vinegar, sauerkraut, and pickle brine, as well as the aromatic smells of hams, shoulders, and bacon, hickory smoked and hung along the walls on great iron hooks. Row upon row of canned vegetables, meats, and fruits were arranged in tiers on the homemade shelving Daddy had built for that purpose. On the top shelves sat the glass containers of peas, beans, beets, carrots, and corn. Below them stood the pints and quarts of sausage, ribs, and tripe. Cole slaw, jellies and jams, and apple butter were proud neighbors to colorful jars of peaches, pears, and spiced apples. Raspberries, blackberries, and cherries were arranged in long rows atop a concrete slab that ran along the rear wall, waiting to provide succulence to endless pies and cobblers. In the far corner, elevated onto a concrete slab rested the big oak vinegar barrel. Each fall we bagged the seconds from our Northern Spy, Granny Smith, Red and Yellow Delicious, and Baldwin apple trees, and Daddy took them to a nearby cider press. The cider was emptied into three 10-gallon milk cans, transported home, and lowered into the icy water of our milk cooler. We enjoyed it for nearly two weeks before it began to harden. Daddy and Pappy then poured it into the oak barrel and let it "work" in the full sunlight of the yard. When it was completely fermented, the barrel was carried to the cellar and the contents were used exclusively as vinegar.

In addition to the food stored in our cellar, Daddy and Pappy dug an underground cellar into a slope near the top of the orchard, lined it with straw, and cached bushels of potatoes, onions, and apples in the dark interior. They then boarded up the entrance to prevent the invasion of animals. The temperature in the interior was sufficiently cold to retard spoilage and adequately warm to prevent freezing. Typically, the food remained preserved until January.

It is true that nearly all my memories of the farm, of home, of Mommy and Daddy, of Mammie and Pappy, and of my brothers and sisters, are in some way associated with work: hard work, exhausting work, unrelenting work. However, there were diversions, delights, and consolations that compensated. While weekdays and weekends, whether spring, summer, winter, or fall, were filled with work, there were also times to play. Normally, these times occurred when Daddy was away or on Sunday afternoons between returning from church at 1:00 pm and starting the barn work at 5:00 pm.

I played ball, standing in front of the garage, throwing a sponge ball against a barn door, or batting a ball between the yard and the pig lot, always pretending the Phillies were playing. When the weather was inclement, or it was wintertime, I read or spent time with my baseball cards. On rainy summer days I loved to take a book, climb up in the haymow or the corncrib, and read. Listening to the rain pounding against the tin roof, I inevitably fell asleep.

In the winter, I played in the barn, the chicken house, the garage, or some other enclosed place. Keith and I spent afternoons in and around the haymows. We jumped from the loft down into the hay, or we played cowboys and Indians, carving guns, bows, and arrows from the branches of maple trees and sumac bushes, then made bowstrings using the twine that tied chicken feedbags. Sometimes, when severe weather conditions restricted us to indoor activities, we put jig-saw puzzles together on the kitchen table or played board games of Monopoly, Chinese Checkers, Parcheesi, etc.

By third grade I had learned to love books. On the final day of my third-grade school year, my teacher, Edie Erb, permitted me to take a schoolbook for the summer from which I read and reread "Rumpelstiltskin," "Billy Goats Gruff," "Tar Baby," "King Midas' Touch," etc. A year or so later I found a set of six books in our attic (*Heidi, Little Women, Eight Cousins, The Bucket Brigade, etc.*), which Mommy's family had been given when she was a girl. They had been stored in our attic for years, since neither she nor her sisters had an interest in them. I read them multiple times during my early teens.

The one-room school houses in Decatur Township were visited monthly by a county book truck that circulated dozens of books between six schools. As a fourth grader I read 76 of those to win a school-wide reading contest (there were only 16 students in the eight grades). First prize was a copy of Collodi's *Pinocchio*. A year later I won a copy of Lofting's *Dr. Doolittle*. Meanwhile, I memorized a sufficient number of Bible verses in a contest at church to be awarded Craig Massey's *Indian Drums and Broken Arrows*. As was my custom with books I enjoyed, I treasured and reread them many times.

On Friday and Saturday nights, our entire family, including Mommy and Daddy, gathered around the radio and listened to *Amos and Andy, Jack Benny, Gun Smoke, The Lone Ranger,* and other popular broadcasts. Theodore Epp's *Back to the Bible Broadcast* on Saturday nights inspired me to read more than a dozen of the *Danny Orlis* novels. Daddy had discovered that these novels, as well as similar ones, could be purchased at the Christian book store in Lewistown. By the time I was in junior high school we had a library of three or four dozen of these books for young people. At about the same time, Daddy began taking us to the Lewistown public library where I discovered a section of sports novels for boys and read ten or twelve in one summer. As much as I enjoyed reading, however, it simply filled the time when I could not play baseball.

As surely as I had to work long hours and was denied a few of the pleasures available to other boys, living on a farm more than compensated for the sacrifices. I was unable to play on a baseball team until my sophomore year of high school, but the years of lifting, chopping, and shoveling enabled me to compete with bigger, stronger players. My one regret is not for myself. Living on a dairy farm required that all of us contribute to the family welfare. Daddy had to limit each of us children to one school activity, because we had to help him with farm work. Joe and I played baseball. Keith and Dave played football. Bill played basketball. Ruthann played softball. As a result, Keith and Bill never had the opportunity to display their skills in other sports. Both were good baseball players.

In retrospect, my childhood home was atypical of most mid-twentieth century American homes because it was a farm home. There was always work to do without regard to age, size, gender, or disposition, but the most impacting difference was the twenty-four hour presence of my father. When my Dad was away at Lewistown or McClure, our family was relaxed and time was enjoyable even though he always assigned work.[6]

---

6. I have always disliked the word "chores," because "chores" sounds like an incidental task such as taking out the garbage or mowing the lawn. We did not have "chores." We had "work."

If we finished our work before he returned, I played ball or read. When Daddy reappeared, he brought with him the tension that always gripped our home. We were afraid of his moodiness and the consequences of not pleasing him.

———⟨∞⟩———

Once each year, usually during the Thanksgiving holidays, Daddy shot three or four pigs, and we assisted in the cleaning, scrubbing, and sectioning of the carcasses. Then we carried wood and made the fires, carried water for cleaning and cooking, trimmed meat for sausage and fat for lard, rendered the lard and stirred the steaming meats and broths in the large heavy kettles as the pudding meats were prepared for scrapple. Afterward we cleaned and dried the kettles, then carried salt, dumping it into the kettles so that it covered the hams and shoulders that had to be cured. Afterward, we built hickory fires in the smoke house, so the meats would be preserved through the coming months. In the late 1950s, when finances were more tenuous, we butchered beeves, hogs, and chickens weekly, placed the different cuts into a display case that daddy built on the bed of our truck, and traveled to Lewistown where he sold the meat, eggs, and produce house to house.

The bed of that truck holds many memories. Keith, Billy, and I rode the back of that truck when we took grain to Murray's Mill to be

The blue 1946 pickup truck in which I passed my state drivers' test. On this occasion Joe, Dave, Susie, and RuthAnn are eating a picnic lunch.

ground into the "chop" that was fed to chickens, pigs and cows. Those summertime rides were cool relief from hot fields and overheated farm buildings. We huddled down amongst the grain bags, held onto our hats, watching the countryside fade away behind us. We rode in the same fashion to church on Sundays and Wednesday nights. Mommy swept clean the truck bed each Saturday evening, spread a blanket on which we boys were to sit, and on Sunday morning we climbed aboard and rode the twenty plus miles to church. In cooler weather she provided a heavier blanket into which we wrapped ourselves against the cold.

I never received an allowance, but there were occasions when Keith and I were given dimes and nickels for our labor. When we were old enough to drive tractors for the neighbors during silo filling or threshing, John Goss, one of our neighbors, would sometimes slip us fifty cents for two or three day's work. When we were in our young teens, Daddy paid us a quarter for chopping down Canadian thistles in the meadow with a corn chopper. Many of the thistles were tall and often we were pricked by the sharp thistles as the falling plants toppled on us. It was hazardous, but the reward of a quarter made possible the purchase of a sponge ball at Joe McKinley's general store.

Keith and I were regularly called upon to "go to the store." Mommy would take Daddy's wallet from the kitchen cabinet, finger some change from the billfold pocket, snap it closed and instruct us to "walk up to Joe's" and buy some thread, or paraffin, or

Corn choppers had 24-inch handles attached to a sharp blade.

rat poison. Always I asked if I could buy a baseball card, and most times she gave Keith and me a penny or two. Baseball cards in the 1950s were packaged as a single card with a piece of gum. I opened those cards with bated breath, fearful that my penny had bought a sixth copy of Enos Slaughter or Jim Delsing. Duplicate copies of Del Ennis or Willie Jones, however, were fine because Phillies cards were my treasure. And discovering that a package contained a Richie Ashburn, Robin Roberts, or Granny Hamner sent me at night into my box of saved cards to read and memorize for the hundredth time the information on the card backs. Sometimes I persuaded Keith to buy a baseball card with the promise I would trade my gum for his card. Shameless thievery required no subterfuge.

A life is the product of both choices and circumstances. Some choices result from a free will that is subject to conscience and passion, mechanisms for which the individual must ultimately accept responsibility. Conversely, many circumstances lie outside volition. Scripture teaches that human beings are born with a disposition and a genetic reality already in place. Further, God mysteriously and miraculously has set in motion His cosmic design and purpose under which all individuals live. My destiny has been to spend my early years on a farm in Decatur Township in central Pennsylvania. My parents and my siblings were also providentially appointed. They were and are ineffable blessings. If I were given the choice of mother and father, of brothers and sisters, I would choose the very ones I experienced. They were and are wonderful, loving people, and I feel privileged in every way. To be sure, there were agonies, abrasions, and neglects. But love covered the sins, both mine and theirs.

It is true that growing up on a farm meant there was constant work. Concomitantly, however, the demands of labor taught important lessons and inculcated a consciousness of God's mercies and blessings. Farm people learn early that sovereignty is exclusively a divine property. Thus, I am grateful that during my early years I learned that a meaningful life requires hard labor, that work has no terminus, that idleness leads to dissipation, that dignity is ornamented by accomplishment, that obstacles can be overcome with patience and resolve, that individual behavior affects family honor, and much more.

Submitting to God's providential determinations and love, it is with gratitude and wonder that I look back upon my early years.

TRACTOR ACCIDENT

I fell under the right rear wheel of the WC.

By the time I was born in September 1942, my grandfather had begun the transition from farming with horses to a more mechanized operation utilizing tractors. He had already sold the farm's first tractor, a Fordson, and replaced it in 1940 with an Allis-Chalmers WC. The WC was a marvel in and of itself because it featured rubber tires, replacing the earlier steel-wheeled models. It was a symbol of Pappy's success as a farmer and gave him a measure of distinction and satisfaction when neighbors stopped by to inspect the new purchase. That tractor holds a particular place in my personal history as well, but for an altogether different reason.

Although the tractor revolutionized our farming methods it did not wholly replace our horses for at least two reasons: (1) gasoline during WWII was scarce and rationing made it difficult to obtain amounts needed for a fully mechanized farm operation, and (2) nearly all the farm's implements were adapted for horses. Converting horse-drawn apparatuses to tractor-mounted hitches and drawbars involved more than discarding single and double-trees and was, in almost all cases, impossible. A new tractor meant an expenditure of $750-$1000 whereas a pair of quality work horses could be bought for $200-$300. In addition, the cost of acquiring implements that utilized the tractor's power take off and hydraulic systems was financially beyond the means of most farmers. Thus, although tractor sales soared in the years after WWII, the transition from horse to tractor was, in most cases, gradual.

The horse drawn double-tree (left) was replaced with the tractor drawbar (right).

The important exception to this slow change on our farm was a two-bottom plow that Pappy purchased with the WC. A 30-acre field that had taken a full week to till could now be completed in two days. Thus, on a weekday morning in the spring of 1945, after spring rains had thawed and soaked the soil, Daddy determined to hitch the plow to the WC and begin the plowing that preceded the planting of crops.

Both the tractor and the plow were kept in the wagon shed next to the barn, so following breakfast Daddy opened the large wagon shed doors in preparation for the day's work. His designs were to hitch the plow to the tractor and begin turning over the sod in the field across the road from the barn. He and Pappy hoped that by week's end a crop would be planted.

The previous day's rain had created mud puddles in front of the shed so that, as the great 8' x 10' doors were pushed open, the bottoms of each dragged through the mud. The tractor had been backed into the shed because it required hand cranking to start the motor, and the crankshaft was installed on the front. Its gasoline tank had been filled the night before after Daddy and Pappy had combined efforts in mounting 150-lb. wheel weights to each of the rear tires. The added weight assured that the wheels of the 3,500 pound tractor would not slip as the machine negotiated the hilly and dampened fields.

Turning the crank was dangerous because the engine sometimes backfired, violently spinning the crank counter-clockwise. When this happened the metal handle clubbed the arm and hand of the person holding the crank, delivering severe bruises and often breaking fingers and arms. Daddy taught Keith and me to be extra careful when we crank-started machinery, and usually insisted on doing it himself. "Put the gearshift in neutral," he directed, "Turn on some gas (open the throttle), … open the choke." Then he punctuated, "Turn it (crank) slowly until it's at the bottom of the stroke …, then give it a hard pull upward."

Pappy standing behind the Allis-Chalmers WC while Daddy tends a horse. A wagon shed door stands open.

In spite of his advice to us, whenever the motor would not immediately start for him, he lost his temper, violated common sense, and gave the crank three or four continuous furious turns. If the motor backfired in the midst of his tantrum, the crank inevitably delivered a painful blow across his hand or wrist. Expletives followed along with punishment to the tractor, crank, or anything that was within arm's length. I once saw him bend over in pain holding his wrist after the starter backfired, then suddenly grab the crank, draw back his left arm, intent on throwing it into eternity, and hit himself on the same wrist as he tried to hurl it into the pig lot. Ironically, he could be a marvel with machinery, ingenious at repairs and innovative with labor-saving devices.

Years afterward when he explained what happened on this spring morning, he always emphasized the need to follow proper procedure when using a crank. He readily admitted that he had failed to do so on this day.

At this time I was two and one-half years old. Daddy loved to take me along when he drove the tractor, or lift me to the tractor seat to play while he worked nearby. I would pretend to drive, opening the throttle,

I was two and a half years old when the accident occurred.

pushing on the brake pedal, and opening the accelerator. Frequently, he sat me on his lap as he came and went to the fields. So it was within the bounds of convention on this busy morning that he took time to lift me to the seat of the WC as he was about to crank start it. Children playing on machines are attracted to moving parts: the gear shift, the knobs and buttons that are controls, and, of course, the steering wheel. As he picked up the crank, I mimicked the humm..humm sound of a tractor engine, pretending as a child does, that I was actually driving. He methodically stepped between the rear tire and the body of the tractor, pushed the gearshift into neutral, and opened the choke. He then moved to the front of the tractor and inserted the crank head into the crankshaft.

It is impossible to be definite about what next took place. Apparently, as he positioned the crank I leaned forward and pushed the gearshift lever into first gear. Regardless, the transmission was engaged when Daddy turned the crank. Unexpectedly the motor started on the first stroke. The tractor lurched forward. Off balance, I fell down in front of the huge right rear tire.

At the moment the engine turned over, Daddy jumped backward and to his right in order to get out of the way of the moving tractor. Just as quickly, he saw me fall and watched in horror as the rear wheel of the tractor flattened me against the ground, pressing my head and upper body into the mud.

The garage door next to the tractor was not fully opened, and as the tractor passed, the newly attached wheel weights caught on the door's 4 x 4 support that ran horizontally along its base approximately 12" off the ground. The support took most of the tractor's weight, and the 12" allowed enough clearance that I was not crushed.

Daddy could do nothing but watch since other machinery stored in the wagon shed prevented him from moving around to the rear of the tractor where he would have been able to throw it into neutral. The tractor meanwhile continued riding on the 4 x 4 until suddenly the door gave way and was pushed farther open. The widened opening caused the tractor wheel and wheel weight to slide off the support and fall back onto the ground. It had ridden on the support only about four feet, but in that space I was spared. As the riderless tractor exited the wagon shed, Daddy jumped aboard, shut off the motor, and turned to where I lay prostrate in the mud. Picking me up, he saw the abrasions where the tire had left its marks across the left side of my face but retained hope that it might not be serious because my head was not misshapen. He noted also that there seemed to be little bleeding.

Daddy immediately called in the direction of the house, "Hazel! ... Hazel!" Mommy knew from his tone that something terrible had happened but assumed it had happened to Daddy. As she exited the house and hurried along the yard steps he hollered again, "The tractor ran over Dennis!"

Pappy, who was in the lower barn, heard the report and came running. He instinctively knew that a doctor was necessary. His car was parked next to the barn, and assuming that he should drive because I required both Daddy and Mommy's attention, he headed to the house to retrieve his keys. When he returned to the scene, however, Daddy announced that he would drive.

Mammie was busy in the house when Pappy entered. He quickly explained that he was about to drive Daddy, Mommy and myself to the doctor's office in McClure. Assuming the injuries might be fatal, the alarm in his voice warned Mammie that an emergency was at hand. She grabbed towels instructing Pappy to give them to Mommy who by now had climbed into the car holding me on her lap. Careful not to worsen the situation, Mommy removed a bit of mud from my face, but decided not to try to do too much. She would later say that her lasting memory was more about concern for my muddied condition than for my bloodied cuts and scrapes.

Everything happened in seconds, so that afterward the principals in the spectacle were unable to piece together with exactness the details of the near tragedy.

There were no telephones. These were country folk, with notions and reactions indelibly rural. No thought was given to taking me to a hospital. Neither my mother or father, my grandparents, nor Keith or I had ever been to a hospital. Children were either born at home with the help of a mid-wife, or in a doctor's office if it was equipped for such occasions. Many times, however, the country doctor arrived at the home after the delivery and tended to whatever needs might remain. On this day we headed to the doctor's office in McClure.

McClure lay seven miles to the east. Three of those miles were un-paved road, but it can be assumed that Daddy hurried. Heavy traffic did not exist, but still it took about twenty minutes. The doctor's office was in his home. Daddy parked the car, helped Mommy step up onto the house porch, and knocked on the door panel. There was no immediate response. Daddy then banged against the door itself, and soon the doctor appeared.

Daddy offered a brief explanation of events as the doctor laid me on a table, pulled back the muddy clothing, and began examining. He noted that my breathing was normal, and that there seemed no threat from exter-nal bleeding. After a few minutes of hurried examination, he sat back and announced that he was sending me to the Lewistown Hospital for internal examination. His cautioned that I appeared to be alright, but at the least, my left ear needed stitching, and x-rays would provide a more complete diagnosis. He then phoned the hospital to alert them that an emergency was on the way. Finally, he wrapped me in a clean cloth and returned me to Mommy and Daddy.

From the doctor's office in McClure to the Lewistown Hospital, Mommy sat in the front seat holding me. For the first time she realized that the front of her clothing was covered with mud. She reached for one of the towels Mammie had thrown into the car, and as best she could while holding a two-year-old child, began cleaning mud from her blouse.

Neither she nor Daddy said much in transit. Prayer is sometimes a human reflex, an acknowledgement that we are hopelessly unable to effect change and recognize that our hope is in a transcendent God performing the miraculous. Nonetheless, neither Daddy nor Mommy had yet accepted Jesus as Lord, so prayer was awkward. Although either or both may have silently called for help, there was no spoken invocation. Adding to the distress was the guilt Daddy was experiencing. Self-reproach consumed him. He had permitted a two-year-old to play on a running tractor. Penitent, he confessed that he should have double-checked to make certain the tractor was not in gear. Intermittently he referenced the trauma of watching helplessly as the tractor tire ran over his child.

Mommy was consoling. She assured Daddy that it was an accident, that no one was to blame. Her composure resulted from the intuitive belief that I was not seriously hurt. She would tell me many years later, "You seemed to be normal. You weren't in a lot of pain or at least you didn't seem to be."

It was about 10 am when they pulled into the hospital parking lot. Daddy pulled alongside a parking space marked "EMERGENCY PARK-ING." As he got out of the car, an orderly stepped outside and directed them toward the emergency room. A nurse took me from Mommy's arms and bade my parents follow her. Inside I was given immediate attention. A doctor examined me for internal wounds and within minutes reassured Mommy and Daddy that I did not have life-threatening injuries. After that news, the examination slowed. I was washed and dressed in a hospital gown. The doctor informed my parents that, except for my torn ear, no other stitching was necessary.[1] He permitted Mommy to hold me while he did the sewing. At about 1 pm a nurse came into the room informing us that I would be held overnight for observation. Mommy indicated that she would stay with me. The nurse firmly advised that such was unnecessary. Mommy asked Daddy if he would go home, get some clean clothes for her, then call his mother who lived in Lewistown. She wanted to stay nearby and knew Grandma would welcome her. When the doctor found out the details of their plans and realized they lived twenty miles away, he again assured them that I would receive proper care, would be sleeping much of the time, and it would be better for all concerned if they were to get their rest and return in the morning. Mommy was at first dissatisfied with the arrangement, but a gracious nurse invited both of them to stay with me for

---

1. I have carried a scar behind my left ear all my years, but I have never been conscious of it except when I wash my hair. The space between that ear and my head is a bit larger than the space on my right side.

as long as they wished and offered to get them something to eat.

Neither Mommy nor Daddy liked to be beholden, nor did they feel comfortable receiving what they regarded as special treatment. They knew that Pappy could do the barn work alone, and that Mammie would care for Keith, but after a conference, they decided to go home and return to the hospital as soon as the barn work was completed the following morning.

D addy and Mommy arrived at the hospital early the next morning. I was in a crib when they came into the room. A nurse was present, and Mommy inquired whether I had eaten. The nurse responded that she had offered oatmeal, but I refused and asked for an egg.

At 9 am the doctor who had examined me the day before stopped in the room. Mommy remembered her relief when she was told, "Take him home. He's as good as new." As she had all her life when informed of good news, she cried.

In later years when recalling the morning of the accident and the ensuing events she could not remember the return drive home, nor could she recall when the stitches were removed. She did, however, distinctly recall that it was a beautiful day, and she remembered that the tractor and plow were still standing in the place where the accident had occurred when she and Daddy pulled into the driveway. Twenty-four hours earlier a little boy had miraculously escaped death, but now a field needed plowing so that seed could be sown, so that the farm where the boy lived might prosper. There was work to do. While Mommy put me to bed for my afternoon nap, Daddy hitched the plow to the tractor and began plowing thirty acres.

SCHOOL
◇◇◇◇◇◇◇◇◇◇◇◇◇◇

Keith and I - First grade, September 1948
Twelve years later we graduated together.

During the summer of 1948 my parents spoke with Emmet Hoffman, a neighboring farmer who was to be my first-grade teacher in September. Seeking his advice, they weighed the wisdom of sending me to the first grade as a five-year-old. Their inde-cision was founded upon the concern that I would have to walk alone one mile to Krick School.

Although Emmet's teaching creden-tials were limited to a certificate that he had earned after spending a couple of se-mesters at Susquehanna College and the many years he had been teaching local children, his advice was valued.[1]

My parents knew Emmet well, both as a teacher and as a friend. In fact, he had, fifteen years earlier, taught my

My first-grade teacher was Emmet Hoffman, a neighboring farmer.

---

1. At that time a college diploma was not required to teach, and most states granted provi-sional certification because there were few teachers available in rural America who had completed degree programs.

mother at the same school. When she disclosed that I could recite the alphabet backward, he encouraged my parents to enroll me. The practical value of my feat was never questioned, but my mother's concern about walking alone across fields, over a bridge, and through woods was allayed when Emmet suggested that my four-year-old brother Keith accompany me. Perhaps his advice was intended for the short term, but for the next twelve years we attended school as classmates.

Krick School[2] was a traditional rural American school. The schoolhouse was set on a stone foundation, had a bell suspended in a tower high above the entrance, and boasted six shuttered windows that were opened each school day to provide light for school activities.

Inside the one-room structure was a coal-burning stove that sat at the rear of the room to the immediate left of the school door. To the im-

mediate right of the door was a small table on which rested a porcelain water crock and a metal bucket that was carried twice each day by two students to the neighboring Loht farm, where water was pumped from a hydrant alongside one of the farm buildings.

The one room Krick School that Keith and I attended through fourth grade.

The filled bucket was then carried back to the school and emptied into the porcelain crock. Paper cups were foreign to rural schools, so the teacher provided a tin or ceramic cup out of which the student drank, rinsing it afterward with a splash of water.

Tasks such as carrying water, cleaning erasers, or using the hekto-

---

2. Keith and I were part of an unusually large class (7) for that era and locale. Larger families had characterized my mother's generation when the building housed as many as thirty-six students (1931-31), but the post-WWII years rarely saw more that 18-20 students in the combined eight grades. Our class was an oddity. The seven included Keith and me, Henry Kline, Gary Knepp, Billie Lash, Laray Renninger, and Jim Aumiller. As best I can recall, the remaining members of the school in 1948-49 were: eighth graders Harold Reisman, Janet Renninger, Luther (Bud) Knepp, and Mary Bubb; seventh graders David Dillman and Lynn Renninger; sixth grader Eugene Aumiller; fifth grader Calvin Knepp; fourth grader Donald Aumiller; third graders Ronnie Goss and Rennie Mitchell; and second grader Alice Harbst.

graph were normally reserved for older students or those who had proven themselves responsible by completing seat work on time and displaying good manners. Being chosen for these special duties was a prestigious reward.[3]

The teacher's desk sat on a riser at the front of the room. This platform granted tacit authority to the teacher as he or she was able to survey the classroom by looking down upon student activities.

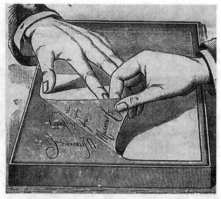

The hektograph permitted teachers to produce multiple copies from a single master.

Along the left wall, adjacent to the teacher's desk, was a four-foot wide bookcase enclosing shelves that held textbooks, board games, and a container of ink used to refill the individual ink wells built into the top of each desk.

The center of the room was occupied by five rows of six desks where students studied, ate, and on rainy days, played board games. Youngest pupils were "doubled up," so that two children shared a desk. Thus, during my first two years, Keith and I sat together in a two-seater at the front of the room, slightly to the right of and looking up at the teacher's desk. Keith sat on my right. The desks were wooden with iron frames bolted to the floor as a two-piece (seat-desk) structure. The seats in the front row were not attached to desks so that individual grades could be called forward, and students could be seated in front of the teacher's desk where lessons were reviewed.

It was from my front-row desk on the opening day of school that I suffered a five-year-old's trauma when I realized Daddy was returning home and leaving Keith and me to the new and foreign world of public education. Feeling deserted, I cried in front of my teacher, my classmates, and the "big" kids who comprised the upper grades. Mommy was not there to comfort me. Eight months pregnant with my sister RuthAnn, she had remained home with Billy, not yet two years old. In retrospect, the circum-

---

3. In the hektograph (also spelled "hectograph") process, which was introduced in 1876, a master was written or typed with a special aniline ink. The master was then laid face-down on a gelatinous substance that absorbed the ink from the original. The gelatin was in a pan about 9×12 inches and about 1 inch deep. After removing the original, plain paper was laid on the gelatin, and the ink bled off the gelatin onto the paper, making a copy.

The inside of Krick School was similar to the one pictured here at the Herbert Hoover National Historic Site in Iowa. It featured the customary portraits of Presidents Washington and Lincoln, a wood-and-coal stove, two blackboards, and a small bookcase. Neither electricity nor running water were installed.

stances were beneficial. Had she been at school she may have indulged me, whereas Daddy tolerated no such nonsense, and I was forced to quickly adjust. Besides, Mary Bubb and Janet Renninger, the two oldest girls at Krick, spent the next few days doting over Keith and me. The result was that I have a most favorable recollection of my first year of school.

Keith's adjustment to formal schooling was less dramatic but more protracted than mine. On our second day, following afternoon recess, I sat alone at our desk anxiously trying to explain to my teacher the reason my four-year-old brother had disappeared from the playground and gone home.

Fifteen minutes earlier, Keith had assumed that the afternoon recess was really dismissal, and despite my efforts to restrain him, exited the playground and started walking home. I spent the remainder of the school day scared for the punishment that awaited Keith the following day. Curiously, Emmet seemed unconcerned, but after dismissal, he packed me into his blue sedan and drove me home to make certain that Keith had arrived safely.

Two or three days later, seated at the same desk, I watched in disbelief as Keith again violated the unwritten code of behavior. He opened a strange brown paper bag at lunchtime and began eating Emmet Hoffman's lunch.

Upon arrival at school each morning, custom was for the teacher to collect the brown-bag lunches, write each student's name on the corresponding bag, and store them in the teacher's desk. Then, at lunchtime, after excusing those who went home for the noon meal, the teacher retrieved the lunches, announced the name on each bag, and one at a time, hungry boys and girls claimed their treasure. On this particular day, Emmet was engaged in the administration of discipline to two older boys who had been fighting during the earlier recess. He had taken them "outside," which meant there was tension and sobriety "inside."

Before exiting, Emmet directed that we need not wait for his return but should find our lunch bags in his desk and begin eating. Cautiously, we lined up and made our way onto the platform. Reaching into a teacher's desk was voyaging into foreign and dangerous territory. No one spoke as we were also conscious of the plight of the delinquents who remained "outside" with Emmet. Intrigue was heightened for us first-graders because no one was there to identify our lunch bags and none of us could read. The more enterprising asked older students to find their bags, but Keith and I were last in line and waited deferentially.

When our turns came, three bags remained. There were names, however, on only two of them. I recognized the letter "D" on one, supposed it was mine, reached into the desk, and claimed it. Keith was last in line. He selected one of the remaining two bags – the one without a name – and we returned to our seat.

I opened my brown bag, removed the fried ham sandwich that Mommy had packed, unwrapped the waxed paper holding the sweet pickle she knew I loved, and began eating. She had also packed an apple fresh from our orchard, and a piece of Poor Man's Pie.[4] I ate hurriedly, because I was anxious to go outside and play.

Mommy had programmed me to "look after Keith." My instructions were explicit: "On the way to and from school do not walk ahead but wait for Keith;" "alert the teacher when Keith needs to go to the bathroom;"[5] and "tell Emmet if you have a problem." With that mandate, I checked to see if he was eating.

---

4. Poor Man's Pie was a simple and quick dessert when Mommy was otherwise occupied. Onto a bottom crust she spread a mixture of flour, salt, brown sugar, light cream, and butter. It was topped with a bit of cinnamon and baked for 45 minutes.

5. The "bathrooms" were, of course, outhouses. There were two, one for boys and another for girls. Keith's first paddling occurred as a four-year-old a few weeks later when, after being told not to go into the girl's bathroom during recess, he was found exploring the forbidden world.

At once I was seized with the catastrophic realization that he was eating someone else's lunch. The contents of his bag were foreign: There were sandwiches with "store-bought" bread and meat, "store-bought" potato chips, and a thermos filled with coffee. Paralyzed with the reality that my four-year-old brother was a thief and would be severely punished when Emmet discovered the larceny, I pleaded with him not to eat the sandwich, certain that a paddling was in store.

Every student knew that Emmet kept a paddle atop his desk. Each time we were called to write our letters or numbers on the blackboard, it lay in full view. And sometimes when he lectured or conducted classes at the front of the room, he absentmindedly picked up the menacing instrument and used it as a pointer. Regardless, it frightened the students, and the thought of Keith being struck by such a weapon filled me with terror. Keith, as though the entire universe continued to turn in perfect concord, paid no attention and continued eating.

In a few minutes, Emmet re-entered and resolutely strode to the front of the room. The miscreants who had been fighting remained "outside." I imagined they were locked in the coal shed or tied to one of the posts that fenced in the school playground. The room quieted. Emmet seated himself, lifted the lid to his desk, reached into the cubicle, and withdrew the remaining lunch bag. Picking it up, he turned it over, opened the top, looked at the contents, then glanced down at Keith and me. He said nothing, but I knew Keith had been found out. The bag was returned to Emmet's desk.

I waited for the explosion, imagining an impending execution. Instead, as though it were part and parcel of his lunchtime routine, Emmet reached for a stack of homework and began grading papers. Minutes passed. No explosion. He walked to the back of the room, drew a cup of water from the porcelain jug, drank, and returned to his desk. Concluding that everyone had finished eating, he excused us to spend the remainder of the lunch hour on the playground. Relief swelled. Making certain that Keith was at my side, I headed outdoors.

It was a beautiful fall day for play, but my first concern was for the two reprobates who had been punished. I searched this way and that. They were not to be found; neither in the coal shed nor in the outhouses. Older students surmised they had "run away," not just from school, but due to the magnitude of the injustice they had suffered, they had run away from home and would not again be seen. Of course, the juvenile explanation implied Emmet would convulse with regret when he realized the two recalcitrants had permanently withdrawn their charms from his classroom. Further, a sixth grader surmised that Emmet would experience serious casualty when parents were informed of the miscarriage of justice.

Normal activity resumed and soon afterward the clanging of the school bell called us back to classes. It seemed Keith's larceny was forgotten. Or so I thought.

The remainder of that school day was uneventful. After classes were completed, Emmet dismissed his charges, locked the school door, climbed into his sedan and drove away. Keith and I, along with a half-dozen others who walked to and from school began the trek homeward.

Krick Road, so-named because of the school, was a dirt road that ran through the wooded countryside, bounded by a leisurely flowing creek, extending a half-mile southward, where at the intersection with our farm lane, Keith and I turned west. From there, we walked unaccompanied toward home. September's corn filled the fields, the tall stalks obstructing our view of the countryside including our farm buildings until we rounded the final knoll in front of our house. Suddenly, my heart stopped. Emmet's car was parked outside the entrance to the cornfield ... Keith's sin had found him out after all.

Fifty yards into the field, we spotted Emmet talking with Daddy. Our first impulse was to sneak past, but Daddy had seen us and called, "Boys! Come here!"

Daddy had been bindering corn that afternoon in preparation for filling the silo when he noticed a cloud of dust rising on the adjacent road and knew a car was approaching. Minutes later he saw Emmet's car pull alongside the corn field and stop. Then he watched as Emmet got out and began walking into the field toward him. Daddy turned off the tractor motor, and the two men greeted. Fifteen minutes later Keith and I appeared.

In the interim Emmet had returned Keith's lunch to Daddy and had shared the afternoon incident. Both men were laughing good naturedly at Keith's *faux pas*. Daddy asked Keith, "What did you have for lunch today?" Keith could not recall, either because the food he had eaten was unfamiliar, or more probably because a four-year-old is unable to retrieve such trivia. In any case, Emmet had altogether enjoyed the irony of a student eating a teacher's lunch and had wanted to share the fun with Daddy.

As a first-grader Keith was only four years old and forced to compete with children nearly two years older. His playing field was radically tilted, and he struggled with routine matters that he would later not only conquer but vanquish. One of those early requirements was to fill the inkwell that was recessed into the desk we shared.

A wooden stylus and the nibs that students inserted for penmanship classes.

Once each week the teacher distributed pens and nibs that had to be inserted into the stylus. Each student was provided a blank sheet of lined paper on which penmanship was to be practiced. In preparation for the activity, inkwells had to be filled. A can of ink was passed from desk to desk where, with tedious care, each child carefully filled the inkwell.

When it was our turn, Keith intercepted the ink can, removed the inkwell from the recessed slot in our desk, and with the careful deliberation of a four-year old, poured a quantity of ink from the can into the inkwell, closed the can and passed it to the desk behind us. All that remained was for him to return the inkwell to its slot. In his attempt, however, the top came off the glass container. Ink streamed across the desk and ran down the slanted desktop toward us. Trying to stave off the disaster of ink-soaked shirts and pants, both of us used our arms and chests to block the flow. Suddenly we were ink disasters. Emmet rushed to secure cloths from a supply of rags on a shelf at the back of the room, wetted them with water from the ceramic water container, and told Keith and me to clean up the mess. Stunned silence filled the room. By now, not only were Keith and

An inkwell and cap exactly like the one that spilled at Keith and my desk.

I wet with water and ink, but our desk and our books had been damaged. Janet and Mary, the older girls who had befriended us on opening day, volunteered to help. They washed the desk, wiped the floor, and sponged the ink from our clothes. They even took time to wash ink from our faces and arms. In the end, we survived, but our desk remained permanently discolored.

In contrast to those sometimes anxious moments there was much enjoyment at school. Recesses and lunchtimes sped by with games of "Balley Over," "Drop the Handkerchief" (a variation of "Duck, Duck,

Goose"), "Three Deep," and "Prisoner's Base." On rainy days there were board and card games such as "Monopoly," "Parcheesi" and "Rook."

The education I received during my elementary years in one-roomed schools might be justly criticized as provincial. There was little contact with the world of national and international events, and even information regarding state and local communities was scarce and infrequent. It was a time that predated electronic media, and it was a location beyond the circulation of daily newspapers. The McClure *Plain Dealer* arrived Thursdays, but it contained only local news, and neither our school nor our home had telephones, television, or relatives who kept up with the news. The county sent a book-truck to the school once each month, but seldom did our school reading or conversation reach beyond children's stories, baseball, or standard American history. Regardless, retrospection and my life of reading argue that my early schooling was fraught with advantages. Since there were eight grades, I was exposed daily to lessons designed for older students. I received individual attention and rewards. I was also influenced by the Christian values, circumstances and teachers that I encountered in that one-room school. Emmet Hoffman, my first teacher, recognized my love for mathematics and motivated me to work ahead of my classmates; my second-grade teacher, Mertie Baker, nourished my love for baseball, reinforced my self-esteem, and helped me to assert myself; my third-grade teacher, Edie Erb, brought history alive with stories, poetry and music; and my fourth-grade teacher introduced me to the "fun" of social games and activities.

Emmet was a no-nonsense disciplinarian. His presence was intimidating. (Ironically, stern inside the classroom, he was personable and somewhat reticent as a neighbor). His emphasis was rote: arithmetic, writing and reading in that order. I had already learned to count and "do numbers," so that while my classmates sometimes struggled with basic addition and subtraction, I was "rewarded" with more difficult exercises. He demanded compliance and meticulous attention to detail. Completing my homework conjoined an effort to be the best student with staying in Emmet's good graces.

Mertie Baker was the favorite teacher of every child who ever frequented her classroom. She demanded respect, but never forgot that we were

EMMET HOFFMAN

children. An obstreperous fourth grader might be
sent to stand in a corner, but always the castigation
ended with an embrace and the assurance that she
loved each of us. She laughed at herself and taught
us not to take our mistakes too seriously.

The teacher who had the greatest impact on
me, however, was my third-grade teacher, Edie Erb.
Her passion for learning was visceral. She cried
when she read stories of the boy, Abe Lincoln, losing his mother. Tears fell when she reverently re-

MERTIE BAKER
My second grade teacher

cited "In Flanders Fields." And when the entire assembly of students sang
"Battle Hymn of the Republic," her voice rose as she marched up and down
the aisles. It was from her that I learned to love language, the music of poetry, and the power of literature.

Marian Doebler was in her first year of teaching when I was a fourth-
grader. New to both the area and the classroom, and well into her first
pregnancy, she struggled to find the productive balance between disciplined classroom management and a relaxed, amicable classroom ambi-
ence. The result was an academic year compromised in favor of extended
social activity. Classes on any given day were postponed and replaced with
a marathon of Monopoly, Rook, or similar games. Her rationalization was
that the games constituted a kind of practical education.

While fourth-grade class days many times were barren of academia,
Mrs. Doebler introduced our school to worthwhile and enjoyable traditions
and celebrations foreign to Decatur Township. It was she who held a "Hal-
loween Night," for families including grandparents, parents, and siblings,
replete with a costume party and caramel-candied apples. The evening of
fun was climaxed when Mrs. Doebler tied towels around each first grader
and herself, knelt on the floor beside a tub of water, and "bobbed" with us
for apples. She gave us "treats" at Christmas, each wrapped in decorative
paper with a personal note. The entire school was surprised with donuts
on Groundhog Day, valentines on Valentine's Day, and an Easter-egg hunt
on Good Friday that featured individually wrapped packets of candy to be
shared with families. The relaxed academic and scholastic atmosphere of
her classroom many times violated the *raison d'etre* of education, but her
students loved her, and moms and dads dismissed her laxness, attributing
much of it to the fatigue and discomfort that accompanied her pregnancy.

KRICK SCHOOL SEPTEMBER 1951
Keith and I were in the fourth grade when this school picture was taken. (Left to Right) Keith Morgan, Park Lash, Rennie Mitchell, Ronnie Goss, Shirley Brower, Laray Renninger, Jim Snook, Calvin Knepp (Rear), Richard Shilling(Front), Dennis Morgan, Lynn Renninger, Larry Snook, Alice Harbst, Kay Harbst, Mrs. Doebler (Rear), Billie Lash, and Gary Knepp.

Sequestered against the impassivity and detachment associated with suburban and metropolitan schools, students in one-roomed country schools were blessed with teachers and parents who were neighbors and whose relationships extended beyond the classroom. The familiarity produced close accountability. The improper behavior of a neighbor's son or daughter at school was revealed at every evening supper table and quickly traveled to all sides of the local community. Anonymity, the ally of indiscretion, was altogether alien. Everyone knew everyone else's children. In such a setting surreptitiousness was impossible. The collective eye of the community produced welcome moral and civil restraint. Inevitable change, however, was imminent.

The end of WWII introduced the beginning of the Cold War with the Soviet Union. It also introduced the 1950s, a new economy, and a new pragmatism. John Dewey and William James, atheist educator-philosophers, convinced a nation of legislators that one-room schools could not compete with the collective programs of regionalization generally and vocational training particularly.[6] Dewey's pragmatic curriculum began the displacement of Christian transcendent values and introduced the existential philosophy of Naturalism. Science was given a new emphasis and liberal arts was moved to a rear seat as the struggle to find comfort in immediacy reversed the earlier mindset that had underscored spiritual preparation for a future life. One-room schools were closed in favor of regional schools and vocational training.

Teachers and administrators were no longer friends and neighbors with Judeo-Christian values emphasizing character, but strangers whose secular values emphasized utility. The *good* life was defined by material comfort, not moral restraint. Thus, an era ended in both my life and the lives of rural Americans. Until that reform, moms and dads had enjoyed an intimate relationship with public education. Afterward, parents lived with a new anxiety. They were alienated from the decision-making processes of education that affected their sons and daughters.

Fifth grade was my interim between the old and the new as Decatur Township prepared for change by building a regional school (Decatur School) at Shindle, a hamlet near the center of Decatur Township. Krick School was abandoned, and until the new building became operational, dispossessed students were bused to Center School, another one-room building six or seven miles away, where we were strangers forced to find new friends amid an established fraternity. Children who had formerly walked to a local school, were now transported to a distant school in a strange vehicle by an unfamiliar driver. I walked one mile to a bus stop with Keith and Bill.[7] Each morning we stepped aboard a big, yellow school bus and were transported to a world beyond the simple familiarity we had known.

It was sixth grade, however, that formally began the passage that moved my brothers, sisters, and me away from a strictly provincial

---

6. William James (1842-1910) was an American philosopher and psychologist, and the first educator in the United States to offer a course in psychology. He was a leading thinker of the late nineteenth century and has been labeled the "Father of American psychology." John Dewey was an American philosopher, psychologist, and educational reformer whose ideas have been influential in education and social reform. Both were proponents of the philosophy known as pragmatism.

7. Bill was a first grader. Ironically, just as Keith and I sat at the same desk during our first year, Bill and I spent his first year seated together.

DECATUR SCHOOL 1953
The opening of this regional school in 1953 marked the end of the one-room school era.

consciousness. We attended Decatur Elementary School, a brand-new facility. Although the majority of students were from rural areas, they were no longer intimate. The moms, dads, and children represented in these classrooms were not from farm families, but men and women who commuted to work in towns and then returned at day's end to a "country" home. We became conscious that we were "farm" kids, strangers to the system.

The year at Decatur School also introduced me to a new reality. For five years I had been the top student in my class,[8] but in sixth grade Howard Hackett, a farm boy from another end of the township, outperformed me in every academic area. It was a necessary lesson in humility and a reminder that I had to accept limitations. For consolation, I rationalized that Howard was not a good baseball player.

A year later, the same yellow school bus that had transported Keith, Billy, and me the few miles to Center School, now picked up Keith and me at 6:45 am each weekday morning and carried us twenty miles to Burnham Junior High School (grades 7-9). We were thrust into a setting of "town" kids, all of whom seemed more sophisticated, and for the first time, I listened to conversations about going to college. The notion of college was not a consideration for us, and the exchanges among our new friends continually reminded us of the

---

8. My second-grade teacher, Mertie Baker, persuaded my parents that I should be "skipped" to the third grade. As a result, I spent that second year in school as a third grader. The following September, in the annual rotation of teachers, Edie Erb, replaced Mertie and vetoed the maneuver. She maintained that every grade contributed important social skills as well as academic ones and neither should be neglected.

distance between them and ourselves. At Burnham Junior High, the idea of college was chimerical.[9]

My junior high and high school years were distinctly divided into three years of anticipating playing baseball and three years of actual participation. In seventh, eighth, and ninth grades I was a farm boy who stood on the perimeter and fantasized about being a part of the athletic and social life of my classmates. I longed to play baseball during the spring of ninth grade. I saved some Christmas money, earned three dollars in three days working for neighboring farmers, and was thrilled when Daddy added the two dollars that permitted me to buy my first baseball shoes. Unfortunately, his anxiety over the farm's needs, his reluctance to become involved with town people, and his concern that we children would become worldly, soon resulted in a change of mind, and in late February he informed me that I was not permitted to go out for the team.

That summer, on evenings after the family had gone to town and I was alone at the farm, I laced on those shoes and walked and ran in the fields pretending I was a player. I avoided wearing them in the yard or when I was throwing a ball against the barn, because I feared someone might stop by and think it peculiar that a kid who was not on any team was wearing baseball shoes.

During that spring I listened from the periphery to every lunchroom conversation about the high school games. I envied the kids who played and wondered if I could compete. I never dared to assert myself, for not only was I not on the high school team, but I had never been on any team. In fact, I had never worn a uniform or competed against another group of organized boys.

Happily, all of this changed in the spring of 1958. One February evening at the barn, Daddy told me I could try out for baseball and simultaneously told Keith he could play football. It was a compromise

---

9. It was not until my final year of high school that college took on a personal connotation. I was struck with the reality that remaining on the farm promised only the monotony of hard work and the stress of an uncomfortable father-son relationship. College, on the other hand, provided an escape from both and an opportunity to continue playing baseball.

that ensured one of us would always be home to help with the work. A few weeks afterward Uncle Paul met Daddy and me at Aurand's Sporting Goods store in Lewistown where he supplemented the few dollars I had saved and bought me a $15.00 MacGregor glove. Years later I learned that it was an outfielder's glove, large and cumbersome, and I should have bought a smaller model, but at the time it was a dream come true. That glove was my high school companion and later went to college with me.

When March arrived and baseball practice began, I was both scared at possible failure and so excited that I couldn't sleep. I got up every morning and checked the weather. I kept a bat in my bedroom and practiced swings. I suffered trepidation each time I heard talk at school about players who "threw smoke," or were "strong as an ox." I worried that I would not make the team; I worried that Daddy would change his mind; I worried that I would not have a ride home after games.[10] Finally, I worried about what position I should choose. Since I had never played on a team, I had never played a position.

Finally, on a cold March afternoon, following the school day, candidates were assembled behind first base, where we were lectured on the virtue of being on time and the transgression of not hustling, and then directed to run to the position for which we were trying out. I hesitated slightly, deducted that my chances were best where numbers were least, and went to shortstop which was occupied by only one other player. At the time it seemed judicious, but I learned the following day that my competition was the team captain.

When the squad was announced before the first game, I was thrilled to get a gray wool uniform (#5) with green piping and a hat lettered with school initials. It didn't matter when I learned it was an older style uniform that had no lettering, nor did I mind in the least sitting on the bench for most of the season. I was on the team.

Every player seemed accomplished. I struggled sometimes in practice not knowing how to position myself or where to throw the ball. I still was not an active participant when the morning-after-the-game conversations took place outside the cafeteria, but I could "sit-in." Then, with eight games remaining, I played in my first high school game, against

---

10. There were rumors that school officials were unwilling to provide transportation since I was the only player at my end of the county and the cost of transporting one person such a distance was excessive. It turned out to be untrue. After games and practices, the school reimbursed my coach to drive me the twenty miles to my bus stop.

CHIEF LOGAN HIGH SCHOOL BASEBALL TEAM 1959
I was a high school junior in the spring of 1959 when the team photo was taken.
Front Row Left to Right: Tom Wert, Mgr., Denny Morgan, Ron Moore, Don Mast, Ron Gingrich, Dennis Young, Lee Fisher, Mike Erb, Terry Smith, Dick Gingrich, Jack Zeigler, Mgr. Back Row: John Monsell, Ron Armstrong, Jack Crozier, Dick Cummings, Ron Lewis, Bill Kupple, Gary Klinger, Gary Rowe, Andy Leeper, Joe McMullen, Don Fuhrer, Coach.

arch-rival Lewistown.

In the fourth or fifth inning of a game in which we were badly beaten, I was inserted as a pinch-hitter. Gary Sprout, a right-handed pitcher who would later play football at the University of Colorado, gained further anonymity that day by being the first pitcher to face me. He threw hard for a high school pitcher, and I remember being so nervous that I forgot to announce myself to the umpire as a pinch hitter. Settling myself in the left-handed batting box, my goal was to avoid striking out. I determined my best chance for success was to begin my swing as the pitcher began his windup. I started so early, in fact, that I had time to stop and take that pitch. It was out of the strike zone. I relaxed a bit after that pitch realizing he was not as fast as I had surmised. I lined the next pitch to the center fielder, who charged but was unable to make the play as it went off his glove for an error, and I became a member of the team.

I played every inning of every game for the remainder of my high school career. I replaced the captain, hit leadoff, and dreamed of immortality. By my junior year, I was captain and an integral participant in the morning-after-the-game conversations.

By my junior year, Keith and I shared the same classes. Both of us received good grades, but our academic achievements foreboded nothing in particular. We had no counselors or advisors who recommended college or directed us toward specialized vocations. Neither Mommy nor Daddy had experience with secondary education, and each had, in fact, reservations about its practical value. The fact was, in our house we never spoke about goals, vocations, or dreams.

Baseball made my last three years of high school a special time, but there were many painful factors. Neither Keith nor I were part of the social fabric of our class. Classmates dated, went to movies and dances, visited each other weekends and summers. We were isolated 20 miles away without transportation. While our friends went off to college, neither of us entertained any notion that we would be able to leave the farm. Graduation for us was more than a parting from friends; it was a final and complete separation.

ADDENDUM

During our years on the farm and especially those preceding high school, Keith and I spent countless hours playing ball in the yard and behind the barn (from my high school years onward Billy became an even more frequent baseball playmate). After writing the preceding article, I asked Keith to read and edit it. He returned the following commentary:

"I can identify with the uncertainty about choosing a sports position. Until Dad allowed me to play, I had never paid any attention to football or had any interest in it. It was like being designated to take out the manure on a cold freezing night. I had no idea whether or not I wanted such a chore.

On day three of the first practice I was asked what position I would try out for. I did not know the names of the positions, so when the person next to me said, "halfback," I said, "halfback." We started practice immediately, but I twisted my ankle badly during a tackle since I did not know to put my head down when running with the ball. I was home for several days. When I came back to practice the coach said he thought I had quit.

I was tested for running time in the 100-yard dash. I was not the fastest but not the slowest either. Then I was assigned to guard, and spent the rest of my junior year on the bench. I was only 14 and around 160 pounds.

Afterward, I was handed a sheaf of papers with cryptic names, circles, and squiggly lines and told to memorize them. I never figured out how

Keith played varsity football as a 15 year-old high school senior.

to do that and wondered if anyone else did, since there were no classes on the game of football, and no one ever explained the rules or penalties. Only the referees seemed to know when anyone was doing anything wrong and the only way to find out was to get caught doing something wrong. The line coach used to teach how to hit someone illegally and not get caught. It was a confusing game to me.

I played as first team for the junior varsity but sat on the bench during the varsity games that first year. There was a lot of bad and old equipment which the junior varsity inherited. I got a bad callous on my right foot because one of the cleats on my shoe was defective.

One afternoon line coach, Steve Prisuta, put me in a tackle practice with Lester Murphy, the starting varsity guard and self-styled mean guy. We met head to head in a tackle drill and the collision cracked my helmet in half. I must have blacked out, because Prisuta looked like he thought I was dead and asked if I was alright. I remember that Lester Murphy was slow in getting up because I dumped him (carrying the ball) pretty good. It gained me his respect because he never ridiculed me again. Then Steve said, "This kid wants to play football." Afterward he told Head Coach Andy Radi to put me in a game. After that I began spending some time with the varsity as a linebacker and defensive lineman.

I never expected to earn a senior award and was surprised when they gave me the green and white leather jacket. Actually, it did not mean much to me, so I gave it to my brother Dave when I went away to college. I had worn it only a few times. I admit that despite my attention deficit to baseball when you were after me all the time to play behind the barn, I really enjoyed the times we played on teams. Belltown is the only one I remember. I think I liked baseball more than any other sport. I liked playing tennis but did not play it with anyone much - (spent a lot of time hitting the backboard at a court in Baltimore) and can't help but wonder if baseball would have been a better path for me because I understood it more. I never played baseball after I left the farm.

Thank you for the time I did spend playing baseball. I am sure I would not have participated in any sports if it had not been for your preoccupation with playing on a team."

EDIE ERB

"On some fond breast the parting soul relies,
Some pious drops the closing eye requires;
Ev'n from the tomb the voice of Nature cries,
Ev'n in our Ashes live their wonted Fires."

"ELEGY WRITTEN IN A COUNTRY CHURCHYARD"
THOMAS GRAY

Edie Erb was born on January 17, 1888, and died on March 1, 1985. Forty-two of those years were spent in the back country of Mifflin County, sharing with common folk—in the recesses of nondescript one-room schools—her love of learning. Her labor produced no Miltons, no Caesars. Her name hangs in no hallowed hall. But this may be said, and this is sufficient: there was at least one whom she touched, one on whom was imparted a thirst for learning, one in whom was inculcated a sense of wonder, of something transcendent, greater than numbers and words and lessons, something spiritual that imbues numbers and words and lessons with significance, something that passes from spirit to kindred spirit, something whose source is the mind and person of God. And thus, it must be said that her labor was sacred, because her labor was to share the truth for which all men thirst, and without which living can have no ultimate meaning.

In the fall of 1950 Edie Erb was my third-grade teacher at Krick School, a one-room country schoolhouse at the extreme eastern end of Mifflin County, Pennsylvania, that housed grades 1-8. She had begun her teaching career four decades earlier, in the fall of 1908, and continued uninterrupted through the spring of 1951. By then she had turned sixty-three, and the hardships of wintry weather, long school days, and arthritis had taken their toll. In May she notified the Board of Education that she was retiring. I was only eight years old, but her impact upon my life during her final teaching year cannot be overstated.

The eight grades that occupied the schoolhouse were comprised of twenty to twenty-five students who lived within a three-mile radius. There was no public transportation, so each morning the schoolyard welcomed boys and girls who had walked the fields and unpaved roads carrying books and lunch bags. During inclement weather a few children rode to school in modest coupes and sedans, and there were singular days when a small boy or girl might arrive with an escorting parent on a tractor or horse, but as all were unaffected country people, unpleasant conditions generally went unnoticed.

Edie, too, traversed the three miles from her home on foot. Not one to complain, she faithfully unlocked the building at seven-thirty week-day mornings and stood by the open door welcoming freshly scrubbed faces. On fall and winter days she started a fire in the pot belly stove at the rear of the room and, on the coldest mornings, huddled with us around its cast-iron warmth. Country women and girls did not yet wear pants and jeans, a practice denounced long ago in the Pentateuch and thought to have a lit-eral application by 20th century reformed Christians. Modesty was a Godly virtue. Thus, through sleet and snow she mustered her way wintry mornings wearing a heavy overcoat and a scarf tied under her chin. On rainy days she sported an umbrella, sharing its protec-

A wood and coal burning pot belly stove warmed the schoolhouse.

tion with the children who joined her along her route. In the classroom she stood at the front in a crisp dress or skirt that ran well below the knee, her shirt buttoned at the throat with a fashionable pin. In the teacher's closet next to her desk rested a pair of comfortable shoes, which she retrieved mornings and removed afternoons, donning heavier walking shoes for the trek homeward. Like the rest of us she used the outdoor toilet and drank water from the five-gallon porcelain jug at the back of the room.

Although she was unmarried, the pejorative term, "spinster," did not apply. She was anything but reclusive. Her moral rectitude, self-discipline, and commitment to excellence were virtues manifest in the community.

She participated in quilting bees, helped neighbors prepare meals during summer days when grain was threshed, and on Sundays stayed after services to oversee church finances. It was, however, her love of learning, compassion for children, and energy for living that most captivated her neighbors and set her apart as a teacher.

By the time I arrived in the third-grade "Miss Erb" was beginning her 42nd year as a teacher in Decatur Township, arguably the most rural sector of Mifflin County. Her familiarity with the township and its inhabitants predated her teaching.

Edie was born on the Jacob "Pappy" Lawver farm, located near the eastern boundary of the county. While a baby, her parents moved for a brief period to Beavertown, a hamlet fifteen-miles eastward, where her father was employed at a tannery. Sometime in 1890, the family returned to Decatur.

She had herself attended Krick School for eight years at the end of the 19th century, developing an insatiable thirst for learning. She found excitement in books and yearned to share the truths of their contents. While most of her girlfriends, succumbing to the demands of farm life, "dropped out" after the eighth grade, Edie committed herself to a high school education.

McClure High School lay seven miles to the east, set back off State Highway 522, the closest paved road in the area. The highway was accessed by a seldom traveled three-mile dirt road that ran from the Wright farm where she lived to an intersection four miles from McClure. It was and still is farm country. After packing her lunch in the wee hours of weekday mornings she climbed into the cab of a neighbor's flatbed truck which transported local farmers' milk to a processing plant beyond McClure. Patiently enduring the hour-long ride, she waited in the vehicle while the driver made his stops: methodically hoisting heavy ten-gallon cans of fresh milk onto his vehicle, strapping them into place, and sometimes chatting with friendly farmers before resuming his route. Finally, upon reaching the turnoff that took her to the school, he bid her "good-day" and continued his route. She then walked the one remaining mile to the high school. Evenings she hiked the seven miles back to her home.

Following high school graduation, she became an even greater anomaly as one of the first girls in our rural community to go to college. At a time when few girls graduated from high school, she saved enough money to pay for one term at Kutztown Normal School, then took Normal School

courses offered at Yeagertown until she had garnered sufficient means for
a second year, this time at Shippensburg College. That training enabled her
to receive the certification necessary for a permanent teaching position
and qualified her for a professional career, although she never received a
formal four-year college degree.

By the fall of 1908, having completed the training necessary to gain
employment as a teacher, she began her love affair with young people.
Devoted to her students, she was also committed to frugality and self-suffi-
ciency. During her teaching tenure she invested her savings in the purchase
of two farms in Decatur Township, including the family farm where her
parents had lived and where she would spend her remaining days. Concurrently, her sister Jennie married Clayton Wright, a local farm boy, and the
newlyweds were invited by Edie to join her on the family farm.

Raised a farm girl, she planted and harvested, cooked and cleaned,
and was an integral part of the Wright farm family. In later years, she sold
the farm to her nephew, Paul Wright, and his wife Helen. They insisted she
remain in the home and accorded her the same respect and kindness she
had received from her sister and brother-in-law. Her life was fully engaged,
laboring on the farm, helping to raise nephews and nieces, and teaching at
local one-room schools.

At the onset of Edie's teaching career, farming across America was
done with horses, but by the end of WWI most cities and towns had become mechanized. In the far reaches of Decatur Township, however, the
revolution came slowly. Through the 1920s and 1930s, there continued
occasions when she arrived at school on horseback, a rainproof slicker
drawn about her. If confronted with snow, she hitched her horse to a sleigh.
In those cases when inclement weather was severe and made it prudent to
close the school, she was responsible to alert parents before their children
set out in the morning. In the absence of telephones, which did not make
an appearance in our township until 1957, she arose early and rode from
house to house in carriage or sleigh to announce the closure.

Despite her industry on the farm, in the church, and about the community, she was regarded chiefly as a teacher. By the time she retired most
of the township residents, including my mother, had sat in her classroom.
She addressed most parents and many grandparents by their first names,
because she had taught them and knew them personally. These friendships
assured that the schoolyard was shoveled open after snows, the wood or
coal bin was filled on fall and winter weekends, a fresh supply of water was

available at the nearest farm, and the grassy knoll adjacent to the school was always mowed. More than a friendly teacher, she was a friend who taught school.

The influence of philosopher John Dewey's pragmatism upon modern education had its impact after WWII, so that by the time I entered Miss Erb's third-grade class in the fall of 1950, a new emphasis on math and science as they related to vocational training was felt even in the distant reaches of rural America. The former emphasis on classical rhetoric, the arts, and moral virtue was disappearing. As a result, curriculum and methodology in one-room schools reflected an amalgam of past and current philosophies attempting to combine liberal arts with what was considered the more practical vocational programs. In most classrooms poetry, music, and art were becoming secondary concerns, reserved for one or two class periods per week, and references to Biblical theology were disappearing from the curriculum.

Not so in Edie's classroom. Recognizing the ageless value of the arts and the critical roles played by theology and philosophy in providing answers to life's most important questions, Edie continued to emphasize liberal arts as an integral part of education.

Her methods were rooted in both her Christianity and her personal disposition. Sentimental and compassionate, she inculcated truths from Scripture and punctuated lessons with references to personal experience.

Mornings began with a reading from Scripture, a recitation of the Pledge of Allegiance, and a short prayer. Twice each week she led us in singing folk and patriotic songs ranging from the Americana of Stephen Foster to the classical "Battle Hymn of the Republic" and "America, the Beautiful." She had survived the trauma of two world wars, and her devotion to God and country was central to both her private life and her classroom. America mattered. Sometimes she marched proudly up and down each aisle, carrying the flag whose stars and stripes rested daily above the blackboard. Her passion breathed life into history and literature. When reading aloud of the death of Nancy Hanks Lincoln and the resulting pain visited upon nine-year old Abe, she wept. Her emotions overflowed each time she recited John McCrea's "In Flanders Fields," Eugene Fields's "Little Boy Blue," and Walt Whitman's "O Captain, My Captain."+

Until her final years she was a daily participant during recesses and lunch breaks in games of "Balley Over," "Three Deep," "Drop the Handkerchief," and "Fox and Ducks." At noon she sat on a folding chair supervising

Edie Erb is at the far right of the back row. The fall of 1930 marked her twenty-second year of teaching. My mother is second from the right in row 3. My Aunt Beattie is third from left in back row, and my Aunt Iva is standing next to Edie.

the daily softball game, never missing her turn at bat. The interaction endeared her to younger students and warned older ones that she could still wield a no-nonsense stick.

Parents trusted her because they were familiar with her character. She disciplined obstreperous children by insisting they clean the blackboard or carry coal for the pot belly stove. For the more recalcitrant she kept a paddle under the hinged lid of her desk. In the aftermath of its use, she wrote an explanatory note to be signed and returned by the wounded's parents. Irenic and gracious, she dissolved altercations by cultivating relationships with moms and dads.

Once or twice each week she locked the school after the 3:00 pm dismissal and walked home with a student who might benefit from a teacher-parent conference. Sometimes it meant turning into lanes that led to front doors, and spending a few minutes sitting on front porch swings or at kitchen tables chatting with parents. The sojourn meant extra steps and extra time, but she thought it important to maintain friendships. On Back-to-School Night she was flooded with layered cakes, pans of fudge, shoo-fly and whoopee pies, sticky buns, and quart jars of canned goods.

From September until May, her students were her family. She tied the shoe laces of a first grader who didn't yet know how, hugged and held close a third-grade girl whose mother was hospitalized, and walked four miles out of her way to plead with a seventh-grader to return to school after being informed that he was quitting.

When school was dismissed for the summer of 1951, I was unaware that Edie would be retiring. It was not until several weeks afterward that my mother informed me, "Edie will not be your teacher this fall." The disclosure jolted me. Beyond the threat of losing a favorite teacher, her retirement generated a personal crisis.

On the final day of school Edie had called me to her desk. Confidentially, she whispered that she had an extra copy of the fourth-grade reader and wanted to know if I would like to keep it for the summer. I was ecstatic. Although I was not yet in grade four, she had permitted me to read ahead. The book contained many stories I had learned to love: "Rumpelstiltskin," "Billy Goats Gruff," "Tar Baby," "King Midas' Touch," etc. It was a secret treasure of immense proportion, resting on a private covenant between teacher and pupil, and a responsibility of considerable weight. Tearing a page or staining the book would be a criminal offense to be addressed upon its return.

Thus, her retirement, beyond the childish concern that I might never see her again, produced a second distress; it dissolved our covenant. The promise had been that I would return the book to Edie in the fall. Now, I had no way of keeping my part of the bargain. Worse, the private compact was unknown to the incoming teacher.

I took my dilemma to my mother. Mommy told me to be patient and promised that when occasion arose she would speak with Edie. Although she assured me that I would not be prosecuted, I agonized about the outcome.

Weeks passed. Through the hot summer, I went about my farm work, and on rainy days and summer nights I read from the book. Constant, however, was the realization that it had to be returned. Jewels become doubly precious when they are about to be forfeited.

On a muggy Thursday morning that promised a sweltry afternoon, an unfamiliar car pulled into our driveway. Edie and a newspaper reporter from the Lewistown *Sentinel* appeared and spoke with Mommy through the screened door of our kitchen. He explained that he was writing an article on Edie's retirement and wanted to take a picture of her with some pupils. He asked if Keith and I might ride along to the school, promising it would take but a few minutes. Mommy was pleased that we would have our picture in the newspaper. She insisted that Edie and the reporter come wait in the kitchen while she hurried Keith and me to put on school pants and shirts, comb our hair, and wash our faces. Concerned that Armageddon had suddenly arrived, I surreptitiously left the book in my bedroom and feigning innocence crawled into the reporter's car.

Mary Bubb, a seventh-grade neighbor, had also been solicited. She was waiting outside her house near her mailbox when we pulled into the driveway. I slid to the middle of the rear seat as she climbed in, and the three of us sat in silence as the reporter navigated the half-mile to the school grounds.

Inside the one-room building, he positioned Edie at her familiar desk and placed us three school-children alongside where we stood peering over her shoulder at some imagined work while he snapped several pictures. Fifteen minutes later, satisfied that his mission was accomplished, he was ready to return us home. Edie began closing her desk for the final time while everyone started for the car. As we were filing out, however, she called me back.

"You may keep the book," she whispered, as though the two of us were sharing covert information. I was speechless. She smiled, revealing that she had intuitively been aware of my distress. And then, as though an explanation were necessary, she confided "The cover on your book is damaged. I don't think your next teacher will want it."

Edie Erb had, from September to May of my third-grade year, with inherent kindness and compassion, endeared herself to her students. Her love for learning, her concern for the education and welfare of each student, and her insistence on Christian decorum left indelible impressions on everyone who sat in her classroom. But it was her magnanimity in permitting me to keep the fourth-grade reading book that engendered personal and lasting gratitude.

Edie appreciated education as a means to a greater end. She knew it must provide the tools and skills which permitted us to function as productive members of a community, but she believed its purpose transcended mere pragmatism. To live useful lives, we must learn, not only facts, but truths. We must acquire not just information, but a love for that which is true. We must live not merely to fill existential needs, but to

Edie Erb on the day she told me to "keep the book."
Newspaper photo courtesy of Lewistown Sentinel.

prepare for tomorrow. For Edie Erb education involved a kind of worship, an understanding not only of the design of the universe but a recognition of its designer. She concluded that the mind is not isolated from the heart or soul, and a schoolteacher must embrace all three if students are to live meaningful lives.

THE GOOD SAMARITAN

PART ONE

It was a sultry August evening in 1953. The oldest of five children, I would turn eleven in one month and was already familiar with both the hard labor and the unremitting demands of a farm. The end of a twelve-hour work day should have brought release. Cows had been fed and milked and turned out to pasture. Chickens noisily ate the remains of the ground mixture of corn, wheat, and oats that filled the long feeders in the chicken house. Pigs swilled slop, a soup of finely chopped grain sopped with water, from the low troughs in their pens. The day was winding down.

A boy holds the notion that freedom has no contingency. Work completed, he is free to play ball games, read books, or hunt rabbits. Reality informs otherwise. Constraints and obligations are enduring. Barn work was completed early on Wednesday evenings only so that prayer meeting could be attended. Now, Daddy and Mommy, with us five small children, were on our way to church in the used two-door '38 Buick sedan Daddy had bought the previous winter.

Buying that car had become a necessity after his burgeoning family had forced us boys to ride through wintry weather on the open flat bed of our '46 Chevy pick-up. Despite this, during the summer months, we preferred the truck and the refreshing breeze created by its languid 40 mph trips to town and back. Readying the truck for church, however, was extra work as the animal rack had to be removed and the truck bed swept and scrubbed. With all there was to be done in the persistent routines of farm life, it was simpler to ride in the car, even on a sweltering August evening. The oppressive heat enervated. Suffocating days of stifling temperatures had turned into weeks without

Two adults and five children squeezed into our two-door 1938 Buick sedan.

rain. The noon day drone of cicadas presaged ruin. Crops shriveled. Dust rose. Tempers flared.

We three boys, Billy aged six, Keith aged nine, and I, dressed in clean overalls buttoned over white T-shirts, sat in the rear seat, listless. Our dampened T-shirts clung to our backs, while four-year old Ruthann sat prettily in her crisp dress in the front seat between our parents. Mommy, wearing a bandanna to keep her hair in place against the open windows, held both her and Daddy's Bibles. Our one-year old, Susie, was fast asleep on my lap. No one spoke as the long miles took us past the unending hamlets that lay between our home and the back way to Lewistown: Wagner, Shindle, Paintersville, Alfarata, Maitland, and Derry Township. Daddy was angry.

Daddy's patience had been stretched paper-thin thirty minutes earlier when he learned from Mommy that "the boys" hated attending Wednesday night prayer meetings. We never dared complain directly to Daddy, but Mommy was a safe audience. She endured the vagaries and fancies of her children. Prudently, she regularly kept our protests to herself. This time, however, she found them useful for her own purposes. The stifling heat and long days of washing, baking, and cleaning reduced a body. She, too, yearned for a respite, an evening relaxing with the slow back and forth pendulum of the porch swing. Attending prayer meetings demanded continual energy and attention to her children. Her desire for release coupled with her children's complaints gave way. Subterfuge masked her more private motive as she had abjectly told Daddy, "The boys don't want to go to church."

Daddy's days, too, consisted of exhausting farm work, incessant and unvarying, amid the financial strain of growing debt. Reprieve for him was a holiday fishing in a mountain stream, or a twenty-five mile mid-week afternoon jaunt to the Belleville sale barn where a slice of shoo-fly pie and a cup of coffee could be had for thirty-five cents. Or, of course, the mid-week prayer meeting at Calvary Bible Church, twenty miles distant. Church offered an arena where friendly acquaintances respected his exchanges and afforded him the pleasures of male relationships. Wednesday night prayer meetings, more than Sunday services, extended an opportunity to visit and to talk. It revitalized his week. Daddy most certainly knew that his children would rather have avoided the confinements of church and the pleasant exchanges of strangers, but he was fully persuaded that regular church attendance resulted in virtue, and his parental obligation trumped childish myopia. Motivated by moral obligation and colored by selfish desire, we were on our way to church.

Wending the final miles over rolling hills we approached the Heights, the outlying environs of Lewistown, when suddenly, the car began to shake and wobble. Daddy knew immediately. He pulled to the side of the road, abruptly shut off the motor, and ordered us to "stay in the car!" He got out, slamming the door. We did not turn to watch as he twisted the handle that opened the trunk and removed the spare tire, but we came to attention when he called for someone to give him a hand. I passed the baby to Mommy, climbed over the front seat, and stepped from the car. Keith followed and then Billy, until the three of us stood waiting for directions. Daddy was searching the car trunk, tire iron in hand. Seconds passed. Finally, he slammed the trunk lid closed. The car jack was missing. Frustration fomented anger. He turned to us with reproach, "Who was playing with the jack?" It was not a question; it was condemnation. We were guilty by default. He ordered us back into the car.

Meanwhile, Daddy walked to the front of the car and stepped onto the highway preparing to flag a passing motorist. Most folks were home for the evening, suppers eaten, listening to radios, engaged in front porch talk. Intermittently, however, a car passed. It was not in Daddy's nature to ask for help. Asking for assistance wounded his pride. It was tantamount to begging.

Necessity, however, prodded. We needed a jack. In the distance a sporty 1953 Chevy came into view. Reluctantly he stepped forward and began waving. The driver of the approaching car must have seen us stranded on the side of the highway, for he immediately began slowing. The Chevy pulled to a stop opposite Daddy.

Stopping a motorist was bad enough, but stopping one who was driving a newer car compounded his irritation for it meant engaging an "uppity" driver, one of the "town" people whom Daddy distrusted for their education, money, and airs. He had long ago determined that "townies" were supercilious, soft, and depraved. They made their money by working in offices where they hoodwinked country folk.

A friendly face leaned from an open window and asked, "Whatsa matter?"

Daddy approached the polished two-tone blue coupe. Out of earshot in the rear seat of the sedan, we watched the exchange. Within seconds the new car pulled slowly back onto the highway, made a U-turn and drove up behind us. The driver got out and walked to the rear of his car. He opened the trunk, took out a jack and brought it forward. As Daddy reached for the instrument, the stranger waved him aside, fell to his knees beside our flattened tire, and began positioning the jack. Gratefully, Daddy expressed his appreciation and again volunteered to change the tire. He reminded the Good Samaritan that kneeling in the dirt would ruin his clothes. Ignoring Daddy's remonstrance, the new friend examined the flat tire, surmising that a piece of metal or a nail was the culprit, and then began pumping the jack handle. Oddly, he called Daddy, "Jim," as though they were acquainted.

Inside the car we waited in silence. We knew that Daddy's smiles and good-natured responses to the stranger did not preclude a further display of anger. We also knew that childish complaints about the heat or any semblance of impatience would sharpen the consequences. It was scary to feel the car tilt perilously as the jack lifted the axle. A sudden shifting of children's bodies might cause the car to fall and ignite Daddy's anger. With bated breath, we sat motionless. The minutes passed. The flat tire was removed and laid on the grassy slope. Daddy stood ready with the spare. In a few minutes lugs were tightened, the jack was lowered, and tools were returned to the trunk.

"Andy, whad'da I owe you?" Daddy offered.

"Aw, Jim, you don't owe me anything. One of these days I wanna stop and see your farm," Andy climbed back into the Chevy.

"We'd love to have you. And thanks again."

We drove on to church. The hour service, as always, lasted ninety minutes. Two ceiling fans droned drowsily above the overheated room. Pastor Snyder asked for prayer requests. Hymns were sung. Time dragged as we knelt with folded hands pressed against hard wooden benches, while heartfelt prayers of thanksgiving and ardent solicitations for divine grace were spoken. Finally, Pastor Snyder offered a closing prayer and dismissed the congregation.

The evening had cooled, and children were anxious to wander outside into the fresh air, but while Daddy and Mommy visited with friends and exchanged mutual concerns, we patiently remained seated on the benches.

By the time we reached our car, darkness had fallen. It was getting late for a farm family. Although Daddy's presence, as always, was foreboding for the first minutes of the drive home, he soon began to banter with Mommy regarding news exchanged with church friends, and children relaxed from the earlier tension. The two small girls fell asleep. In the rear seat the cool night breeze from open windows stirred tousled hair just as the lights from passing farms stirred imagination. Nothing was spoken of Andy, the "town" man who had helped us. I wondered who he was, where he worked, how he made his living, and how he and Daddy knew one another. And I wondered if he would really come to see the farm.

PART TWO

Sometimes, after Sunday morning church services, our family was invited to drive two miles to 10 Belle Avenue, where my paternal

CORA (BARDELL) SHAWVER
I was blessed with wonderful grandmothers.

grandmother lived with Irv, her second husband. Widowed in 1937, she had remarried soon afterward, but her children seemed not to have bonded with Irv, and he existed as a rather obscure member of the family. Grandma's house stood on the western side of the Juniata River which ran north to south through the town. Belle Avenue ran perpendicular to the river and was the primary conduit that carried Lewistown's workforce weekday mornings from the center of town to the industrial sites located along the western banks of the river. It was located where the river bridge ended, amid a row of similar houses whose front steps faced the main thoroughfare. The homes suggested middle class: millworkers, railroad hands, policemen, and waitresses who went about their lives amid the sadness of anonymity. Save for the family that operated the candy and tobacco store at the end of the street, they held no familiarity for me, and Grandma seldom mentioned them.

Grandma's children, with a lone exception, were grown and gone from the house, which meant she welcomed our company. Visiting Grandma on Sundays meant sumptuous meals and treats that might include a dime with which a boy could buy a comic book from the candy store. Visiting Grandma was fun.

Uncle Don, the youngest of Grandma's eight children, still lived at home. He had graduated from high school the previous spring and was working as a carpenter's apprentice. Everyone knew him as "Nipper," a name coined years earlier after the wide-eyed, mischievous cartoon character who appeared daily in the *Lewistown Sentinel*, the local newspaper. He was athletic and enjoyed playing and entertaining us kids with his songs and stories, and sometimes took us on adventurous hikes. Visiting Grandma was double fun when Nipper was present.

DONALD MORGAN
We kids loved him.

On a warm spring Sunday in 1954, after church dismissed, we received one of Grandma's invitations to noonday dinner. We eagerly accepted and expectantly drove to Belle Avenue where we knew a smorgasbord awaited. Opulent dishes of ham, mashed potatoes and gravy, greens, freshly baked bread, rice pudding, and Daddy's favorite, scalloped oysters, swelled the table. We ate with relish.

It was mid-afternoon when chairs were finally pushed back from the table, and Daddy announced it was time to leave. Nipper interrupted. The following day, Monday, was his free day, and he asked if he might come to the farm and hunt groundhogs. Daddy said that would be fine. Nipper ventured further, "Jim, how about letting Denny and Keith stay overnight? I'll bring them with me in the morning." My heart leapt.

I knew Daddy needed our help with the farm work, but staying overnight was wrought with enticement. I knew it probably meant a fishing trip that evening, replete with sandwiches and a campfire along the banks of the Juniata. I loved watching the lines as my uncle set baits for the catfish and carp[1] that lay close under the bridge that ran across the river. Daddy was torn, considering the extra work our absence would cause, balancing it against boyish hopes. Then, turning to Mommy, as if he needed her approval, he asked, "Hazel, wha'd'ya think?"

Without reservation, she gave her blessing, and I began romancing staying overnight in Lewistown with Nipper. Keith, however, younger by one year, for unspoken reasons wished to go home. Goodbyes were

---

1. Carp are a heavy-bellied fish popular as food in Eastern Europe, Russia, and China but treated as pests in most parts of the United States due to their invasive nature in waters inhabited by more desirable fish.

View from Lewistown looking across the Juniata River Bridge. Grandma's house was third on left after crossing the bridge. American Viscose Corp. is in right background. Riverbank in front of Viscose plant is where we fished.

spoken, children piled into the rear seat of the car, and I was alone with Nipper, ready for adventure.

PART THREE

It was dusky evening when Nipper and I cut slender limbs from the saplings along the shore of the river. The limbs were trimmed and shaped with his pocket knife to allow the bottom ends of the three-pronged sticks to be driven into the sandy bank while the tops formed the forks in which the fishing poles would rest. Next, Nipper weighted the lines with sinkers and baited the hooks. The lines were then cast far out into the waters that flowed under the bridge. After the sinkers grabbed the river bottom, Nipper placed the poles into the forked sticks, surveyed his work, and satisfied, laid back on the grassy bank. Fishing required slow patience.

We glanced from time to time to see if the fishing lines evidenced the tug and pull of a hooked fish, but our concentration was for the most part on the river. Nipper told of its history: over there, where a young boy, years earlier, had drowned; down further, on the far side, where a small boat had overturned, and two occupants were saved by passersby; and here, near our campsite, where a great carp had been taken.

Nipper walked to the water's edge and cleaned his hands in the cold river water. He returned and spread a piece of folded canvas onto the grass. From a brown paper sack he took sandwiches, laden with slabs of ham left from the noon meal and laid them atop the canvas. Taking an opener from his pack, he pried open a can of beans, and with a spoon that appeared from the same pack, he scooped spoonfuls onto the waxed paper that had held the sandwiches. We savored every bite of the banquet, washing it down with long draughts of water from his canteen.

The grainy dusk had given way to darkness as Nipper directed me to gather stones and place them in a small circle while he began foraging for driftwood. The rise and fall of the river during and after heavy rains had deposited a plentiful supply of broken tree limbs against the river banks. He gathered two armfuls, placed them within the circle of stones, removed a lighter from his pocket and began the tedium of holding the flame against a small stick, waiting for it to flare. At first it failed to catch, but when the empty paper sack was added to a tiny bed of sticks for kindling, he again flipped open the lighter and soon the bag burst into flame. Jamming it further into the bed of sticks, he waited hopefully. Seconds passed, and then, the tinder caught. Methodically he fueled the fire, stick by stick, until the tiny bundle began crackling. Then larger chunks and branches were added, and flames began leaping above the wood.

The fishing all but forgotten, we lay back once more in the darkness. From time to time, Nipper checked the lines for signs of a hooked fish, but our attention was occupied with the sounds of a river at night. Time passed. In the distance a train whistle called. By now the fire had fallen to low embers. It was nine o'clock. We decided our fishing must be limited to "just a few more minutes," because we had to get up early in the morning to go to the farm. Walking to the water's edge, Nipper checked the lines a final time. Suddenly, his voice filled with excitement, "We got one!"

The night came alive. The drama of the moment played the anxious hope of a man against the strain of a fish pulling taut the line. As he maneuvered into position, Nipper explained each strategy. He let the fish run, all the while maintaining tension on the fishing line. Each time he attempted to work the reel, the spindle would whirl as the fish swam farther beyond the bridge overpass. Excitedly, he directed me to reel in our second line so the two would not become entangled. The fish had stopped running, but Nipper's line remained taut. Minutes passed when abruptly, we heard the splashing sound of a fish breaking the water's surface out beyond the bridge, and Nipper began reeling frantically to maintain tension on the line as the fish turned and swam toward us. I was now able to see ripples where the fish's back rose above the water no more than thirty yards away. The fish swam close, then, suddenly, turned and made another run. Again the reel whined. Minutes turned into a half hour. This time the fish swam short of the bridge overpass as fatigue began to erode its resolve. Slowly, Nipper worked the reel, drawing the fish ever closer, yard by yard to where we waited at the river bank. In the darkness, we could see only a few feet, but the fish was no longer splashing. Wearing sneakers, jeans, and a sweatshirt, he began wading into the river, working his way towards the fish. Knee deep into the water, he turned and motioned me down to the river edge. He splashed several steps in my direction, directing me to take the rod. Holding the line high above the water Nipper began slogging out towards the fish. Ten yards from the river bank, he reached down and placed one hand under its belly and lifted, but the fish wiggled and slid back into the water. He held the line taut and began dragging the fish all the way to the water's edge. A second time he reached down, and this time secured the fish. It was a gigantic carp. Cradling it in both hands, he splashed through the water and strode up the embankment, carefully laying his prize on the grassy knoll.

PART FOUR

I carried the fishing pole and the bait box as we marched triumphantly through the night, carefully weaving our way along the river bank in the moonless dark, climbing the path that led up to the rear of the houses that ran along Belle Avenue, and then crossing into the backyard of Grandma's house. We were both fatigued and excited. Inside the house, sleepers had retired for the night. Nipper decided to carry the carp down into the cool cellar where it would be left until morning. He had cleaned and washed it at the river, and he would cut the carcass into pieces in the morning before departing for the farm.[2] Two doors covered the outside entrance to the cellar. Laying the carp on the sidewalk, he lifted them open, picked up the fish, and we descended the steps into the cellar. He laid the carp on a newspaper, atop a work table, took the fishing pole and bait box

---

2. Not considered a food fish by local residents, Nipper cut the carp into small pieces and fed them to the large goldfish that were kept in an outdoor pond at the back of the yard.

from me and set them on a shelf. We washed our hands and dried them using an old towel that he found near the work table. It was time for bed.

It was ten thirty when we ascended the stairs to his second-floor bedroom. The room contained a double bed, a small bureau, a lamp stand, and a chair and flat table that served as his desk. In spite of the furniture, it seemed barren, vacant, a room to be occupied only at night; a room where only sleep and unbroken silence dwelt. A picture of a pretty girl wearing a coat and scarf rested on the table. Nipper had never spoken of her, but I knew that she was his girlfriend. As we climbed beneath the covers, he lowered his voice and asked if I had fun. His whispers remained tinged with excitement as he recounted the conquest of the carp. With long pauses, he recalled the interplay with the fish, his anxiety and exhilaration. The ebb and flow of his voice faded as fatigue and the late hour overcame me. Within minutes I was asleep.

PART FIVE

The gunshot did not awaken me. The room echoed only silence, but I suddenly realized that Nipper was not in the room. I sat upright and peered into the darkness feeling something was amiss. In a strange bed, in the wee hours of morning, I had been awakened and could make no account. The moment seemed suspended. I reasoned that I was at my grandmother's house, in my uncle's bed, that my uncle had inexplicably left the room, and I was alone.

I crawled from the warm bed and crept to the window that looked down onto Belle Avenue. Black night was surrendering to gray morning. Cars parked along the street sat deserted and dumb. The dusky river, torpid and impassive, flowed southward in endless journey. Up river and to the west, two huge water tanks marked the train station. The rails lay idle. The bridge that crossed the river eastward away from Belle Avenue stood in ready wait to funnel seven o'clock traffic from Lewistown to the industries this side of the river. I listened for voices. The house seemed empty. I climbed back onto the bed and waited.

I thought of the farm, Daddy and Keith alone now at the barn. Anxiety flooded my spirit. I would have to atone for my sin. Daddy had not wanted me to stay overnight. I had avoided responsibility. He would be silent, brooding. Time would turn slowly. The faint whine of a siren on the far side of the river, fading, rising, distant, broke the stillness. Muted and fixed, the pulsations seemed imaginary, like faint memory. A flock of pigeons lifted from one of the water tanks and circled the train yard, their dark outline barely visible against the dawning sky. A lone crow perched atop a utility pole directly across the street.

Suddenly, I was aware that the siren was growing closer. It was not the driving alarm of a police car, but the piercing whistle of an ambulance or fire truck. I jumped to the floor and looked eastward up the avenue, fearful. Almost immediately, a white ambulance, its side brandishing the large blue letters, EMERGENCY VEHICLE, came into view. Red warning lights were flashing as it crossed the river bridge and began slowing, cautiously passing the homes along the street. Then, in full view, it stopped and backed onto the sidewalk in front of the house next door. Simultaneously, an escort of police cars appeared, and at once the scene exploded into action.

As I strained to find context for the tableau below, I was startled to recognize my grandmother speaking earnestly with a white-clad female attendant while uniformed medical personnel and policemen, in urgent step, disappeared into the house. Two more white-clad attendants removed a stretcher and a black case from the ambulance and followed Grandma up three cement steps that led to a front room. I watched and waited. The frenzied activity in front of the house next door was rendered all the more mysterious, because there were no other signs of life up and down the early morning street.

It now seemed to me that someone in the adjoining house was in trouble. I had never seen or heard children next door, indeed, I had seldom seen the husband and wife who lived there, and then only from a distance. I surmised that the occupants lived alone, and now, either the man or his wife had perhaps fallen, or become sick, and the other must have phoned Grandma and asked for her help. In turn, she must have awakened Nipper, and the two of them had gone next door to offer assistance. As I watched, a few curious neighbors began to assemble on the sidewalk beyond the ambulance. Two policemen, double parked, stood beside patrol cars, lights pulsating. From the center of Lewistown, on the far side of the river, the wail of a new siren intruded. I wondered if the problem next door included both the husband and the wife. Seconds passed. Inexplicably, the sound vanished, not to come again.

Anxiety for the events next door was coupled with my personal exigency. I had promised Daddy to be home in time to help with the farm

work. He would be angry at my delay. His arm reached beyond the boundary of house and barn. Its grip was pervasive, incessant, forceful. The
morning milking was done, cows were at pasture, chickens and pigs were
fed. I could feel his annoyance, his petulance as he groused at Mommy,
concluding she was complicit in some collective plot to undermine him. I
regretted staying overnight.

My private concern was arrested by four policemen below, who
stepped from the house. They strained against the weight of a body,
strapped supine on the stretcher they carried. Skilled hands lifted and then
slid the bed into its rack. Doors slammed and a convoy of police cars, ush-
ering the ambulance, lurched forward into the street. With sirens wailing,
the procession sped across the river bridge toward surcease and away from
time. Once more, the morning became still.

PART SIX

The remaining participants of the early morning drama quietly
dispersed. I was forlorn, anxious for someone or something to
make sense of what I had seen. Neither the bedroom where I waited nor
the silence throughout the house provided a clue.

Ten minutes passed. Then, a door downstairs, at the back of the house,
opened and closed. I heard noises in the kitchen below. Muffled voices in
a slow staccato of subdued sounds accentuated by long pauses, as though
each articulation awaited an answer. Grandma and Nipper had returned
from their mission. Once more, I got down from the bed, pulled on socks
and blue jeans, and began to lace my sneakers. The soft tread of steps as-
cending the stair stirred my attention, and a moment later Nipper quietly
opened the bedroom door.

Surprised to find me awake and dressed, he asked, "How long you
been up?"

"Just got awake," I lied.

Relieved, he told me Grandma had breakfast ready. "Are you ready to
head home?"

I said that I was and followed him down the steps and out into the
kitchen. Four eggs were frying in a cast iron skillet while Grandma set a
cup of hot chocolate on the table. Nipper poured a cup of coffee and came
and sat beside me. When the eggs were ready, Grandma placed two slices

of buttered toast and two eggs on each plate and brought them to the table. She made small talk to fill the time, but I remained anxious that Daddy would be upset when I arrived home at a late hour. I hoped he would send me to cultivating corn. That would be good. Cultivating corn could be monotonous, but driving a tractor up and down the unending rows during a summer afternoon meant being alone, time passing pleasantly in the uninterrupted fields of imagination. Daddy's grasp could sometimes be forgotten in the reverie of daydream.

Grandma came and sat at the table. Gathering her thoughts, she sighed. Then, as if confiding some sacred, inscrutable truth, she bent toward me. "Denny," she paused, "Do you remember our neighbor, Andy?"[3]

Suddenly, a bolt flashed backward in my memory. Andy? ... Andy? The Andy who changed our tire? The Andy who wanted to visit our farm?

She placed her hand atop mine as if to soften the impact of her revelation. "Tell your dad that Andy shot himself last night. He committed suicide."

The day became anesthetized and listless as I ate the toast and eggs and drank the hot chocolate. Nipper was absorbed in reflection. Irv returned from his midnight shift at the laundry, went immediately upstairs and disappeared into the bathroom. I heard water running into the tub and knew he would sleep before eating his noontime meal. When we finished breakfast, Nipper and I lingered in the kitchen while Grandma cleared and washed the dishes. She then dried her hands and brought my baseball cap from the hallway closet. She bent, kissed me, and asked if I had a good time. Nipper assured her that he would return before dark, and turning, led the way to the garage. In a few minutes we climbed into Irv's black Buick Roadster and started to the farm, crossing the river bridge, leaving the town proper, and passing the villages that lay between Lewistown and the farm. We rode in pregnant silence, Nipper considering the night's confusion of people, events and circumstance. I was submerged beneath a more pressing reality. Daddy wanted me home. There was work to do.

The carp, forgotten, lay silent in the cool, dark cellar.

---

3. Andy Cohn was Grandma's next-door neighbor at 10 Belle Avenue in Lewistown where she lived with her second husband, Irv Shawver. Andy was out of work, possibly because of a dismissal at the American Viscose Plant where he had worked for many years. Newspaper reports indicated that he seemed despondent in the days preceding his death.

I'M GOOD THE WAY I AM

There's a certain Slant of light,
Winter Afternoons –
That oppresses, like the
Heft of Cathedral Tunes –

Heavenly Hurt, it gives us –
We can find no scar,
But internal difference,
Where the Meanings, are –

None may teach it – Any –
'Tis the Seal Despair –
An imperial affliction
Sent us of the Air –

When it comes, the Landscape listens –
Shadows – hold their breath –
When it goes, 'tis like the Distance
On the look of Death –

EMILY DICKINSON

Winter 1952. A cold February Sunday afternoon. 3:00 pm. The porch thermometer just outside the kitchen door held steady at eleven degrees. A foreboding sky, gray and fixed, stretched from horizon to horizon, promising continued cold and threatening snow. Melancholy, heavy with ennui, hung dreadfully in the lassitude of afternoon silence. The day was in abeyance.

Sunday dinner had been eaten without conversation. Twelve toasted cheese sandwiches had been placed on a plastic serving dish and set in the middle of the long table around which sat the family. Keith, Bill, and I occupied one end while our little sister, RuthAnn, sat in a highchair between

Mommy and Daddy near the stove. Sobriety had marked the meal—a solemn stillness interrupted with cautious spoonsful of steaming vegetable soup.

Two hours had passed. My eight-year-old brother Keith was behind the kitchen wood stove, playing with the set of Lincoln Logs that had been a Christmas gift from my maternal grandmother two years earlier. A few pieces were missing, but it was one of our few toys that occupied children on a day that was to be spent indoors. Occasionally, the clatter of the logs announced that Keith had dumped a project and begun a new one, but his amusement remained passive and contained as the afternoon droned. RuthAnn and Billy were taking naps.

Play on raw wintry days presented for us older children one of two options. We could either retreat to the barn or remain in the warm kitchen, the only heated room in our house. Keith had chosen to entertain himself behind the kitchen stove. Heat radiated in uneven waves into the spacious room, but the walls of the house were not insulated, and even though windows were reinforced with blankets and towels, and faded throw-rugs were stuffed against the base of the kitchen door, occupants of the room huddled near the stove, alternately moving close to and retreating from the hot belly.

Daddy had gone to his bedroom for a Sunday afternoon nap. It was his respite between a morning of barn work, services at Calvary Bible Church in Lewistown, an evening of more barn work, and a return to worship for the evening service. The inertia of the day was solemn and slow.

I elected to go to the barn. The ground floor held the body heat of cows, calves, and horses and supplied adequate warmth to play cowboys and Indians or cops and robbers on days Keith was willing to brace the cold. When I was alone, however, I shot baskets on the upper barn floor. There was no heat, but it was shielded from the wind, and the rigor of playing basketball kept a body warm. If it was too cold, I played imaginary baseball games in front of the calf pens on the ground floor by swinging a bat at pitches delivered by major leaguers.

I pulled my heavy barn coat over a sweatshirt and sprinted with my basketball across yard and barn bridge to the entryway that opened to the second-floor mows and granaries.[1] On this day being outdoors was un-

---

1. The ball was not an actual basketball, but a volleyball that I found in the weeds next to the baseball field at Kisacoquillas Park where our church had gone for a late September fellowship and picnic supper.

pleasant. My warm breath was visible in frosty vapors, and I hurried until I was inside the barn where I removed my coat, confident that shooting baskets would keep me warm. The homemade rim of a basketball hoop was nailed to one of the twelve by twelve jambs that formed the twenty-foot ladders that reached up into the mows. There was no netting, so that shots entering the rim bounced against the jamb and rolled to the end of the barn floor. The flooring was uneven, splintered in places, making dribbling tedious, but I shot basket after basket into the wire rim, each time running across the floor to retrieve the ball.

Despite the day and the cold, I loved the hours. Imaginary games, heroic performances, and the dreams that somewhere ... someday. ...

As the hours passed, the sweat inside my shirt turned to chill. When I began to shiver, I threw on my coat, opened one of the trapdoors that led down into the first-floor where the cattle were penned and climbed down. Contrasted with the frostiness of the upper barn, the lower portion seemed warm. In any event, it was more enjoyable than being confined in the house.

I again discarded my coat and picked up the baseball bat that I kept at the far end of the stables. It was a discarded Del Ennis model that I had taken from the trash barrel next to the ball field at Belltown after watching a summer evening game. The handle was cracked, but it was a treasure. Returning home on the evening I found the bat, I went to the garage, found three one-inch brads and drove them into the handle. The nails protruded a bit, so I used the hammer to bend and pound the ends flush into the wood. Taking a spool of electrical tape from Daddy's work bench, I wrapped a thick supply over the nails, careful that the grip was smooth and free of creases. The bat was 34 inches long and weighed 34 ounces when it was new. Over the years I preserved it with linseed oil which added to its weight. It was much too long and heavy for a nine-year-old to swing, but I had seen older men choke their bats, and on frigid Sunday afternoons, within the confines of the barn, that choked bat and my childhood imagination transported me to a big-league world.

Eventually the fascination of play gave way to fatigue and a hungry belly. Propping the bat back into its corner, I gathered my coat, thrust my hands into its large pockets, and headed for the house.

The earlier mid-day cold had been prelude to a heavy snowfall—one of those slow, silent storms that first deposits tiny granules which rattle through the needles of pine trees and rustle against leafless maples and oaks, and then, in soft, soundless cascades of white, empties itself into a panorama. Despite the cold, the beauty of the moment held even a nine-year-old. I stopped and stood motionless, surveying the landscape, sequestered in a breathless interlude, while an unseen presence hovered upon the landscape. I forgot the cold and became a solitary being. There is no stillness like that of forgotten time. For a moment I was suspended in communion with the unseen presence.

My chin was tucked into the folds of my collar and soon the moisture from my breath froze against the heavy mackinaw. It was a warning to get indoors.

An inch of snow already covered the buildings and roads. By the time Daddy, Keith, and I would begin the evening barn work, several more inches would fall. I kicked loose the snow on my pant legs and shoes and opened the kitchen door.

There is a sadness, perhaps a despair, in seeing your mother sit alone at the kitchen table on a winter Sunday afternoon, abandoned as it were, pensive, occupying some deep-felt loneliness by putting together the pieces of a jig-saw puzzle. A beige plastic radio sat on a shelf to the right of the kitchen door, its signal modulating as Charles Fuller, a radio evangelist, broadcast his thirty-minute *Old-Fashioned Revival Hour*. It was Mommy's favorite Sunday program. Sometimes she sang with the music of old-time hymns, but on this day, she did not look up. The program was solemn, its message urgent, emphasizing the nearness of Christ's second coming with the exhortative verses of the hymn *Jesus Saves*. Reverend Fuller was illustrating his message of Christ's relationship to believers with personal allusions to his marriage. His depictions were warm, ideal, soapy—magnifying the breaches in Mommy's relationship with Daddy and adding further gloom to an already leaden day.

A doorway at the far side of the room led to an unheated summer kitchen which, during winter days, served as a pantry, refrigerator, and cloak room. On the left wall, behind the cook stove, were pegs where we hung our heavy coats and caps. On the floor Mommy kept a large cardboard box for shoes. I hung up my coat and stocking cap and deposited my shoes.

A Hoosier cabinet rested against the right wall. On its sideboard sat leftovers from meals: slabs of cured ham, crispy pieces of fried chicken, a crusty roast of pork swimming in succulent gravy, smoked sausages and open pans of pon haus; dishes of creamed rice, grapenut pudding, po-

Behind my sister Beth is the Hoosier cabinet where Mommy stored leftovers during the winter months.

tato and macaroni salad, sweet and sour pickles; pies of all sorts: custards, cremes, and meringues, mince-meat and fruity pies of raisin, sour cherry, peach, apple, and berry; thick slices of cakes: angel food, black walnut, devil's food, whoopie pies; cookies: oatmeal, molasses, peanut butter, ginger snaps; homemade soups: rivel with plenteous chunks of dumplings congealed in dark broth, vegetable with chunks of beef immersed in heaps of beans, peas, carrots, tomatoes, and corn, chicken with rich homemade noodles swimming in hearty broth; the doughy goodness and fragrance of freshly baked loaves of bread, cinnamon and jelly rolls; apples, mellowed from the dug-out cellar in the orchard; a five-pound block of cheddar cheese in its waxed casing; walnuts waiting to be cracked open ... all for the taking ... an apple stuffed into a pants pocket, a fistful of cookies, a piece of cake crammed into the mouth ... eating between play and work ... on the run.

Grabbing two pieces of fried chicken, I returned to the kitchen, laid the food on a napkin and pulled a chair to the table beside Mommy.

"Are you cold?" she asked.

"I'm okay."

"It's gonna snow."

"Already started."

She looked up at the kitchen door window, now aware she had been transfixed in thought. "Oh my, it is," she affirmed. I had broken her concentration.

Returning to the puzzle, she studied some pieces set off to the side.

"Wanna help?"

"Nah."

"What'er'ya gonna do?"

"I think I'll read."

She did not respond, but I intuitively knew she wanted me to stay. I began studying the puzzle.

The puzzle pictured one of those wintry bucolic scenes common to greeting cards and jigsaw puzzles. The focal point was the back porch of a framed white farmhouse with two vacated rocking chairs sitting behind an ornate bannister. In the right foreground was a small pond, undisturbed, sheathings of ice showing near its edges. Its placid surface mirrored a red barn and horse corral set in the background. An abandoned rowboat with one paddle sat motionless in the near corner of the pond. There were no signs of movement, no wind, no ripples, no birds or animals, just a pastoral moment frozen in time.

Mommy had completed the border before I sat down, so I began gathering pieces that contained the blue water of the pond. When I had a dozen or so, I began piecing them together.

"Are we going to church tonight?"

Sunday night was my least favorite time at church. Ordinarily I would not have asked, because attending the Sunday evening service was a *fait accompli,* but the snowstorm posed possible intervention.

"I don't think so. Daddy said if it snowed, we'd stay home."

That was good. I didn't feel like hurrying through the barn work, then washing and putting on clean clothes in a freezing bedroom. Worse, the thought of sitting for an hour, pretending to listen to the preacher, and then kneeling for an additional thirty minutes on the hardwood floor during prayer time was insufferable.

"Do you like going to church?" I asked.

She looked up, momentarily off-balance.

"Why'd'ya ask? Don't you like it?"

"I like it when we have church picnics."

When the weather permitted, groups from the church regularly met evenings at Kishacoquillas Amusement Park, located near the church. It featured a large picnic area with charcoal grates where Sunday School classes could enjoy the adventure of an outdoor barbeque and the fellowship of a Bible study. After eating, children could walk around the grounds, ride in the rowboats, or pass the time with friends. The attraction for me, however, was a ball field, complete with bases and a backstop. Usually there were five or six other boys who brought baseball gloves, and we spent the remaining daylight in the never-ending excitement of hitting a ball and running around bases.

"I like when we go to the park." I continued.

"I thought you liked Mr. Peeples."

Henry Peeples was Keith's and my Sunday School teacher. He was a nice man who patronized us by inquiring about cows and gathering eggs and making hay. He had no interest in ball games. When our class went to Kishacoquillas Park for a youth picnic, he wore church clothes. It wasn't that he was formal, but it was an indication that we shared no common ground. Mommy never understood the reason we avoided him.

"Ya know," she interjected as though sharing a confidence, "there will be all kinds of people in Heaven. We're supposed to love everyone." Her chastisement was successful. I felt guilty for making her defend Mr. Peeples.

I had put together five or six pieces of the pond and now attached them to the border.

"Good," she cheered. The plaudit was a ploy to keep me as company. Psychology 101 properly applied was always effective.

I heard the radio broadcast in the background, listened as Dr. Fuller gave the altar call to accept Jesus "while there was yet time." Mommy sat immobile, her mind drawn to matters more serious than puzzles. Minutes passed as she listened intently. Intuitively I knew where she lingered.

"Do you think Jesus will come soon?" I asked.

She did not look up but paused to gather words that would not frighten a nine-year-old boy. The notion of the second coming terrified me. A trumpet sound, loud enough to be heard world-wide, graves opening, and the possibility of being left behind kept me awake nights. But death was an even greater dread, so that even during these early years I hoped that the second coming would take place before I died.

"We don't know for sure, but the Bible tells us of signs that will occur just before He returns, and it seems many of those things are happening. Daddy says it could happen any time, ... and Reverend Snyder and Billy Graham believe it will happen soon. Pointing toward the radio, she added, "Dr. Fuller, too. He agrees we're in the last days."

The wall clock above the refrigerator hummed in the lull of late afternoon. Keith emerged from behind the stove, unfolded a blanket that lay atop our kitchen rocking chair, laid it on the warm floor beside the stove and laid down to sleep.

The broadcast finished, Mommy arose from her chair, turned off the radio, went to the kitchen cupboard, took down a cup, and carried it to the stovetop where a kettle pot of coffee was kept warm. She filled the cup and set it by the puzzle.

"Would you get me the milk?"

Our milk was kept in a large covered sauce pan on the bottom shelf of the refrigerator. When more was needed, Keith or I was sent to the milk cooler in the milk house. We used the saucepan as a dipper, pushing it down into one of the ten-gallon cans of milk that was sitting in the icy waters of the cooler. We first had to stir the contents in a circular motion until the cream that had risen to the top was homogenized. Then filling the dipper, we wiped it with a cloth and carried it to the house. Mommy liked milk in her coffee.

While I poured a bit of milk into her cup, she went out to the summer porch and returned with two molasses cookies. In the course of my years on the farm, I saw Mommy, her mother and father, and numerous neighbors dunk molasses cookies into their drinks. Usually it was coffee, though during the war years, Mammie and a few others grew to enjoy Postum,[2] and on occasion when neither was available, they dunked their cookies into glasses of water. I was spared the habit, since I never cared for molasses cookies.

"Would you like a cookie?" she asked.

"You eat them," I deferred.

Reseated, her mind returned to the puzzle.

"Why don't you start working on the rowboat?"

I didn't answer but began searching for red pieces while she looked to complete the white house. My own mind, however, was fastened on the second coming.

Combinations of family Bible study, vacation Bible school, and Sunday School classes had convinced me that anyone who smoked cigarettes, cursed, told lies, drank beer, danced, went to movies, or gambled, was bound for eternal perdition. I realized that Hell might include a few people I actually knew—classmates, neighbors, uncles and aunts—bad people. It didn't seem unreasonable that bad people would go to Hell. I associated Heaven with good people and Hell with bad ones.

Regularly, during morning devotions, I had heard Mommy pray for her dad's salvation, but it had somehow seemed abstracted. Bad people went to Hell, not Pappy. Now, suddenly, on this cold February afternoon, the radio message and the puzzle merged. According to Dr. Fuller an inescapable judgment awaited everyone. The rocking chairs in the puzzle pic-

2. Postum is a powdered beverage made from roasted wheat bran, wheat, and molasses. Although the Post Cereal Company explicitly stated in its advertising that Postum did not taste like coffee and was not a coffee substitute, the drink enjoyed an enormous popularity in the US during WWII when coffee was rationed and people sought a replacement.

ture were empty. Where were the people who had lived on the farm? It was a beautiful farm and suggested that they had been good people. I thought of Pappy's rocking chair. I knew Pappy was old. I knew what happened to old people. I was suddenly struck with the realization that judgment awaited Pappy. I remembered that Mommy prayed for his salvation. Trepidation welled within me. Pappy had never accepted Jesus as his Savior.

"Mommy, what will happen to people who aren't saved?

On a weekday afternoon months earlier, Pappy had stopped at the farmhouse to borrow a shovel. He needed it to clean the small chicken house he had recently built at his new home. After locating a shovel in the wagon shed, he placed it into the trunk of the Ford sedan he drove, then came to the house for a drink of water and to visit with Mommy and us kids. Daddy had gone to Wagner's Garage in McClure for some machinery repairs.

It had become obvious to even a nine-year-old that Mommy was her father's favorite—a special bond evidenced by her constant concern for his health and his distress when she seemed fatigued by the demands of a large family. Privately, he also worried about the emotional bruises she sometimes suffered as a result of Daddy's petulance.

"Pop, you want something to eat? I made raisin pie."

With the slightest of deliberations, he seated himself at the kitchen table. Raisin pie was one of his favorites, and although he had recently been told to lose weight in the face of his sugar diabetes, his self-discipline wavered. Mommy cut a piece of the pie, placing it on a dinner plate, then set a knife and fork next to it. As he ate, she shared the most recent family news: five-year-old Billy had learned to open the front door by climbing a kitchen chair; she had driven to her sister Beatty's house yesterday to leave some old flannel shirts that could be used for braiding rugs; the baby chicks Daddy had ordered would be at the post office any day.

She did not sit with him but continued to prepare the apples, raisins, and orange peels that were ingredients for mincemeat pies. Allspice, cloves, cinnamon, sugar, and salt had been emptied into a bowl and waited to be mixed with the venison, cider, and peach juice that gave the pies their singular flavor. Though she watched as he ate the pie, she was preoccupied with his health, fearing the day she would lose him.

Two nights earlier, at the urging of his mother, Daddy had attended a revival service at the First Church of the Brethren in Lewistown where she was a member. When an invitation to accept Christ as Savior was given, Daddy responded by going forward and receiving counseling. Deeply moved by the experience, he insisted his family return with him to hear further teaching. Thus, the six of us piled into our 1938 Buick sedan the following evening and set out for the 7:00 pm service.

At the conclusion of the evening sermon, as Daddy had done the previous evening, Mommy responded to the evangelist's invitation to walk to the front of the assembly room and ask Christ into her life. Afterward, she met with a counselor who prayed with her and read some promises from Scripture. Later, as we traveled home, she was so happy that she cried. I had been seated beside her when the altar call was given and wanting neither to go to Hell nor be separated from my mother, I had gone forward with her.

In the days that followed, despite Mommy and Daddy's new-found joy, I remained unsure. I had expected an identifiable change—some inner sensation that would provide proof of my salvation. A deacon, Raymond Lawver, had sat with me, turning his Bible to Romans 10:9-10 and assuring me that I was now saved. In the days that followed I claimed that Scriptural promise, but I was not at peace.

Mommy and Daddy's conversions, however, proved to be life-changing. The excitement of their relationship with Christ produced new energies and concerns. In the weeks following, they shared the gospel with family, friends, and loved ones, but their first response was to announce the following morning that family devotions would be a regular part of our day. Thus, for the duration of my years on the farm, each weekday morning saw us gathering near the kitchen stove where we listened as Daddy read and commented on a chapter from Scripture.

Mommy eagerly read her Bible, asked questions of Daddy, took notes during Sunday School and church, and invited Pastor Snyder to dinner so that she might gain a deeper understanding. As well, she had a new concern for her children, her siblings, and her parents. Eternity now loomed large, and she took seriously both Christ's admonition to share the good news of the gospel and His warning that Hell awaited those who rejected God's love.

With the fervor of a new convert she looked now to speak with her father on this day when he came to borrow a shovel to clean his chicken house.

He sat eating his pie.

"Pop?" She was cautious, apprehensive, personal. "I'd like for you and Mom to go along to church tomorrow night."

Fearing an immediate and conclusive declination, she quickly added, "We have a guest speaker. I'd like you to hear him."

He didn't look up. Finishing the pie, he took the table knife, scraped the last morsels onto his fork, and lifted them to his mouth. As he chewed and swallowed, he sat forward slightly, holding the knife in his left hand, the fork in his right, thoughtful, ruminating.

"What time?"

"The service begins at seven. We'd leave at six."

Hope grew large.

"Do you wanna take a piece of pie for Mom?"

He nodded, but his mind was unsettled. He wished to please his daughter but had little interest in attending church.

Mommy had poured cider and peach juice into the large canning pot she had set atop the table. The venison had been ground and now she scraped the meat into the liquid, adding the spices, sugar, and salt, and began mixing the ingredients.

"I'll ask Mom."

She knew him too well to assume a definite answer at that moment. Privately, however, her heart leapt at even the possibility. She cut a wedge of the raisin pie, wrapped it in a sheet of waxed paper, slid it into a brown bag, and laid it atop the table.

Fearful that prodding might irritate his sense of autonomy, she said nothing more until he had gathered the coat he had removed before he sat down and moved toward the door. With a hint of anxiousness, she urged, "Could I know tonight? There was awkward silence. Then, quickly summoning discretion, she added, "So that I can tell Jim."

He placed the bag containing the slice of pie in his coat pocket and opened the door to leave. "If you want, take Denny with you. He can walk back after you discuss it with Mom."

Telephones would not arrive in our community for another half-dozen years. Waiting for a response from a neighbor required patience. Information would be shared the next time fence was mended, or quilts were sewn, or greetings were exchanged at the general store. On this afternoon, the fastest way to get Mammie's response was to send one of us boys with Pappy.

I rode in the front seat of his blue Ford. Neither of us spoke on the five minute ride, but I was accustomed to silence when riding in a car. Pappy and Mammie drove twenty-five miles to the sale barn in Belleville on Wednesdays with few words between them while I sat in the back seat, looking out the windows or reading. Besides, Daddy seldom talked as we rode to McClure or Lewistown, and even when Keith and I rode on the back of the truck bed to church or the feed mill, we did not talk.

Years before the construction of his house, Pappy had built a large shed that served as a kind of concession stand for the annual Samuel-Lawvers Church Picnic. By the time he and Mammie took residence the picnic was no longer observed, so Pappy converted the structure into a one-car garage. It stood adjacent to his new chicken coop about 150 feet from the house. Parking the car outside the garage, he removed the shovel from the car trunk, and carried it toward the chicken coop. Meanwhile, I bounded toward the warm house.

Pappy and Mammie had been living in the house for several months, but its rooms still held the smells of drying lumber, recently laid linoleum, and fresh paint. It was a simple retirement home; a cement block, two-bedroom, one-bathroom ranch with a small porch facing the dirt road that ran in front. Entrance at the rear was through a summer porch to which Mammie retreated on hot summer afternoons and evenings to braid carpets, crochet doilies, and mend clothes. Sometimes she served hot suppers on the porch to avoid the overheated kitchen, but most months it sat barren, a drying and cooling room for freshly-made noodles and pies, and an anteroom with a coat tree and cardboard box for shoes and galoshes. Forgotten in one of the corners was a shepherd's crook cane someone had given Pappy years earlier. A mop, broom, and dustpan were propped against the wall nearest the door that opened to the kitchen.

The kitchen was small, featuring a center table and chairs for four. A large laced homemade doily of flowered embroidery decorated the tabletop. To the left of the entrance sat a refrigerator, topped with an electric clock resting on a smaller white doily. Pappy's wooden rocking chair occupied the adjacent corner, one of Mammie's small, quilted blankets folded across one arm. A teacher's desk and chair that had braced more than fifty years at Krick's School faced against the left wall. The desk's center lid lifted and served as a repository for her King James Bible, the most recent copy of *The McClure Plain Dealer*, and during meals, the embroidered table doily. Beyond the desk, an archway opened to a short corridor that led to the bathroom on the left and the cellar door on the right. At the end of the hallway were located the two bedrooms.

A second archway at the left side of the rear kitchen wall led to the adjoining living room. Next to the archway sat the fourth table-chair used only when company was present for dinner. An electric stove and a row of cabinets continued along the right wall and sat on either side of the kitchen sink and faucets. A small broom closet was located just inside the summer porch door in the right corner.

My sudden appearance at the back door provoked no curiosity on Mammie's part. I routinely walked to her house when I had free time. She always stopped what she was doing and fussed over me. Putting aside her sewing, knitting, or braiding, she would ask how Mommy was doing, or whether Mommy needed help with canning or baking or cleaning. Frequently we played Chinese Checkers. She would retrieve from a bedroom closet the large, heavy, homemade board that had been in her possession since girlhood, along with a small velvet pouch that contained the six sets of colored marbles ordered from the *Montgomery Ward Catalog*. Placing it on the kitchen table atop the doily, she let me set the marbles in place while she poured herself a cup of coffee or Postum, then came and sat opposite me. She loved to play. The game was a moment's respite. In the beginning she pointed out advantageous moves, sometimes letting me win, but later, if I beat her, or if I failed to pay attention and just went through the motions of being interested, she beat me soundly.

I took a peanut butter cookie from the jar she kept atop her kitchen counter, all the while keeping my eyes on her wall clock, reminded that I must not stay too long because Daddy would soon return from Wagner's Garage to begin the barn work. Finally, Pappy opened the summer porch door, removed his shoes, and came into the kitchen. The afternoon was waning. He slumped into his favorite rocker, beginning the slow cadence of a man in thought.

"Mom?" he hesitantly asked. "Hazel wants to know if we will go to church with her tomorrow night."

Mammie did not immediately answer. Privately though, she was delighted to be invited. Her decision, however, would defer to Pappy's disposition and comfort. He was now sixty-three, habitually in bed by 8:30 pm, and not inclined to venture far from home. On the other hand, she seldom had opportunity to travel to Lewistown, and since moving into her own house, almost never saw Daddy's mother whom she always admired.

"Do you wanna go?" she asked.

He did not answer but pursed his lips as though any decision involved pain. The chair rocked methodically back and forth prolonging the moment. Finally, as though released from the grip of a paralysis, the rocking halted.

"Hazel wants us to go."

And that was it. ... The father pleasing the daughter despite his apparent preference to stay home.

Mammie turned to where I was seated at the table. "Tell Mommy we'll go."

Pappy offered to drive me back with the news, but he had taken off his shoes and coat, and I wanted to walk anyway.

It was true. I enjoyed running the half mile to the farm. I imagined I was racing someone, running bases, or catching long touchdown passes. I put on my coat and headed for the door. When my feet hit the dirt road in front of Pappy's house, I began running both to keep warm and to win imaginary ball games. Mommy was sliding the final mince-meat pies into the oven when I burst into the kitchen. Pungent aromas of warm clove, orange peel, and cinnamon permeated the room.

"Mammie said they'll go."

The evangelist's text was from Luke 16—the rich man and Lazarus. It is the story of two men who lived long ago. One, the rich man, lived hedonistically, unmindful of both God and fellowman. The other was indigent, distressed, miserable. Both died. Lazarus went to Heaven while the rich man was consigned to Hell.

The Reverend Jimmy Johnson stood in front of the assembly, on a raised platform, behind a lectern, and began his message. Part preacher, part thespian, he gave a complete performance, milking every line of Scripture, dramatizing the rich man's rejection of a righteous life, sensationalizing the anguish of the flames. Fire and brimstone were in full display. Mommy sat on the left side of her father, her mother to Pappy's right, three rows from the front of the church. I sat on my mother's left, the aisle seat. Reverend Johnson read from the King James version of the Bible,

"And (the rich man) cried and said, 'Father Abraham, have mercy on me, and send Lazarus, that he may dip the tip of his finger in water, and cool my tongue; for I am tormented in this flame."

He laid his Bible on the pulpit, stepped around the lectern, and came to the front edge of the platform. The moment was protracted. Suspense heightened.

"The tip," he began, "The tip! ... the tip of one finger! ... How excruciating the torment must have been for the rich man. The Scripture says, 'He cried out!' ... Cried out! ... That means he screamed. Screamed for relief!"

The urgency and momentum of his message grew with alarm.

"There are two points the Scriptures make. Two, ... that I do not want you to miss. First, the rich man asks for help! Send Lazarus with cool water."

"This will be the plea of each one of you who rejects Christ in this life. But note what the Scriptures tell us." Again he paused ... "There will be no relief ... Father Abraham reports, 'It is too late! Lazarus cannot come to you, nor can you go to him.'" Raising his voice to the heavens, Reverend Johnson shouted, "IT WILL BE TOO LATE!!!"

The preacher returned to the lectern. Now he modulated his voice. A hush had fallen across the room. With quiet concern, he implored his listeners, "Each of you must make a decision as to where you will spend eternity ... with Lazarus in the bosom of Abraham ... with our Lord Jesus Christ ... or...," he choked, nearly in tears, ... "with the rich man... begging for relief from eternal torment. It is up to you: ... Heaven ... or Hell!"

The message had lasted barely twenty minutes. Exhausted, Reverend Johnson took his seat at the rear of the platform. A second member of the evangelistic team responsible for the music approached. Turning first to the organist and then to the congregation, he asked everyone to turn in the hymnal to "Jesus Saves," adding that anyone wishing to make a public profession of faith should come, during the singing, to the front of the church to meet with a counselor.

Standing in the pews, the soft strains of the hymn echoing through the dimly lit auditorium, tears ran down faces. Thoughts of spending a hopeless eternity, alienated from loved ones in some dark lake of non-consuming fire moved some to step into the aisle and fall to their knees before the altar. Others, fearing for loved ones, prayed.

The hymn ended. Reverend Johnson stood a second time asking that the altar call be extended a bit longer. He began another hymn:

> *"Just as I am, without one plea*
> *But that Thy blood was shed for me*
> *And that Thou bid'st me come to Thee*
> *O Lamb of God, I come! I come."*

Mommy, hopeful, beseeching, choked with emotion, turned to her father.

"Pop?"

Eternity hung in the balance. She was a child saying goodbye for a final time, a little girl about to be abandoned by her most loyal and beloved friend. She placed her hand on his lower arm, "Do you want to be saved?"

There is a time when argument is so certain, so convincing, so sure, that doubt cannot be entertained. Rejection at that point moves beyond reason and becomes personal.

Without looking at his daughter he submitted, "I'm good the way I am." Guarded, firm, final.

"Are you sure?" She was sinking below the brim.

He made no further response. All was defeated, lost, ended.

Mommy looked up from her puzzle. She had just begun to assemble the white pieces that constituted the farmhouse. Looking beyond me, she stared far into the distance. My question had reawakened the anxiety surrounding her father.

"Mommy, what will happen to people who aren't saved?"

Heretofore, her misgivings had remained private, unspoken. Now, on this cheerless Sunday afternoon, I was asking her to state formally the terrible conviction of her innermost being. As though she was passing final sentence upon the fiber of her own life, tears gathered. With tremulous voice, measured, pitiful, she submitted, "They will go to hell."

RUBBER BALLS

By Chivalries as tiny,
A Blossom, or a Book,
The seeds of smiles are planted—
Which blossom in the dark.

EMILY DICKINSON

I owe something of special gratitude to Daddy. ... something never spoken, never acknowledged, but appreciated as "smiles that blossom in the dark."

At regular intervals, the sponge rubber balls that I incessantly threw against the barn doors as a young boy, the balls that provided so much pleasure for me, tore and fell to pieces. A new ball at Joe McKinley's General Store cost 25 cents. I was apprehensive about asking Daddy either for money or a new ball. Instead, I always approached Mommy.

Although entreaty was never treacherous with her, manners demanded a rather obsequious approach, "Do you think I can have a quarter for a new ball?"

Mommy deferred. "Look in Daddy's wallet," she would say.

Daddy kept his wallet on the bottom shelf of the right side of the white kitchen cabinet, just above the kitchen sink. It was a plain black leather wallet with a billfold and a small buttoned change purse. I would carry a kitchen chair to the sink, stand on the seat, reach into the cabinet and take out the wallet. There were never dollars in the billfold, and many times the change purse was empty. However, when it contained 25 cents in coins, Mommy usually permitted me to take the money and walk to the store to buy my prize.

I'm certain that she informed him afterward of my request, but not once did I hear my father complain either about the money or the time I spent playing with those rubber balls.

THE APOLOGY

F riday, the 30th of August 1957 was hot, sweltering, one of those summer days when the sun seems fixed overhead, and heat rises from baked earth and tin roofs in enervating waves. Newly washed laundry hung from the clothesline in the yard, the whites strung farthest away from the dirt road that ran in front of the house so as to escape the billows of dust that rose as Park Weader, the mailman, passed at twelve o'clock in his worn blue Chevy. Cows lay in the meadow in the shade of maples and oaks methodically chewing their cuds and switching their tails to drive away pervasive flies. The family dog, a black and white shepherd, lay phlegmatic in the shade of the corn crib, his breath rapid and labored in the heat. Fields and buildings awaited relief from the long summer.

I was fourteen, about to turn fifteen in September. My brother Keith was a year younger. In a few days we would enter Chief Logan High School as tenth graders, leaving Daddy with the interminable demands of the farm. [1]

The summer had seen barley, wheat, and oats harvested. The grain had been dumped into the granaries which rested beneath and alongside two huge hay mows on the upper floor of the barn while the straw had been baled and stored in the straw mow, a recessed area adjacent to the granaries. The hay mows themselves were only half-filled. The June cutting of alfalfa and clover had been raked, baled, and stored in the mows, but there had not been the usual late summer cutting. The heat and drought had taken its toll. Instead, farmers anticipated the financial strain of purchasing additional hay from out-of-state suppliers. The drought depleted men in the same way it diminished crops. Now, the summer's closing yield, unending rows of stunted corn that had matured through the heat of July and

---

1. The new Chief Logan Joint High School at Highland Park, just outside the borough of Lewistown, was not completed until 1959. In the interim, grades 10-12 met in the old Yeagertown School which had formerly been part of the Burnham High School District.

August, stood ready to be cut and brought to the silos.[2]

Daddy had spent the early morning in the field in front of the house with a corn chopper, opening the first rows of mature corn so that the binder could pass through and begin its operation. Opening a cornfield in this way prevented damage that would otherwise result when machinery first entered the field and trampled the stalks. Once there was room for the binder, Daddy would cut several acres at a time, dropping sheaves throughout the field where Keith, Billy, and I followed with wagon and tractor. Either Keith or I picked up the sheaves and threw them onto the wagon while the other built the load by placing them in an inter-locking pattern so that lurches and abrupt stops could not dis-lodge them. If sheaves lost their purchase and tumbled from the wagon, work was slowed, time was lost, and loose grain was wasted on the ground. Billy, who was ten, drove the tractor. The work, more tedious than difficult, occupied our morning. Corn was the final gold of summer, requiring many

Corn shocks at the eastern end of the farm. Endless hours were spent planting, cultivating, and harvesting corn.

hands to harvest. Daddy was anxious to finish the crop while his boys were available.

By the time we sat down to a breakfast of ham, fried noodles, eggs, cereal, toast, and hot cocoa, the early barn work had been completed: cows were fed and milked, pigs had received their ration of corn, and chicken feeders had been filled with mash. The milkman, too, had come and gone, carefully lifting the four ten-gallon cans, each labeled B-16, onto the flat-

2. The corn that would be used as grain involved a more difficult process and was not har-vested until late October. By that time the ears dried so that the husks could more easily be removed, and the grain would not mildew in the granaries. In the same way that corn for the silos was cut, tied into sheaves, and thrown onto the ground by the binder, so corn for grain was harvested. However, while silage corn did not need to be shocked for drying, grain corn had to be both shocked and the ears husked. Shocking required that three or four men follow the binder, picking up the sheaves and setting them upright in shocks. It was important that some moisture remained in the stalks so that the ears didn't break off and fall to the ground. The corn would not be husked until later when the stalks were completely dried. Finally, after the husking was completed, the stalks were picked up, brought to the barn, and used for bedding the animals.

bed of his truck. The day was fraught with work.

Daddy returned thanks for the morning meal, picked up his fork and was about to eat.

"Hazel," he brusquely complained, "there's pepper on these noodles. Irritated, he pushed the noodles that she had set before him to the side of his plate, apparently convinced that the Creator he had just petitioned was equally disgusted. Mommy had not yet sat to eat but remained at the stove stirring a mixture of cocoa, sugar, salt and milk into a dipper (saucepan) that would be heated to make hot chocolate. She left the chocolate, came and scraped the peppered noodles onto an empty dish, returned to the stove where she forked a fresh portion onto Daddy's plate, then set it in front of him. He resumed eating.

Between mouthfuls, he announced that on Labor Day, three days hence, we would take a holiday and go to the stock car races at Port Royal, a hamlet one hour distant, if, and only if, we had by that time hooked up the silo filler and opened the corn field. That would allow Daddy sufficient time, while we boys were at school, to begin shredding the corn for the silage that was the winter staple for our herd of cows. Effusive reactions to news were foreign to our family. Thus, the declaration of a day at the races was greeted with silence. Daddy's pronouncements were not open for question or comment. Domestic government was not democratic.

Nonetheless, I welcomed the trip. It provided a break from accustomed labor, even though our enthusiasm was often tempered by his quixotic moods. I assumed Keith felt similarly, but I was uncertain. We never talked about our parents; in fact, we seldom talked to each other. "As soon as devotions are over," Daddy directed, "get the corn choppers from the wagon shed and finish opening the field, then hitch the wagon to the tractor. I'll help when I've finished fixing the meadow gate."

The meadow gate consisted of three strands of barbed wire attached to a fence post. The old post had broken, so while Keith and I began our work, Daddy took the strands one at a time, stretched each taut and then stapled it to the new post. The work required steady hands. Should the wooden fence stretcher slip, the barbed wire would be jerked through the hands tearing the flesh. It was a man's job.

In spite of the heat, the day was not unpleasant. As we swung the choppers, cutting off the stalks, Daddy joined us, filling the time by recalling days when he hunted rabbits in the same cornfield. Memory, colored by nostalgia, ofttimes paints past events with a golden brush that, in reality, were mundane. On this morning the good times Daddy recalled were swelled with hyperbole. He talked of the days he had hunted with his brothers. The number of rabbits they bagged and the expert marksmanship he described did not cohere with our experience, but we willingly accepted the fanciful because we benefited from his good humor. And, of course, he talked of the Labor Day races at the Port Royal Fair. It was tacit confirmation that we would be going to the fair primarily because he wanted to go.

The morning passed quietly. We finished our work and were leaving the field when we saw Mommy, standing in front of the clothesline in the front yard, waving the white dish towel that signaled dinner was ready. It was twelve o'clock.

She cooked three meals daily, not as a chore laden with fatigue and ennui, but with the duty and pride that complements a good housewife and mother. She knew we would be hungry and knew her signal was more than a reminder, it was an invitation both for us to rejoin her world and for her to be included in ours. We belonged to her just as surely as her dish towel called us home.

We ate the vegetable soup, rich with the meat and broth from the shanks of a beef. Newly churned butter was spread generously onto freshly baked bread. There were fruity pies and layered cakes for dessert. Meals presupposed hungry bellies.

Daddy reminded again that we would be setting up the silo filler. As I finished dinner, he instructed that I should fill the grease gun and begin greasing the filler's cogs and wheels. He and Keith would remove from the wagon shed the ten-foot sections of pipe that had to be bolted into a forty-foot length, then lifted by rope and tackle so that the entire unit could be attached to the filler and reach upward to the opening atop the silo.

The power needed to turn the great blades that chopped the green corn stalks and forced them up the pipe stem into the silo came from two pulleys: one on the tractor that drove the second, attached at the rear of the filler. The belt-driven system was difficult to align, and once in place, the tractor remained fixed for the days it took to fill the silo. The paddle-shaped blades served a dual purpose. Their rapid spinning chopped the stalks into fine pieces and also created a wind tunnel that forced the chopped silage fifty or sixty feet upward and blew it into the opening at the silo top.

It was two o'clock by the time I finished greasing the machinery. Daddy and Keith had begun to bolt the pieces of pipe together.

Aligning the bolt holes of each heavy piece required patience and

strength. Keith and I watched
as Daddy stood atop the filler,
an adjustable wrench in hand,
maneuvering and bolting. His
awkward stance atop the filler,
the strain of holding the heavy
sections in place, and the deft
and delicate touch needed to
couple the pipe set Daddy's
equilibrium on a precarious
edge. Twice he lost his grip on
the wrench, watching it clatter
against the machine as it fell to

Belt alignment between tractor and silo filler had to be precise.

the ground. With each failure, his frustration mounted. As I crawled a second time beneath the machine to retrieve the tool, it came to his attention that Keith and I were standing idly below waiting for him to finish the pipe. Provoked that time was wasting, he fulminated, "You and Keith can start the tractor and line up the belt."

We immediately turned to the task. I brought the belt from the garage while Keith climbed aboard the tractor and drove it into position five or six yards from the filler. The belt was a 30-foot loop of flexible leather used to link the rotating pulley on the tractor to the rotating shaft on the filler. For it to remain in position and turn the pulley on the filler, the two rotating shafts had to be parallel. This meant the tractor pulley had to be in an exact position. It was not an easy exercise and often frustrated experienced men. If it was not centered, the belt would spin off the rotating shafts, sometimes at high speeds and posit danger. To further exacerbate the annoyance, each time the belt spun off, the tractor had to be repositioned. In so doing, the wasted time pressed upon Daddy's reserves.

I unrolled the belt and lifted it onto the pulleys while Keith backed the tractor into position until the belt was sufficiently taut to prevent slipping. I indicated all was ready, and Keith gradually employed the tractor clutch. The weighty belt began to turn, slowly at first, then accelerating. As it neared full engagement, however, it jumped from the pulley and spun to a stop on the ground in front of the tractor. No one spoke, but at once we set about to repeat the operation. Daddy, continuing to wrestle with the pipe, hollered, "Put some dressing on the belt." The dressing was a sticky substance that helped the belt adhere to the pulley surface. Keith waited while I ran back to the garage and brought the "stickum." I applied it as best as I could and then stood back while Keith again engaged the clutch. The belt immediately spun off.

As tension mounted, we re-positioned the apparatus for a third time. By this time Daddy had stepped down from the filler and came and stood beside the belt. He was livid as he took the stickum in his right hand, ready to apply a second treatment if the belt remained on track. He found a stick

of wood in the nearby pig lot, came and held it with his left hand against the belt, hoping the resistance might keep it in place. He motioned Keith to let out the clutch. For a third time, the belt began to turn, and for a third time, it spiraled off the pulley.

This was the straw that broke the camel's back. Daddy's temper turned vitriolic. He heaved the stickum far down toward the creek that ran below the pig yard and jumped up onto the tractor. Keith, reacting to the tantrum, moved aside and sat on the tractor tool box, mounted above the left rear tractor wheel.

Keith sitting atop the tractor tool box

As Daddy hoisted himself, Keith rose to jump down from the tractor. Off balance, he was not prepared for the shove of Daddy's hand. Jumping and falling simultaneously, Keith fell to the ground and slid down the 15-foot embankment below the silo.

There was stunned silence as we waited for Keith to pick himself up. Guilt-ridden, Daddy struck the steering wheel violently with his left hand and jammed on the brakes. In a fit of temper he kicked the OFF switch and jumped from the tractor. He was about to walk away toward the garage when I was overcome with the indignation of what he had done. Impulsively I muttered, "I think you should apologize."

I had never confronted my father or even dared to openly disagree with him. Dogmatism and temper were a frightening combination. Confounded by the audacity of my remark, he was at first dumbfounded, glowering in disbelief. Then, incensed by what he considered my obstinacy, he strode toward me. The fury of the moment was paralyzing. He placed his hands on my shoulders and shoved me backward away from the tractor and toward the house. "Take your things and get outta here!" he shouted. "You're not in charge of this farm!"

Screen door entrance to the kitchen

I retreated farther toward the house. "I mean it," he yelled, "Pack your clothes and get out!" He immediately turned on Keith who had climbed back up the slope and was standing near the tractor. "You go with him," he yelled, "I get more done without you guys. Just pack up and get out!"

I didn't see Keith's reaction. I hurried toward the house, lost and convoluted, in an abyss of uncertainty. The screen door that gave entrance to our kitchen had a half-inch hole in the netting near the knob, and as I reached to open it, I strangely remembered the times Mommy reminded us to keep the door closed. It passed through my mind that this might be my last entrance. His cruelty devastated my psyche. The farm was my home, as much as his. The fields, the buildings, the animals were as much mine. The hours plowing, seeding, cultivating. The walks through meadow and woods. All of it had been down payment and investment, so that, in the same way it had taken possession of him, it had become mine. The work, the endless work. The sweat, the tears, the fantasies, the disappointments, had bound me to the farm as one is bound to a steady place, a rock secure and unyielding. Gone. Gone. Crippled, I opened the screen door and began crying. Not sobbing, not wailing — private, hidden, a deep wound without blood flowing.

It is difficult to objectify a moment so terribly emotional. Where the spirit is torn, the anguish is visceral. And though time endows the soul with a philosophic and forgiving mind, a cautious posture is adopted lest the resulting scars are again opened by even a wayward blow. Restoration is slow and incremental. Repeated violation may preclude further vulnerability and prevent the soul-to-soul embrace desired by fathers and sons.

Mommy had heard the tirade. She was in the winter kitchen making noodles, her apron white with flour. She had heard, had watched Keith and me coming from the pig lot, saw us entering the yard. She didn't ask what had happened. She, too many times, had felt the laceration of his temper. She knew the sting of his verbal abuse. She did not speak as tears welled in her eyes. I choked, "What should we do," whispering, as though he might overhear.

Foremost in my mind was the possibility he would come to the house. I was scared. Though he had never struck me, though his lack of self-restraint seldom resulted in physical assault, I had seen his terrible temper, his violent tantrums: driving a pitchfork into the flesh of an unsuspecting animal, breaking the hind leg of a cow with a baseball bat, swerving sharply around the corner of our driveway so that our blue pickup truck rolled over onto its side smashing the animal rack above the truck bed. He regularly threw tools in frustration, damaged farm machinery, made hurtful accusations. As incidents multiplied over my early years, I grew afraid of his outbursts, avoiding moments and situations that might have flowered into a closer, warmer relationship.

On a cold January day in 1952 Daddy took Keith and me along to Harrisburg to see the Pennsylvania State Farm Show. We stayed the entire day, viewing the latest farm machinery, admiring prized animals, watching demonstrations of new farming techniques, and sampling food from vendors. The entire show was held inside several sprawling buildings, sufficiently spacious to house thousands of patrons as well as multitudes of livestock and exhibits. About two o'clock, fatigued from hours of standing and walking, we wandered into the large arena where the State Police Show was about to begin. Daddy measured the need to arrive home in time for the evening milking against our desire to watch the proceedings. He announced that we could stay a bit longer. While we lingered, the day-long rain that had soaked the grounds outside turned to sleet. When we exited at four thirty, the first flakes of a heavy snow already blanketed the ground. The parking lots were unpaved fields, and beneath the layers of snow and ice was a soft layer of mud. Dozens of cars were stuck in the mixture. Drivers worked feverishly as wheels spun, first backward and then forward, trying to break free of the morass. Strangers joined to free tires from grooves and ruts worn deep into the soil. At the edge of the field, a tow truck dragged a muddy blue Ford coupe *toward the highway. Already late for the evening barn work, Daddy started the motor of our 1938 Buick sedan, slowly let the clutch engage and pressed the accelerator. The rear wheels spun, but the car did not move. We, too, were stuck. All about us, frustrated drivers spun wheels. Daddy let the motor idle, opened the driver-side door, stepped out and studied the situation. It was about fifty yards to the paved road. As he considered possibilities, we saw the tow truck back up to another car, watched a man in muddy overalls attach a chain to the front bumper of a disabled car and begin towing it out onto the pavement. The driver of the truck then climbed out, removed the chain, and walked to the open window of the towed car, held out his hand and was paid cash.*

As we waited, the truck driver reconnoitered the field. Fat and muddy, with unshaven face, he waddled to the next stalled car, looking to take advantage of the moment. Wearing a heavy leather jacket and stocking hat, his raspy voice asked the driver, "Need some help?"

Daddy climbed back into our car. The motor was still running with Keith and I huddled in the warmth of the sedan. I knew Daddy could not afford to have our car towed, and I knew he would not ask for help. He sat for a few minutes in poignant stillness, then impulsively rolled down his driver-side window and threw open the door. Leaning back into the car he directed me to slide into the driver's seat.

"Push the clutch all the way to the floor and put it in first gear," he began, "And when I holler, let it out real slow."

I had experience driving our pick-up truck about the farm. I was eight or ten years old when, for the first time, he had told me to get behind the wheel. I knew how to depress the clutch, put the vehicle into first gear, and slowly release the pedal. That first time I had steered just a few feet until Daddy called, "Whoa." I had watched as he stood on the truck bed, selected one of the locust fence posts lying beside him, set it into place, then picked up the thirty-two-pound sledgehammer and pounded the post into the earth. He seemed to have greater endurance and strength than neighboring farmers. I admired him as beads of sweat streaked his face. He did not complain of tired muscles or long days, even though the work was arduous and constant. I had, however, also witnessed his fierce outbursts and knew that I must pay close attention to my driving. Setting a hundred fence posts in place was monotonous, but Daddy did not tolerate a lapse of attention. Starting or stopping too quickly would have caused him to lose his balance and have thrown him from the bed. The consequences of not paying close attention taught young boys to do as they were told.

On this wintry January day, his irrepressible will defied reason. He strode recklessly to the back of our car. "Let her out," he called. I slowly released the clutch. I felt the rear of the car rise and we began to crawl forward, a few inches, a few feet. In a rage and with a rush of adrenalin his meaty calloused hands had grabbed the car bumper and lifted. As I steered toward the paved road, the driver-side door opened. Still raging, he pushed me toward the middle of the front seat and climbed in, quickly taking the controls. Slowly we made our way, the wheels cutting two-inch tracks in the mud and snow, ever moving toward the paved road lest we lose momentum and sink back into the mire. As we pulled up onto the main road, I saw blood on both his palms where the icy metal of the rear bumper had cut into the flesh. He did not look at the cuts but maneuvered through the traffic until we turned onto the highway that would take us home.

Neither Keith nor I spoke. Blood greased the steering wheel and smears soaked into the cuffs of his jacket. With his left hand, he reached into his rear pocket and brought out a red bandanna. Glancing at the wounds he saw his right hand had the more severe cut. Wrapping the cloth around it, he kept the left fist clenched to staunch further bleeding. We had long ago learned that he would not acknowledge pain. We also knew that he would disregard any of our comments or questions as impertinent and irritating.

For the next hour we sat in strained silence as Daddy concentrated on driving through the storm. The wiper blades of the windshield compacted the heavy flakes into slush that slowly melted to water and ran along the sides of the windshield in varied patterns. After twenty minutes I let my head fall back against the seat and pretended to sleep.

Beneath the punctuations of Daddy's life, below the temper, the inferiority, the defeats, the failures, coursed regrets. His dreams ran beyond the fields of Mifflin County. His passions called him to vague enchantment. He yearned to give expression to those passions, but circumstance bound him close to the ground, and in the darkness of frustration he failed to recognize the heaven about him. The reciprocity of love that he sought was precluded by self-absorption.

As we neared home, the thought of barn work transported us to more immediate concerns. Daddy's moody silence had held us in abeyance for more than an hour. Now, without warning, he became penitent. Recognizing that his outburst had stolen all joy from our day, he broke the silence. "Listen," he reached out, "We'll get right to the barn work as soon as we're home. You guys feed the cows and bed the stalls, and you can go to the house. I'll do the rest." His beneficence, genuine and well-intentioned, was not a reprieve, but a command. I wondered how he would manage to operate milking machines with hands raw and bloody, but I did not volunteer to do the milking. His remorse had opened a door. Momentarily, he was approachable. It should have been an opportunity to draw close, to accept his attempt at apology. Instead, his gesture created discomfort. History had formed a callous. I had become guarded. Walls constructed for protection were difficult to penetrate. I did not respond.

It was seven thirty by the time work at the barn was finished. Mommy dished hot soup into bowls while we sat about the table waiting for Daddy. Meals never began until Daddy was seated and had asked a blessing. As he sat, I noticed he had washed the wound and Mommy had dressed it with a clean bandage. The "Amen" spoken, I did not look up but broke saltine crackers into my soup and began ladling the chicken and noodles to my mouth. The clatter of spoons against glass bowls gave life to the silence.

Mommy had not yet sat down. Serving herself last, she carried a hot bowl of soup to her place and joined us.

"Jim," she prodded, "how was the Farm Show?"

"There are no crackers on the table," he grumbled.

I froze. I had used the last of the crackers Mommy had set atop the table. She immediately arose, went to the kitchen cabinet and brought a second sleeve of Saltines. Daddy opened the package, reached in and withdrew a half-dozen crackers. Placing them in his right palm, he used his left hand to grind them into bits and poured the contents into his soup. In relief, I stared at my bowl and breathed.

The hour passed — slow and uneven.

"Aw," he returned to the earlier frustration, "that car. A little bit of snow on the ground, and there's no tread on them tires, and we were stuck. I didn't know if we were gonna get home. You can't depend on nothin'."

"The boys said they liked the police show," she redirected the focus.

"Yeah, he rejoined, "if we hadn't a' stayed for that, we wouldn't a been stuck. It lasted an hour and a half."

Despite his mood, plainly, he enjoyed his food. He ate with relish, commenting, "That's good soup."

When he had finished and put down his spoon, Mommy picked up the empty bowl, went to the stove, refilled it, returned and placed it in front of him.

The moment lagged as we continued to eat. I finished my soup, carried the empty container to the pot above the stove and ladled a second portion for myself. As if a friend had joined us, Daddy remarked, "Hazel, you should have seen that police show. It was really somethin'." He crumbled more crackers into his soup.

"Some a' those stunts were really good. Eight brand new police cars ran a figure eight, cuttin' in and out, right in front of each other. They just missed smashin' up. It was the darnedest thing."

"Tell about the clowns," Keith implored.

"Weren't they somethin'." He grinned. "How about the one in the barrel?"

As part of the show, a stunt man dressed as a clown had leaped into a barrel in order to avoid a passing car. The barrel had fallen over, and a second car then veered sharply, tilting on its side until it had cleared the barrel. The spectators gasped audibly at what had appeared to be a near accident.

The animus passed. As quickly as his temper had erupted, he was now placated, but his equilibrium teetered on the precipice of a cliff. He spoke glibly of the Farm Show, the food, the animals, the people. I thought of the times, after long hours and days of demanding labor, feeling a need for relief, when he announced magnanimously that the following day's work would be set aside so we could go fishing. A day of fishing with Daddy was, however, a day of foreboding, fearing the sharp tongue, the irrational tantrum. I did not want to go fishing, but he solicited no input from wife or children. If we were to participate in the respite, we had to remain within his bounds. He wanted to fish. Failure to effervesce resulted in reproach and tirade. We would go fishing whether or not we found it enjoyable. The cruel edge to his magnanimity was that we were restricted to his world. Thus, we grew accustomed to his delights, his interests, his concerns.

G o down to Mammie's and stay there until I talk to him," Mommy instructed. I did not hesitate. As if escaping the menace of an approaching storm, I exited through the summer porch door and began the trek to my grandmother's house. The flight, however, afforded little relief. As I made my way past the knoll of the meadow, out of sight of house and barn, obscured by tall corn, I knew the affair was not ended.

Seven years earlier my grandparents
had built a retirement home at the far eastern end of the farm. A simple two-bedroom home, nestled in a grove of maples
and oaks, it had been a comfortable retreat
until my grandfather's death the previous winter. Since, Mammie lived alone.
Her days continued much as when Pappy
was alive, listening to the Philco radio as
she cleaned, sewed, quilted, cooked, and
looked forward to visits from family. She
especially anticipated the two evenings
each week when Daddy, Mommy, and all
seven of us kids arrived to watch her TV,
a gift from her only son, Bud. It sat in her
living room where the fascination of west-

Pappy and Mammie's retirement home was
built on the eastern boundary of the farm.

erns and situation comedies drew us. Her house was as familiar as our own.
We seldom drove past without stopping for cookies or cakes or to just loiter. She was family. Her nights, however, were lonely and long if one of us
grandchildren, after finishing work and eating supper, did not walk down
the dark dirt road and stay overnight with her.

Long before I set foot on the gravel driveway, I saw her in the front
yard watering the flowers that grew in beds she had planted next to the
house. She wore a faded blue apron over a blue dress and a flowered bonnet
that shielded her head from the hot sun. In her right hand was a digging
trowel for weeding and loosening dirt. As I approached, she straightened,
placed the heels of both hands against her sides so as not to soil the apron,
and remarked, "It's hot. Let's go in the house." She gathered from my non-
response that something was amiss.

We walked around to the back, but before I entered the sun porch, I
removed my shoes and turned down my pants cuffs, emptying the dirt and
soil that had collected during the morning work. It was a custom of those
who farmed. Farm wives understood that laboring in the fields meant that
dirt and chaff could not be avoided, but it did not provide license to dirty
a clean house. Inside, she propped open the windows, though no breeze
stirred. Removing her apron, she folded it neatly and laid it on a small table
stand near the door. Placing the trowel atop the apron, she came and sat
down in the rocking chair that had been my grandfather's. A hand fan lay

on the window sill next to the rocking chair. She picked it up and began fanning her face in slow, tedious cadence.

The sun porch was an add-on room large enough for the rocker, table stand, dinner table, and two chairs that were its only contents. A broom stood in a far corner and a fly swatter hung from a nail above the table stand. I seated myself at the table. "Daddy's mad. Mommy said I should stay here until she talks with him."

She knew that I had been crying. She did not answer or ask what had happened but arched forward as elderly people do when rising to their feet, straightened and went into the kitchen. I listened as she opened the refrigerator door and poked inside the ice cabinet until a waxed paper sack of cookies appeared. Closing the door she returned to the porch, brought the three molasses cookies to the table where I was seated, and laid them before me. She resumed her seat in the rocker.

I began nibbling at the cookies, but I didn't feel like eating. Besides, molasses cookies were among my least favorites. Since my earliest years I had observed the relish with which my grandparents had dipped molasses cookies into cups of coffee or Postum and eaten them delectably. My grandfather, on occasion when coffee was not readily available, immersed them into a glass of water before he took the soggy contents to his mouth.

"Wanna watch TV?" Mammie asked. I knew she suggested watching television to divert me from the moment. She was as familiar with Daddy's temperament as I. The years spent on the farm, living in the same house with him, had plainly demonstrated his temper and irascibility. I turned on the TV, but the recurring images and emotions of the afternoon's events held me.

Although Mammie was neither worldly nor sophisticated, her simplicity was genuine, guileless. She had no art for words, no time for currying favor, but her love and concern were constant as was evidenced on a cold January day the following winter.

A snowstorm was imminent. During the day temperatures had fallen and a gray calmness had settled over the land as though nature was listening to distant, sad music, foreboding and ominous. At twilight, while Daddy, Keith and I were occupied with the evening barn work, the snowfall began. For an hour large, light flakes fell in the silent fields, pinging against farm windows and rattling through bare tree limbs. Then, in ever increasing fury, the vast skies darkened, the winds gathered force and the great blizzard came. Granules of snow, hard and crusted, blew in furious sheets, portending the immense snowfall that would be deposited.

During supper Mommy whispered to me, "Mammie needs someone to stay with her till the storm is over." I had just come from the barn and had no desire to bundle up a second time, leave the warmth of the kitchen stove, and spend both the night and possibly the next day at Mammie's house. Duty, however, was built into both the moral fabric of Christian commitment and the supplication of a mother. I promised that I would walk down to her house before the roads drifted shut, but I dallied in the warm kitchen another hour, postponing the unavoidable mission.

When I finally stepped outside, the landscape was already a winter wonderland. Despite the fierce wind, layers of new snow were creating mystical shapes out of mailboxes, fence posts and buildings. With wool gloves I pulled my stockinged hat down over my ears and face, thrust my hands into my coat pockets, and began wading bootstep over bootstep the half-mile to Mammie's house.

The following morning it took a couple of hours to clear the deep snow from the walkway in front of her house and to shovel a path from her back porch to the driveway. Mammie sat inside her living room window watching me, tapping on her front window for my attention and pointing to an area I had bypassed. Finally, finished, I walked around to the back of the house where I pushed a heavy layered drift from her back steps. It was nearly 11:30 when I climbed the porch steps and stepped into her kitchen. She was not effusive, not demonstrative, but the table before me indicated her appreciation: fried chicken, canned peas, a boiled potato, bread and jelly. Love, in one of its many colors, established an indelible memory of her kindness.

CARRIE EDNA (SNOOK) ARNOLD
To know her was to love her.

By the time I arrived into this world, Mammie was 51 years old. I was the first grandchild, and as such, received a huge portion of her time and affection. As soon as I was old enough to sit between them

in the front seat of their Ford, Pappy and Mammie included me wherever
they traveled. In an era that predated seat belts, bucket seats, fast food and
convenience stores, I sat with my feet atop the gear box, the gear shift between
my knees, and ate the pieces of orange or slices of apple that Mammie care-
fully peeled and sectioned. I went with them on overnight trips when they vis-
ited Uncle Bud and Aunt Arvella or helped any of their friends and relatives
with farm or housework. When we stayed overnight, I slept between them,
careful not to disturb Pappy because Mammie insisted he needed his sleep.

Two years prior to my birth, Pappy, needing help for his expanding farm,
had invited Daddy and Mommy, newlyweds, to move permanently into the
farmhouse where Mommy had been raised and where I would spend my
growing up years. To provide adequate privacy, Pappy installed a separate
kitchen and the two older folks contented themselves with smaller quarters
while the two families conjoined to share farm work and responsibilities. Dis-
cord was minimal amid the excitement of learning to farm and the delight of
starting a family.

That farm was and always will be my home, and the pleasant memories
and lasting fondness it holds results in large part from the love and time lav-
ished by grandparents. I spent much time in those early years with Mammie.
Her presence was welcome relief for Mommy who was often pregnant and oc-
cupied with other small children. By the time I reached fourteen, a deep and
permanent bond had developed between us.

The remainder of the afternoon was spent on tenterhooks as I
feared the inevitable confrontation that awaited. The TV was on,
but at regular intervals I wandered out to the porch where Mammie sat.
Looking out from her porch window, I wondered where Daddy was, what
he was doing. I was convinced his anger was unabated, that some greater
pain was yet to follow. I speculated as to Keith's whereabouts. He had not
followed me. Had he and Daddy resumed readying the silo filler? ... had he
simply gone to his room? Once I thought I heard the sound of truck tires
against the loose gravel of Mammie's driveway, but it was my imagination
playing with the sounds of the day, reminding me of the lingering incident.

As painful as the earlier volleys of his tirade had been, I dreaded more
the icy gulf that would follow: an evening at the barn, mute, revulsed by
his physical presence, hopeless of redress or restoration, despondent, an
evening in purgatory. And in the crater of our relationship, my incessant

hunger for his recognition, sympathy, love.

Mammie asked no questions that afternoon, made no commentary, busying herself at the porch dining table, stuffing and hand stitching a set of small pillows to match the color scheme of her sofa. A hand fan lay on the table beside her. Despite the heat of the day, the porch seemed cool, ventilated by four screened windows and shaded by trees just beyond the house. In the quiet of the afternoon, a wall clock above the kitchen refrigerator ticked off seconds. At four o'clock I turned off the TV as Art Linkletter's House Party began pandering to an afternoon audience of housewives and senior citizens. I sometimes enjoyed the banter, especially the interviews with children, as often Mommy listened to the program on our kitchen radio. Sometimes at dinner one of us would repeat the funny remarks made by House Party children. Daddy would laugh and recall for us similar experiences from his past. The House Party was a fun show, but on this afternoon, it was uncomfortable.

The tedium of the afternoon grew. I returned to the porch where Mammie continued to stitch the pillows. A palpable stillness rested on the landscape. A continual chorus of cicada prophesied the end of summer. From distant woods, crows intermittently gave emphasis to the afternoon silence with peremptory alarms. The earth was waiting, summer ending with a whimper. My mind wandered to the farm and the tractor and silo filler standing idle next to the silo in back of the pig lot. It seemed strange and far away, surreal in contrast to the earlier flurry of events. Since it was not possible for one man to thread the belt between the tractor and filler, I supposed Daddy was now in the garage sharpening the huge blades that spun inside the filler or else working in the barn.

A storage shed stood thirty yards below Mammie's house. As I watched, a crow landed on its roof and began a clarion caw-caw. Two squirrels on the branches of an oak rising in a grove just beyond, began barking at the crow's invasion. It paid no attention for several minutes, then, ready to meet the consequence of its recent raid on a nearby bird nest, flew skyward. Immediately, sparrows attacked, causing the crow to veer and dive in attempts to avoid the sharp forays of the small birds. The battle raged, the crow straining to free itself, but losing altitude as it was driven sideways. Seconds passed, and just as abruptly as they had arrived, the sparrows were gone, abandoning the crow, satisfied their efforts had thwarted further sallies. The heat of the day returned.

Mammie was always busy. In addition to the duties of house, garden, barn and field, she found time to stitch, braid, crochet and embroider.

O n the floor beside Mammie rested a cardboard box filled with scraps of various colored cloth awaiting her next project. Eventually she would weave the pieces into long braids that would later be sewn together to form the colorful throw rugs that were inherent to the floors of most farm houses. She loved both the work and the resulting compliments that acknowledged her handiwork, and though she had not yet finished the pillows, she was anxious to begin the rug. The busyness of daily routine veiled the loneliness that followed Pappy's death in February. She struggled to reshape a sense of identity. As a wife she had been content as a helpmeet, for it was Pappy's energies that had dictated the momentum of her life. Now he was gone, and it fell upon Mommy and us kids to fill the vacuum and enfold her within the sphere of family.

The role of work, of industry, cannot be overstated in the lives of Mammie and Pappy. It was the grand design of life. God helped those who helped themselves. It assured provision both for today and tomorrow. Conversely, idle hands evinced defective character and led to wickedness. Pappy dreamed of extravagant barns with opulent cattle. He enjoyed the praise of neighbors, and he understood that hard and diligent labor resulted in material reward and spiritual satisfaction.

Mammie did not quite share his vision, but she, too, frowned on idleness, fearing it was the devil's workshop. A virtuous life must avoid indolence. So, she worked. From sunup to sundown she toiled, obsessed with a sense of cleanliness and order. In an age preceding telephones, she was prepared for both strangers and friends who came to call. Spotlessness was imperative, and neither flecks of dirt nor floccules of dust were tolerated.

She attended Samuel's Church every Sunday, wearing her Sunday best and placing her dollar quietly into the collection plate. When the congregation sang from the hymnals, she followed the words but did not sing aloud. After Pappy died, she rode with John and Nettie Goss, her neighbors, to church. They stopped in front of her house on Sunday mornings, welcomed *her to the rear seat of their car and then, two hours later, dropped her off on their return. She looked forward to the service and visitation with the friends and neighbors she had known since girlhood.*

She read her Bible daily, marking the place where she finished with a purple ribbon that had one end bound to the book's seam. Finished with her evening reading, she lifted the lid to the old desk that sat next to Pappy's rocker in the kitchen and laid the black King James Bible into its protected place. The desk had once sat atop a platform at the front of the one-room Krick schoolhouse where a solitary teacher taught eight grades of country children. Each of Mammie's four children had attended the school and was acquainted with the old desk. Thus, the Bible and the desk alike were sacrosanct.

I thought it curious that she never underlined or highlighted significant passages of Scripture, and it was not until I was much older, and she had passed away that my mother recalled for me favorite verses that Mammie recited. "Enjoy the days of thy youth before the silver bowl is broken," she had warned from the book of Ecclesiastes. That she never used scripture to admonish her grandchildren may have resulted from observing Daddy's dogmatism, convinced that harsh and unfeeling remonstrance was cruel and ineffective. She regarded Daddy's Biblical knowledge, however, as superior to her own and was attentive during his times of exegesis.

At mealtimes she bowed her head before eating, although I never heard her pray aloud. Pappy waited to eat until she looked up, then went about his meal, satisfied that her petition included the both of them. When I ate at her table, she asked me to "say grace."

At exactly 5:00 pm our blue Chevy pickup truck pulled into Mammie's driveway. I had gone back into the kitchen and was sitting in what had been, just six months previous, Pappy's rocking chair, leafing through the pages of the *McClure Plain Dealer*, the four-page local newspaper that arrived every other Thursday. I sometimes read articles when I recognized names, but generally disregarded the paper's banality. Though I didn't hear the truck, I was aware that Mammie had risen from her sewing and gone to the window that looked westward toward the driveway. I walked out onto the porch. Through the open window of the cab Daddy called to her, "Tell Dennis it's time to do the barn work."

"I'll tell him," she submitted.

The truck turned in the gravel driveway, climbed back onto the dirt road and sped away. As cruel as it seemed that he didn't wait to give me a ride, I was glad I didn't have to climb into the cab with him, and that I had ten or fifteen minutes to collect myself before going to the barn. I said a cursory goodbye to Mammie, then quickly exited by the porch door and started up the dirt road.

I usually ran the half mile between the farm and Pappy's house, pretending I was stealing bases, running down long fly balls, or catching winning touchdown passes. On this late afternoon, however, my mind was not on games.

During most spring and summer months our cows were pastured overnight in the meadow adjacent to the barn. Early mornings would find them bedded beneath one of the larger shade trees at the far end of the pasture from where Keith and I took turns fetching them for their early morning milking. It was a pleasant duty. Cows never hurried, but with udders heavy, leisurely plodded toward the barn where they were milked and fed. Afterward, they returned to the meadow. Curiously, for evening milkings, cows did not need calling, but gathered inside the meadow gate, waiting for it to be opened. The quotidian regularity would continue until the colder temperatures of November when they would be bedded and kept inside the barn. As I ascended the knoll beside the meadow, I saw that Daddy had already opened the meadow gate and the herd was filing into the barn yard.

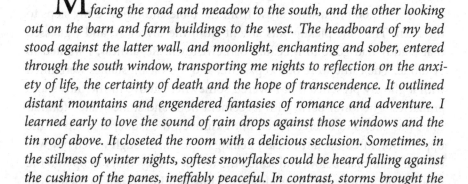

*M*y upstairs bedroom was a corner room with two windows, one facing the road and meadow to the south, and the other looking out on the barn and farm buildings to the west. The headboard of my bed stood against the latter wall, and moonlight, enchanting and sober, entered through the south window, transporting me nights to reflection on the anxiety of life, the certainty of death and the hope of transcendence. It outlined distant mountains and engendered fantasies of romance and adventure. I learned early to love the sound of rain drops against those windows and the tin roof above. It closeted the room with a delicious seclusion. Sometimes, in the stillness of winter nights, softest snowflakes could be heard falling against the cushion of the panes, ineffably peaceful. In contrast, storms brought the lament and wail of something wild and momentous. My room was a cloister, sequestered and private and personal.

In the earliest days and nights, before Mammie and Pappy moved into their own home, and before Mommy and Daddy's first babies arrived, the bedroom belonged to the newlyweds. A stovepipe from the living room wood stove ran upward through the center of the room, supplying a modicum of heat on the few winter evenings when the living room was in use. Generally, unless there was company to entertain, the room below and the stove remained idle as the kitchen was the center of activity. Walls and ceilings throughout the house lacked insulation, and noise from the downstairs reverberated throughout the house. An occupant of a second-floor bedroom could decipher conversation from the kitchen below.

Neither Daddy nor Keith nor I spoke as we went about the barn work. Perfunctory motion masked the tension. I went about a wooden way, far from the feeding and watering of animals, anxious to escape the pressing weight of the moment. When Daddy had finished the last cow, he went to the milkhouse, rinsed the milkers, lifted the heavy milk cans into the water cooler, and disappeared. A few minutes later Keith and I closed the barn and headed for the house.

The disquietude of the afternoon lingered at supper. Daddy was not at the table as we ate the fried sausage and mashed potatoes. Beans, lettuce, and carrots were still plentiful in the garden, but Mommy had opened a jar of canned peas to escape going outside into the wilting heat. Beads of condensation ran down water glasses as we ate in silence.

It was 7:00 pm when I arose from the table and retraced my steps to the barn. The blue pickup was absent from the driveway, and I guessed that Daddy had gone to McClure or Lewistown. Regardless, I wanted to be alone. The cattle were out to pasture, and the vacant stables were filled with a ghostly presence that hovered somewhere above in the mows and granaries. The lower barn, with its cement floor and stone-walled foundation, was cool and offered relief, but I climbed the ladder that led to the upper floor, lifted open the heavy ceiling trapdoor through which hay was thrown to animals below, and scaled the wooden rungs that ran up into the mows. The mows were close, almost steamy, but I lay down in their seclusion, while the tension and the heat of the day beat upon me.

Convoluted in self-pity and reflection, the minutes passed. The hour from supper to bedtime was usually a time of retreat. I often hurried through evening meals so that I could fetch my baseball glove and a ball from the cardboard box Mommy kept behind the porch stove, take my place behind the barn, and enter my imaginary big-league world. Night baseball games were broadcast at eight o'clock, at which time I returned to the house, sat next to the radio in the kitchen and kept score of the Phillies games on a sheet of paper torn from my school tablet. On this evening, however, I could not escape the real world.

The events of the day continued to pulsate. Attempts to concentrate on peripheral matters surrendered to immanent despair. Indulging in despondency, I fell away from the moment, no longer conscious of time.

Suddenly I realized darkness had fallen. The spaces and cracks in the barn's boards and rafters where beams of sunlight had shone earlier now exuded a shadowy spookiness, creaking and groaning as the temperatures cooled. I rose from my perch and climbed down to the barn floor, exited through the upper barn door, and trudged to the house.

Mommy had cleared the kitchen of supper. Pots, pans, and dishes had been washed, dried, and stacked into the kitchen cabinet. In their stead, containers of vanilla, cream of tartar, sugar, and flour sat atop the kitchen table alongside cake pans as she prepared to beat egg whites for an angel food cake. She informed me that I did not have to stay overnight with my grandmother. Understanding that I was upset, she had sent Billy to take my place.

Many nights, after Daddy went to bed, I kept Mommy company, working on jigsaw puzzles, rocking one of the babies, or listening to her concerns. Some nights I worked with her, cutting up chickens, canning vegetables, snapping beans or podding peas. On this night, however, I went to my room.

My room lay at the far-right end of the main upstairs hallway. On the other side of the corridor were three doors that opened: to the attic stairwell, Keith's bedroom, and a walk-in closet. Light from Keith's room could be seen in the space below his door, and I knew that he, too, had gone to his room.

Despite open windows and screened doors there was little ventilation in the house. An all-day baking from the hot sun resulted in heated air trapped in the upstairs bedrooms. I lay atop my bed, still wearing Levi's and a T-shirt, reading anew my baseball cards as I laid them in patterns on my bed. The cards were my favorite retreat. Stored in boxes, I cached them beneath my bed. Their pictures and statistics had long been committed to memory and breathed life into my fantasies. I separated them by teams, compared their stats, and always handled them as fine and treasured pieces. The house was quiet, but outside, every creature of the night had joined in full-throated chorus.

At about 8:30 I heard the pickup on the road behind the barn, and seconds later Daddy pulled into our driveway. After parking in front of the garage I heard his step on the walk outside the kitchen, and minutes later heard the screen door to the kitchen screech open as he entered. There was a brief muffled conversation with Mommy, after which she came to the wood stove beneath my room and lightly tapped on the pipe that ascended to the roof overhead. "Daddy bought ice cream," she announced. Her voice was filled with the anxiety that anticipates rejection. She hoped that I would come downstairs, that doing so would expunge the day's hostility. Her greatest concern was lingering tension, whether between Daddy and her or Daddy and us kids. Personal equilibrium was impossible when her family was disquieted.

I did not answer. I was struck with the cruel irony that while his temper had alienated him from his children, it had also estranged each of us from one another. I understood Mommy's distress, but my own wound prevented my reaching out to her. Each of us would have to survive in isolation. I could not go downstairs.

"Denny," she softly called, "Are you coming down?"

"No." There was neither defiance, nor spite, nor anger, only the exhaustion of defeat.

She returned to the kitchen. Stillness permeated the house.

Ice cream in the summertime was a treat. On evenings when Daddy arrived home after dark with a half-gallon of vanilla, we clamored to the kitchen where Mommy scooped spoonfuls into individual bowls and watched all seven of us kids enjoy the bedtime banquet. Even the times Daddy bought maple walnut or cherry vanilla, his favorites, we seldom complained. Ice cream on a hot summer night was delightful.

I heard my younger brothers and sisters tumbling out of bed for the ice cream. In minutes they were gathered in the kitchen where the jingling of silverware against saucers reached my room. It seemed obvious that the ice cream was an inducement to restore civility. I was not, however, deluded into believing he had become sensitive to my pain. Rather, he knew Mommy would not be mollified until her children were repaired, and ice cream seemed an apt vehicle.

Suddenly my attention was arrested by his heavy tread on the stairs. Intuitively, I knew he was coming to my room. His appearance on the stairs was not just an irregularity; it was a departure from universal order. He had never before come upstairs after we had gone to our rooms. It signaled approaching judgment. The tension of earlier events became compounded.

In the lower barn, at the back of the stable, sat a feed bin. It was filled with "chop," a mixture of ground grain and nutrients which was fed to the cows during their morning and evening milkings. When the lid was not closed tightly, it attracted mice. If discovered, the trapped mouse could not escape, but darted to a corner where it waited trembling, resigned to doom.

As the footsteps drew near, I trembled with nausea. At that moment I hated my father. When he reached the top of the stairs and turned toward my room, I sat upright. Reaching the end of the hallway, however, he inexplicably turned toward Keith's room. I heard Keith's door open and a brief exchange of words, their tone somber and officious. Keith's door closed and before I could gather myself, the knob of my door turned. Invasive, he pushed open the door without knocking. Leaning into the room, he declared, "I apologized." Stern, impenitent, impersonal, he did not wait for a response. He spoke and was gone.

I was accustomed to the timbre of his voice. At 5:15 mornings, when he tapped but once on the stove pipe that ran up through my room and announced, "Time," the tenor of his voice was fraught with gravity and tinged with threat. It was time to be in motion, to get to the barn, or to go for the cows. Delay was irresponsible and ground for consequences. I was shaken on this night, however, not just by his tone, but by the violation of my privacy. My room had been a haven, inviolable, sure, a refuge. A few times Mommy had come to my room, bringing newly laundered clothes or asking for help with something in her world. Always, she knocked. Personal space was sacred. Daddy's violation was unconscionable.

I spent the next hour wrestling with grisly dread that he would return. I could not go downstairs into his presence, nor could I leave the house. The former suggested I was being confrontational, the latter that I was sulking. Either would worsen the already menacing situation. Thus, I sat on my bed, the baseball cards impotent to relieve my despair.

My brothers and sisters finished their ice cream and returned to their beds. The minutes dragged as the house quieted, the stillness charged with the tension of the day. My mind wandered, revisiting my abrasions with extended self-pity. The windows of my room were propped open, letting in the myriad sounds of night. Katydids, crickets, tree toads, frogs, and cicada called and answered from the maple trees in the yard and the swamp in the meadow. Far away at the foot of Jack's Mountain came the forlorn whistle of a train. Near the barn an owl complained. I turned off the bed lamp and sat on the side of the bed facing the southern window staring out into the night.

How long I sat in lost thought I do not know, but my self-absorption was finally interrupted by soft tapping on the stove pipe. "Are you okay?"

"I'll be alright." I answered as convincingly as possible. I didn't want Mommy to worry.

"Why don't you come down? Everyone's in bed."

I didn't answer immediately, uncertain that "everyone" included Daddy.

Finally, I acquiesced, "Okay."

As though guilty of ignominious transgression, I surreptitiously made my way downstairs to the kitchen. I sat on the old couch in the corner of the kitchen while she ironed. The ironing board was directly in front of the kitchen screen door, and although no breeze stirred, it was cooler there than the rest of the house. A sprinkler bottle rested on one end of the board while clothes were piled on the table.

For several moments neither of us spoke. Wistfully she asked, "Do you want some ice cream?"

"No."

I rose from the sofa, went to the sink and found a glass. Opening the tap I let the cool spring water fill my glass. I drank half of the contents, poured the remainder down the sink, and returned to the sofa.

"Daddy didn't used to be like this." Her voice was hushed, and she did not look up as she drove the iron over the fabric of a shirt. "He's had a lot on his mind." Teary-eyed she continued, "When we were first married, everyone remarked what a nice person he was."

She was thinking out loud, pausing between thoughts. There was no need to respond.

At the far end of the meadow one of the cows bawled, provoked by the heat and flies. Mommy's mind ran into the past; the loving and loveliness of early days, the heartaches of more recent times. She remembered the time she almost left him, a time before they had children, "before she became a Christian," before she learned that Jesus wants us to pray and trust that "all things work out for the good of them who love God."

She recalled the difficulties, especially for Daddy, of living under the same roof with her mom and dad. "I will always love Pop, but he interfered sometimes. He thought everyone should work all the time. He was very critical of Daddy. Mom would tell Pop to stay out of it, but Pop was stubborn."

I had seen firsthand some of the ugly exchanges between the two men. As a little boy I heard my grandfather criticize Daddy for the way he was bagging grain. The three of us were in the upper floor of the barn. Daddy had filled burlap bags with grain to be taken to the mill while Pappy was in one of the mows throwing loose hay onto the barn floor to be used later that evening to feed the cows. When Pappy was finished, he came into the granary. Without speaking he loosened a bag of grain Daddy had just tied, dumped some of the contents back into a bin and retied the bag. It was a direct and ugly confrontation. Both men were angered.

"If you don't like it, you can do it yourself!" Daddy slammed the granary door behind him. I followed him out of the barn and up toward the corn crib. When he reached the steps of the crib, Pappy came out of the barn and started down toward the stables. Talking to no one in particular, but loud enough for Daddy to hear, with head down, he complained, "It has to be done right."

"What?" Daddy challenged. If you have something to say, say it like a man. I'll tell you something, you're not a man!" Daddy was about to enter the crib, but now he slammed the door closed, turned, and strode toward the house.

I hesitated, not knowing what to do. Pappy stood motionless next to the milk house as Daddy disappeared. Trying to avoid both men I started back toward the upper barn. As I passed Pappy, he looked toward me, and I saw that both eyes were filled with tears. It seemed unfair that a grown man should be hurt so deeply. Daddy never cried.

MY GRANDMOTHER CORA'S FAMILY
Back row, left to right: Daddy, Uncles Dick, Bill, and Don (Nipper). Front row: Aunt Helen, Cora, and Aunt Mary. My grandfather, Uncle Bobby, and Aunt Lolly had already passed.

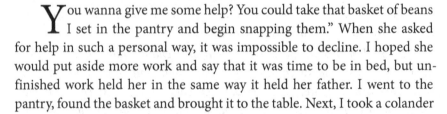

You wanna give me some help? You could take that basket of beans I set in the pantry and begin snapping them." When she asked for help in such a personal way, it was impossible to decline. I hoped she would put aside more work and say that it was time to be in bed, but unfinished work held her in the same way it held her father. I went to the pantry, found the basket and brought it to the table. Next, I took a colander from the kitchen cabinet, set it beside the basket, and began to snap off the ends of the string beans. The broken ends fell back into the basket while I dropped the edible portions into the colander.

For several minutes we worked in silence, the creaking of the ironing board and the crisp snapping of the beans the only sounds.

"Why does he get so mad?" I looked up from my work.

"He has that Morgan temper. They all have it. Mary, Dick, Helen. They say Daddy's dad had a bad temper, so I guess it came from him. Uncle Bill is not like that. And Grandma, she doesn't get mad." There was a pause. "She gets upset sometimes, but she doesn't have a temper."

She stopped for a moment, her right hand holding the iron, her left resting on the ironing board, her motion suspended while she analyzed the intemperance she had observed since her marriage. "They never say 'sorry.'"

The revelation was hushed, as though she had surrendered classified information. "Now that's not entirely true," she softened. "Daddy apologizes sometimes." There was another pause. "Sometimes, it's my fault. I don't let things go, and I make it worse. Your dad's not perfect. None of us are. Apologizing is hard for some people."

She finished the ironing and began placing the newly pressed clothing into piles. Completed, she asked, "Almost done?"

"Yeah."

"Let's go to bed."

I put the colander of beans into the refrigerator, set the basket aside to be emptied in the morning, and headed for my room. She waited until I had mounted the stairs, then turned off the light. Her bedroom door closed, and the house was still.

Morning came quickly. I was sound asleep at 5:15 am when I heard his rap against the stovepipe.

"Time!" he called. It was a call I had heard hundreds of times, always imperious with a sense of foreboding, but on this morning, it was a siren.

Rousing myself, I tugged on my Levis and shirt and pulled socks from a drawer. Holding sneakers and socks in one hand, I opened my door, called to Keith, and as I headed downstairs heard the kitchen door close and knew Daddy was on his way to the barn. I speculated about his mood, wondering how yesterday's events would color the morning. Sometimes, at 6 am, he would switch on the radio in the milk house. It was an indication that he was in a good mood. Most stations did not begin their broadcast schedule until later in the morning, but WWVA in Wheeling, West Virginia, signed on early in order to accommodate listeners who worked in the coal mines. After a briefing of news, the station announced which mines would operate on that day. It was of no interest to us, but at 6:15 the *Bob and Ray Program*, a home-spun comedy was aired. Daddy loved the humor and many times repeated their jokes later in the day. When I slid open the door to the barn, he was in the milk house assembling the milking machines. The radio was not turned on.

Not knowing if he wanted me to fetch the cows or to remain in the barn to feed the stock, I asked, "You want me to get the cows?"

"Yeah. I'm gonna try to set up the silo filler. You go ahead with the milking."

A light fog covered the lower meadow where the cows lay under oak trees. The grass was wet, so I stayed on the dirt road, running the quarter mile to where I crawled between the strands of barbed wire, careful to avoid the electric wire that ran inside the barbed fence, and stepped into the meadow. A few cows had to be prodded to their feet, but in a minute the herd was trekking methodically in the direction of the barn, their udders heavy with milk. The fog was lifting, and I was shortly able to see Keith opening the meadow gate, anticipating our arrival. Leaving the meadow, the cows filed into the barnyard as Keith ran ahead, opened the stable door, and watched each animal methodically enter its assigned stall. As he closed the stanchions one by one, I headed for the milk house where the milking machines were stored.

Assembling the machines, through one of the milk house windows, I saw John Goss, our neighbor, standing just outside the barn gate. At about the same time Daddy appeared from behind the barn, a quizzical look on his face.

"John, you have trouble?" Daddy queried.

"Your hogs were in my corn." John announced. "Your two sows got through the fence and crossed the road into my corn field. I chased them back down to the opening and waited till they squeezed through, but I wouldn't trust them. They'll find that hole again."

"John, I'm awfully sorry."

"Aw, it's nothin'," he chuckled, waving the back of his hand at Daddy. "I just wanted you to know your fence has a hole in it."

"Well, I really appreciate it. I'll get to it right away."

"Aw, finish your milkin'."

"Boys'll do that. I'll get to the fence."

John saw me as I carried one of the machines from the milk house into the barn. He took a moment to look toward the stable, and I heard him tell Daddy, "Those boys work hard. You got good help."

"Yeah, they do a pretty good job." Daddy brushed the compliment aside.

John turned to go, "I gotta get back."

Affected by the kindness of his neighbor, Daddy repeated, "John, I apologize for the trouble."

"No trouble," John reiterated, "some things can't be helped. Foolish to get upset."

"Well, anyway, I apologize."

FEBRUARY NIGHT

The morning after the storm

The icy sting of snow blown fiercely against the face of a thirteen-year-old boy, stranded on a bitter cold February night in a remote field on our farm is never to be forgotten. The sheets of white drifting across frozen terrain, the haunting sound of gales howling through dark groves of pine, and the stealthy darkness of an ominous sky remain indelibly fixed in the memory.

Icicles, where yesterday's snow had begun to thaw atop rooftops, hung heavily from the eaves of house and barn. Great stalactites, three and four feet in length, that had dripped for a few midday hours, were now fixed in the dark. The mercury thermometer outside the porch had registered minus four at 6:00 pm and continued to fall through the night while the rusted weather vane atop the barn changed direction with each polar gust that beat against the buildings.

The Sunday evening church service was cancelled due to the cold. Barn work completed, an early darkness descended prematurely. Daddy had rinsed and placed the milking machines on the metal racks of the milk house to dry for morning. The barn door was closed for the night, and he and my brother Keith had hastened to the warmth of the kitchen in our farm house. It was my turn to take the manure we had just cleaned from the stables to the field adjacent to the meadow on the far side of the frozen crick.[1]

Resolved to get the job done quickly, I went to the house, tugged on an extra pair of jeans, wrapped Mommy's scarf over my ears and face, pulled high the collar on my heavy coat, and stepped out into the night. Reaching the barn, I opened the outside gate of the barnyard where the tractor and spreader were parked, pulled myself up onto the tractor seat, and turned the ignition key. The motor started at once, and within moments I steered through the open gate onto the snow-covered road that wound across the cement bridge, turning left onto the lane that ran east on the far side of the meadow. The Arctic wind was penetrating, and I was already shivering as I crossed the bridge and drove onward into the darkness. I huddled forward on the tractor to escape the cold metal seat. Stuffing my right hand into my coat pocket, I closed the fingers of my left hand inside my glove and steered with the back of my wrist against the cold metal wheel. I was driving the smaller of our two Allis-Chalmers tractors, and it occurred to me that Daddy ought to hitch the bigger tractor to the spreader so that my job could be completed more quickly. As it was, the smaller tractor now inched and plodded through the sea of snow eight or ten inches deep.

The sky cast an eerie blackness above the drifts as though something foreboding and sinister lurked in the darkness. Billows swirled furiously in front of me. With each blast I turned away from the wind and huddled close to the tractor. The combination of darkness and blizzard made locating the fence rows impossible. Unable to determine where yesterday's manure had been spread, and more concerned with my discomfort than my duty, I purposed to empty the contents quickly, return the machinery to its place underneath the barn overshot, and retire to the warmth of the house.

Pulling into the field I realized the gale prohibited spreading the contents leeward. I would have to drive to the far end of the field and head into the blast before I could trip the lever that set in motion the wheel-driven conveyor chains. The chains would then push the spreader's contents into the rear spindles and throw it backward onto the snow-crusted ground. Daddy had warned both Keith and me that delay on such a night might cause the manure to freeze onto the chains and result in their jumping from the pulleys. That would mean serious complications. It would be necessary to return to the barn, find forks and shovels, and make a second trip to spread the manure by hand – an extra hour in the frosty night.

Reaching the eastern end of the field, I turned the tractor into the

---

1. The alternate spelling "creek" was foreign to the rural folk of central Pennsylvania.

Neighbors helped clear the road in front of our house after the storm.

wind, threw it into neutral, and jumped down to trip the lever that drove the conveyor chains. The drifting snow momentarily blinded me, and I hunkered behind the tractor waiting for the fury to subside. A minute passed. My hands and feet felt numb and my legs quivered involuntarily as I bounded back onto the seat, threw open the throttle, and began steering into the darkness.

The sound of a ratcheting cog slipping against the chain it should be turning was always frustrating, regardless of the weather, but on a frigid night, it was devastating. Above the wind I could hear the clack-clack-clack of metal butting metal, and I immediately brought the tractor to a halt. I knew the chain had jumped from its track. In utter dismay, I pounded my hand against the steering wheel, knowing what lay in store. For a moment I sat defeated, unable to gather myself. Feeling the victim, I kicked the gear-shift into neutral, a gesture of protest against a pitiless universe.

Jumping down from the tractor, I tugged at the pin that hitched the spreader to the tractor. It was wedged and would not release. I removed my gloves to get a better grip, and began jimmying the pin, but it refused to budge. Manipulating cold metal with cold hands on a freezing night was one of farm life's cruelties. Personal discomfort, however, had to be borne without complaint. I had learned that private wounds must never bleed publicly.

I decided it would be faster to turn off the tractor motor and run back to the barn rather than unhitching the spreader. I would grab a fork and shovel and run back to the field. Perhaps, it would warm me.

I jumped from the seat and sprinted into the wind, my face numb. The blowing snow stung like sleet. Keeping my hands pocketed as I ran, the icy crust beneath me cracked and gave way with each step. After only a few yards exhaustion slowed me to a walk. To worsen matters, my breath had formed an incrustation of ice inside the scarf and was now chafing my lips. I removed the glove from my right hand, reached inside the scarf, scraped the ice loose from my face, then resumed my retreat. When I crossed the bridge and turned toward the house, the pole light that stood between the house and the barn turned on. For a moment I entertained hope that someone might appear to lend help, but the house door remained closed, so I continued directly toward the barn. The sliding door that led into the stables was jammed with ice, but a kick from the inside of my right foot dislodged it sufficiently so that I was able to push it open. The stable was a refuge, and I immediately came and stood trembling against the nearest cow, pulling off my gloves and placing my hands inside the warm flank of her hind leg. She quivered from the sudden intrusion.

I dreaded returning to the field, and for several minutes I speculated on the consequences of waiting until morning to unload the spreader. By then, however, the manure would be one huge clump of ice, too heavy to move, rendering the spreader, which was needed the following morning, useless.

Outside, the wind howled against the creaking barn. A pigeon, holed up in the wind-sheltered ledges of the barnyard loft, cooed, reminding that I must not linger. The manure was freezing on the abandoned spreader. Working my fingers back into the gloves, I walked to the far end of the stable, selected a pitch fork and shovel, and turned to go.

There are gestures, whether patronizing or solicitous, that cannot be forgotten because they lift us from despair. About to turn off the barn lights, I heard the sliding entry door open and saw Daddy step into the barn. He was wearing a heavy coat, wool cap, and gloves. He had also buckled on a pair of boots and was prepared to go out into the night.

"Trouble with the spreader?" he asked.

"Chain came off the track," I explained.

"Where's the tractor?" he wondered.

"I ran back. Thought it would be faster," I offered.

I knew he did not like the tractor left in the field, but I also knew he appreciated that I had no intention of bothering him with my problem, especially on a raw winter night after he had gone to the warmth of the house.

He glanced at the shovel and fork, surmising I was headed back into the cold night. Affected, he reached and took the fork. Turning toward the door, he directed over his shoulder, "Come on."

We started back across the bridge, heading into the drifting snow to the distant field where the tractor and spreader had been abandoned. In the cold and dark of that night, as we hurried to stay warm, I felt his presence though no word was spoken. He had not upbraided me for leaving the machines, nor did he blame me for the breakdown, and for all the times I had been afraid of his temper, his outbursts, his cruelty, I knew on this night that I was safe; I was with my dad, and he would rectify and remedy the situation. We strode hurriedly, collars buttoned, caps pulled low on our heads, the snow continuing to swirl about us, across the bridge, up the hill on the other side of the crick, and into the field.

Approaching the implements, he raised his voice above the storm's fury, directing me to start the tractor. I climbed aboard, anxious to please him. The motor started immediately, and I turned to await further instruction. As Daddy climbed into the spreader and began pitching the manure into the field, a blast of savage force swept over us, the snow blinding our vision, and the wind throwing Daddy against the side of the spreader. He dropped the pitchfork and held to the side of the spreader to maintain balance. For a full minute he hunkered down in the cavity of the machine, head down, both hands clinging to its side to avoid falling. I held tightly to the steering wheel of the tractor and waited for the gust to subside. When it abated, I peered back at Daddy. Fighting to keep his balance against the gusts, he took the handle of the fork and returned to his work. He motioned me to drive forward so that he could spread the contents of the load. I cautiously advanced the tractor, careful not to lurch as he worked. Moving slowly east to west, I steered while he labored. Twenty minutes … arduous … afflictive … the wind unremitting … treacherous … a second gale throwing him off-balance, landing him atop the manure. Finally, holding to the side of the spreader, he shouted for me to stop. I disengaged the clutch and waited. Dropping to his knees and using the brute

Daddy emptied the spreader of its contents after the wheel driven chain jumped off the cogs.

strength of his arms and hands, he forced together the unfastened chain links and rejoined them. By now his shoes and overhauls were stained with manure. Anxious to escape the elements and the ordeal, he jumped from the spreader and climbed aboard the tractor hitch, shouting into the night, "Let's get outta here."

It took another twenty minutes to reach the barn, park the machines, put away the fork and shovel, and close the gates. Both of us were numb by the time we reached the sanctuary of the house. I huddled next to the stove, peeling off the layers of clothing. Daddy went immediately down to the cellar shower to wash and change clothes.

Fifteen minutes passed before he appeared in the kitchen in stockinged feet, wearing clean work pants and a fresh white T-shirt under a flannel shirt. "Hazel," he said to Mommy, "Is there any soup left from supper. I need something hot."

She took a covered pot of vegetable soup from the refrigerator and set it atop the stove. She brought a bowl from the kitchen cabinet, set it at his place on the kitchen table, and returned to the stove to stir his soup. I remained close by the stove still trying to get warm, listening to the banter between the two of them. I marveled at Daddy's strength and willpower. Despite his caprice, and at times, his temper, he was a bulwark. We went to bed evenings impervious to alarms of the night. He made our world impregnable.

He really enjoyed his food. Spoonfuls of hot soup with a handful of crushed saltines were eaten with relish. He did not talk. When

Daddy enjoyed his meals but was sometimes difficult to please.

he had finished, he found the book he read nights and went to bed. Mommy carried his plate to the kitchen sink, rinsed and washed it, and set it to dry atop a dish towel. She told me to get a pillow from my bedroom and bring it to the kitchen, so she could warm it in the oven bin before I took it along to bed. Warm pillows in unheated bedrooms on winter nights were luxurious, but there was something more in her request. I intuitively knew when Mommy wished to talk. I suspect the same intuition that informed me of her needs told her that I was unsettled, that some of the things I wanted from him on that night were identical to her own longings.

When I climbed into bed later that night, I was not ready for sleep. I appreciated what Daddy had done for me. He had sacrificed personal comfort for my welfare. My gratitude was sincere. The bonding of two lives, however, is incomplete unless there is a spiritual response of one to the other, a giving back of some part of the gift, a demonstration of intellect and emotion that the other is special. It had not happened. He had built a bridge but not crossed over. I was left on my own island.

In the years that followed, the events of that night grew phantasmal, distant, dispirited. There was a great white oak that stood regal on the hill above our farm. It towered, transcending all other trees in the surrounding wood. A centurion, it had withstood the storm and fury of the decades. When I left home for college it was intact. But in succeeding years, a great bolt of lightning broke one of the massive arms, and its magnifi-

The great white oak that stood above our house. By my teenage years, it had grown to nearly twice the size pictured here.

cence and might were compromised.

Like the oak, the rugged man of that February night grew vitiated and tired. He became more impatient and self-occupied, sometimes insensitive to children and grandchildren. No blame is cast. Age and health can weary. Simply put, he was no longer an imposing figure. Even in his decline, however, he remained aloof, and the bond I hoped for on that February night never was realized.

In the passage of my own years, nonetheless, I think of him when I see hungry men eating, or when I am buffeted by life's thrusts and jolts, or on bitter winter nights when I am alone. The memory of that February night haunts, and sometimes in my loneliness, I entertain the hope that again, in eternity, he will smile and beckon, "Come on," and I will be able to walk beside him, free of the cold, the exigency, the darkness.

PAPPY'S DEATH

Charles Lester Arnold

January 29, 1887 – February 12, 1957

I was fourteen when my maternal grandfather, Charles Lester "Pappy" Arnold, died at our farm on Daddy's birthday, Tuesday, February 12, 1957. He was seventy. Although he was diabetic, somewhat overweight, and on heart medication, his death felt sudden. I was shaken by the abruptness, the finality. There had been no closure—he was vibrant, warm, fully alive the previous evening when I visited at his house. I was unaware that he was, in fact, having health issues. To a young boy, he seemed untouched by the advancing years, as though the inertia of his life moved above the slower cadence of others. He was never old, never frail, never slowed. Thus, there was no portent that the end neared. That evening at his house was the last time I saw him. Too young to notice his foibles and failings, he was simply my grandfather, unblemished, receptive, kind. His death awakened me to mortality.

Most of my memories of Pappy are associated with the farm, with hard work, and especially with his rocking chair. After spending long days of labor in the fields or at the barn, following evening supper, he unhooked the shoulder straps of his bibbed overalls, removed his shoes, and sat in the rocker. He loved to hold one of us grandchildren on his lap and endlessly rock while the old chair creaked in rhythmical monotony. He hid peppermint or wintergreen candies, licorice, or Chiclets in his breast pockets encouraging us to search for the surprise.

Although he enjoyed time with us, relaxation was counter to his disposition. When work awaited he was single-minded, preferring that small children "stay in the yard," and older children "get to work." When I was eight or nine and old enough to work beside him, he expected me to plant corn in straight rows, seal silo doors all the way to the top, and strip milking cows to prevent mastitis.[1] Character was embedded in carriage, and proper carriage meant working hard, not wasting time, and always completing an assignment.

Pappy had long been establishing himself as a successful Decatur Township farmer. On January 8, 1911, he had married my grandmother Carrie Edna Snook, a nearby farm girl, and concurrently leased the farm that would become my home. The couple purchased it outright in 1923 and continued to operate it until his retirement in March 1950 when my parents bought the acreage and a sufficient quantity of the livestock and implements to maintain a dairying operation. The remainder of the animals, some of the implements, and a portion of the hay, straw, and grain were auctioned at that time to pay for the cost of building his new home within a wooded area near the eastern boundary of the farm and to provide a nest egg for the couple's retirement.

Deeply rooted habits and routines are not easily displaced. Although Pappy relinquished formal title and jurisdiction of the farm, in a

Friends and neighbors knew him as "Charl." His grandchildren called him "Pappy." Proud and taciturn, his greatest love was labor.

---

1. "Stripping" a cow involved extracting all the milk from the udder. Cows improperly milked could develop mastitis, a serious inflammation.

large sense, his love for farming and its routines remained a need he was unable to vanquish. His very being was inextricably alloyed to the farm. Although he sold it, he never surrendered his right to work it.

Pappy's intrusions, however, irritated Daddy. On early mornings, during breakfast or family devotions, the sound of a tractor motor or the clanging of machinery was an unwelcome announcement that he had returned. To Daddy's mind, it was the older man's reminder that a farmer should be at work by that time of morning, an indictment for negligence, idleness, indifference. The result was a smoldering antagonism between the two men. Wives grew uneasy, fearful of taking sides, lest mother and daughter suffer division. As a result, Daddy felt alone in his quandary. Pappy's death on Daddy's birthday was for my father both cruel irony and a welcome release from bondage.

A mong my earliest memories of Pappy is a Saturday morning in early October when I was five. Mommy awoke Keith and me in our upstairs bedroom and brought us down to the kitchen where we dressed in the warmth of the wood stove. Both of us were excited. First, there was no school and second, we were going to help Pappy make our annual batch of apple butter.

The process had begun the previous evening. During the week Pappy had alerted several neighboring farmers and a few relatives of the task at hand, and after Friday barn work and suppers were completed, they began arriving in coupes, sedans, and buggies. Two of Pappy's brothers, Sam and Art, came with their wives, Mertie and Mabel.[2] Pappy's oldest daughter, Beatty, brought her husband, Stewart. Walter and Mabel Wright, long-time neighbors, were there to lend a hand.

The kitchen table had been pushed aside to provide sufficient space for the work. Workers sat in straight-backed chairs around a 20-gallon galvanized tub half-filled with salted cold water into which peeled and quartered apples were tossed.[3] It had been Daddy's job to pick the apples from the orchard in the days preceding, place them in burlap bags, lift them onto the bed of our pick-up truck, and store them in the wood house. Mommy and Mammie then transferred the apples to buckets, rinsed them

---

2. Pappy was the oldest of thirteen. All but one lived with their families within easy travel of our house.
3. Salt prevented oxidation and browning.

at the hydrant just outside the wood house, and carried them to the kitchen. The willing workers, armed with paring knives brought from home, filled their laps or aprons with Granny Smith, Northern Spy, and Red and Yellow Delicious apples. Each apple was pared, cored, quartered, and tossed into the tub. Cores and parings were discarded into empty buckets and later dumped into the pig lot where pigs gratefully awaited the treat.

The evening was industry, but it was also social. Men spoke of milk cows and crops, women of neighbors and children. Compliments and good will flowed amid promises of reciprocal visitation.

Taciturn, Pappy sat next to the wood stove at the rear of the room, farthest from the door. He relished moments when labor produced visible, measured results: bags of apples and gallons of apple butter. For him, the process was important only in that it led to production. Personal value was tightly attached to a product.

For Pappy, the evening also reflected his success as a farmer. Esteem was tied to corn in the bin, straw in the shed, animals in the barn, fruit in the orchard. He appreciated the deference and respect neighbors bestowed as a result of his hard work and the farm's increase. God helped those who helped themselves. He was thought sagacious by a community who admired his doggedness, his endurance, his success. He seldom volunteered information, but when asked would demonstrate the correct way to shoe a horse or milk a cow. In a circle of friends he was the least verbose. Instead, Mammie or a familiar neighbor would draw him to the center, directing, "Ask Charl."[4] His word was binding, his promises kept. His brothers and sisters sought his advice because he was the oldest, the most experienced, the most reliable.

He did not discuss problems or difficulties. He asserted explanations and solutions, never with ostentation or arrogance, but with quiet assurance. His opinions

MAMMIE AND PAPPY 1950

---

4. "Charl" was his nickname. From birth, it remained the appellation used by family and friends throughout his life. Those less acquainted addressed him with the more formal "Charles."

were clipped: conclusions, not comments that evoked conversation. Still, he was well-liked, ever willing to be a neighbor, perhaps less inclined to help than to take over a task. He was impatient with fellow-workers until work was completed, unable to sit until the acres were plowed, the corn was planted, the crop was in the barn. Leisure was altogether alien. Evenings, after supper, he walked his fields of tasseled corn, surveyed the acres of wheat, oats, and barley, inspected his animals, curried and preened his horses, and always, he prepared for the morrow, greasing machines, sharpening knives, oiling harness. He sometimes visited neighbors by "dropping in." In an era that predated telephones he liked to inspect and compare and perhaps brag about a new animal or machine.

The early-morning daylight remained grainy with an October chill as Keith and I tied our shoes, slipped into warm jackets, and headed outdoors. Breakfast would wait. Pappy was already stationed behind the wood house, stoking the fires that heated the great black cast iron kettles by now bubbling with the sweetness of cider and apples. The mixture was about to be transformed into the sugary dark brown spread that would be eaten on sandwiches, crackers, and pancakes.

We intermittently watched the work and played near the fire, sometimes throwing kindling wood and small sticks beneath the cauldron. We had been awakened early because Mommy, in Pappy's absence, had to help at the barn with the early-morning milking. That left my grandmother to prepare breakfast and tend Billy, our one-year old. As Pappy worked he sometimes stepped back from the heat, removed his weathered fedora, and placed his right hand on my shoulder. For a few minutes, he watched the process with us. He smelled of perspiration as did all the men who sweat-worked at farm labor. Although intrusive, the odor was inoffensive. Pappy was large and safe and his nearness was welcome. As busy as he seemed, his hand on my shoulder welcomed our company.

He carried a large red railroad bandanna in the rear pocket of his bib-overalls, and as he rested from the work, he would step back from the hot kettle to wipe his brow and the back of his neck. The red bandanna was central to his person. Except for church days when he wore his dark blue Sunday suit, the bandanna always spilled from one of the pockets in his bibbed trousers. Evenings, after supper, he sometimes took me into his rocking chair and began a slow, back-and-forth cadence that ceased only when he fell asleep. That bandanna often bulged uncomfortably in his rear pocket, so he would reach down and stuff it into one of the breast pockets in his overalls. Redolent with dried perspiration, it would rest against my head so that forever afterward I associated the bandanna with that odor. On this cool, October morning, before resuming the slow monotonous stirring of the boiling apples, he stuffed the dampened bandanna back into his rear pocket.

Like the red bandanna, the conventions of a dairy farmer were both practical and habitual. From as early as I can remember, and lasting until he became ill in his final years, one of Pappy's more inveterate customs was attending the Wednesday farm sale at Belleville. It was a ritual more sacred than attending church on Sunday.

Activities at the sale barn began about 10:00 am, so Pappy arranged Wednesday farm labors to permit time for the thirty-mile excursion. In his mind the weekly trip was necessary as it permitted him to stay abreast of farm prices, dicker with neighbors about crops, machinery and animals, and sometimes buy a milk cow or sell a litter of pigs. Social life was appurtenant. Mammie rode along as a kind of hostage compelled by circumstance. She did not relish the long trip, the summer heat, the winter cold, or the long hours waiting alone in the car, but she worried about his health and assuaged her anxiety by accompanying him. They were tethered by the warmth of love and the demands of duty.

After I reached four or five, I became part of the weekly trip. I sat in the back seat, the bib of my stiff Sunday overalls pushing uncomfortably against my throat. A one-pint mason jar placed beneath the passenger seat was my bathroom. They took me along, possibly to reduce Mommy's responsibilities, but also because I enjoyed watching the sales, sitting with Pappy high up in the indoor arena, and drinking the bottle of soda pop he always bought for me.

Pappy enjoyed the morning horse sale that was held in a makeshift outdoor arena. Dozens of farmers lined both sides of a grassless lot as the great work horses and the smaller, sleek carriage animals were paraded in front of them. The cadence of the auctioneers and the mingled smells of horses, chewing tobacco, and food invigorated and excited.

After the horse sale was concluded and before moving inside the main building where the other livestock were auctioned, it was time for our "dinner."[5] From the concession area Pappy would buy an orange pop for me and two pieces of pie, mincemeat for himself, and shoo-fly for Mammie. Then we would walk to the parking lot where Mammie waited in the car with the apple butter sandwiches she had packed and the chicken she had fried that morning. A second Mason jar offered cold cups of coffee. While Pappy sat on the folding chair he carried in the trunk of the car and drank the coffee, Mammie laid his dinner on the running board and poured a cup of coffee for herself. She then returned to the car, opened the bag containing the pie, took her slice of shoo-fly, and began the savory repast of pie dunked in coffee. There were always cookies for me.

Amish buggies at Belleville Sale Barn

Most of the patrons of the Belleville sale were Amish, thus the parking lot was principally occupied by horses and buggies. Curiously, many of the Amish wives waited in their buggies in the same way and for the same reasons that Mammie waited in the car. The ladies crocheted, knitted, or mended. Most sat alone, not venturing from their refuge to visit one another, but simply awaiting their husbands.

Pappy enjoyed the company of men. In addition to the trips to Belleville, on Saturday evenings he and Mammie regularly visited neighbors, the women churning butter or finishing a quilt, the men at the barn boasting about their horses or the most recent crop, but always engaged, never idle. On occasions of the McClure Bean Soup Celebration, or a local fair or church picnic, Pappy was there with the other farmers, inspecting new machines, renewing old friendships, and continually discussing farming.[6]

---

5. "Dinner" was the Pennsylvania Dutch term for lunch.
6. The Bean Soup Celebration is held in September in McClure, PA, a living memorial to all veterans of all wars. It was started by the Veterans of the Civil War of McClure and nearby communities. On the second floor of Joseph Peter's Blacksmith Shop in Bannerville, PA, on July 23, 1883, a group of Civil War veterans met to organize the Grand Army of the Republic Post. Their first formal session was held on October 20, 1883. Regularly, this group held their own bean soup festival, but in 1891 they invited the public. Since then, the citizens of McClure have continued this annual bean soup tradition.

   Though soup is the main attraction, the Festival and Fair includes exhibits, a horse show, amusements, rides, concessions, displays, and Civil War re-enactors. It has turned into

Site of the original McClure Bean Soup Festival

Most nights he was in bed by eight-thirty or nine o'clock, worn by the day's labor. He slept through any and all distractions. After he moved into his new house in 1951, as a nine-year-old, I often crawled into bed beside him. Although this relegated Mammie to sleeping in the guest room, she willingly indulged me. Before closing his eyes, he turned on the small brown Bakelite radio that stood atop Mammie's sewing machine stand, the sewing machine itself folded within. He tuned to *Fibber McGee and Molly, The Great Gildersleeve, The Tom Mix and Groucho Marx Shows,* and other popular nighttime programs. Ten minutes later he was asleep, unaware that the radio had lost its signal or that Mammie had turned it off.

Pappy was a farmer and his interests seldom strayed beyond his family and his farm, but he also enjoyed friends and welcomed their visits. A good neighbor who was generous with his means and ready to lend a hand, he was, however, judgmental. Privately he criticized those who retired too early from their fields, farmers who overworked their horses, laborers who took shortcuts, and anyone who was just sitting.

On a summer evening when I was about twelve, the barn work finished, I was playing ball behind the barn when he and Mammie stopped at the farm. He knew that I had worked long hours in the field that day, harvesting oats and bringing it to the granary, but he could not suppress the notion that time was being wasted. He momentarily disappeared into the granary while Mammie went to the house. In a few minutes he reappeared to inform me that cobwebs needed to be cleaned from the oats bins. I listened with no intention of complying. To his credit he did not badger, but went his way, and I continued to play ball. His work was his

an eight-day event that draws 40,000 to 60,000 people annually. (http://www.visitcen-tralpa.org/things-to-do/McClure-bean-soup-festival)

raison d'etre. Idleness was, indeed, the devil's workshop.

The last time I saw him was the evening before he died. He was somewhat weakened physically as he was only a few days out of the hospital where he had undergone a checkup for his diabetes. After supper, Mommy said that he had called and wanted me to bring Joey, our newest baby, to his house. Joey had been born the previous November, and the difficulties of wintry weather coupled with Pappy's declining health reduced the frequency with which he had seen the three-month-old baby. Now, he missed his grandchildren and wanted to hold Joey. I was fourteen and old enough to drive our pickup truck the short distance to his house. RuthAnn went along to hold the baby. We did not stay long. I handed the baby to him in his rocking chair, and while RuthAnn and I busied ourselves with Mammie's Parcheesi board, he rocked Joey. After an hour, Mammie reminded him that the baby had to return home. There were no indications that this was a farewell. He gave the baby to Mammie, who wrapped him warm again in his blanket, and RuthAnn and I took our leave.

February 12, 1957, was not unlike any other winter day. Clear and cold, it was a school day, and by 6:45 am Keith and I were standing in the warmth of Joe McKinley's country store awaiting the yellow bus that would transport us twenty miles to Burnham Junior High School where we were in the ninth grade. Billy and RuthAnn attended the Decatur Elementary School at Shindle, while Susie, Dave, and Joe were not yet of school age. The day passed routinely for me, attending classes, talking sports with friends, eating the brown bag lunch of Lebanon bologna sandwiches, cookies, and milk, and then, at 3:00 pm, boarding the same school bus that returned Keith and me to "Joe's" store at 4:30 pm from where, each afternoon, we walked the remaining mile to our house.

While we older children had passed the day at school, Mommy and Daddy attended to the daily demands of the farm. At 1:00 pm Mommy placed a turkey into the kitchen oven to roast for Daddy's birthday supper and then turned her attention to baking a cake. Joey was sleeping on a small changing table where Mommy could watch him, while Dave, almost two, was taking his afternoon nap in the living room. Susie, soon to be five and still in her nightie, was playing in the kitchen.

In the early afternoon Pappy and Mammie drove the four-tenths of a mile from their home to the farm so that Pappy could shell corn for his chickens. He had built a chicken house on his own property because his work ethic did not permit him to be idle, and he enjoyed the busyness that raising chickens required. Upon hearing their car pull onto the grassy knoll in front of the house, Susie climbed onto the couch by the kitchen window, from where she watched the outside activity and waited for her grandparents to come inside.

The new corn crib on the left was built into the side of the wagon shed.

There were three corn cribs on the farm: one adjacent to the chicken house, one next to the pig pens, and a newer one that adjoined the wagon shed. The chicken house was located directly north of the other farm buildings, half-way up an incline that crested two hundred yards beyond. At the base of the incline rested the pig pens and the lower shed. The house stood apart, fifty yards east. By late winter the other cribs had been emptied to feed the animals, so that only the new crib contained corn. Upon arriving at the farm, Pappy found our wheelbarrow and went to the empty crib at the top of the rise to load the corn sheller and move it down to the new crib.

Pappy collapsed after moving the corn sheller from the upper to the lower crib.

Shelling corn was a two-person job, and Mammie, concerned for his health, helped Pappy load the 150-pound machine into the wheelbarrow. Pappy then transported it to the new crib. Maneuvering the heavily loaded wheelbarrow down the incline may have exhausted him because, as he opened the crib door, he collapsed to the ground. Susie looked on from the house with a child's eyes, not realizing that a crisis was at hand.

Suddenly, she saw Mammie appear at the kitchen door and heard her blurt, "Come quick, Hazel, I think Pop's dead!" The two women hurried from the kitchen and ran down the embankment to where Pappy was lying. Mommy held his head as he gasped for breath several times and then fell lifeless. Although he appeared unconscious throughout these frenzied moments, neither woman relinquished hope. Knowing that immediate help was needed, Mommy ran back up the slope to the house and from the kitchen phone dialed the closest neighbor, Chip Sheriff. There was no answer. She tried a second neighbor, Emerson Bubb, who responded immediately to the distress in her voice. He promised that he and his wife would be there within fifteen minutes. With the reassurance that help was on the way, Mommy tried to telephone Daddy.[7] She was unable to reach him at first, but finally located his whereabouts and apprised him of all that had taken place. She then called Dr. Leipold, the family doctor, seven miles away in McClure. Before leaving his office, the doctor called the ambulance unit from McClure and directed them to the scene.

After completing the phone calls Mommy left Susie to watch the babies and returned to the area of the corn crib where Mammie and the newly arrived Bubbs waited. Propriety dictated that the body should be removed from the ground and laid in a proper place. It was decided to lift his inert form into the wheelbarrow and transfer it to the house. The frantic activity of those first moments following Pappy's collapse now became more passive in the resignation of death. Emerson, Mommy, and Mammie lifted the body onto the wheelbarrow and pushed it up the fifty-yard slope toward the yard surrounding the house, with Mommy holding Pappy's head as if he could be comforted. Then, mounting the three cement steps that led into the yard, they brought their burden to the house, lifted him from the wheelbarrow, carried him the dozen steps through the doorway into the kitchen, and laid him onto the couch. Pappy's body now rested supine with the head directly beneath the window from where Susie had witnessed the spectacle.

While awaiting the doctor's arrival, Mommy dressed Susie and continued preparations for supper. Soon Daddy arrived, and shortly afterward, Dr. Leipold appeared and examined the body. After pronouncing death, the doctor asked Mammie routine but necessary questions regarding the deceased's physical disposition prior to collapse—information required for the death certificate. Mammie, still wearing her apron and using it to wipe her eyes, pushed despondency aside and politely answered each query. Afterward the doctor called the mortuary for a vehicle.

It was now approaching 4:30 pm, at which time Keith, Billy, RuthAnn, and I would be stepping from school buses in front of Joe McKinley's store

---

7. Mommy did not phone Daddy initially because he was not within ready distance to be of help. In later years no one could remember exactly where he was on that day, but Mommy guessed he had gone to the feed mill or a garage in Beaver Springs.

and beginning our walk home. Aware that the arrival of four unsuspecting children would further attenuate the energies necessary to meet the already burdensome demands of the afternoon, Mommy and Daddy decided to phone Don and Catherine Rush, friends from church who lived about five miles distant, and request their help. The Rushes welcomed the opportunity to assist and insisted that all of us children, excepting baby Joey, be brought to their house until proprieties were addressed and matters quieted. Catherine offered to feed us supper and put us up for the night.

After the call was ended, Daddy climbed into our pick-up truck and set off to intercept us on our way home from the bus stop. Moments afterward a hearse arrived, and attendants transferred the body from the sofa to the waiting car. And now, in the quiet of the aftermath, Mammie could no longer contain her grief. Sitting next to the couch where the body had lain in state, looking out the kitchen window toward the corncrib, her features contorted. She laid her head against her right arm and sobbed.

Daddy met us as we passed neighbor John Goss's farm about a half mile from home. He informed us rather matter-of-factly, "Your grandfather's dead, I'm taking you to the Rushes." It was a pronouncement, void of emotion, permitting no reaction on our part. It was the first and only time I heard him refer to Pappy as "your grandfather." He seemed coldly detached, as though he felt no personal loss and was unwilling to consider what a grandfather's death might mean to grandchildren.

Keith, Billy, and I held RuthAnn, Susie, and Davey on our laps as we squeezed into the cab. Subdued, we rode in silence to the Rush farm, where we were welcomed by Mrs. Rush, who fed us supper and busied us with diversions in the form of puzzles and comic books. Mr. Rush was at work, but Danny, who was my age, was home, and I spent the evening with him, reading his comic books and playing board games, The hours passed in protracted angst.

It was nearly 9:30 pm when Daddy returned, loaded us into our Chevy pick-up, and started the trek home. Twenty minutes later, we pulled into our own driveway. As we entered the house, Mommy stood by the kitchen sink, busying herself. The moment pleaded for a word of compassion, the touch of a hand, but custom had not prepared us for such an event, and attempting to avoid the reality that had befallen, I went immediately to my bedroom.

Between our departure and return, Mommy's brother and sisters had been notified. When they arrived at about 8:00 pm, Uncle Bud and Aunt Ivy had taken Mammie to her home and made arrangements to stay with her. Daddy had finished the barn work.

Throughout the afternoon and evening, circumstances had forced Mommy to repress her private anguish. Her mother had needed comfort, and her small children had needed care. It would not be until later, in the silence of that night, that her bereavement gave release to weeping. From my upstairs bedroom I heard her crying and came downstairs. She assured me she would be okay and insisted I return to bed. She drew mightily upon the sacred promises of Scripture for assuagement, even as life's vicissitudes required emotional submission. Her father's death was a deep wound, a loss profoundly personal that had to be expressed privately.

I remember little of the remaining week. We attended school. I dreaded Saturday and the finality of the funeral. I recall seeing the body in the open casket at the service at Samuel's Church, holding back tears, conscious that he had refused to acknowledge his need for the Savior, wrestling with the notion that I would never see him again.[8] He had been the quintessential grandfather. Tender-hearted and gracious, he demonstrated his love for me each time he bought me a bottle of pop or hid a candy in his overall pockets or held me on his lap while driving the tractor, and it has been anguishing these many years to accept that he slipped into eternity before I told him that I loved him.

---

8. This is detailed in the chapter, *I'm Good Just the Way I Am.*

NEIGHBORS
◇◇◇◇◇◇◇◇◇◇◇◇◇◇◇◇◇◇◇◇◇◇◇◇◇

JOE MCKINLEY[1]

PART ONE

Ol' Joe took down the block of cheddar from the top shelf and carried it to the counter. He unfolded a sheet of butcher paper, placing it beside the block. From a back shelf he brought his butchering knife and began trimming the waxed casing before cutting two slabs of cheese and placing them, not onto the paper, but onto the scale atop a display case.

Daddy never trusted Ol'' Joe's scale.

"Is that scale clean?" objected Daddy, his voice laden with contempt.

---

1. Joseph Melvin McKinley was born at Spruce Hill, Juniata County, in 1893 and died at home in 1963. He never married but lived with his sister, Margaret "Maggie" (McKinley) Beatty, at what had formerly been the home of their parents at RD#2, McClure. The general store that he operated and ran for forty years, McKinley's Store, sat next door to the house. We knew little about his private life, except that he closed the store on Sundays, and every now and then was seen leaving or returning home in a Chevrolet that he had purchased new in 1957.

    I was married and living in New Jersey when he died, but some of my brothers and sisters attended the funeral. He is buried on a gently sloping hillside, five hundred yards from the store, in Lawver's Church Cemetery, beside the remains of Maggie and his mother, Mary Alice (Kepner) McKinley. His sister vanished, as it seemed, immediately after her brother's death, most probably going to live with relatives, and the empty house and store were sold by mid-summer. My brother, Bill, attended the sale, and with all of us, later remarked that something phantasmal, something essential and spiritual, had been torn from our farm community, so that afterward neighbors drove past on summer evenings in silence, reminded of the passage of their own fleeting lives through the same quiet corridors of time.

Ol' Joe moved slowly, awkwardly, his body worn from labor and stiff with the hunchback he had suffered since boyhood. He muttered woodenly, "Thirty-five cents," as though the transaction was tedious and perfunctory. He knew my father, standing on the other side of the counter, was reading the scale, and he knew that the thirty-five cents was already warm in the pocketed hand that had fished the quarter and dime before ordering the cheese. Daddy laid the change on the counter as Ol' Joe creased the worn paper and again folded it over the block before returning it to the shelf. Neither man spoke. Joe scooped the coins from the counter, deposited them into a stained cigar box, and retired to his three-legged stool behind the counter. Two decades of intercourse with local patrons had resulted in a kind of indolent indifference, a lassitude that ignored Daddy's insinuation.

The country store was a one-room building standing adjacent to the house where Ol' Joe lived with his spinster sister. Although both brother and sister were above scandal, the wives of patrons believed it queer that a house should be devoid of visitors. Thus, country gossip whispered, speculated, and watched as only Joe and his sister passed through the doors of the main house.

Inside the store were walls lined with shelving on which sat canned goods, yards of cloth, and glass bottles containing sundries ranging from molasses to medicines. Horse collars and harness decorated wooden pegs. Kegs of nails and crockery containing pickles were shoved into corners. Fly paper, black-fouled with dead insects, hung from the ceiling. Ointments, salt, pepper, and vanilla rested inside one of two glass cases. Outside, thirty feet from the screened entrance, on wooden blocks, sat two fifty-gallon drums. A one-gallon measuring can rested atop each drum. The smell of coal oil and kerosene drifted into the store.

Daddy stood near the door, pausing to read a handbill that announced the sale of livestock at a nearby farm. The circular was tacked to the wall adjacent to the door. As he studied the listings, a slow realization that the three men playing cards near the back of the store had heard his protest about the dirty scale and were intently watching, tempered his anger. The three wore work overalls and sat astride wooden crates in front of an overturned keg that served as a table. They were neighbors, familiar and friendly, but they had not greeted my father when we arrived. At the front, a wood-burning stove occupied the space to the left of the only window. Near the stove, barely audible, a small radio was broadcasting a ball game, its signal alternately fading and rising. I withdrew near the radio and listened. The tallest of the men playing cards attempted to mollify the tension. "Jim, this your boy?"

Daddy deflected the inquiry, "How are ya', Max?" His answer was cool, disinterested, final.

Turning to me, he enjoined, "Come on."

As I exited behind him I saw Max look knowingly at his two companions. Ol' Joe did not look up from the newspaper he was reading.

Part Two

The following day dawned to a cold September drizzle. It was a school day and the routines of early morning were long underway when Keith and I were awakened at six o'clock. Daddy had gone to the barn, and Mommy had started a fire in the wood stove that was warming the kitchen. From my bedroom directly above the living room, I could smell the wood smoke, and I heard her feet on the wood floor as she walked to the bottom of the stairwell that led to the upstairs bedrooms. She opened the stairwell door and called that it was time to dress for school.

My brother Keith and I scrambled out of bed, tugged on socks, jeans and flannel shirts and bounded down the stairs. We were in a hurry. There were forty-five minutes to dress, eat, attend to toiletries, gather our books, and walk the one mile to the bus stop. Mommy reminded us that the wood we had split and stacked in the wood box behind the stove was depleted, and that after school, we were to renew her supply. The kitchen was not yet warm, so we slipped on jackets and sat at the table waiting for the bacon, eggs, cocoa and toast that were school morning staples. The linoleum floor felt cold through our socks. After breakfast was served, Mommy began packing our lunches, and by the time we gobbled the last crusts of toast, she had wrapped fried meat, jelly sandwiches, and slices of apple pie in waxed paper and placed them into brown bags.

During summers and school weekends it was customary to gather in the kitchen after breakfast and listen as Daddy read from the Bible, but on school days, before leaving to catch the bus, Mommy stood at the kitchen door, waited until we had bowed our heads, and quietly asked Divine guidance and protection for us. Though we were anxious about being late, these brief delays were a welcome contrast to Daddy's prolonged

The winding mile road that led up the hill behind our barn to our bus stop

meditations.

As we passed the barn, Daddy called, "If the rain stops, we're gonna fill silo when you get home." We were accustomed to work after school, but Daddy's reminder seemed unwarranted. Neither greeting nor encouragement flowed easily from him.

The mile road that led to the bus stop ran up the hill behind our barn and then flattened into a sinuous lane that ran past John Goss's dairy farm. The morning rain had turned to a heavy mist, and we hurried to avoid the damp chill and to be on time. If we arrived a few minutes early, we knew Ol' Joe's store would be open, and that he would have started an early morning fire in his wood stove. On most mornings Keith and I stood inside the store's lone window and watched for the yellow bus. Ours was the first stop on the route to school, so the bus was always empty when the driver opened its folding door and saw us scramble up the two steps. We sat near the back where friends joined us as they were picked up at similar stops on the twenty-mile ride to school.

Our walk to Ol' Joe's store was usually uninterrupted. Sometimes, however, John Goss emerged from his barn to tease, "Ya gonna miss the bus." He enjoyed the joke, and we appreciated his greeting. Most mornings his brown and white beagle lay in front of the house, insouciant, passive. Ironically, a passing car or bicycle seemed to irritate the sleepy dog, and it would race barking into the road for a few yards and then retire once more, but it never bothered pedestrians. If John was near, he sometimes hollered after the barking animal, but it had little effect.

Neither Keith nor I talked as we hustled around the final bend and noted with relief that the bus had not yet arrived. As we crossed the highway Ol' Joe welcomed our arrival by holding open the door to the store. We brushed by him and politely took our place near the window. The radio had been tuned to the morning news, and the telegraphic staccato of Western Union tickers dramatized the somber tone of news from distant London or Berlin or Moscow. The remains of a cup of coffee sat on the counter beside a rumpled jacket. Ol' Joe had seen us coming and had dashed to open the store and start a fire. Providing a warm shelter for school children was obligatory, a tacit reminder of the Golden Rule in a community where kindness was assumed. The absence of overt acknowledgment did not signal ingratitude or indifference, but resulted from the stoic practice of a community as uncomfortable with neighborly applause as with encomium. As we watched and waited, he busied himself with a newspaper. He would postpone his breakfast until after we were on the bus and duty had been discharged.

We sat in abeyance for ten, then twenty minutes, listening for the strain of the bus engine in its climb on the grading that ran past the store. As the minutes passed anxiety that we may have missed the bus began to grow. If the bus had gone Daddy would be angry. We knew that waiting a bit longer in the store was an imposition on Ol' Joe, but we did not wish to spend the day at home. That meant a day of labor. Daddy would put us to work. Besides, Keith and I were dutiful students who completed assignments on time and feared falling behind. Returning to school after an absence was awkward, and the discontinuity required, not only catching up, but living with the presumption that some irrecoverable event or lesson had taken place that rendered us intruders.

A few days earlier, on a misty cool morning, I had come upon a spider's web outside the entrance to the chicken house, glistening in the early light. Tiny beads of moisture on the web shone like glassy jewels. I tried to capture a bit of their beauty by tearing loose some of the strands, and in doing so, poked a hole in its lace. The disfiguration disturbed me. My meddling had disrupted the web's elegance and symmetry. However, it was the revelation of the following morning that more deeply haunted me. I discovered that the web had been repaired. My intrusion was no longer perceptible. It occurred to me that if I did not get to school, my place might be taken. I was dispensable.

Recognizing our growing concern, Ol' Joe put down the paper. Looking over his spectacles he reassured, "Bus hasn't come yet." The hands of his wall clock asserted 7:30.

Like Ol' Joe, the clock labored faithfully at its tedium. Often while we waited during those early mornings, I watched him mount his two-step ladder and push the minute hand ahead until clock time and radio time corresponded. Amid the slow rhythms of his country store, time mattered. Glancing at the clock, he came from his seat behind the counter and opened the door to listen. "It's comin'," he announced.

Keith and I picked up our books, moved outside and waited. In another minute the yellow bus pulled to a stop. Neither Keith nor I spoke to Ol' Joe as we crossed the black top road, mounted the bus steps, and found our seats. As we pulled away I saw him locking the store door and walking back toward his house. On the heart of the virtuous is written duties. Ineffable, tacit, Ol' Joe's kindness left indelible impressions.

SAM ARNOLD

PART ONE

The barn and wagon shed could be seen through the netting of our kitchen screen door. Windows were propped open. Heat, palpable and enervating, produced beads of perspiration above the brow and down the back. The family sat in the stultifying closeness of the room as Daddy read from his Bible. Breakfast had been eaten, tractors fueled, machinery greased and oiled. Mowed grass in the field above the pasture lay waiting to be tedded and raked before noon dinner. The afternoon would be endless, moving heavy bales from field to wagon to hay mow. Daddy's reading droned. Children squirmed restively, awaiting release.

The hum of a motor interrupted the morning. A black coupe turned off the hard dirt road in front of the house and pulled into the driveway next to the barn. Sam Arnold, straw hat in hand, slow with a sixty-year-old's stiffness, crawled from the car. He stood idly for a moment then placed the hat on his head. He fetched from his pocket the paper pouch that held his tobacco, pinched a wad between forefinger and thumb, padded it into his left jowl, then slowly made his way toward the barn.

Sam was one of my mother's many uncles. Farm people. He should have been family, but Daddy said he was an Arnold. That implied provinciality, dullness, ignorance. To make matters worse, Daddy thought the Arnolds were imbued with good fortune. Sam's cornfields were not visited with weeds.

With angled gait Sam continued toward the barn, assuming that a farmer, by this time of day, should be found either in the barn or at the fields. Through the screened door we saw him disappear into the building. Daddy, his attention arrested by the visitor, laid down the Bible. "Hazel, have prayer with the kids. I'll see what Sam wants."

SAM ARNOLD
One of Pappy's twelve siblings

Sam reappeared just as the screen door slammed behind Daddy. He waited as Daddy walked to the end of the yard, opened the hinged gate, and made his way toward the barn.

Mommy did not ask us to kneel for prayer but hurriedly abbreviated her thanksgiving and supplication. She wished to clear the breakfast dishes and unclutter the kitchen should the visitor come to her house. As soon as I heard her, "Amen," I tugged on my baseball cap and headed outside, allowing the kitchen screen door to slam behind me. It was infrequent that a neighbor stopped by, either to visit or attend some business. Regardless, any caller stirred excitement, and I was anxious to hear.

Sam was leaning with both arms against the top of the barn gate waiting for Daddy. He seldom spoke, but his easy smile and slow cud posed no threat. Daddy asked, "How'er ya doin'?"

Sam nodded affirmatively. "Jim, you still want those pigs?"

There was a long pause. "Aw, Sam," Daddy sighed, "I don't think I can take them."

"Why not?" the older man queried.

"Well, to tell you the truth," Daddy hesitated, "I just don't have the money right now."

"Pay me when you get it."

"Naw, I don't wanna do that."

Sam's insistence was emphatic. "Pay me when you get it."

"Sam," Daddy submitted, "I'm gonna level with you. I really appreciate your offer, but I have some bills I haf'ta pay, and," he paused a second time, "I'm gonna haf'ta borrow money, so I'll just wait 'til I kin afford it. Sell those pigs and get yer money. I don't wantcha ta' wait."

Sam spit tobacco juice onto the ground, continuing to chew with thoughtful cadence. There was awkward silence. "Gonna bale hay?" he nodded in the direction of the field where the mown hay lay drying in the early sun.

"Yeah, the boys'll rake it up this morning."

Sam smiled at me in approval. "Good workers," he nodded in my direction. Removing his hat and wiping perspiration from his brow, he warned, "Gonna be a hot one."

He turned back to Daddy, "Well, I'll letcha get at it."

He spit a final time and then moved from the gate and ambled toward the coupe. There was no further exchange. Climbing into the car, he steered back toward the dirt road where billows of dust rose and slowly settled as he faded into the distance.

PART TWO

The following morning at breakfast, Daddy announced that he would be going to the blacksmith shop in McClure, a settlement of houses and shops seven miles east. He told Keith and me to empty the wagon of yesterday's final load of bales, assuring us that he would be back before we could complete the task. Thirty minutes later, family devotions completed, he took two dollars from the kitchen cabinet and made his way to our pickup truck parked behind the barn. The clouds of dust that rose from behind the departing truck signaled an easing of the tension that surrounded us when he was present, and reminded that we had work to do before he returned.

Early morning heat trapped inside the mows was oppressive, and Keith and I sweat-worked to unload the hay. Dry dust hung in the still air. Each bale was bound by two wires that compressed eighty pounds of

A load of baled hay just like the one Keith and I unloaded on the day Sam brought the pigs. This picture was taken a few years later with Susie and Bill atop the load.

dried alfalfa into a four-foot bundle. Bales were lifted by the wires, thrown from the wagon and stacked four tiers high onto the barn floor where they would later be transferred to the mows. Conditioned by long hours and days spent with Daddy, neither Keith nor I spoke as we wrestled with the bales.

The monotony of the work was suddenly broken by the sound of a truck on the dirt road in front of the house. It pulled to a stop in front of the barnyard as the driver shut off the motor, climbed down from the cab and walked toward the open doors where Keith and I continued to unload the hay. The grunts of pigs could be heard coming from the rear of the truck. I jumped from the wagon and walked to the far end of the barn bridge where the driver now waited.

Wearing the same straw hat he had worn yesterday and working his cud of tobacco with the same thoughtful cadence, Sam asked matter-of-factly, "Where's yer dad?"

"Blacksmith."

"When'll he be back?"

"Said he'd be here before we finished unloadin'."

The smell of pigs captured my attention. I motioned in the direction of his truck, "Pigs?"

Typically, two females from each litter were kept for breeding and the others were sold or butchered.

"Yeah," he drawled. For a minute he studied the situation. Then, abruptly, as though discovering a solution, he directed, "Open the gate to yer pig lot."

I hesitated. A day earlier I had listened to Daddy's resistance to accepting the pigs, but now a neighbor's kindness argued for compromise. Sam felt my concern. "I'm gonna back in there and leave these pigs for yer dad," he explained. "You tell 'em not ta' worry 'bout the money." With that he started toward the truck.

Keith had been standing slightly behind me, listening. Now he turned and ran to the heavy wooden gate that opened onto the pig lot. Loosening the leather strap that held it closed, he swung the gate open, then stood aside as Sam slowly backed the truck into the lot. Well inside the gate, the truck stopped and Sam, stepping down from the driver's seat, walked to the rear. I stayed near the barn. Peering from behind the truck bed he looked to where I was standing. Motioning with his head, he asked, "Wanna gimme a hand?" I knew someone had to climb onto the bed and chase the pigs down the ramp, and I knew it was easier for a fourteen-year-old boy to wiggle aboard than it was for a sixty-year-old man. I had been, however, hoping to escape direct involvement should Daddy ask questions.

I took the animal prod Sam extended and jumped aboard the platform. The prod was a simple cane with an arched handle that could be used to catch calves and sheep. Sam let down the ramp, and I began pushing the six shoats toward the chute with the prod. One by one they placed front hooves onto the ramp, then stumbled forward and slid down the gate into the lot. Sniffing and grunting, they ran down the sloped lot toward the muddy creek that lay beyond the gate.

Beech-Nut chewing tobacco

Sam pushed the ramp back onto the bed and closed the truck gate. I handed the prod to him. The odor of perspiration and the fetor of pigs hung on his person. Sweat beaded his brow and dark stains showed under his armpits. He removed his chew and flung it into the pig lot. Methodically, he reached into the breast pocket of his coveralls and took out his pouch of Beech-Nut chewing tobacco.

Leaning against the cab he dug his thumb and forefinger into the sack, lifted the fresh shreds to his mouth, closed the pouch, and stuffed it back into his pocket. The morning heat had become wilting. I was aware that several dozen bales still waited on the wagon bed and that Daddy's return was imminent.

Sam hunkered down in the shade cast by the truck cab. His stubbled face was tranquil, probing. Reaching for the animal prod he began poking the dirt. Without looking up, he asked, "How many cows ya milkin'?"

Keith wandered into the shade next to the barn. I had been waiting to close the gate but now came and sat on the ground near Sam.

"Fifteen. Couple are dry." I wondered at his question. "You have a lotta cows?"

"Same as yer dad."

There was a lengthy pause. "Yer Pappy milked thirty."

His reminder was pregnant with implication. A few years earlier the farm had been doing well, but everything seemed to change after my grandfather died. To Sam's experienced eye, the farm was failing.

"How's yer mom?" he continued to look down at the prod.

When Pappy was alive, Sam and his wife, Mertie, visited regularly and sometimes ate with us. Pappy, Sam's brother, would bring Mammie for the meal and, while the men talked farming, the women caught up on neighborhood news. Mammie and Mertie, best friends since girlhood, fussed over newly made quilts and doilies or recently canned jars of food on the cellar shelves. Sam complimented my mother's cooking.

"Tell yer mom," he offered, "she should stop over with Carrie. Mertie would like a visit."

With that he rose to his feet, the early aches of arthritis evident, and opened the cab door. "I'll letcha git back to yer work. Stay outta the sun." The truck moved forward, through the open gate and onto the driveway. In a minute, summer dust again obscured the departing truck as it disappeared down the road.

DADDY

The penetrating chill of a January evening hung oppressively in the grey twilight of Sunday. Earlier a mixture of rain and sleet had frozen atop ground and against buildings. The temperature had dropped into the teens and an ominous calm portended an approaching snow storm from the North. Frost could be felt in the nostril as darkness fell. It was a time to be inside. However, barn work awaited. Animals had to be fed. Cows had to be milked. Pens and stalls had to be cleaned.

I tugged my way into two pairs of pants, pulled a sweatshirt over my flannel shirt, and zipped my overcoat to the collar. My sheepskin-lined leather aviator cap that my Uncle Bud had given us kids fit snugly over my head, the wool warm against the back of my neck.[2]

Stepping from the kitchen door, I sprinted across the yard and down the slight embankment that led to the barn. Bounding into the barn, I slammed closed the stable door. The barn was pleasant, the familiar odors provoking a synesthesia of warmth. Cows, stanchioned, turned to survey the intruder. Hungry bellies anticipated fodder and grain. Despite the shelter of the barn, their breath condensed in steamy trails, reminding of the cold. I walked to the entrance of the silo and began climbing the forty-foot, cold metal ladder that led to the chopped corn silage. Picking up the metal silage fork propped against the silo wall, I felt its chill through my

leather gloves. I worked quickly, carrying forkfuls to the opening of the entryway, then dumping them into the shaft that ran down to the barn floor. Bushels of silage were needed to feed fifteen milk cows and the four heifers that were tied in the

Tending the stock was a daily routine for Keith and me.

calf pen. I heard Keith enter the barn below, and I knew he would begin

---

2. Uncle Bud was Pappy's oldest, nine years older than my mother. He had completed aviator lessons and on a summer afternoon in the early 1950s, he landed the piper cub he was flying in the field in front of our house. We kids were in such awe of his aviator's cap, goggles, and jumpsuit, that he gave us his cap.

to carry the feed to stalls. Barn work was carried on methodically without conversation. There was seldom a need to hurry, since much of the work waited until milking was completed. Everything about farming seemed to require patience.

Experience told me just how much silage was needed. Finished in twenty minutes, I climbed out of the silo and descended the metal ladder. Keith had nearly finished carrying silage to the stalls, so I opened the feed bin stationed in the entryway in front of the manger, found the feed scoop, dug into the ground mixture of corn, wheat, oats and molasses, and began spreading the "chop" over the mound of silage in front of each stall. The work was routine, my mind engaged elsewhere until I heard Daddy arrive and enter the milk house. He assembled the electric milking machines and began the systematic process of attaching the teat cups to the udders of, first one cow, and then the next. It would be another forty minutes until milking was completed.

Keith and I took turns nightly, one of us throwing hay down from the mows while the other fed the pigs and chickens. The hay-mow rested above the stables, out of the warmer portion of the barn. It was lit by a single dim bulb. Neither of us liked leaving the lower level for the isolation and confinement of the cold and dark upper barn, which consisted of a central threshing floor, flanked by mows, each having a granary at the rear. On the lower level, the stables and stalls, separated by alleyways, housed the cows. Given a choice, Keith and I always opted to feed the pigs and chickens, even though it, too, meant going into the cold and working alone. Somehow, the howling wind and creaking boards of the upper barn, in the darkness of winter nights, was foreboding.

All barn work, however, was ancillary to milking the cows. Selling milk paid the bills and put food on the table. Its importance was underscored by Daddy's reluctance to trust us boys with such critical work, fearing that we would not properly "strip" empty the udders. An unemptied udder could result in mastitis, an infection that spoiled the milk and could result in the death of the cow. He usually concentrated on the milking and depended upon Keith and me to attend to appurtenant labors.

The most strenuous activity, morning and evening, was cleaning the "drop," a long trough that ran along the rear of the stalls where the cows were stanchioned. It collected both the solid and liquid waste that had to be carried by shovel to the manure spreader which was pulled by tractor to its station in front of the open barn door. We could not begin the process until Daddy finished milking and all other chores were completed, because opening one of the barn doors on such a cold night resulted in sweeping drafts of cold air that was neither good for cattle nor comfortable for us.

After milking was out of the way, calves had to be bucket-fed "Calf-A", a mixture of milk and supplement purchased from the mill, and pens had to be bedded with fresh straw. Finally, the tractor had to be hitched to the manure spreader, the heavy tracked door of the straw shed pushed open, and manure had to be carried to the spreader.

The tractor and spreader were parked beneath the barn overshot, an eight-foot projection of the barn's upper story that hung above and outside the straw shed. Pulling the spreader into position involved starting the cold tractor motor and sliding open a seven by ten foot, two-hundred-pound door. The door was constructed of timber sufficiently heavy to prevent the large animals from pushing it open. Although it slid on metal tracks, moving it required dropping a shoulder, using the weight of the body as leverage, and exerting a full effort.

The wind had picked up, and the first flakes of the norther swirled as I climbed onto the tractor seat. At the same time Keith futilely attempted to push against the sliding barn door, but the earlier rain had frozen the heavy door onto its metal track. He began alternately throwing his weight against the door and kicking it, trying to break loose the ice. In spite of his efforts, it remained fastened to the track. Atop the tractor seat, I turned the key in the ignition. The engine groaned, rolled slowly over once and stopped. In the bitter cold, the machine's oil had turned to sludge, and the battery was unable to start the motor. I knew Daddy would be angry if I was unable to start the tractor, because it meant he had to interrupt the milking, start the tractor by hand, and then wait for us to finish cleaning the barn before we could close up and retire to a warm house for the night. On the other hand, continuing to press the starter would drain the battery. A damaged battery would create financial strain if it had to be replaced. I jumped down from the seat, walked toward the stable, and braced for his outburst. I knew his temper would be on edge. Countless times, Keith and I had witnessed his reaction to adversity. His equilibrium seemed always to teeter on a precipice. A weak battery, a jammed door, or the oncoming storm might set the flint to tinder. Once kindled, it would turn to fury, resulting in broken machines, wounded cattle, and scarred emotions.

He took the news as though a thousand-pound weight had been

placed on his chest. Sighing the sigh of the condemned, he set down the milking machine he was holding, strode to the entryway and walked out into the cold night toward the wagon shed. The tractor crank was kept atop a bench in the shed, and he quickly emerged with the handle in hand. No word was spoken as he determinedly walked to the front of the tractor and inserted the crank. Starting the tractor with a crank was an ordeal. It required a man's strength and it was somewhat dangerous because the handle sometimes failed to disengage. A recoiling handle could break a wrist.

Directing me to climb onto the tractor seat, turn on the ignition key, and open the gasoline feed, he gave the crank a violent turn. The motor sputtered but failed to catch. A second and third turn failed. He ordered me to adjust the choke. Rage began playing with his psyche. In a frenzy he gave the crank three continuous turns. Simultaneously, the engine started and the crank kicked hard, striking across his wrist. Enraged, he heaved the crank toward the pig pen. For a long moment he stood silent, eyes closed, teeth clenched against the pain. Then, determined, he turned to open the sliding door and gave it a hard shove. It remained fixed to the track. The culmination of multiple frustrations became maddening. He retreated a few paces, then in spontaneous fury, ran and smashed into the door. It jumped from the track and crashed to the cement floor, breaking its small glass window. He had also hurt his shoulder, but refused to acknowledge the injury. Instead, he walked back into the barn leaving Keith and me to move the broken door, pull the tractor and spreader into the barn, and begin cleaning the stable. He milked the few remaining cows in strained silence, went into the milk house where he rinsed the milking machines, then rigidly slammed closed the milk house door and disappeared in the direction of the house.

It had begun snowing heavily. For thirty minutes, armed with shovels, we carried manure to the spreader, opened bales of straw, and bedded the cows. Normally we opened the stanchions and chased the cows out of the stable to the straw shed while we scattered the straw, but now the broken door let in the cold and snow, and the hour being late, we simply threw straw under each cow and turned out the lights. It would take a few minutes more to drive the spreader to an outlying field and empty its contents, but the barn work was finished.

I knew there would be constricted silence in the house for the remainder of the evening. By the time I would empty the spreader and step out of the cold into the warm kitchen, younger children would have escaped to their rooms, and Mommy would have already felt the sting of his clamor against life's circumstances, against the world, and being the most palpable of its objects, against her. I knew, too, that in the morning, activity would blur and blot the previous evening. There would be no reference to previous events, no conversation. Ironically, I knew Daddy privately suffered remorse for his temper, but as though he were handicapped, his disposition lacked a mechanism for apology. Locked into his own prison, absolution resulted from engagement with the people of his church, his Bible study, but not from relationships with family and neighbors.

KENNY LOHT

New days should bring new beginnings: clean, unencumbered, bursting with possibilities. Yesterday's chaos should not be visited upon today's promise. History, however, teaches that the consequences of yesterday's sins reach beyond the immediate hour.

The morning broke cold and still. Roosters crowed another day's arrival. The world lay glistening in a veil of white. Banks of newly drifted snow gave strange and beautiful shapes to familiar buildings and woods. Birds flitted in and out of shelters, foraging. From the barn could be heard the rattle of stanchions as hungry cattle waited. Outside the house, the scraping of a shovel on the cement walk meant that Daddy was clearing a path to the barn.

The sliding barn door still lay on its side as I entered the barn. Snow had drifted over it and blown into the straw shed. Daddy was in the milk house, putting the milking machines together and preparing to milk.

"Throw down silage," he instructed. It was Keith's turn to climb into the silo, but he had not yet made his way to the barn, and protest was not permitted. Keith and I would have to settle our dispute on our own time. I climbed the metal ladder and began working. Fifteen minutes passed. "That's enough," he shouted up the silo shaft. I climbed down and saw that Keith was already pouring chop over each cow's portion of silage.

Daddy emerged from the milk house, carrying a milking machine in each hand. He opened the switch that operated the electrical mechanism, stepped into the first stall, and attached the first milker's hose to the vacuum line that ran overhead. Bending down, he fastened the four cups onto the first cow's teats. He then picked up the other machine and repeated the process in the next stall. Milking was tedium.

Snowbound on a Decatur Township farm in the 1940s and 50s meant hauling milk cans to the main road by horse or tractor or, if neither were possible, feeding it to animals which resulted in a serious loss of revenue. The milkman could not make his way to some of the barns and milk houses that lay back among secondary roads and dirt lanes which were not plowed. A few farmers rigged tractors so that the ten-gallon cans could be placed aboard and transported to opened roads by driving across fields where the snow was less deep. Daddy had not yet been able to configure an apparatus to fit our tractors, so on this morning, he was resigned to financial injury.

By 6:30 am Daddy had finished milking and was washing the machines in the milk house. Three ten-gallon cans of fresh milk sat on the milkhouse floor while three additional cans from last night's milking waited in the cold water of the milk cooler. Some would be fed to pigs, but most of the precious commodity would be dumped into a snowy bank where it would freeze and eventually soak into the ground.

It was my turn to feed the chickens and pigs. I had just left the barn and was slogging my way to the pig pen when I heard the distinctive putt-putt sound of a John Deere tractor coming across the field in back of our house. I stopped and waited. Kenny Loht, a neighbor, came into full view as the tractor drove onto the main road and then into our driveway. He shut off the tractor motor, jumped down, grinned in my direction, and asked, "Are you the one who brought all this snow?" I laughed at his friendliness. He seemed always in a good mood.

I thought him a pleasant mystery. Everyone in the valley knew him as "Fuzzy." From May to October he worked shirtless in the fields, exposing a thick growth of curly black hair that covered his darkly tanned and heavily muscled body. On hot days, chaff and dust, embedded in perspiration, stuck on his chest and back, appearing grotesquely uncomfortable, although he seemed oblivious. Not wearing a shirt ran counter to the Christian modesty of neighbors, but his good nature and genuine affability excused the anomaly.

In spite of the neighborly dispensation granted Kenny, Daddy and Mommy required us boys to wear shirts, and directed that we were never call him "Fuzzy." Respect demanded that he be addressed properly.

"Where's yer dad?"

"Milk house," I stated.

He started for the milk house, and I hurried to complete my assignment, not wanting to miss the excitement of having a visitor on a morning when we were snowbound.

When I returned Daddy and Kenny were lifting the three full cans from the cooler. The other three cans from the morning milking stood nearby. I waited near the doorway, careful not to get in their way.

"I can get only three cans on the tractor," Kenny explained to Daddy. "I'll take the three and come right back for the others. If I hurry I can get all six out to the road before Fred comes."

I could tell Daddy was delighted with this unsolicited and unexpected gesture. Resignation was displaced by possibility, despair by promise. Fred Arnold was our milkman, but his flatbed truck was unable to negotiate the drifted snow in our farm lane. It was incumbent upon us to get the milk to Fred or lose a day's supply.

Now, a savior had arrived. Kenny Loht was attempting to be a good neighbor by salvaging at least a part of our milk production. His tractor could carry three cans. If he hurried, he might save all six.

Kenny hoisted a can of milk and made his way toward the tractor. He set it on a small platform behind the seat, then turned to help Daddy who was carrying the second can. The two men lifted the next can into place beside the first, then brought the final can, careful not to spill the valuable liquid, and tied it securely onto the platform. The urgency of the moment precluded conversation. As soon as the three cans were tied in place, Kenny jumped aboard the seat, switched on the motor, and headed the tractor back across the field that would take him to Fred Arnold's truckstop.

I had not yet fed the chickens, so while Daddy waited for Kenny, I went about my work. In the entryway to the chicken house were stored the bags of chicken feed, cracked corn, and crushed sea shells that were fed twice each day to the brood of chickens. It was easy work. I emptied the feed and corn into the long metal feeders, placed the seashells into their dispensers, rinsed and refilled the drinking fountains, and was exiting when I again heard the putt-putt of Kenny's tractor in the field behind our house.

Daddy had moved the remaining three cans outside the milkhouse, and it took but a few minutes for the two men to load the tractor a second time.

"Thanks again," Daddy shouted above the loud putt-putt of the tractor motor. Kenny immediately mounted the tractor and began turning around for his departure. Daddy walked back into the milkhouse to close up.

As Kenny pulled alongside where I was watching, he paused and leaned toward at me.

"What happened to the barn door?" he asked rhetorically. He smiled, and I knew that he knew. All our neighbors knew. I liked Kenny. He always said hello and gave me some time, but I was embarrassed by the innuendo. The curiosity surrounding Daddy's temper extended to every neighbor. Their reaction to Mommy and us kids was fraught with pathos, thinking us innocent victims of fateful circumstance. As Kenny drove away he turned back to me as though we shared a secret and winked.

—————

JOHN GOSS

The dog lay outside the stable door in the January cold, waiting to be fed. A smallish shepherd, he was used to Daddy's sharp commands and vicious kicks. He was used, as well, to the table scraps that were thrown carelessly beneath the corn crib where he stayed nights or dumped onto the cement floor outside the stables during the day. The crib stood elevated on four stone legs so that, in summer, the dog could use the crawl space as a refuge. On hot days the crib was rife with the smell of dog. In winters, he found his way to the wagon shed and crept under the farm wagon. On this January night, he intuitively knew there would be no food until the barn work was completed. He waited outside the stables.

John Goss was kindly disposed toward animals, people, and life. He was ever ready to help his neighbors.

Besides the unwarranted abuse he

suffered from negligence and passivity, the dog seemed disposed to a foul mood. When visitors or neighbors appeared, he bared his teeth and snarled. Frequently, callers remained in their cars until Daddy chained the shepherd to the crib. He was not permitted in the stables. We had for long watched the livestock tense in the presence of the dog, and often he nipped at the heels of horses and cows. Neighbors said he was mad, but Daddy liked the idea of having a dog, so the vagary was tolerated. His presence assured that rats, weasels, and other varmints were scarce. Explicably the dog was afraid of Daddy. When Daddy spoke, the dog cowered and stealthily stole away. When he was directed to fetch the cows from the meadow, Keith or I ran quickly to open both the meadow gate and the barnyard door so that fleeing cattle could escape the snarling animal and pass into the barn without breaking down the portals. The second the dog appeared in the pasture, cows laden with heavy udders, sprinted for the safety of the barnyard and away from the menacing dog.

Shep was a threat to us children only at feeding time. Mommy placed table scraps on a tin pie plate and told us to carry it to the dog. Either Keith or I cautiously approached the wagon shed or corn crib, waiting for the low growl. If the dog was tied, we crept close, threw the plate in front of him, and retreated to the safety of the yard. If he was loose, we hurled the platter in his direction and raced for the house. Neither of us volunteered to feed him.

Now he lay outside the stable door.

Inside the barn, chores were concluding. Cows had been milked and were being released from metal stanchions to exit into the barnyard while stalls were bedded with fresh straw, and mangers were cleaned and filled with new hay. An older Holstein was in heat. Keith and I knew that meant Daddy would leave us to finish the rest of the work while he drove to John Goss's neighboring farm to ask John for the use of his bull. A cow remained in heat for only eight to ten hours and required immediate attention if breeding were to be successful. The survival of a dairy farm rested upon replenishment of the herd. In a little while John would comply with Daddy's request and walk his bull to our farm.

John Goss and his family always greeted Keith and me when we passed his house. John was genial, good-natured and enjoyed lively banter. When I walked home evenings after a ball game, he would appear at the entrance to his barn and ask, "Did'ja hit a home run?" Sometimes I stopped for a few minutes and talked, or watched him milk his cows, and wondered at his manner. He never seemed to be angry. He stroked his cows and spoke in low tones as if they shared an understanding. His affection for animals was genuine.

Daddy was gone for less than thirty minutes. By the time he reappeared cows had been watered and were back in their stalls. The straw shed, where the watering trough stood, was empty except for the cow in rut. Shep had not moved from his place outside the stables. A calf, recently weaned, poked its head between the wood slats of its pen and called for its mother. The older cow turned where she was stanchioned and stared. The calf had become a frustration for Daddy. Three other calves had learned to drink readily from a bucket, but this fourth resisted. Daddy was resolved to forcefully wean the recalcitrant animal.

In the milk house he dipped a ladle into a milk can and emptied milk into a bucket. He then added a scoop of powdery supplement and stirred the slop until the powder dissolved. The bucket contained a rubber teat from which a young calf could suck milk. He approached the calf pen with patience spent. I followed him, holding the bucket. He entered and strode to the frightened calf that had cowered into one of the pen's corners and faced away from him. Straddling the calf, he grabbed its neck, lifting it up and backward until its front legs were airborne. His temper was frightening. He twisted the head so that the animal lost its balance, fell on its side and was pinned to the floor. Calves were weaned with a teated bucket.

Sitting astride the fallen calf, he placed the index and middle finger of his left hand into its nostrils and with his right hand forced open the mouth. At that signal I squirted milk from the bucket teat into the calf's mouth. The animal struggled to breathe normally. Foam came from the nostrils. I squirted a second time and a third. The calf swallowed. I inserted the teat into the open mouth. Daddy relaxed his hold. The animal swallowed but did not suck. The process was repeated. A third attempt was unsuccessful. His patience exhausted, Daddy threw the calf aside. "She'll drink when she's good and thirsty," he cursed and exited the pen.

I took the bucket to the milk house, covered it with a clean cloth, and went into the stable to wait for John. Our obligations ended, Keith went to the house. I stayed with Daddy because he needed someone to signal him

The calf's nose was wet with milk from the bucket.

when John appeared with the bull. I knew also that the dog lay just inside the gate, and when John appeared, Shep would snarl and try to nip the bull's rear ankles. Only Daddy would be able to make the dog move away from the bull. If the bull broke away, it could be dangerous. I sat atop a stack of feedbags at the front of the manger, watching the cows wrap long tongues around mouthfuls of hay, and waited.

In the interim, Daddy had climbed up into the silo and was throwing down silage for the next morning. Both of us knew that John needed time to complete his own barn work before he would be able to snap the bull's nose ring into a staff and lead the burly animal the half-mile to our farm. Ten minutes passed when I heard the jingling of the bull's chain and knew that John was coming into the barn. The bull had been tied to the barnyard gate away from the dog, and John, seeing me, matter-of-factly stated, "Denny, ya haf'ta move the dog."

I hollered up the silo shaft to Daddy, "John's here."

John and I waited for Daddy to climb down. When he appeared the two men exchanged cursory greetings and Daddy asked, "Where's the bull?"

"Ya haf'ta move the dog," John explained.

Daddy walked outside, opened the gate, and walked threateningly toward the dog. "Git outta here," he shouted. The dog obsequiously tucked its tail, lowered its head and slunk away toward the pig lot where a missing slat in the fence allowed him to crawl through. He disappeared into the darkness.

John again fastened his staff to the ring in the bull's nose, untethered it from the hitching post, and began leading it toward the straw shed. Inside, the gate was again closed. John removed the staff, and the bull was freed to be with the cow.

The two men and I retired to the stable. The top of the Dutch door that separated the stable from the straw shed was opened so the men could monitor the bull's activity. John attempted small talk, "Jim, how many ya milkin'?"

"Fifteen," Daddy answered. There was awkward silence.

John was standing against the calf pen. The unfed calf poked her nose between the boards and began sucking at John's pant leg. John spoke to the calf, "Not weaned yet, huh?" He squatted and let the calf take his finger.

Feeling a need to explain the calf's behavior, Daddy complained, "She won't take the nipple, John, so she can just go hungry for the night."

John protested mildly as though he were chastising a favorite child, "Jim, ya gotta feed em." He paused. "Where's the bucket?" he asked.

Daddy walked to the milk house and retrieved the bucket. He handed it to John, "If you can get 'er to drink, go ahead. She wouldn't drink for me."

John took the bucket, opened the pen gate and went inside. He set the bucket aside and slowly, cautiously, approached the young calf. The innocent critter stood facing him. "Now, now," he soothed. "Yer hungry, ain't cha?" He patted its head. As it quieted, he reached for the cloth that covered the bucket. Placing it over the calf's eyes, she momentarily resisted, but John quickly brought the nipple of the bucket to her mouth and squirted a spray of the liquid against it. The tongue licked, and as John gently pushed the teat into its mouth, the animal began sucking. As it did so John removed the cloth and continued to pet the calf. Daddy said nothing as he watched John patiently tend the calf until the milk disappeared. Finally, he handed the empty bucket to Daddy. The other calves stood in a far corner surveying the activity. With an impish smile, John stepped from the pen. He had made a point. "Learned that from Sam," he offered.

The men resumed their vigil, intermittently watching the cow and the bull, but mostly passing the time in polite conversation. Fifteen minutes passed. Leaning against the lower portion of the door, John grew quiet. Straightening himself he studied Daddy mysteriously, then asked, "Jim, what'sa matter with yer dog?"

"Whad'dya mean?" Daddy seemed surprised.

"Nasty," the older man retorted, "He's gonna bite somebody."

"Na-a-w-w," said Daddy, "He growls, but I don't think he would bite."

"I dunno," responded John. "Everybody's afraid of him." He paused. "How'd he get that way?"

"Whad'dya mean?" Daddy grew defensive.

"Do the kids hit him? Seems to me he's scared."

Daddy didn't answer.

It had been an hour since Keith had gone to the house. Fatigue had settled over the long day. Satisfied that the bull had successfully performed, John took the staff in hand and walked into the straw shed. The bull permitted the staff to be clipped to its ring and the neighbor led the way out through the gate.

Closing the gate behind the departing bull, Daddy called, "John, thanks. I'll pay you tomorrow."

"Take care a' that calf," he reminded. He gave a tug against the bull's halter and the two began moving toward the road that would take them home. When he had gone as far as the wagon shed, he turned, momentarily surveying the area, and spoke a final time, "Take care a' that dog. Don't treat him so bad."

PAPPY

July 4th was celebrated with a picnic as members of Lawvers and Samuels Churches conjoined at the far end of our cow pasture, amid a grove of oak and maple. Benches, folding chairs, and tables were carried from the churches and set up in likely places of shade. Friends and neighbors, resplendent in freshly washed aprons and overalls, bonnets and straw hats, arrived by carriage and car, amid throaty hellos and welcoming hands. It was a holiday for quiet conversation, good-natured argument and reminiscence. Hampers laden with country food were set on planks placed on trestles and covered with white cloths. Ladies, up since dawn, labored, not only to feed their families, but to make certain visitors and neighbors were fed. The satisfying pleasures of good times were demonstrated in an opulence of fried chicken, fruity pies, and layered cakes.

Reverend Zechman, pastor of the Samuels congregation, arrived. He served as the *de facto* guest of honor and the invocatory. The Pastor and his wife surveyed the gathering, moving cordially among the families, stooping to touch children, shaking hands with men, and complimenting ladies. The patronization was welcome. Plates overflowed with slices of ham, ladles of potato salad, and scoops of baked beans. Jugs of cold lemonade and crocks of home-made root beer sweated in the warm sun and were emptied by thirsty hands. A good time was being had by all.

In the backwaters of rural America this was the surviving patriotic ripple of the concussion of revolution that occurred two hundred years earlier. Yesteryear's conviction had been paid in blood. It demanded tribute. Annual salutation had spawned convention, first thoughtful and somber, now, eroded by decades, festive and jubilant.

The meal finished, farmers, jowls swelled with tobacco, gathered near the weather-beaten wooden platform that would serve as a bandstand for the three o'clock concert. A few sat on folding chairs, others leaned against tree trunks or sat with backs braced against stumps and spoke in languorous tones. From time to time an animated voice argued the superiority of an animal or crop, but the afternoon drifted.

Reverend Zechman approached the circle of men at the bandstand. John Goss sat, legs folded, on one of the chairs, poking between his teeth with a stem of timothy grass. He spoke. "Reverend, did you get enough to eat?"

The Pastor patted his stomach appreciatively and smiled. "I guess I'll find some shade here with you boys." He offered to no one in particular, "Haf'ta save a seat for the missus, you know. She wants ta' have a good seat for the concert."

The minister's college education and refined manner evoked no admiration from the farmers. Instead they regarded him with a curious pathos usually reserved for the weak. Suits and stiff collars were acquaintances, not companions. Regardless, Reverend Zechman enjoyed the company and looked forward to the concert.

The concert was a recent custom. In the years following Daddy and Mommy's move to the farm, Daddy had encouraged his relatives and friends to Sunday dinners, especially during the summer when food could be prepared and served picnic style. Mommy readily acquiesced. One of the relatives was his uncle, Russell Riegle, director of the Lewistown Band. The musicians were an assorted collection of amateurs from the county seat who practiced the marches of John Philip Sousa and paraded for local affairs. During one such dinner Russell volunteered the efforts of his band at the Samuel-Lawver's Church Picnic. In a short time band members became eager participants, enjoying the friendliness and food and the deference accorded by simple country folk. The concert thus became a mixture of patriotic and religious music highlighting the day's activities.

Beyond the mingling of men at the bandstand, older women cleared tables and gathered in groups of three and four, their conversation flowered with compliments and punctuated with knowing looks: a daughter-in-law pregnant again, new curtains hanging from a neighbor's window, pies to be baked for tomorrow's dinners. Younger women gossiped while attending small children. Above the scattered picnic sounds the day moved passively.

Charles Arnold, my grandfather, joined the group of men. "Pappy" was Mommy's father. A strong emotional bond had formed between him and his youngest daughter long before my father married her. However, after the young couple accepted Pappy's offer to live in the same house and share the farm work, the relationship suffered continual abrasions resulting from conflict between father and son-in-law. Pappy was an inveterate traditionalist, his ideas ensconced in years of successful farming. Corn was planted the first week of May; silos were filled the third week of September. Hay was harvested the first week of June, wheat the second week of July, oats two weeks afterward. Obdurate, laconic, private, Pappy presumed his deadlines and methods were understood and would be observed.

Inexperienced and anxious, Daddy experimented and guessed at procedures. When his efforts failed to meet expectations, the older man intruded, climbing aboard the tractor himself, criticizing mistakes, and sometimes taking the bucket from Daddy's hand. Petulant, irascible, exasperated, Daddy's wounds festered. His responses became barbed and personal. Weeks passed as the two avoided each other. They worked separate fields, divided the labor, seldom spoke. As a result, the bond between father and daughter became strained, uneasy. Mommy found herself a mediator. She and her mother commiserated. Mammie was asked to "talk to Pappy." Despite the women's efforts, the chasm widened. The families stopped taking meals together. The trivial became formal. Introverted from youth, Daddy's insecurities erupted with displays of temper, feelings of inferiority.

Just as his farming routine had become entrenched, so Pappy's attending church on Sundays, although perfunctory, was habitual. He did this, not because it filled a vacuum in his life, but because he held the notion that a good man was a church-goer. It was a social and moral requirement. If an additional prod was necessary, he was reminded that women did not go to church unescorted unless they were widows or spinsters. My grandmother would have worshipped without him, and that would have meant embarrassment. Thus, sitting in the same seat, in the same pew every Sunday morning, Mammie and Pappy were regular. Regular, too, were the pokes in Pappy's ribs as Mammie fought unsuccessfully to prevent him from snoring.

Unlike Mammie, Pappy had not grown up a church-goer. In fact, his mom and dad never darkened the doorway of a church, though they were neither profligate nor apostate. Moral and wholly respected by neighbors and friends, they felt no need to endure a lengthy sermon on their day of rest. Pappy answered critics simply, "God helps them that helps themselves. I'm as good as any man." Case closed.

Ironically, it was church attendance that had exacerbated Pappy's irritation with Daddy several years earlier. For a brief time after moving to the farm, Mommy and Daddy had spent Sunday mornings with Pappy and Mammie at Samuel's Church, but the sermons seemed bromidic and staid. The young couple were new Christians, having recently "gone forward" during revival services at the Brethren Church in Lewistown where Daddy's mother was a member. Jimmy Johnson, the guest evangelist under whom noted minister, Billy Graham, had been converted, preached a series of emotionally-charged sermons that convinced many, including my parents, to accept Jesus as their Savior. The excitement of those messages was in stark contrast to the soporific homilies of Pastor Zechman at Samuel's. Thus, when my parents failed to appear in their accustomed place on Sunday mornings, it was left for the older couple to provide answers. Pappy, finding little that distinguished one church from any other, fumbled for explanation in the face of curious inquiry.

On this July 4th holiday, his discomfort was compounded, first by the presence of the Reverend, and then the idleness of a day when his farm work had to be postponed for no profitable reason. Finding a seat near John Goss, his mind was detached from the friendly conversation, absorbed with cows to be milked, grain to be bindered, gardens to be hoed. His absorption was interrupted by John.

"Charl, whad'dya think a yer brother sittin' here with the preacher?"

Pappy smirked, recognizing Sam, but gave no reply.

"Sam, when's the last time you was ta' church?" John kidded. The men enjoyed Sam's unease.

Sam smiled, continuing to chew his tobacco methodically. He turned to his brother. "Charl, that's a good stand a wheat ya have in the field nex'ta the road."

"We're gonna open it tomorrow," Pappy responded. "Jim planted that."

Everyone knew Daddy as "Jim." He had not sat with the men. Farming conversation for him was tinged with ennui. Unlike them, love for the field and fold was alien. He had learned a bit of the jargon, could explicate some nuances of crop rotation and argue the advantages of alfalfa over clover, but his exchanges were often contentious and defensive. The fact that these men enjoyed the bantering, that their wrangling simply filled time, went unnoticed. His sense of inferiority had birthed a cynic. Since attending the Brethren Church, he had become guarded, distant. He felt the pariah. He had not heard the compliment. Panegyric, it might have been anodyne to a crumbling relationship.

Daddy visited, instead, with Russell Riegel, withdrawing to a more comfortable sphere, not with neighbors or in-laws, but with his uncle. Ironically, Russell represented still another circle for whom Daddy felt disdain — town dwellers, a subclass of humanity whose disposition he considered cavalier, whose character was allegedly negotiable, and whose behavior he viewed contemptuously as fluctuating between patronage and subversion. Despite these properties, Russell was somehow more agreeable company than these neighbors — these farmers whose fundamental transgression was simply that they were farmers. Perhaps, the attraction lay in the fact that Russell seldom if ever conversed. Instead he lectured, dismissing the comments and queries of listeners by speaking over and above their interruptions. A peacock without feathers, he boasted *ad infinitum*. Conversation was both unnecessary and futile as Daddy sat with Russell.

Thus, in a larger sense, Daddy sat alone, away from everyone—withdrawn from both the kidding that somehow pricked the tender bruises of old wounds, and the applause that might have formed the substance of needed friendship and self-esteem. His behavior was, in the end, habitual avoidance and renunciation of persons and practices that were, in reality, distortions of his own coloration. The acceptance and alliance he so much desired resided in his own neighborhood, needing only his willingness to be a good neighbor.

KEITH KIDNAPPED
◇◇◇◇◇◇◇◇◇◇◇◇◇◇◇◇◇◇◇◇◇◇◇◇◇◇◇◇◇◇◇◇◇◇◇◇◇◇

D addy served on the Chief Logan Joint High School Board of Education from September 1954 to June 1961. Ostensibly, his reasons for doing so resulted from exasperation over increasing school taxes and transportation costs. When asked for the reason he threw his hat into the political ring, he assumed a rather truculent defiance declaring, "Somebody had'a put a stop to those politicians." His motives were not again questioned.

An incident in the fall of 1956, however, might have revealed his actual incentive. He was in back of the barn on a warm late afternoon, greasing the fittings of our Papec silo filler, anticipating the arrival of his two oldest boys from school, so the three of them could begin filling the silo with corn silage. As he reached beneath the machine Mommy shouted from the house fifty yards distant, "Jim, you have a phone call."

She was standing on the front porch steps outside the kitchen screen door. For several moments he did not respond. She knew that he had heard her, but she also knew that a second appeal might badger him. When badgered his retort might be heard, not only over the phone, but throughout the surrounding countryside. Judiciously she walked to the edge of the yard. Placing both hands on the railing of the yard gate, she obsequiously pleaded, "Jim?"

The reception of phone calls at our house was a study in personality and disposition. If Daddy was away, calls were a welcome respite. Mommy enjoyed conversing with the neighbors. Answering the phone meant catching up with community life: the Hostetlers had a new horse; the Goss's dog died; or Aunt Effie had visited Uncle Reuben last Sunday. Ladies on our ten-party-line expected and welcomed three or four friends to pick up receivers and listen in. Advice to alleviate sore throat, tomato blight, and molting hens was readily dispensed. A telephone was

Our wall telephone connected to a ten-party line.

a good thing.

Daddy, on the other hand, was not so disposed. A phone was a disturbance; a violation of privacy. Folks got along fine before the arrival of talk boxes; people were friendlier, happier, and it might be added, electrical lines strung through fields and along highways changed weather patterns. Rainfall decreased, crops failed, and cows went dry. The new technology was provoking.

"Who is it?" he shouted back irritably, certain that the caller wanted his money or his time.

"It's the school. Keith missed the bus."

Keith and I were ninth graders at Burnham Junior High School, twenty miles from our farm. We were model students in scholarship and decorum, completing assignments on time and behaving ourselves. Neither of us was troublesome. We were, however, "Decatur kids," a euphemism for "farm kids." As such we were bused from farms and hamlets to Burnham, a metropolis of some two thousand souls who were every bit as blue collar as farm people, but had the distinction of living in a town. This provided subtle arrogation for social conceit, and in my father, instilled resentment.

Daddy had been kneeling, grease stained, his hands black from the grease pump. He arose reluctantly, considering possibilities.

Plainly annoyed, he scolded, "Well, whadda they want me to do?"

Mommy didn't answer.

He started toward the house, stopping at the fifty-gallon gasoline drum to pick up a soiled rag and wipe his hands. The drum, fitted with a pump handle, hose, and nozzle, supplied precious fluid for the farm tractors, cars, and trucks. He gave the handle a half-turn and let the fluid wet his hands and wrists. Rubbing them together to loosen the grime, he turned the rag to its clean side and wiped them dry.

He didn't speak as he brushed past Mommy and strode determinedly to the house.

Mommy followed at a distance, listening from the porch but not entering the house. Her concern was not with the interruption of her activity or the possible inconvenience of driving twenty miles to rescue her second-born, but simply for Keith's well-being. Where was he? Was he sick or injured? Did he need a ride? Personal and logistical circumstances were secondary.

Daddy aggressively picked up the phone. Accusingly, he asked, "Who is this?"

At three o'clock each school day afternoon, a secretary in the administration office opened the speaker to the school's public address system and announced the arrival of school buses. Dismissed, students hurried from classrooms, ran to lockers, and exited the two story building to board their particular bus.

Monitors patrolled the bus area. They were teachers cursed with the most servile of after-school assignments. Inattentive to duty, they usually retreated to some remote area where, in small groups, they commiserated while condemning administrators.

Meanwhile, students in flight from the throes of the classroom, fought to be first to board their buses so that they might experience the pleasure of sitting at the back of the bus, far from the scrutiny of a bus driver whose misanthropy and distrust centered on teenagers. These were the malcontents, the juvenile delinquents, the criminal element. They hung out in school bathrooms, smoked cigarettes, and wrote sexual epithets on bathroom walls. When threatened, they retaliated. Not with sticks and stones, but with stealth. When a teacher's back was turned, they made unintelligible remarks or obscene gestures. They were regularly assigned detention, but "skipped." Keith and I sat nowhere near the rear of the bus.

Keith and I were the first to board the school bus each morning for the one-hour ride to junior high school.

A dozen yellow buses were parallel-parked next to the curb of the street that bounded the school. The bus that took us home to Decatur Township was half-filled when I boarded. Beckoned by a few familiar faces, I chose a seat near the front on the street side of the bus, away from the heavies in the rear. Keith arrived a few minutes later and sat on the curb side three seats in back of me.

Although Keith and I were in the same grade, I was a year older. Conventional wisdom decreed that brothers sharing the same classes were destined to be social misfits and academic failures, wandering the earth as aliens suffering identity crises. Thus, we had different courses with different teachers in different locations. I was tracked as an "academic" student, while Keith bore the shame of a "regular" or "general" student. His label resulted in a different set of friends and classes, and cruelly, the social stigma of lower specie.

The junior high school principal was James "Jimmie" Leader. Lacking rapport with both students and teachers, he closeted himself in his recessed office where he was seldom seen and less frequently heard from. On occasion he appeared in corridors as students passed from one class to another, glowering with the proverbial chip prominent on his shoulder. Obstreperous seventh graders cowered in his presence, but ninth graders had long learned that his bark incurred no bite whatsoever. The more brazen of them were openly recalcitrant, reducing him to a caricature, ludicrous and ineffectual.

As pathetic as his image was, it was further damaged by an unfortunate incident that occurred away from the school. Jimmie Leader had mistakenly shot a farmer's cow (or so the rumor ran).

JIMMIE LEADER
Junior High School Principal

During the fall deer season several years earlier, Jimmie had donned hunting regalia, packed a rifle, and set out for the hinterlands hoping to bring back a trophy buck. At the end of a long, uneventful day, he was returning to his car when shots nearby brought him to attention. Sequestering himself against a tree in the gathering twilight, he strained in the direction of the report. At first, he saw only the expanse of woods in front of him, but as he peered intently into the grainy light, his eye detected movement in nearby brush. He slowly brought the rifle into position, waiting for the animal to step out into a clearing. Minutes passed. Finally a form emerged and began grazing. Jimmie centered the animal in the gun's sight and fired.

Initially, the incident was quashed, but in time, too many were accepted into his confidence, and the inevitable found its way into the public corridors of the school. Self-deprecation was foreign to Jimmie's disposition, so he assumed a defensive posture, denying the obvious. When his back was turned in a hallway or on the playground, some wag would "moo," and to the delight of students, anger would flash in the reddened face and Jimmie would overreact. He was the continual butt of jokes.

The final students seated, the driver closed the bus door and waited for the queue of vehicles in front to pull away from the curb. At that moment, Jimmie Leader, on a personal, clandestine patrol, made his way alongside, scowling, hoping to thwart a future convict. When he turned away from our bus, some wayward lad, seated on the curb side, leaned out of an open window and mooed.

Jimmie wheeled about to identify the culprit. On the bus, kids snickered, looking straight ahead, holding their collective breath. In a moment, Jimmie marched to the bus and began banging against the yellow door, demanding entrance. The driver, compliant, opened.

Jimmie stood for a moment, tense, fumbling, searching the faces. Then glaring recognition flashed in his devilish smile. Slowly raising his right hand, he triumphantly extended his accusing index finger in the direction of my brother, motioning him to come forward. The iron hand of the law enveloped our family with ignominy. Keith was a captured criminal.

How and where Keith was occupied during his incarceration I did not know. Immediately following his apprehension, my bus pulled away from the curb and headed for Decatur Township. During the next hour, as classmates and friends were deposited at their various stops, I speculated on Keith's condition. What goes through the mind of a thirteen-year-old about to face a firing squad? I imagined his tremors were only slightly less severe than facing a mortified father. Worse, what courses through the mind of a brother about to face Jim Morgan?

Later, I found out that Daddy had threatened to call the police if Keith was

Keith was the guilty party.

not returned home, and the threat had been a thunderclap that reverberated through the school's main offices. At first, when they realized their
work day was to be extended until the issue was resolved, staff members
somewhat resented the behavior of the student who sat in Jimmie Leader's
office. But as the delay became protracted, their scorn turned upon Jimmie.
My brother had actually done what they had only fantasized doing. In any
case, secretaries and assistants shook their heads in ridicule at Jimmie's
most recent buffoonery.

The serpentine bus route from school to my stop ended at Joe McKinley's store. The remaining mile to the farm was traversed on a dirt road
whose daily traffic consisted of two vehicles: a flatbed truck, driven mornings by Fred Arnold, our milkman, and the afternoon car of Park Weader,
our mailman. Paul Revere's mission nearly two centuries earlier on a similar road was only slightly less urgent and much less stressful than mine. I,
too, was about to send shivers up and down the land as I sped home to
sound the alarm.

On warm days, Mommy left our kitchen door open for ventilation, but insisted that the screen door behind it remain closed to
keep out flies. As I negotiated the sidewalk that ran in front, I could hear
Daddy inside. I realized immediately that my news was old news. Daddy
was incensed, delivering diatribe against the known world and specifically
broadsiding educators and "city people."

"What happened?" he asked as I entered, his voice tinged with indictment. "Were you there?"

Absolving myself, I explained, "I wasn't sitting with him. I guess he
yelled something at Mr. Leader."

Of course I knew what he had done, but discretion informed that I
should avoid the storm. "Those bastards called and want me to drive to
Burnham and pick him up," Daddy ranted. "I told them if they don't get
him home in one hour, I'm coming to that school with the police."

I feared that a confrontation was inevitable, that Daddy would not be
easily mollified. I also knew that Keith was in for it.

As I would later learn, the first phone call had come from a school
secretary informing Mommy that Keith had been detained. The

news upset her, and her equanimity broken, she called for Daddy. Daddy was the handler of crises, the solver of dilemmas, the settler of disputes. Unfortunately his choice of weapons was, more often than not, a hammer and an axe. He demanded of the secretary that she should put Jimmie Leader on the phone or else he would call the police. Ameliorating Daddy was impossible. She found the principal. There was no discussion, only the dictum that Keith was to be returned home immediately if not sooner.

Daddy's temper on this day must be understood in the context of the stress a farmer experiences to complete chores while the sun shines. Getting corn into the silo before the stalks dried in the field was critical, an exigency just short of emergency. Things could not be put off until tomorrow. Besides, tomorrow would introduce its own stress. Tomorrow's anger would then be refocused—on Keith, or Mommy, or me, or whomever was nearby when his personal lightning struck.

At five o'clock on this September afternoon, the vitriol was directed at the subversives who had kidnapped Keith, and particularly the henchman, Jimmie Leader. Daddy had been standing near the phone when I entered the house. Mommy was seated next to the kitchen table, peeling apples, dropping the quarters into a pan of water at her side, and placing rinds and cores into her apron. I went upstairs to change out of my school clothes, but I could make out Daddy's sporadic and by now desultory allegations as he waited for Jimmie Leader's arrival.

"I'm gonna put an end to this," he threatened, "Next board meeting we may haf'ta fire a few people."

He sat down, opposite Mommy, resting his elbows and clenched fists on the table. He made no gesture, but it was obvious his mind was in full gear. "Those people think they can do anything they want."

He arose abruptly and went to the kitchen sink. Taking a glass from the cabinet above, he turned open the spigot and let the warm water that had lain in the line run over his hand momentarily. Then feeling the cool spring water flow, he filled the glass and drank thirstily.

Forty-five minutes had passed since Mommy had taken the phone call.

"Jim, maybe Keith did do something. I don't think they would just take him off the bus."

Her speculation was met with cold resistance. "I don't care what he did. No one is taking a kid off a bus without a parent's permission. I decide how he gets punished, not the school."

Out-voted one to nothing, Mommy redirected the moment, "He should be here by now."

With new resolve, Daddy strode to the phone. This time the junior high school office was vacant. The call, however, was rerouted to the superintendent's office. Roy Wilson, with whom Daddy spent school board meetings one Monday evening each month determining the philosophical and methodological directions of local education, greeted him as a life-long friend. Agitated, Daddy presented his case against malicious and inhuman torture, and Roy, sensing that a cooling down period might induce reason, invited Daddy to his office on the morrow.

While Daddy and Mommy waited in our farm house, Keith's misadventure took a turn. Capitulating both to Daddy's demand and the frustration of a prolonged day, Jimmie Leader had directed Keith to his personal car and started the twenty mile drive to the abandons of Decatur Township. He was aware of Daddy's outrage and understandably reluctant to engage a parent who appeared irrational and menacing. The twenty miles passed in deafening silence.

The dirt road from Joe McKinley's store to our farm was seldom traveled.

Serendipitous circumstance now played its part in the day's events. Heavy rains that autumn had pitted with ruts the dirt lane that ran from Joe McKinley's store to our house and may have on this afternoon saved several lives. As Jimmie was about to pull off the paved road and enter the narrow lane, he protested to no one in particular, "Is this the only road? How far is it to your house?" Keith, who had no desire to spend additional minutes with the kidnapper, seized the moment, volunteering, "I can walk."

The effect of a storm is seldom as great as its thunder. Daddy went to the school next day, but instead of a confrontation with Jimmie Leader, he met with Roy Wilson, Superintendent of Schools. Roy disarmed him. He complimented Daddy's concern for education, eulogized Keith and me as exceptional students with impeccable character (the kind of which any parent would be proud), and served Daddy two sugared donuts with coffee. If Daddy saw through the sham and politic of compliment and eulogy, he was in the end convinced of Roy's sincerity. Sugared donuts were Daddy's favorites.

ROY WILSON
Superintendent of Schools

If the kidnapper got away scot-free, the victim did not. As Keith rounded the final turn in the road, Mommy got up from her chair, pushed aside the apples, wiped her hands on a dishcloth and went into the yard to meet him. Keith was rather nonchalant, as though he was arriving from school on any other day. "Anything to eat?" he greeted her.

Mothers are affected by such ploys. Not so fathers. Daddy passed him in the yard. "Change your clothes," he ordered, "We have a silo to fill."

LEAVING HOME

I graduated from high school in June 1960. A few months earlier, during an evening when Daddy and I were alone in the barn, I off-handedly remarked, "I think I might like to go to college."

He was standing between two Holstein cows, his back to me, looking down at the electric milking machine beneath the cow to his left, waiting for her to be finished so that he could place the teat cups on the cow to his right. He didn't look up but bent down, placing his hand on the cups to strip the last squirts of milk from the udder. Finished with the first cow, he methodically moved the machine to the next and repeated the process.

"Did you feed the pigs?" he asked.

I nodded, "Yeah."

I knew he was ruminating, somewhat off-balance and surprised. This was entirely new ground—a subject never conceived much less broached. I was nervous, awkward, aware that he was weighing the repercussions of my leaving the farm, considering the financial cost and labor loss to the family, struggling to coalesce the pragmatic with the ideal. In addition, my announcement may have carried a personal sting, a sense of failure that he could not afford to help a son go to college, or perhaps self-reproach for the financial strains and plight of the farm. Whatever emotion stirred, he did not respond.

"If you're finished with the pigs, you can pull the spreader up to the door."

Cleaning the stables morning and evening was a requisite part of maintaining a herd of milk cows. Most mornings Daddy's priority was to finish the milking before the milkman arrived at 6:45 am. As a result, cleaning the stables was delayed until other work was completed. His directive to "pull up the spreader" meant he was nearly finished with milking, and I should begin the remaining task.

He removed the milking machine from the last cow, carried it to the milk house, and poured its contents into the funnel atop the ten-gallon milk can. I began opening the stanchions, watching each cow exit into the barnyard. The stables emptied, I climbed onto the tractor that was parked under the overshot that ran alongside the barnyard and started the motor. The spreader was already hitched to the tractor, and in a matter of moments both machines were positioned to begin the evening's final duty.

Meanwhile Daddy removed the pulsators from the milkers, placed them atop the highest of the two shelves he had built into the side wall of the milkhouse, and began cleaning the other components.[1] He rinsed the buckets and teat cups, hanging them from the metal rack standing below the shelves. I shoveled manure from the stalls and carried it to the spreader. The work was not difficult, but in the tedium I dismissed the possibility that he was going to immediately respond to my disclosure.

Daddy said nothing. Still in the milkhouse, he lifted the funnel from a milk can, removed the filter that was used to strain the precious liquid, and tossed it into the rusty bucket he kept for that purpose. Finally, he lifted the ten-gallon cans up and over the side of the milk cooler and dropped them into the

The milk cooler, which held four ten-gallon cans of milk, was located in the milk house.

cold water. I marveled at his strength. Each one hundred pound can had to be hoisted up and over the four-foot front wall of the cooler and carefully lowered into the water. He did it with ease, often continuing conversation as though the work was effortless.

Finished with my work, I opened the barnyard gate and watched the herd, conditioned by daily ritual, amble through the opening and head for the meadow pasture. As I did so, Daddy closed the milk house door, exited the barn, and latched the barnyard gate. When the last cow was safely inside the electric fence that ran around the perimeter of the meadow, I closed the meadow gate, and the two of us headed for the house. The issue of going to college seemed closed. If he later shared any concern or frustration with Mommy, I never found out, although Mommy's silence regarding the incident indicated that he probably never mentioned my remark.

The notion of attending college had germinated two years earlier when

---

1. A pulsator is a device that sits atop the milking machine and regulates the vacuum pumping action, which draws milk from the teats.

I attended Percy Crawford's Pinebrook Bible Camp outside of Strouds-burg, Pennsylvania. Don and Catherine Rush, friends from Calvary Bible Church, had a son, Danny, who was my age. His parents were concerned that he had few friends and found socializing difficult, so when his mother discovered that we had formed a passing friendship based upon our mu-tual love of sports, she determined to cultivate the relationship.

In the spring of 1956 telephones were installed in the homes of Deca-tur Township residents, and Danny's mother began phoning on Sundays, inviting me to spend afternoons with Danny. She drove the five miles to my house, took me to spend the afternoon with him, then returned me in time for my barn work. In the late spring, eager to facilitate and maintain our friendship, his mother and dad presented my family with a second-hand bicycle hoping that I would sometimes peddle the five miles to their house and free them from picking me up and taking me home each Sunday.[2] His parents also encouraged me to accompany them to a Major League baseball game in Philadelphia on Labor Day. It was for me an event of momentous proportion—my first big league game. I sat with the Rush family behind third base, mesmerized, watching my heroes play the New York Giants.

I continued playing basketball, football, and baseball with Danny on Sunday afternoons, but our friendship was limited. He did not attend Boys Brigade or any of the church sponsored programs that afforded socializing.

At school he took what were designated "commercial" cours-es which qualified him for secretarial or office work, while I studied "academic" subjects in preparation for college study. Both pursuits smacked of irony. He had no desire to become a secretary, and I had no intention of going to college.

DANNY RUSH

As a final demonstration of their desire for Danny and me to spend time together, Catherine and Don requested that Keith and I accompany Danny to Bible Camp at their expense. Reluctant to accept charity, Daddy acquiesced when it was pointed out that it would benefit our spiritual life, and the camp was endorsed by Donald Barnhouse, a radio evangelist to whom he listened. Thus, in the summer of 1957, Keith and I, along with Danny, found ourselves campers at Pinebrook Bible Camp. Not only did that week

---

2. My brothers and sisters were initially excited about the bike, but we soon discovered that it was designed as an industrial bike to be used for deliveries by grocers, dairies, and the like. It was heavy and impossible to ride for any distance.

affect my future pursuits, but it reinforced my spiritual development as I observed for the first time the lives of Christian young people whom I admired—especially athletes.

On the final Saturday of that week counselors and campers played a softball game. One of the counselors, Don Crawford, was enrolled at The King's College in Briarcliff Manor, New York, where he played baseball. I discovered subsequently that he was Percy Crawford's son, and that Percy was the founder and president of the college. After the game Don complimented me on my play. He must also have spoken to his father, because later that afternoon as Percy was walking his dog past the baseball field where I was playing with several other campers, he called me over and asked where I was planning to go to college. Dumbstruck, I answered that I didn't know. The truth was I had never considered college. He told me that King's had a good baseball team and offered a Christian education. I thanked him and returned to the game, but at intervals over the next two years I romanced the notion of playing baseball in college, never really believing it possible.

PERCY CRAWFORD introduced me to The King's College.

Baseball was the focal point of my life. Since my earliest years I held big league players in esteem and secretly entertained hopes that I would some day be noticed by professional scouts. As my senior year of high school approached, I was keenly aware that my hope of playing professionally hinged on that final spring. I also knew that attending college would extend my chances, but the reality of actually enrolling was not only unfeasible, it was illusory. Simply, there was no money.

A few days prior to revealing my secret to Daddy, I had sat in a high school study hall listening to two of my friends talk about applying to Penn State University. Curious about the courses, the cost, the campus, and the other logistics of college life, I conjectured college to be an extension of high school. Although neither of my friends had visited a college and were as uninformed as I, both appeared confident of the future. Their conversation stirred my imagination. Inchoate as the idea was, and as unrealistic as it seemed, I wanted to

Baseball was the highlight of my high school experience.

pursue my baseball dream, and I realized that I must get Daddy's approval
before anything could be set in motion.

Two days passed. We were again in the barn for the evening milking. Daddy had just begun the milking process while I was placing fresh straw in an adjacent calf pen. We had not spoken in the interim.
The silence between us was nearly audible. From the far end of the barn
could be heard the faint hum of the electric motor that supplied power for
the milking machines, and intermittently stanchions clacked as cows in
their stalls ate the chopped grain that lay in the cement manger.

Squatting beside a cow, about to remove the teat cups, Daddy broke
the stillness, "How're you going to pay for college?"

His suddenness startled me. I looked at him momentarily, stopping
to consider.

"I don't know."

"Did you talk to anyone at school?"

He was referring to teachers, guidance counselors, and such. I had
never hinted at the subject with anyone. Teachers were distant icons, not
personable friends. Guidance counselors were a recent phenomenon to the
educational process and served mainly as administrative assistants. They
seldom met with students and treated college selection as though it were a
private matter between parents and children.

"No."

The moment was protracted.

"Where would you go?"

"I don't know."

If I was to rally any support, it was important to mention a Christian
college. Daddy's theology was narrow, and I knew he would not consider a
liberal, secular college. I had seen a few college advertisements in Daddy's
favorite reading, *The Sword of the Lord*, a clarion newspaper published by
John R. Rice. Its articles and advertisements were polemics for fundamental Christianity. The paper's primary collegiate thrust was an acclamation
for Bob Jones University in South Carolina. Thoughts of Bob Jones University, however, engendered images of stern decorum, coeds not permitted
make-up or jewelry, and students assigned detention if caught smiling at
the dinner table. As much favor as it would have curried, I could not enter-

tain the possibility. I machinated a compromise.

"I saw an ad in *The Sword of the Lord* for Tennessee Temple College."

It was true. But I hadn't read the accompanying article. Instead I had checked their baseball schedule and recognized none of their opponents. I cynically supposed their teams might play against churches instead of colleges.

"At Pinebrook, Reverend Crawford told me that King's was a good Christian college."

Daddy returned to the milking, and I resumed bedding the calves. Throughout the evening my imagination raced with fanciful hopes, but there was no further discussion.

More than a month passed. I was enjoying the high school base-ball season, but school itself had assumed a foreboding aspect. Graduation loomed. Finality with consequences. For most students, the closing weeks were sentimental, celebratory, with weekend parties, school dances, and desultory conversation. The monotony and uneventful routine of school days were taking on new colors as classmates suddenly found value in something they were about to lose. Unlike mine, however, their distress was momentary. The days following graduation would find them preparing for college and, by September, old friendships would be replaced by more vibrant ones.

For me, the end of school fomented no excitement. Instead, melan-choly weighed heavily upon my days and nights. I was severing ties with everyone and everything that offered romance and escape from farm life. Awaiting were hot summer days in the fields and dark summer nights alone. After-school and weekend social life was reserved for kids with ac-cess to cars and money.

My school relationships were restricted to school hours and the ban-ter of study halls, cafeteria, and locker room. I did not invite teammates to the farm. Theirs was a world of movies, TV, and "hanging out." I was not permitted to go to movies, we had no television, free time was scarce, and Daddy would not have permitted "hanging out."

I did not go on dates, though there were attractive girls whose friend-ships I cherished. Dating required money and a car. Daddy could not afford to pay an allowance, and transportation was limited to the farm pickup truck. The car was too valuable to be entrusted to teenagers.

Springtime passed. The final high school baseball game was played, so I no longer arrived home too late for field work. Instead, planting, fertilizing, and cultivating began each afternoon as quickly as school clothes could be exchanged for work overalls.

On a Friday evening in May, I had just come from one of the fields when Daddy informed me that he was going to Lewistown, and I was to do the milking. He said the cows had been fed, and I should turn them into the pasture when I was finished.

I never minded milking cows, especially when I was alone in the barn. The work was not difficult, and the solitude was pleasant—a time for fancy. I went directly to the milk house where I busied myself with assembling the milking machines. In a few minutes, through the milk house window, I saw Daddy come from the house and make his way to the garage where the truck was parked. I went about my jobs—carrying one of the milking machines into the barn, switching on the motor that powered the system, plugging the suction hose into the vacuum pipeline. Amid my oblivion, Daddy appeared in the doorway.

He came and leaned against the calf pen behind him, carefully considering his words. "I have an idea."

I said nothing, just looking in his direction.

"Mommy and I were talking," he paused. "If you want to go to college, maybe we could buy two sows, breed them, and sell the pigs." He explained, "I can get you a job at McClure working in the plant with me. You won't be able to go to college this year, but … if you put your money away, you could save enough to start next September."

Stupefied by the suddenness of his proposal, I stood speechless.

"How does that sound?" he asked.

"Good," I managed.

"What I would do is go to Belleville and buy two young sows. We'll get Sam to breed them with his boar.[3] You buy the feed and after they come in,[4] we'll divide the pigs. You take half and sell them, and I'll keep some

---

3. Mommy's uncle, Sam Arnold, who lived nearby, kept 4-6 boars which he loaned for breeding purposes.
4. "Come in" was a common euphemism for giving birth.

for butchering and sell the others. We could have three litters by the time college starts."

Experience had taught me never to respond negatively. "I'll see they get fed," I offered. As an after-thought, I added, "Should I buy grain from you or from the mill?"

"You just pay for grinding it. We'll use the corn that's in the crib."

I was genuinely grateful, but emoting was foreign to both of us.

"Thanks."

Neither of us spoke. Affection has a language, but it must be practiced for its usage to be comfortable. Daddy had no such tongue. The pause embarrassed.

"Well, I gotta get going." He turned to go.

I redirected, "When will we buy the pigs?"

He returned to the moment. Thrusting his hands into his pockets, contemplating the week's schedule, he announced, "We can go to Belleville next Wednesday."

He bore a sense of relief as he left, pleased perhaps that he could contribute, grateful that the moral obligation that burdened him was momentarily lightened.

The summer of 1960 passed. In August I began working the 7:00 am to 3:00 pm shift at the McClure Cabinet Factory, a company that bought various gauges and kinds of steel, then custom cut, folded, welded, and polished the resulting cabinets to fill what were mostly government contracts. Minimum wage was one dollar per hour, so that, following deductions, I was taking home $28 each week.

Change was gradually enveloping the farm. Financial strain was increasingly evident. Here and there a roof leaked, a loose board needed to be nailed, cobwebs appeared in corners. The supports were sagging.[5]

5. Daddy had been working from 3 to 11 pm at the cabinet factory for over a year. The principal income was no longer from the farm. There were other changes, both subtle and obvious. The herd of milk cows had been reduced from 30-35 in the spring of 1950 to 20 or less at the decade's close. By the time I graduated from college in 1965, there were fewer than a dozen, and two or three years later, Daddy dissolved dairy farming altogether. More conspicuous were the departures of sons and daughters. In the summer of 1960 Keith moved to Lewistown where he stocked shelves, carried groceries, and nurtured his own notions of attending college and pursuing a career in art. When I departed that fall, the

Daddy did the barn work mornings, and I handled evenings. In the pig lot behind the barn, two sows, heavy with young, rooted and rolled in the mire. By month's end there would be twelve piglets, and by November I would have my first return on our investment. Daddy and I seldom spoke about the pigs, but he fed them every morning, and I put corn and mash into their pen in the evenings.

I played baseball that summer for both McClure and Paxtonville, riding after work the fifteen miles to Paxtonville with a plant co-worker who welcomed my company and sometimes came to my games. On the evenings when I played for McClure I walked the half-mile from the cabinet factory to the local field.

Road games for either team presented a problem. I had no consistent transportation. Most evenings after Paxtonville games, I rode the fifteen miles back to McClure with one of my teammates, then hitchhiked the remaining seven miles to the farm. Fortunately, the sight of a boy in a base-ball uniform usually struck pathos into the hearts of motorists, because I seldom walked, especially if it was raining. There were, however, times when I was unable to solicit a ride along Route 522, and the long miles of dusky highway resolved me to quit rather than endure the hardship. The resignation never lasted, as the next day brought with it renewal. Baseball was my *raison d'etre.*

Excepting baseball, my life took on a predictable monotony: planting and harvesting crops, milking and feeding livestock, and punching a clock from 7:00 am to 3:00 pm. A friend, Paul Everly, picked me up at 6:30 am each weekday morning and dropped me off at our front gate each afternoon. On most afternoons after work I played with my little brothers, Dave and Joe, or took them with me to the barn or fields or wherever I worked about the farm. The three of us enjoyed riding in the pickup truck to the mill or to Joe McKinley's store. When the weather turned cold, they rode beside me in the cab while I told stories and listened to their adventures. In the summertime, they climbed aboard the truck bed, nestled close against the cab, and let the wind cool the heat of the day.

The summer passed. No more baseball games to play on weekday

---

farming fell upon Bill, only fourteen, and my sisters, RuthAnn and Susie. The struggle to make ends meet further intensified when Mommy became pregnant in the spring of 1964. My sister Beth was born on October 28 and within six years Mommy was forced to take a job at a shoe factory in Beaver Springs. The struggle to maintain financial equilibrium and personal dignity choked attempts to continue farming.

evenings or weekends. I listened to Penn State football on Saturdays and watched Philadelphia Eagles football on Sundays. I was aware that friends from high school were now at college. I felt forgotten, isolated, confined. On a late September afternoon I arrived home from the cabinet factory to find the latest *Sears and Roebuck* catalog on the kitchen table. Transistor radios had become an American obsession, thanks in part to the explosion of rock and roll music and increasing amounts of leisure time for the middle class. That evening I thumbed through the pages and became fascinated with a battery-operated AC-DC portable Zenith radio whose eight transis-

A Zenith 755 transistor radio was my first investment.

tors would permit me to listen to games and music outside the walls of the house. My history with money was limited to the pennies I spent on baseball cards and the nickels my grandmother gave me to buy cowboy comic books during the week each summer when Keith and I as small children stayed at her house. Three years earlier I had saved three dollars, hoping to buy a baseball glove and shoes for my sophomore year, but my weekly allowance of twenty-five cents was canceled by family needs. I had never had money to spend.

I knew that going to college depended upon the money I was earning at work, but the romance of tuning to baseball games from St. Louis, New York, and Chicago, and listening to the same rock and roll music I enjoyed on bus rides to and from school, was seductive. A few evenings later, I gave two of my uncashed checks to Mommy. In turn, she wrote a check for $60, and I filled out the catalog order form and mailed it.

Until I left for college one year later, that radio was my companion. I never played it when company was present, and I knew Daddy would disapprove if I took it with me to the fields, but at 8:00 pm on summer nights I lay alone in the yard and listened to games. On winter nights I was no longer confined to the kitchen radio, but took my new Zenith to my bedroom.

On the Friday afternoon before I left for college, Mommy and I were alone in the kitchen. She was packing cardboard boxes with my clothes, folding linens and pillow cases, making egg salad for sandwiches, and giving attention to the dozens of preparations necessary for the trip to college and residence in a dormitory. I helped by carrying socks, shorts, T-shirts, and trousers from my bedroom down to the kitchen. I had packed my baseball glove and spikes into a separate bag sitting atop the kitchen table.

Mommy noticed and asked, "Are you taking your radio?"

In the months following its purchase, my brothers and sisters sometimes asked to use the radio. They were not interested in music or sports, but many evening family shows were popular with children, and they enjoyed the novelty of listening to a portable. The result was that my recent purchase became *ipso facto* the family radio. They listened to *Gunsmoke, The Lone Ranger, Sergeant Preston of the North-West Mounted Police, Roy Rogers,* and other such programs. An understanding evolved that, before expropriating it to my bedroom, I would leave it on the kitchen shelf each evening until those early shows were over.

Already wrestling with the guilt of deserting brothers and sisters, I could not take their radio. "No," I assured Mommy, "let the kids use it." She did not reply, but I knew she was pleased that it would stay on the shelf.

O f course, the greater part of my days was spent at the factory. I would have liked to work overtime when it was available, but the 5:00 pm farm work was always before me. Keith was gone now from the farm, working at the *Giant Food Store* in Lewistown. Evening farm work fell entirely upon my fourteen-year-old brother Bill and me. When Bill arrived home from school, he too, changed clothes and came to help at the barn. As I milked, we cleaned the stables and carried manure to the spreader. Bill climbed the ladder to the upper barn and threw down hay bales, opening them and placing the loose fodder in the mangers. When milking was completed, one of us mounted the tractor and drove the spreader through the darkness of fall and winter nights to the outlying fields while the other scattered straw and bedded the cows.

CHARLES WILLIAM MORGAN
Bill was an athlete and my constant playmate.

Bill was a hard worker. By 6:30 we were usually back inside the house.

On Saturdays, Bill and I bagged grain to be ground at the local mill in Beaver Springs, cleaned the chicken house or calf pens, swept cobwebs, or occupied ourselves with some of the dozens of jobs intrinsic to farm life.

On Sunday mornings, after milking the cows, everyone went to Calvary Bible Church in Lewistown. I felt displaced from high school friends, ambivalent about college, and restive of farm life, but Sunday afternoons made life tolerable.

My grandmother, who lived fifteen minutes walking distance, had a television set. In the late fall, she shut off the water and heat, packed some belongings, and went to Lewistown to stay with my Aunt Ivy for several weeks. The

Autumn Sunday afternoons were spent at Mammie's house watching Philadelphia Eagles football.

television, however, remained, and every Sunday, after arriving home from church, I quickly ate something and sprinted to her house to watch the Philadelphia Eagles. She hid the house key for me in a guarded crevice and left a warm blanket on her sofa. For two and one-half hours I lost myself in the drama of that football season. I became so engulfed, in fact, that on Monday, December 26, when our family went for Christmas dinner to Uncle Bill and Aunt Faye's house, I begged to stay home because I wanted to listen undisturbed to the championship game. Mommy, however, made plain the impropriety of spurning the invitation of valued relatives, so I compromised and went. The game was not televised, but I listened while closeted in a spare bathroom.

As winter thawed and the spring of 1961 reminded that my days on the farm were quickly passing, I grew increasingly aware that I would be leaving something more than home. The farm had been an emotional and spiritual investment. A part of my being was inextricably affixed, not to animals and crops, not to buildings and fields, but to the past: to the struggles, the joys, the dreams, private and personal, and to the relationships of family—relationships about to be disrupted, reshaped, or perhaps, disjoined. Bill and I had spent countless work hours together and had established a special bond through our love of athletics. My leaving meant that most of my obligations would be transferred to him. RuthAnn and Susie already worked long hours at both the house and barn. Now, they would be condemned to field work as well. With Dave and Joe, my distress was even greater. I had changed their diapers, given them baths, and held them on my lap from the time they were babies. Their love for me was un-

The most difficult part of leaving home was saying goodbye to Dave and Joe, here dressed for church.

conditional. My absence would seem to them like abandonment.

In early August I apprised my boss at the McClure plant that I would be leaving at month's end. That evening Daddy asked how much money I had saved.

"I don't know exactly," I responded, "I have to count my checks."

He looked at me, then asked Mommy incredulously, "He didn't put his checks in the bank?"

His tone made it plain that she was receiving the blame. Actually, I had been aware for some time that the checks needed to be deposited, but I vacillated, hoping that someone with experience would either go with me or do it for me.

"Where are the checks now?" he turned to me.

"On top of the refrigerator."

A vase sat atop the refrigerator which rested in a kitchen corner. Beneath the vase Mommy kept a doily as a dust cover. Faithfully, on alternate Fridays when I came from work, I slipped my check beneath the doily. I had no concern that a family member would remove it, and I was unaware that checks needed to be cashed within ninety days of their issue. The refrigerator top appeared as secure as a safety deposit box.

Daddy got up from his chair and went to the refrigerator. He lifted the doily and began fingering through the checks, looking at the issue dates, and placing them in a chronology. I watched him count them a second time.

"Where are the others?" he asked. "There's only twelve here."

It was obvious from his displeasure that checks were missing, but I neither knew how many I had, nor did I have any idea where they might be.

Daddy was disgusted that I could be so careless. "Well, you better find them!" he warned.

He left the kitchen and went to his bedroom. I suspect he took leave so that he would not lose his temper. Upon reflection, his retreat may also have been out of consideration for my contributions to the family in the preceding months. Since working at McClure, somewhat routinely, I had helped when dollars were scarce: ice cream from Joe McKinley's store, a loaf of bread for supper, lunch money for brothers and sisters at school. On several occasions he had asked permission to cash one of my checks because of family needs. Still, there were missing checks for which I could give no account. My naiveté deserved criticism no doubt, but his displeasure was mitigated by my past willingness to share.

While he was gone Mommy searched the house: my bedroom, their bedroom, she even walked to the garage and rummaged through the compartments of both the car and truck. Meanwhile I turned out the pockets of all my clothes, including my Sunday pants. In twenty minutes everyone returned to the kitchen.

Daddy modulated his voice, "I'll talk to your boss at McClure. I think they will reissue the checks, but there will be a charge. I can't believe you did this." He shook his head in disbelief. No one spoke.

After a few minutes, he changed the subject.

"We have to sell your pigs before you leave," he declared.

The twelve piglets born the previous August had been sold at the sale barn in Belleville, as had a second drove of thirteen in March. The final batch of nine shoats, although ready for market, was a disappointment as one of the sows bore only two piglets.

The pigs had sold for six dollars per shoat so that after the last ones were marketed I had $100. That money would be added to my checks to give me nearly $700 when I left for college.

Checks to replace the missing ones were reissued at no cost. The factory had just taken on a huge government contract for aluminum medical cabinets to be installed in veterans' hospitals. Daddy was the only welder on his shift who had experience with aluminum, and the company was not about to alienate Jim Morgan because his son had made a juvenile mistake.

In the final weeks of August I saw Daddy infrequently. He arrived at the cabinet factory weekday afternoons at his welding station a few minutes before I punched out. His welding skills kept him occupied on Saturdays, and on Sundays we attended church mornings, and he rested afternoons, fatigued from his long week at the factory. We never spoke about my leaving, but I could sense it was on his mind. Uncle Bill came to visit my last Sunday afternoon at home, and the two men sat in the kitchen and talked while I pretended to be occupied on the porch.

"Aw, it's hard," I heard him tell Bill. There were long pauses between sentences. "I guess they'll all leave."

AUNT FAYE AND UNCLE BILL
They were regular visitors at the farm.

Bill was methodically peeling a green apple with his pocket knife. Mommy had set saltine crackers and a block of cheese on the table in front of him. When the apple was pared, he cut a thin slice, laid it on a cracker with a wedge of cheese, and thoughtfully held it while he listened. It was one of those commiserations that evoke discomfort.

"You recall when you left home?" Daddy asked.

Bill nodded. "When Dad died." Again he reflected on the past. "I went to work in Lewistown; worked there until the war."

Uncle Bill enlisted in the army shortly after the Japanese bombed Pearl Harbor. He was sent to Panama, guarding the canal for the duration of his military duty.

"If you remember," he continued, "Mom didn't stay at Paintersville long.[6] She went to live with the Shawvers and then moved to Lewistown. I didn't get back there much."

The Shawvers were a farm family who lived nearby. They had befriended my paternal grandparents, Cloyd

THE SHAWVER FAMILY
They welcomed my grandmother into their farm home.
Left to right: George, Burt, Anna, and John

6. After my grandfather, William "Cloyd" Morgan died of tuberculosis in 1937, my grandmother, unable to pay the rent, was forced to move. Burt and Anna Shawver, a nearby farm family with whom a close relationship had been forged, offered assistance. Grandma and three of the children moved in with the Shawvers, while older children Jim, Helen, and Bill went to work and found apartments in Lewistown. Thirteen-year-old Mary went to live with her Uncle Sam in Massachusetts. Eight weeks later Grandma found a job at the Lewistown Laundry, enabling her to rent an apartment on Shaw Avenue, and bring Mary and Helen home.

and Cora, and their children, when the family moved from Lewistown to Paintersville in the early 1930s. During the ensuing months while Cloyd spent his final days in a tubercular sanatorium, they were generous with the foodstuffs their farm supplied. Acquainted with the financial straits the family faced following Cloyd's death, they welcomed his widow and her small children into their home until Cora could find work and an affordable apartment.

It was obvious that while neither Daddy nor Bill wished to dwell on the pain of leaving home, memories of earlier times moved them away from Daddy's present discomfort.

Recalling the time of his father's death, Daddy added, "Dad died in thirty-seven." He paused in thought. "I was about the same age as Denny."

Daddy got up from his straight-back chair, walked stiffly to the table, cut a chunk of cheese, and scooped three crackers onto a plate. He took a Barlow knife from his pocket, cut the cheese into bite size squares, and returned to his chair. As he talked he absentmindedly stabbed one of the squares with the small blade of the knife, took it to his mouth, then laid the knife aside, and munched at the crackers.

"After he died, I went to work in Lewistown, too." His voice grew wistful, "The old place at Paintersville holds so many memories."

Bill continued to listen as Daddy reminisced, "Evenings when Dad came home from work, he sometimes walked down by the railroad tracks, and I used to walk down and stand with him and watch the freight trains." As if to underscore the passage of time, he noted, "I was just a kid."

"I think Mom was glad to get away. Dad wasn't there, and we didn't have a lot. How old were you when you enlisted?" Daddy asked.

"Twenty, I think. Maybe twenty-one. Helen and Mary were gone by then, so it was just Mom, Lolly, Dick and Nip. And Dick enlisted right after I did. Really, it wasn't home anymore."

Sentiment and nostalgia had exacted a kind of paralysis. The two men, as though signaled by some psychological warning that they must not wander too far into the past, got to their feet. Clinging to yesterday rendered today impotent. It was time to move on.

Home would never be the same.

TRIP TO COLLEGE

In the wee morning hours of Saturday, September 2, 1961, seated in a blue and white, four-door 1956 Oldsmobile sedan that had seen its best days long before he bought it second-hand, Daddy pulled from the driveway in front of our home and steered onto a highway that ran to a world both foreign and frightening. In his pocket was fifty dollars he had borrowed for gasoline and tolls. He was taking his son to college—to Briarcliff Manor, New York—to a world geographically and culturally remote from our home—a world far more distant than the six hours it would take to arrive.

Mommy rode by the passenger-side front door on the old-style one-piece front seat. Between Mommy and Daddy, in a cardboard box, rested the egg sandwiches, slices of double-layer devil's food cake, and jars of water that would serve as noon dinner. They had agreed to stop "somewhere" and buy coffee.

In the rear seat, behind Mommy, rode Uncle Bill. He was part of the excursion because loaning a brother fifty dollars warranted an invitation. Besides, Uncle Bill was compelled to come along by the notion that something mysterious and exotic lay ahead.

I sat with Uncle Bill in the rear seat. Stuffed between us were brown paper bags filled with underwear, socks, a pair of sneakers, a baseball glove, and other belongings that would not fit into the car trunk.

The men passed the first hours recalling similar trips: Daddy's experiences as a CCC boy in 1934 during the Roosevelt administration;[1] Bill's trip as a soldier to Panama in 1942 during WWII. They spoke of boyhood and people and places from long ago. Memory faded into romance. Nostalgia became relief for Daddy's private disquiet as the miles intensified the pos-

WILLIAM LEWIS MORGAN
Uncle Bill rode with us. Ironically, he died ten years later while bringing his own son home from college.

---

1. See endnote.

sibilities of a disabled car, of being stranded in a foreign country, of insufficient monies to meet imagined expenses.

A second, more remote anxiety also visited. An oldest son was going to college. The effect might make attending college fashionable for other sons and daughters. Such a trend jeopardized the well-being and operation of a farm. Daddy's private concern was unspoken, but years afterward, in her final days, Mommy alluded to conversations from those times wherein Daddy became melancholy as though a fatal end was imminent. On this day, as the hours passed, conversation waned. By the time we reached Allentown and Easton, fatigue and monotony had replaced the early excitement and the miles along Route 22 in New Jersey vanished in silence.

We arrived sometime between six and seven in the morning on Sunday.[2] The parking lots were empty. Service people had not yet reported to work. At the main building, which featured both administrative offices and dormitories, we found a lone switchboard operator who informed us that the dormitories would not open until nine. I had lived sufficiently long with Daddy to know that he was aggravated and would not accept waiting until nine. He approached the switchboard operator a second time insisting that he could not wait two hours. Acquiescing, she suggested that copies of dorm assignments might be found amongst the folders, posters, index cards, and other paraphernalia lying atop tables in the lobby, but that no one was permitted access except assigned personnel who would arrive around nine. He informed her that he would "just take a look." Almost immediately he found my room number, and ignoring the operator's disapproval, the four of us began mounting seven flights of stairs to my new world.

Within the next hour Mommy unpacked bags, scrubbed the bathroom, hung my clothes into one of two closets, and made my bed with

---

2. We stayed on Saturday night at Wyckoff, NJ, in the home of Bruce and Marcy Baker, friends from Calvary Bible Church in Lewistown. Bruce had graduated from Wheaton only two or three years earlier and had taken a position with the Christian Service Brigade, then based in NY. He would, a few years later, become the field representative for the Christian organization. He had invited us to stay overnight, suggesting it would break up the trip, save money, and permit us to arrive refreshed on Sunday morning. He warned that the odor from a nearby pig farm sometimes drew complaints from Wyckoff residents, but doubted that a farm family such as ours would be offended. Two years later Bergen County purchased and shut down the piggery.

Main building of The King's College

clean sheets and pillow covers. Daddy and Uncle Bill carried belongings from the car until everything was deposited at the bottom of the stairwell, then, curious about such an unfamiliar and remote world as college, decided to survey the campus. I transported the final items to the top floor, then remained with Mommy, lining bureau drawers with newspaper, searching the hall closet for a broom and dust pan, and washing windows. The single-hung windows, each with twelve panes, looked out over Westchester County. Tarrytown, Scarsdale, Valhalla, and the wealthy estates of suburban New York lay to the south. To the west flowed the Hudson River, the traffic on the Tappan Zee Bridge visible on clear days. Between the college and the river, the tops of trees obscured smaller villages that had formed centuries earlier as river communities. In another month the picturesque autumn foliage would be resplendent in shades of red, yellow, and orange.

For me, however, the day held no adventure. I was withdrawn and cheerless, anxious for everyone to leave before other incoming students began arriving, convinced they would discover that my belongings were packed in shopping bags, embarrassed that my mother had brought a care package of saltines and jelly in a tin container. I felt ashamed, inferior, inadequate. I supposed all parents of college students wore ties and jackets; assumed all college students had eaten in restaurants, ridden in new cars, wore nice clothes. I imagined that I alone was ignorant of proprieties and protocols. The hour passed slowly. Daddy and Uncle Bill returned and sat facing each other on the straight-back chairs that belonged to the room's two writing desks while Mommy completed her tasks. Daddy wondered aloud if traffic on the way home would be heavy and reviewed with Uncle Bill directions that would take them to the Garden State Parkway and home.

Home is never so attractive as when we are strangers in some foreign country, intruders with no offering, attendees lacking finery. Daddy had cast aside personal anxieties and private misgivings to fulfill moral and familial obligations but doing the right thing does not always quell the tempest within. My new country rendered my father an alien, and though his love for me had countermanded other considerations, the presentiment of an unaccustomed world turned him homeward. It was time to say goodbye.

The investments that constitute a parent-child relationship make even partial relinquishment difficult. The years of nurture and sacrifice fasten an inextricable emotional and spiritual grip. Ironically, for such a bond to last, freedom must be granted.

Uncle Bill stepped out into the corridor leaving Daddy and Mommy alone with me to say good-bye. Daddy announced that he wished to have prayer. His love and concern were genuine, and his prayer for my well-being was sincere, but I also knew that invoking the Almighty's vigilance eased the tension of the moment and supplanted a direct display of affection. It was just as well. Had he been affectionate, I would not have responded in kind but would have shrunken and felt awkward. I would have responded not with love, but propriety; not with appreciation, but resentment. I wanted release from the moment. In his prayer he asked God to "watch over Dennis." I hated when he called me "Dennis." Mommy called me "Denny." It was warm, accepting, affectionate. My teachers called me "Denny." My grandparents, relatives, and friends called me "Denny." Daddy called me "Dennis."

The walls I had constructed were, at the time, impregnable. A lifetime of immoderate temper and cruelty precluded the kind of response for which he hoped. I had learned to protect myself against his cruel sallies.

The invocation was finished. In a futile attempt to bridge the distance between father and son, Mommy hugged me, and whispered, "We love you."

There was awkward silence. Mommy wiped her eyes with her handkerchief. She asked if there was anything else she could do. I assured her I would be okay. She choked back tears and said she would pray for me. She gathered up the things that would be returned to the car, looked at Daddy and implored, "Jim, say goodbye."

Finality was hard—the letting go of yesterday. Affection could not and did not flow easily. Something visceral, naked, defenseless was missing. The moment demanded more than he could give. For a moment he stood paralyzed, contemplating the separation, then lurched forward and extended his hand. He said nothing, but tears welled in his eyes. Unable to speak, with a turn of his head toward the door he motioned to Mommy that they must go. He did not look back as he exited, not because he was indifferent or uncaring, but because he possessed no means for such an end.

ENDNOTE

The Civilian Conservation Corps was created on March 21, 1933, as part of President Franklin D. Roosevelt's "New Deal." Applicants had to be between the ages of 18-25 and be unemployed or have an unemployed father. War veterans of any age could also join. The men committed to a six-month enrollment that could be extended for up to two years. CCC workers were housed and fed on-site at campsites and earned about $30 per month – with the requirement that $25 be sent home to their family. Daddy designated that his money should be mailed to his father, who was suffering from the tuberculosis that he had contracted as a 16 year-old boy while working at the Harbison Walker brick plant in Mount Union. The camps were run by the Army but were a civilian organization. Daddy was inducted into the 336-W-Junior Corps on Thursday, August 2, 1934, at Fort Hoyle on the Aberdeen Proving Ground, Harford County, Maryland. He entered his birth date as February 12, 1916, in order to meet the requirement that members be 18 years of age and listed his address as Lewistown RD (Paintersville). Official records say he was 5'8", weighed 125 pounds, and was assigned to work in forestry. The Corps medical records indicate he was missing nine teeth which strongly suggests poor dental hygiene, a condition not uncommon at that time. Interestingly, he was discharged August 27, 1934, for desertion at Waterville, PA. Official papers indicate he had been absent from Camp S-129 (S was the designation for forestry) since Monday, August 20 and had taken all of his personal belongings with him. As was true of many deserters, in all probability, he went home for the weekend of August 18-19 never intending to return.

CHRISTMAS 1961

What though the radiance which was once so bright
Be now for ever taken from my sight,
Though nothing can bring back the hour
Of splendor in the grass, of glory in the flower;
We will grieve not, rather find
Strength in what remains behind;
In the primal sympathy
Which having been must ever be;
In the soothing thoughts that spring
Out of human suffering;
In the faith that looks through death,
In years that bring the philosophic mind.
                    "ODE ON INTIMATIONS OF IMMORTALITY"
                                WILLIAM WORDSWORTH

PART ONE

The Greyhound bus station in Harrisburg was lonely on the cold rainy December evening of Friday, December 22, 1961. I waited outside the terminal, anxiously watching for Daddy's blue and white 1956 Oldsmobile sedan. Rivulets of water emptied into a nearby storm sewer while oil-smeared pools collected in the streets. Whining tires threw sheets of spray along the dirty sidewalks as commuters hurried home at the end of the work week and last-minute Christmas shoppers jockeyed for parking spaces. The five o'clock light had turned grainy in the last moments before darkness descended. I had been standing outside the station since 3:00 pm.

MY FRESHMAN YEAR
The King's College

At 8:00 am I had taken a final exam that marked the completion of my first semester of college. The instructor had sat behind the rows of students, reading a fashion magazine and mindlessly drinking a cup of coffee. She seemed as bored with Psychology 101 as we freshmen. Adding to our dis-

THE KING'S COLLEGE
Briarcliff Manor, New York

pleasure, students who completed the two-hour test early were required to sit and wait so as not to disturb others who continued to pore over the confusion of multiple-choice questions.

Ms. Parker enjoyed her stature as an academician. Bombastic and pedantic, her lectures were stilted and tedious. She lacked an educator's capacity to convert theoretical postulates into pragmatic applications. She was fascinated by Pavlov's dogs, but failed to consider the consequences of determinism. Her favorite topic was Freud, and her orations, pregnant with sexual insinuation, sermonized as though sex was scandalous and foreign to the Christian life. Psychology 101 was ninety minutes of ennui.

One hour later I was traveling home for Christmas, anxious to see my family, especially my little brothers, Dave, 6, and Joe, 5. Two weeks earlier, when going home for the holidays seemed impossible, Mommy had written to encourage me to find a student from central Pennsylvania who had a car, was going home over the semester break, and had room for a fellow traveler. My alternative was to remain at The King's College, because, as she had explained, Daddy simply did not have the money to drive to New York City, take me home, and then make the return trip two weeks later. She told me to pray about it and assured me that God would provide a solution. An hour after receiving her letter, I read on the dormitory bulletin board that Layton Shoemaker, a classmate, was looking for students who were traveling toward Pittsburgh and were willing to share travel expenses.[1] I immediately arranged with Layton to be dropped off in Harrisburg and wrote home so that Daddy would know where and when to meet.

---

1. Although I did not know Layton well at the time, we became good friends as soccer teammates during our final three years at college. Following graduation he spent his remaining years as soccer coach and athletic director at Messiah College near Harrisburg, PA.

After the Psychology exam, I returned to my dormitory room, tossed some clothes and a toothbrush into a paper bag, removed a package from my closet containing a Christmas present for my little brothers, and headed for the college parking lot where Layton and three others were waiting. He packed our things into the trunk of his green and white '57 Chevy, invited us to climb aboard, and soon we were headed south across New York's Tappan Zee Bridge. The Garden State Parkway connected with Route 22 in Union, New Jersey, which would take us west to Harrisburg. I sat quietly in the left rear seat, anxious that Daddy might have difficulty in finding the Greyhound Bus Terminal.

I did not know Layton's other passengers. I learned that the girl sitting beside me was Janet Perry, an upperclassman, but there was little conversation, and by the time we turned onto Route 22, only Layton and I remained awake. The day was overcast, and as we turned west toward Pennsylvania's capital city, rain began to fall. The tires of passing cars threw cold spray against the Chevy, and I weighed the complication that falling temperatures and snow might interpose on an already worrisome situation.

A few minutes before 3:00 pm Layton pulled alongside the Greyhound terminal, removed my bag from the car trunk, wished me a merry Christmas, and then headed for Pittsburgh with his other travelers. I was alone in a strange city, in a strange depot where dozens of other strangers lethargically accepted the monotony of waiting for their buses by reading newspapers and magazines, smoking cigarettes, or engaging in detached conversation about the weather.

For the first minutes after my arrival, I stood back against the shelter of the terminal, away from the wind and rain, but soon realized this did not permit a full view of the street. Knowing that Daddy was unfamiliar with Harrisburg, I thought it best to move near the curb where he could more easily find me, even though it meant getting wet. Twenty minutes passed. My clothes grew damp, and I began to shiver against the cold. The light wind was turning to gusts. I moved back to where the terminal shielded against the elements, returning now and then to the curb edge to be more visible.

At four o'clock I went inside the building and made a collect call home. It was my first collect call, and I was anxious about the procedure. Did it require more than the dime I fingered in my pocket? Would Mommy be circumspect about receiving such a call? Had anyone ever called her collect? I silently rehearsed several times, "I would like to place a collect call," as I approached and opened the door to the booth. Inside, I rehearsed once more and reached for the phone. I was ready. Dropping the dime into the slot I dialed zero. Abruptly, as though she had been waiting for my call, the operator responded. Her tone was belligerent, whining, as though I had interrupted her nap, "Yesss?"

Flustered, I blurted, "May I make a collect call to my mother?"

I immediately regretted the phraseology. It sounded obsequious, asking the operator for permission to make a call. Worse, telling the operator that I was calling my mother made me feel childish. It also assured me that the operator was listening to my conversation. I imagined her to be dull. She most likely spent her days watching soap operas, gossiping, filing her nails as she sat at some recessed stall in a dingy building, bored, supercilious, drinking a cup of cold coffee and reading TRUE CONFESSIONS magazine. I listened as she placed the call, heard the phone ringing at the other end of the line and my mother diffidently inquiring, "Hello?"

"Will you accept a collect call from Denny?" the operator asked.

Not familiar with procedures, Mommy spoke directly to me, "Denny, where are you?"

The operator interrupted, "Will you accept charges?"

"Well," Mommy hesitated, "Yes, how much does it cost?"

"Go ahead, sir," the operator directed me.

I told Mommy that I was still waiting at the bus terminal and was concerned that Daddy might not be able to find me. She assured me that he would arrive soon and asked if I had something to eat. I said I was fine and, worried that extending the call was expensive, determined that I had best return to the sidewalk.

The fact was that I had sixty-five cents with which I could have bought some food, but I worried that I might have to make another phone call if indeed Daddy was unable to find me. My last dollars had been given to Layton for the ride to Harrisburg. I had saved just enough by babysitting evenings and washing windows on weekends to pay for my ride and to buy a Christmas gift for Dave and Joe. It was wrapped in the package I was carrying.

Nevertheless, there were other factors. Neither my family nor I had ever eaten in a restaurant. I simply did not know the procedure. In addition, there was the guilt of living beyond means. There were a few times when Daddy bought sodas or ice cream cones when we attended the Mc-

Clure Bean Soup, a local festival, or when we spent an afternoon at the annual summer fair at Alfarata, but eating at a restaurant was an unwarranted extravagance, an indulgence practiced by the rich. I imagined my Uncle Bud and his wife Arvella spending dollars in fancy diners buying hamburgers. They seemed to have plenty of money. He drove a new car, and they went on vacations. Our family was different. When we went on a Sunday picnic Mommy packed sandwiches and potato salad and filled our glasses with water at the picnic site. We counted our pennies. I could not bring myself to spend money on food.

As the afternoon passed, I continued to slip back inside the terminal to get warm. Curiously the entrance to the station was through a screen door which permitted wintry drafts to penetrate the waiting room. Still, the room was considerably warmer than standing outside. Buying a sandwich would have entitled me to remain inside the building while I was eating, but I felt guilty just loitering, so I stole into the overheated men's room intermittently, furtively returning each time to the wintry day.

I had tucked the paper bag that held my clothes under my jacket to protect it from the rain, but the package containing the Christmas present was getting wet. I turned up my collar against the wind and thrust my hands deep into my pockets, propping the present against my leg to afford it some cover. Prolonged anticipation enervates, and I thought about sitting on the wet curb to rest, but I quickly realized wet clothes would make me colder. I began to imagine the worst. Perhaps Daddy's car had broken down, or maybe he could not find the bus station, or worse, he may have been in an accident. By now, I was thoroughly chilled.

In the midst of the chill and the wait, I was anxious, too, about my reunion with Daddy. I feared his irascibility. The frustrations of traffic, unfamiliar places, or car problems could light the fuse of his temper. During tantrums his remarks became personal and demeaning, and since he had no capacity for apology, the stings became embedded. I knew he cared about his family. I had observed the pride with which he marched us into church on Sunday mornings and his radiance when neighbors, teachers, and grocery clerks complimented him on the decorum and assiduity of his boys. When one of the family suffered injury or illness he was genuinely affected. Nonetheless, in my nineteen years, neither of us had verbalized or directly demonstrated affection. I suspect there were many times he wished to give his heart voice, but tender moments were awkward, and now, separated for four months, I was discomfited with the possibility that he might fumble for expression. I preferred a stoic greeting and non-committal conversation on the ride home.

I had twice stepped inside the building to warm myself. Each time I slipped into one of the restroom stalls where I would not arouse suspicion, but neither time did I linger, worried that Daddy might have arrived and was searching for me. Entering or leaving the building, I looked straight ahead, trying to avoid any semblance of stealth, as though the ticket manager might think I was engaged in some crime. Quivering against the raw cold, I garnered the courage to enter the station house a third time. This time I stayed near the door, sufficiently chilled that I was willing to be thought recidivistic. If approached, I could quickly step out onto the sidewalk.

On the wall behind the counter of the small concession stand, the face of a pretty girl smiled from a faded Hershey's Ice Cream advertisement, her smile in contrast to the sign's dull green cast. To its right, at eye level, hung a small chalkboard, the word "MENU" scrawled in uneven letters across the top. Listed beneath: "Hot Dogs – 25¢," "Burgers - 35¢," "Cheeseburgers - 40¢." The pervasive odor of hot grease and coffee from the concession stand stirred my appetite. I knew Mommy would have a special supper waiting, but I had not eaten since breakfast, and I recalled a Jack London character so hungry that "his belly began to eat on itself."[2] Four stools, their red vinyl seats worn and cracked, offered seating to weary travelers. A large wall clock hung above the ice cream sign, its plastic cover yellowed with age and smudged with grime. The dusty Roman numerals on its face bespoke something ancient, something frozen in time. From the ceiling an enormous fan hung motionless, floccules of dust clinging visibly to the inert blades. The deterioration, dinginess, and dirt of the place were revulsive.

PART TWO

The routine of farm work is physically demanding, arduous and endless, but it is particularly the daily, unremitting requirements of animal care that most exhausts. Cows must be milked morning and evening. Their grain must be bagged, driven to the mill, and ground for feed. Their hay and fodder must be measured and placed in mangers and troughs. Water must be pumped at regular intervals as animals are loosed,

2. Love of Life, Jack London, (Macmillan 1907).

walked, and returned to pens. In addition, manure must be cleaned from stalls, shoveled to a spreader, and transported to field and meadow. Failure to meet the needs of farm animals can result in their disease and death and the demise of farm and family.

Driving to Harrisburg on this wintery late afternoon meant Daddy was temporarily postponing these critical responsibilities. Such a delay raised the possibility of cows developing mastitis and a resulting decline in milk production. If chickens were not fed, there would be fewer eggs to sell, or a myriad of other complications that could result in veterinary expenses and even the suspension of our milk-selling permit. Either would mean financial burdens that threatened our survival as farmers.

I had too often heard him agonize to Mommy over monies needed for repairs or fuel. I recalled a September day during seventh grade when Keith and I returned home in the late afternoon to announce that the junior high school we now attended required that sneakers be worn for physical education classes. Daddy had no money for extra footwear, but not wanting his kids to be at a disadvantage, he drove twenty-five miles to Lewistown, using gasoline he could ill afford, to borrow money from his mother so that he could buy sneakers for us. I knew, as I waited on this winter evening, that he was concerned for my welfare, but I was also aware that farm responsibilities pressed upon him.

PART THREE

It was nearly 5:30 pm when a blue and white Oldsmobile sedan pulled alongside the curb directly in front of the depot. I was watching from inside the terminal and saw Daddy peering into the building. I picked up my package, pushed open the screen door, and started toward the car. He did not get out but leaned across the front seat and opened the door. I unlocked the rear passenger-side door, placed my things on the seat, then crawled in beside him.

"Have you been standing in the rain?" he asked painfully. It was as though he wished me to controvert what he knew to be true. Guilt flooded over him.

Unable to give expression to his feelings, he pulled from the curb and turned the car homeward. "We'll get some heat in here and get you warm. Mommy has a good supper waiting."

I knew he regretted my circumstances, but nothing further was spoken for several minutes. The only sounds were the whirring of the motor and the slapping of the wiper blades. Outside, temperatures were falling. Large snowflakes wafted downward, illumined by the lights of utility poles and approaching headlamps, melting the instant they struck the windshield. It felt as though the two of us were sequestered in unsought intimacy. I hated the impotence of the moment.

"How's college?"

"Good."

"How long did it take to get to Harrisburg?"

"We left about ten.

Snow was falling with increasing volume, the flakes becoming smaller as temperatures plummeted. Three, four, then five miles passed without conversation.

"Well, we have a new house." The change of topic was momentarily confusing. He looked neither left nor right, his eyes focused beyond the windshield and the glistening, swirling flakes to the snowy road. Then, matter-of-factly in explanation, "We put in a furnace."

No one had spoken to me of a furnace, either of plans to install one or of the actual completion. I was puzzled.

"Where?"

"In the cellar."

My only frame of reference for a furnace was my paternal grandmother's house on Belle Avenue in Lewistown. When our family visited her on cold days, we kids warmed ourselves by standing on the grating at the far end of the corridor that opened into her living room, feeling the warm air funneling up through the opening.

I wanted to engage him in conversation, catch up with events that had transpired during my four months at college, but as we continued through the darkness, it seemed extraneous and incidental, and I let him concentrate on the snowy road.

We traveled north, crossing the Susquehanna River at Duncannon, then passing the small towns that lay alongside Route 22: Amity Hall, Newport, Millerstown. Forty-five minutes brought us to Thompsontown where we turned off Route 22 and began climbing the mountain outside of McCallisterville, the snowflakes becoming small crystals audibly striking the windshield. I realized the temperature was continuing to drop and driving on the mountain road was now hazardous. Slowing sometimes to a few miles per hour, it was nearly 6:30 pm when we reached the foot of the mountain at Beaver Springs and pulled onto Route 522. From there the country was familiar and both of us relaxed, knowing the perils of snowy mountain roads were behind. We had not spoken for some time as Daddy had concentrated on navigating through the snow and darkness, but now his apprehensiveness eased, and as we continued west toward McClure, compassion grew in him. Looking straight ahead, his voice modulated, "When we get home, you stay in the house and get warm. I'll do the barn work."

His sacrifice was genuine, magnanimous, and I was deeply affected. It was a moment when I should have acknowledged his humanity, reciprocated in some way, and beyond all else, gone with him to the barn that evening, but I did nothing. I did not even thank him. Three miles west of McClure he steered off the paved road onto County Line Road, the dirt track that separated Mifflin and Snyder counties. Three miles of ruts, loose gravel, and granulated snow brought us home.

There are singular moments in the course of life that in hindsight seem felicitous and providential, when we stand on the precipice of expression that defines and shapes our character. Riding with my father that evening had been an opportunity to step across the emotional barrier that separated us, but history, and perhaps self-pity, prevented vulnerability. Love, unexpressed, is haunting, and violates the ethos of being. That night I chose to remain alienated. I am still counting the cost.

Saturday dawned clear and cold with temperatures in the twenties. Daddy called at five-fifteen, and I dressed quickly into warm clothes, hurried downstairs, and began lacing on boots over an extra pair of socks. Wrapping a scarf about my neck, I tugged on a heavy coat and stocking hat and stepped outside. Several inches of powdery snow lay atop an icy crust that had formed during the night. Boots crunched through the frozen layers and required extra effort as I trudged my way to the barn.

On clear frosty mornings, first breaths sting in the nostril, but the cold invigorates and impels activity. The rigor and routine of early morning farm work is not quickly forgotten, and I went about feeding the stock and cleaning the stalls as though I had not been away. The noises of the stable—the put-put cadence of milking machines, the jingling of stanchions and the scraping of shovels across cement floors precluded lengthy conversation, but the morning chill was soon forgotten amid the physical strains of lifting and carrying.

Daddy was in good spirits as he briefly caught me up on recent happenings: the cow in the far stall had calved in October—he had afterward sold the calf at the market in Belleville; the cow adjacent to where he was standing had a touch of mastitis—which reminded me to wash the udder and completely strip her when she was milked. It was a morning when all of life seemed animated with cheerfulness.

Daddy seldom talked when we were at the barn or in the fields. Not only did the duties of labor make conversation difficult, but he was seldom disposed to early-morning banter. On this morning, however, his son was home from college, and he found time between the routines to talk. He did not ask about my studies, my friends, or my activities. Rather, he brought me into his world. He spoke of the farm, the correspondence Bible course he was taking, and the Bible class he was teaching at church. He talked of his past. He recalled wintry mornings as a boy, packing sandwiches and going hunting for deer in the woods near his home, walking to a country store in a snowstorm, and eating a big breakfast that his mother had prepared after coming inside away from the cold.

I always enjoyed hearing him talk, and I frequently asked questions in order to prolong such moments, but conversation on this morning passed quickly. Idle conversation contravened the milking that had to be finished before 7:00 am to accommodate the arrival of Fred Arnold, our milkman. Milk that failed to meet the deadline could not be held over to the following day but had to be dumped or fed to the pigs. Fred was a nephew of my mother, pleasant, garrulous, punctual, although his casual manner gave the notion that he was insouciant. Customarily he drew Daddy into conversation, then, announcing he was behind schedule, asked assistance in lifting the ten-gallon milk cans onto his flatbed truck. Each morning he transported our milk, as well as that of neighboring farmers, to the Dairymen's League processing plant in Beaver Springs, fifteen miles east. Each can of milk weighed between 90-100 pounds, and I admired the ease with which Daddy hoisted them over the top of the milk cooler or up onto Fred's truck. Clearly, he was stronger than Fred.

Loosened boards in the hay mow (upper left) needed repair.

By 7 o'clock, the work was completed. I had thrown hay down from the mow while Daddy finished milking, and the two of us had bedded the stalls and pitched dried alfalfa into the mangers. Curiously, while in the mow I had noticed that two of the vertical siding boards near the top of the mow had been loosened by time and weather. As I further inspected conditions, a haunting sense of guilt engulfed me. I was struck with the realization that the farm was failing. Neither hay mow was more than half-filled, and I was reminded that financial straits had forced Daddy to take a second job at McClure. His attention and energy were now compromised, the herd of cows was markedly reduced, and some of the other buildings were showing disrepair. I had abandoned both him and the farm to go to college.

We closed the barn doors and headed for breakfast. The smell of a wood stove and the fragrance of frying food on a cold winter morning are indelible memories, and I forgot the albatross that had weighed in the haymow. Crisp bacon, fried eggs and potatoes, slices of heavily buttered bread, cups of hot cocoa and coffee, and a special treat, grapefruit, laded the kitchen table. At Christmas Daddy usually bought some kind of fruit that was on sale during the holidays. The extravagance was in marked contrast to everyday frugality and thus, this morning meal was tinged with excitement.

Mommy was delighted to have me home and asked if I would like potpie for supper. She knew I loved the homemade yolk-rich noodles, cut into two-inch squares and cooked with thick slices of potatoes in a hearty chicken broth and served with boneless chunks of meat and sweet onion. As breakfast concluded, she asked if I would drive to her mother's house later in the afternoon and bring Mammie for supper. She knew her mother would appreciate being included in our reunion.

Mammie lived alone on a tract of wooded land at the eastern end of the farm where Pappy had built their retirement home, completing it during the winter of 1951-52. Following his death in February 1957, I had stayed with her nights until I left for college, after which my brothers and sisters took turns, walking to her house evenings after farm work was finished. At the insistence of her daughter, my Aunt Ivy, and her son-in-law, my Uncle Paul, she sometimes spent cold winter months at their home in Milroy, a suburb of Lewistown, but always preferred to remain home if one of us kept her company at night. I had been an important part of my grandmother's life before leaving for college, and Mommy reminded that she was anxious to see me.

Part Four

Breakfast over, Daddy announced that following family devotions, if the roads were clear, he was going to Lewistown to buy delousing powder for the cows. Since I would be home for a few days, he figured I could busy myself with the once-each-winter process of shearing and powdering the animals to prevent lice during their period of indoor confinement. The powder was applied along the backbone and tail of each cow after those areas had been shorn. Shearing alone was a tedious process that required constant brushing of hair and oiling of shears, but applying the powder was doubly uncomfortable for it meant breathing the disagreeable chemical that left an after-taste.

Turning his attention to more immediate concerns, he directed Billy, my fifteen-year-old brother, to help me shell a bushel of corn for the chickens and added for both of us, "If I'm not back by the time you finish, the calf pen at the far end of the barn needs to be cleaned." Shelling corn could be uncomfortable when the weather was cold because the corncrib was open and unprotected, but cleaning manure from the warm barn was neither difficult nor unpleasant, and I rather looked forward to doing my part.

We exited the table, located our Bibles, and found seats near the warmth of the stove where we could listen to Daddy's devotional reading. It usually consisted of forty-five minutes of Bible reading and commentary, followed by prayer. Ordinarily, each of us was required to take part in the prayer, petitioning God for forgiveness and guidance, and thanking Him for provision and providential care. It was understood, however, that we must remain silent during Daddy's pontification, which tended toward dogmatism and admonishment.

On this first morning home, I was excited about devotions. I had something to contribute, something I had discovered at college, something about which I actually knew little, but in the egotism of youth, it was something with which I sought to make an impression. Excitement naturally accompanies discovery, but I had not yet learned that new-found revelation ought never to be thrust upon unsuspecting or disinterested company.

I knew my news, though benign, would irritate Daddy. I had throughout my early years been taught by my church generally and my father particularly to venerate the King James Version of the Bible as sacrosanct. I was told it had been exalted by saints, hallowed by church fathers, and beatified by Reformed Christians. More immediately, the notion was validated every morning during family devotions. Daddy insisted the King James Bible be used exclusively; it was God's Holy Word.

With this presupposition entrenched in my thinking, the teacher of my Bible class at college had sounded a thunderclap. He said the King James Version was simply one of many fine but flawed English translations. He alleged it suffered from poor editing, outdated idiom, and worse, its grammar, although classic in style and beauty, was taken from the Latin Vulgate

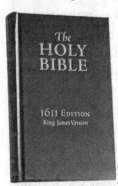

and not the original Hebrew and Greek. His assertions posited a myriad of questions and rocked me with confusion. The logic of his discourse haunted me throughout the remaining weeks of class. Then, prior to final exams, the professor invited students to his study where the issues were further discussed and examined. That hour dissolved my skepticism. He pointed out that the King James Bible was restricted to English speaking peoples, had been in existence only a brief time, and used archaic language no longer discernible. It was as though I had been at sea, lost amid fog and storm, and suddenly discovered land.

Daddy believed the original KIng James Bible was sacrosanct.

Daddy took his place beside Mommy and opened his Bible. Seven dutiful children sat about the circle, lost in the verbose and repetitive nature of the devotional. He turned to the eighth chapter of John and began reading about the woman found in adultery. After reading a few verses, he began to lecture and moralize the passage. His delivery was stilted and emotionally charged with dogma, but to question his commentary was to be adversarial. I waited for my chance. He finally paused to make certain his points were noted.

I leapt at the opportunity. "My Bible teacher at college suggested we use two or three different Bibles when studying, because it sometimes helps to hear something in different ways."

There was stunned silence. I had introduced heresy. He was incredulous, as though I had chosen perdition. Gathering his thoughts, he launched into a tirade, his voice resonating with outrage. "This Bible is God's Word! It is not two different Bibles saying two different things. I'll tell you something, Mister; God's Word is God's Word! These modern teachers are the reason people don't know what's in the Bible." He held his King James Bible aloft for emphasis, "This Bible is *the* Bible and what it has to say doesn't have to be explained by college professors."

Daddy, who was left-handed, now tapped his left forefinger emphatically against the Bible he was holding in his right hand, "This has always told us what God has to say, and this is *the* Bible!"

His disgust was palpable. I felt exposed, a fraud, Judas caught with the thirty pieces of silver. "And I'll tell you something else!" His voice was in a rage, "If you're gonna come around here with your college ideas and the Devil's lies, well, we don't care if you ever come home again!"

I regretted my temerity. It was as though I had miscalculated the weather and found myself suddenly in the midst of a storm – intemperate with gusts of rebuke and excoriating condemnation. The thunder would pass, but the dark clouds of emotion that followed would overcast the day and the remainder of my time at home. On his part, there would be no remorse, no guilt, no apology.

Moved by the irritation of my remarks, he closed his Bible and began to pray aloud, abbreviating the devotional. There was no further denunciation. The edict was explicit and final. The tenor of his voice was unequivocal as his prayer went directly to the issue, "Heavenly Father, we are thankful for the blessings you bestow on us. We are also thankful that you have spoken to us through your Word."

Though there was no direct allusion, I knew that "your Word" was a tacit reference to the King James Version he was holding in his lap.

"And we pray that each of our children will become familiar with its contents and serve you with their lives. And we pray that Satan will not be permitted to lead our children astray with modern teachings that are not in your Word. Heavenly Father, we ask that you would keep the things that are being taught in modern education from invading our home. We ask that you keep us safe even if it means that some of our children are lost to us. Even if it means that you must remove them from our family. We ask these things in the name of your son. Amen."

By the time he finished, I was devastated, vanquished. My winter jacket hung on a peg behind the wood stove, above a cardboard box where Mommy kept hats, scarves and gloves. Immediately I dressed and went to the barn. Reeling from his barbs, I sought escape.

... "Even if it means that you must remove them from our family?" ... What was he saying? ... Was he willing that I should die? ... What did he mean? ...

The barn was warm with the good odor of cattle. I closed the door behind me, walked to the back of the stable where several bales of hay had been loosened to feed the cows, and lay down amid their cushion and fragrance. My mind drifted to college. It had become a sanctuary away from the tensions of home. I was ready to return to my friends and activities, but I was haunted with uncertainties. I hated leaving Mommy, my brothers and sisters, and in spite of Daddy's acerbity, hated leaving the farm. Its obvious decline signaled a need for additional income and attention. I wrestled with the complications and consequences of returning to college.

PART FIVE

It took a long time to rise above self-pity. Daddy's indictment festered. For the remaining days of Christmas vacation, I avoided any direct encounter that could give rise to discussion or debate. When he drove me to Harrisburg to meet Layton Shoemaker for my return to college, I retreated to the back seat of the car eschewing conversation while my Uncle Bill rode in the front.

Back at school, I immersed myself in college life. As Easter vacation approached, I had little money or inclination to travel home. Serendipitously, my roommate invited me to his house in Lancaster where I spent the week tying up carnations in his parents' commercial greenhouses. And then it was baseball season.

My desire to play professionally consumed me. My attention was riveted upon practices and games. Baseball was breath, my *raison d'etre*. The days and nights at the farm seemed far away. I became oblivious to academic responsibilities, allowing my grades to suffer.

At the close of the semester, I opted not to go home for the summer, but accepted a job working at a YMCA day camp for young children near the college. I shared an efficiency apartment with two itinerant workers with whom I had little contact since one spoke no English and both worked nights. At times, I regretted my decision because I worked for minimum wage and suffered through the loneliness of estrangement from friends and family. It especially complicated the concern and love I felt for Mommy and my brothers and sisters. I missed them terribly, but the disquietude that I associated with home overshadowed other considerations.

A pattern was now established. I no longer went home during summers or extended vacations. During Christmas of my junior year, I stayed at the college, walking downtown in late wintry afternoons of the two-week break to clean cages and kennels at a veterinary hospital. At Easter, I went to my girlfriend's home. That summer I worked in the kitchen of a youth camp at Glen Spey, New York. Finally, my marriage in August 1964 irrevocably guaranteed I would not again live in the same house with my father.

Ironically, in the years following, and until his death in 2001 at age 84, whenever I was able to visit, Daddy expected me to participate in devotions. Either he had long since forgotten my violation, or else he suffered no compunction. I have chosen to believe the former.

In any case, even after the intervening years, participation still meant sitting and listening to his sermonizing. Although I seldom disagreed with the tenets of his theology, to the end I wished his delivery was less dogmatic and his tone more genial. Regardless, the daily hour-long session was his pulpit. Though I was no longer a boy and had learned to overlook many of his foibles and vagaries, I remembered to keep my place. If I had dared intrude with suggestion or insight, he would have felt threatened, closed with an abbreviated prayer as he had done on that December morning, and disappeared into his room. There were times I wanted Mommy to share her thoughts and feelings, times when I could have contributed background information by sharing an experience or a book, times I wanted to show my support for the point he was making, but I never dared violate his authority. On that Saturday morning in December 1961, I had forever forfeited my right to contribute when I blasphemed the King James Bible.

To the end of his life, confrontation was futile, ill advised, senseless. Attempts at logic were imprudent. Compromise was foreign to a nature so set upon the familiar. His notions had long been solidified and hardened, refusing any semblance of change to that which he had made sacrosanct. He denounced iconoclasm, refusing to explore foundations of custom or question established practice. Opposing ideas and comments were jettisoned as heresy. When confronted with persistence, he withdrew with umbrage, brooding and sulking, indignant that his argument or his intention was challenged. It is true that on Sundays he enjoyed the men's Bible class at church and contributed thoughts and experiences which were insightful and appreciated, but on the occasion that variance was voiced, he fulminated for days, retiring to his desk evenings where he ruminated, contriving to formulate a reprisal, a defeater, a coup de grace. But mostly his audience for the sequel was limited to Mommy. A follow-up with the person or persons who incited his turbulence would only have resulted in dispute and anger since he had neither the tools nor the temperament for civil disagreement.

PART SIX

Concurrent with the dissolution of the farm had been an erosion of Daddy's Christian commitment resulting in the adjournment of his church attendance. The failing farm aggravated a sensitive wound to his public pride so that his longtime dissatisfaction with ministers, church protocol, and the demands of membership became excuses for apostasy. For several years he peripatetically "visited" four or five area churches, attending for three or four weeks, then impulsively withdrawing for reasons capricious and trivial.

He quit his job at the cabinet factory in McClure in favor of a better paying one as an orderly at Black's Community Hospital in Lewistown. When it closed in 1972, he accepted a job at Selinsgrove State School and Hospital, a residential facility for the mentally disadvantaged. The new job afforded health insurance, a retirement pension, and moderate financial stability.

In 1976 he sold the farm and moved into a custom-made home in Kreamer, a small residential mill-town thirty miles eastward and an easy commute to his job at the State School and Hospital. The day-to-day financial burden of farming was now dissolved, and his life seemed less stressful. He planted a garden, erected an arbor for grapes, and set some half-dozen apple tree seedlings on the back lawn. It was as much of the farm as could be transferred.

By the spring of 1991, Daddy had slowed. My brothers and sisters were now married and established in their own homes, so that visits to Kreamer found him increasingly lonely and alienated. Weekend sojourns of children and grandchildren seemed to him pointedly reserved for Mommy. He looked forward to each homecoming as an opportunity, not to commune, but to once again occupy the center. He was in need of attention and affirmation, but often self-absorption and impatience estranged the very people he wished to see. To combat increasing boredom, he built a workshop, puttering with power tools, constructing coat trees, children's furniture, and knick-knacks. The years drifted.

Part Seven

On a Saturday evening during the summer of 1995, he sat opposite me at his kitchen table. Mommy had cleared the supper dishes, and she and Sammy, my twelve-year-old daughter, had retired to the living room where they leafed through thick picture albums, Mommy reminiscing, pointing to faces, identifying times and places remote while the young girl, decorous and gracious, asked questions. Affection flowed between them. Daddy, too, was recalling images.

His mind ran back to boyhood and his days at Paintersville, a hamlet seven miles outside of Lewistown consisting of two dozen homes, a general store, and a railroad crossing where twice each day steam locomotives could be seen from porches and backyards pulling freight on its way west. A cup of coffee sat in front of him and a plate of molasses cookies rested near the center of the table.

He mused, "Summer evenings, Dad came home from work, and before supper, he walked down to the railroad tracks that ran in back of the house. I would walk with him, and we would watch the trains that came by. Dad loved the trains. He used to point out the different kinds of cars, and

The Paintersville station where Daddy and my grandfather watched the trains.

when the caboose went past, we waved to the man who rode in it. There was just something about those days...."

He caught himself becoming sentimental and changed the topic.

"Ya know, a lotta people depended on the trains in those days," he continued. "When I worked in at the foundry in Lewistown, sometimes in the evening I walked over to the train station and watched the trains. The station was always busy, and during the War, there were soldiers everywhere coming and going. It was just across the Juniata River Bridge, and you could see men in uniforms night and day crossing the bridge. Army, Navy, Air Force, all kinds, coming and going."

Lost in reverie, he became silent. Minutes passed. Feeling him drift far away from the moment I asked, "Did you ever ride the trains?"

"No, not really." He shook his head slowly, wistfully. Noticing the coffee, he lifted the cup with both hands, staring down into its contents. "When I was in the CCC camp we loaded trains, but we didn't ride them or go anywhere." He put the cup down without having drunk. Mommy and Sammy could be heard in the next room.

Wistfully, quietly, he reflected, "Ya know, when I was a kid, I always wanted to ride the trains. ..."Just to see what it was like."

The passing years had begun to soften his once invulnerable rigidity.

It was most apparent whenever he spoke of his father. Barely fifteen and the oldest of eight when his dad began to fail with the tuberculosis he had contracted as a boy, Daddy dropped out of school, enlisted for a brief time in the Civilian Conservation Corps, then stoically waited and watched as the older man spent month after month in a distant and dismal sanatorium, returning for two holidays each year, each time his wasting body confirming the family's fears. His death in January 1937 left a spiritual and emotional void for which the nineteen-year-old never found relief.

"Aw, Denny, those were the days."

For as far back as I could remember, Daddy called me by my formal name. "Dennis," he would say, "Mommy needs you to go to the store." "Dennis, I want you and Keith to clean the chicken house." Or, "Dennis, it's time to go to the barn." Only those few times when warm sentiment surfaced did he call me, "Denny." It made me uncomfortable, as though he were sharing something of great value which I was not permitted to keep.

"Did your dad know the Lord?" I redirected his mood.

"I don't know for sure," he confessed. Momentarily, he turned inward, as though a grotesque reality haunted him. "Mom said he accepted Christ at the sanatorium before he died. The minister of the Brethren Church in Lewistown went to see him, and Mom said that Dad prayed with him."

There was another awkward pause. "I don't remember Dad reading a Bible or going to church, but that ain't what saves you." He pushed back from the table, only half convinced that he would again see his dad. Then with genuine interest, he announced, "I was looking through your Bible."

Sometime after moving to Kreamer, Daddy and Mommy, recognizing their need for worship, had become members of a local evangelical church and had restored daily morning devotions into their routine. As a result, the next time I visited I took along a new Bible I had purchased several weeks earlier.

"What kind of Bible is it?" he asked. There was no asperity to his question, no criticism. His curiosity simply regarded the price, the type of indexing and the concordance. "I looked at Bibles last week, and I almost bought one that I could carry in my coat pocket."

Daddy had a dozen Bibles. They were scattered throughout house, garage, and work shed. Each offered something unique, something that had struck his fancy: colored maps, cross references listed at the end or within chapters, red lettering to indicate the words of Jesus, blank pages for note taking, or easy-to-read type. Each one was heavy with underlined verses and Daddy's annotations.

Knowing that he would enjoy a further inspection, I beckoned Sammy. "Honey, would you bring my Bible? It's lying atop the paper bag that has my clothes in it?"

In a minute she laid the Bible in front of me, and I slid it across the kitchen table to where Daddy sat. Casually he browsed the cover, then turned it to read the spine. For the first time he realized it was not a King James Version.

"Is there a difference in the American Standard Version?" he asked. His dismay was evident, but he maintained an even demeanor. "I don't understand why people are using these Bibles. You know, the Bible says that in the last days we will be led astray by deceivers and false teachers, and I'm just afraid that some of these Bibles are part of that trap."

I did not like where we were headed. Daddy never discussed issues. Radical ideas and unfamiliar terrain were anathema. The world was black and white, and Daddy was its pontiff.

"I don't have anything against the King James Bible." I retreated. "In fact, I think it's a good Bible. I still use my King James Bible."

I continued before he made a final pronouncement, "You know, the King James Bible is an English Bible. The people in France cannot read English. They have to use another edition." I was desecrating the French as I back peddled, but Calvin would absolve me.

"Do you know what I mean?" I obeisantly asked, appealing for conciliation. I wanted to talk of Luther, the Reformation, and the German language, but Daddy was unfamiliar with that history, and I was struck with the reality that he was not being stubborn nor intractable, but simply unable to abandon the mindset that the King James was his Bible, that it revealed absolute truths and assured him of eternal salvation.

He is gone now. I awaken in the wee hours of restless nights, sit at my computer and try to give tongue to something incomplete, unfinished, regarding our relationship. Perhaps, I asked too much. I wanted his approval as a demonstration of his love. I wanted my father to notice me. I wanted to share my small victories, wanted his empathy, and I wanted an irenic moment when he recognized the person mattered as much as the principle.

Forgiveness is easy. My own weaknesses and failings preclude pointing a finger. All has been forgiven. There is no animosity. Only— and this must ever be—the bridge that might have united us was never crossed, and left is the strangeness that a father and son parted strangers.

Incongruity is a part of life, and despite his impatience, his temper, his inner conflicts, he embodied so much that I value. From him I learned discipline, a love of learning, and an appreciation for the aesthetic. He demonstrated that nearly every obstacle can be overcome, that the quality of work reflects the character of the worker, and that promises are binding. He made worship of God the highest priority, taught that God is sovereign, and fully trusted the divine promises that guarantee eternal blessings. Though some of his failures precluded the relationship both of us dearly sought, I am grateful that he, before all others, was my father. Though the pain was real and the alienation lonely, its wake was neither sterile nor barren, neither indifferent nor malevolent. His legacy is not that he failed to love, but that his self-absorption compromised his ability for expression. While I cannot overstate the richness of his contribution, I cannot deny the cruelty of his injuries. I am grateful for the joys and pains that have shaped me, and I confess that my life could not have been so wonderful had he not played his part.

CHURCH
◇◇◇◇◇◇◇◇◇◇◇◇◇◇◇

My earliest memories of formal worship are associated with Samuel's Union Church, a bucolic, sequestered chapel that bordered our farm in Decatur Township. Services were held only on Sundays. The congregation was comprised primarily of neighbors who resided in close proximity to the church so that enrollment was fewer than 100 members. The lot on which the church building sat extended nearly a hundred yards beyond either side of the sanctuary and became *ipso facto* the church cemetery. The oldest markers lay to the east, reaching back to the closing decades of the 18th century, identifying the German farmers who settled the area. They were my ancestors: Folks, Ragers, Gosses, Arnolds, and Snooks. By the end of the 19th century that portion of the cemetery was well-populated, and descendants with the same names began to be laid to rest in the western side. The bodies of my parents and grandparents, my maternal relatives and my neighbors lie there, as well as the ashes of my brothers Bill and Joe. My brother Keith has reserved one of the grave sites

SAMUEL'S CHURCH

for himself and his wife, and when God takes me to His eternal Glory, my body will rest beside those of my brothers and our wives. The reverence, serenity, and simplicity of the site is idyllic, far from "the madding crowd's ignoble strife."[1]

My forebears have been traced to the earliest days of colonial America and the scant bits of information available includes confirmation that most were church-goers, reformed in their faith and deeply committed to the tenets of Biblical truths. Letters of correspondence, military records, and other official documents attest to the role of church and the influence of Christianity in my 18th, 19th, and 20th century ancestry.

Church records indicate my maternal great-grandfather Simon Arnold and his wife Annie were members of the Samuel's congregation, but their children affirm that the family was irregular at best in attendance. My maternal grandfather Charles, the oldest sibling of that family, did not become a regular church-goer until he married my grandmother Carrie, whose family were active church members. Carrie repeatedly taught her children that church attendance was important for civility and refinement. Her family was regular in attendance, and many of her brothers and sisters are buried in the Samuel's Cemetery.

My paternal ancestors, dating back to the years prior to the American Revolution, were also church attending, evangelical, protestant Christians, although the generations immediately preceding me seem to have had only a nominal relationship with Christ. A deeper, more genuine relationship developed during the 1940s after my grandmother Cora gave her life to Christ during a 1930s revival service at the Shaw Avenue Brethren Church. Her testimony resulted in the salvation of her children and their full participation in church activities throughout their lives. It also persuaded her husband to make a profession of faith at the tubercular sanitarium in Cressen, PA just prior to his death in 1937.

One of those early memories at Samuel's Church is participating in the Christmas program when I was 4 or 5 years old.

---

1.   This verse is taken from "Elegy Written in a Country Churchyard" by Thomas Gray.

We pre-schoolers dressed as shepherds or angels and waited patiently on the periphery, ready to join the older children in the finishing chorus of "Away in a Manger." Afterward, each participant received a candy cane with the caveat that it was to be saved for Christmas.

I recall my Sunday School teacher, Mrs. Hassinger, young and pretty, seating us in a semi-circle around a flannelgraph on which she illustrated the lesson with cut-outs of Jesus, Zacchaeus, and a syca-more tree. Curiously, when Zacchaeus climbed the tree to see Jesus, she held the figure sideways as though he was levitating. He looked even sillier when she placed him atop the tree. Instead of looking down to Jesus who was addressing him, he stood full height staring off into the distance as though he were a sentinel.

The congregation at Samuels was both German Reformed and Lutheran. To accommodate the theological differences, two ministers alternated every other Sunday. Reverend Yost held a service for the Lutherans one Sunday (all the Reformed members attended anyway), and then Reverend Zechman preached to the Reformed faithful (all the Lutherans attended) the following Sunday. Despite the historical link to the Protestant Reformation and Evangelical Christianity, wor-ship failed to stress either Bible Study or evangelism, but involved merely a weekly ritual that emphasized living a reputable life. From Daddy's viewpoint, this was apostasy.

Our family worshiped regularly at Samuel's until I was 7 years-old, at which time we began attending Grandma Cora's Calvary Inde-pendent Church of the Brethren on Shaw Avenue in Lewistown.

We made this change for two reasons: first, my father, through-out his life, had a history of disenchantment with ministers. He was seldom supportive of any of them until after they left, at which time one or two would be remembered favorably. Reverend Zechman, the Reformed pastor at Samuel's, was foremost of the apostates and even in perpetuity remained beyond my father's graces. Ironically, Pastor Zechman had married Daddy and Mommy.

The second reason was theological. My Grandmother Cora, who was a member of the Shaw Avenue church, spoke glowingly of the pastor, Harold Snyder, and assured Daddy that the church preached sound Biblical doctrine.[2] Our family began regular attendance there

2. Reverend Snyder was forty years of age when he accepted the pastorate on Shaw Avenue in 1940. By 1948, although he had become popular with the laity, the church's hierarchy

in the summer of 1949,

In 1951 a displaced splinter group (see footnote) from the Shaw Avenue church began erecting a new building at South Pine Street in Lewistown that would later be named Calvary Bible Church. Awaiting its completion, the evicted pastor and his charges worshiped for the next two years at the Lewistown Armory, a few miles from Lewistown.

Mommy, Daddy, Keith, and I were baptized and became official members. We attended both Sunday School and church on Sunday mornings, the vesper service on Sunday evenings, and Wednesday night prayer meetings. In addition, Keith and I went to Boys Brigade on Saturday evenings, and, during the summers of 1951-53, stayed for one week with Grandma to attend the church's Vacation Bible School. I learned Scripture verses, books of the Bible, and became familiar with other Christian kids. Bible School was an especially important time in my life as I began to notice older Christian kids and admire them as role models. I observed for the first time the behavior of teen-agers who dated and boys who played on high school sports teams. I learned that some of the friends I most respected went to summer Bible Camps, had daily personal devotions, and enjoyed a very real relationship with Jesus.

Our family continued to worship at Calvary Bible Church for the next ten years, after Reverend Snyder retired in 1959, and after Keith and I departed for college in 1961. By that time a new pastor, Ralph Norwood, had been hired. The North Carolinian, fresh from his first pastorate in Virginia, possessed flamboyance and a pretty wife whose style of dress sometimes generated whispers of

demanded that he renounce views that included: anti-pacifism, opposition to the Federal Council of Churches, and support of eternal security. Pastor Snyder asserted that the parish was autonomous and was not bound to the denomination's theology. When he renamed the church Calvary Independent Church of the Brethren, the hierarchy filed suit and the church split into two factions. The local court ruled that Pastor Snyder and his followers be evicted. An appeal before the Pennsylvania State Supreme Court was upheld on March 19, 1951. Incredibly, one week later, a groundbreaking ceremony was held at the site of a newly acquired plot on 315 South Pine Street, and the construction of a new church building began. In the interim, a trustee of the Lewistown Armory, a military installation about five miles east of the town center that had been largely vacated after WWII, offered the displaced congregation a meeting place. The newly named Calvary Bible Church would continue at the armory until February 1952 when the Pine Street church was opened.

disapproval amongst the older ladies. His manner seemed dispatch without diplomacy. He had the brashness of a young minister but lacked the grace that results from experience. As a result, an incident occurred one Sunday at Calvary Bible Church that underscored Daddy's personal struggle with inferiority and self-esteem and brought an end to our involvement at that church.

On the previous Sunday, we had learned that one of the deacons had died earlier in the week. Daddy and Mommy approached the widow to express condolences. The widow asked Daddy if he would be interested in some of her late husband's clothes. With Mommy's encouragement, Daddy politely agreed to stop at the house later in the week and take a look. In spite of his sometimes volatile temper, Daddy often charmed strangers and was fully capable of grace and kindness when he socialized. These sensitive demonstrations always seemed to manifest a precarious balance between his low self-esteem and lively ambition.

In any case, on a weekday afternoon I accompanied him to the home of the deceased where he chose a pair of shoes and two sport coats, and afterward profusely thanked the widow. Neither coat was conservative in either cut or color, but one in particular, a purple plaid, was somewhat garish and became the instrument that severed our ties with Calvary Bible Church.

Daddy had few dress clothes and fewer opportunities to wear them, so he looked forward both to the new wardrobe and to the attention it might produce at church. After we arrived home that evening, he slipped into first one, and then the other of the coats, parading in front of us and demonstrating his unspoken delight. He was encouraged by Mommy's affectionate assurance that he was "handsome in those coats."

His pride was nearly palpable the following Sunday when we arrived at church. Daddy was in full regalia, wearing the purple plaid coat. We entered and took our seats near the rear of the auditorium. Reverend Norwood preached. As a new minister, he, too, was trying to make a favorable impression. His sermon was long, his theatrics overdone. Daddy found the minister's youth and extroversion in stark contrast to the reserved dignity of former Pastor Snyder. Afterward most congregants were receptive, gracious, affirming, perhaps even patronizing, although a few skeptics continued to hold reservations.

PASTOR RALPH NORWOOD
A foreigner from North Carolina

For Daddy, however, Pastor Norwood was on trial. The service was a reenactment of Nuremberg with Daddy as the chef magistrate and executioner. He listened with a critical and jaundiced mind. He disliked the new arrival and plainly considered the minister a "foreigner." The preacher was walking a narrow and precarious path. Actually, Daddy had already passed judgment, pinioning Pastor Norwood beneath the shadow of the departed Reverend Snyder. He measured the newcomer's every word, his every gesture, probing for flaws. Judgment was calculated and inexorable.

When the service was completed parishioners exited by passing through a receiving line at the rear of the church where Pastor Norwood greeted members and visitors with small talk, trying to recall names and attach them to faces. His comments were, like his personality, sometimes awkward but generally clichéd and innocuous. He hoped the interaction would produce positive feedback and generate good will. For Daddy the receiving line gave the new pastor one last occasion to ingratiate himself.

Parishioners filed slowly forward, extending hands of greeting, one after another praising and encouraging the new minister. Then, it was Daddy's turn. He extended a stiff hand, but did not speak. Pastor Norwood, in all probability, sensed that Daddy was not yet an admirer. The cleric attempted to seize the moment—an opportunity to grow in the grace of Jim Morgan. As though they were familiar friends, he chortled, "Jim, where in the world did you get that coat?"

Our farm lay twenty miles distant from the church. For all twenty miles, we rode in the midst of a storm. Ralph Norwood and all clergy remotely associated with Christendom were formally and finally denounced. "Never again," Daddy swore, "will I set a foot in that church. Calvary Bible Church can go straight to Hell. They'll never get anything of mine." The family sat in frozen silence as we sped past familiar landscape—racing past the store at Maitland where we usually stopped to buy the potato chips and luncheon meat that helped celebrate Sundays, zooming by the hitchhiker at Wagner who retreated from the berm into a weed bank at the sight of our onrushing car, and spinning the rear tires as we turned off the paved highway at Joe McKinley's Store onto the dirt road that led to the farm. Daddy had been humiliated.

Instead of store-bought meat for sandwiches, Mommy fried eggs. Heavy slices of home-made bread were substituted for commercially produced sandwich rolls, and potato chips were forgotten as we quickly ate and scattered until Daddy's fury subsided later in the afternoon.

We did not return regularly to Calvary Bible Church after that. Keith and I went off to college, and Daddy spent the following months looking for a new church, a new set of faces, and a new beginning. In the years that followed I never asked him about that morning at church, Pastor Norwood, or the purple coat. I did, however, when I returned home in the summer after my freshman year at college, sneak into his bedroom one afternoon and look into his closet for the purple coat. It was not there, as I knew it would not be, but its absence marked for me the sadness that Daddy wore something even worse in its place: a wound, internal and private.

Detachment
That other armor -
For crueler blows.

Applause withheld,
The wounded soul -
Withdraws - topples -
Prepares a firmer hold.

Fixed its public hurt,
Bleeds -
In hidden places.
                              DENNIS MORGAN

Vacation Bible School at the Lewistown Armory (1952)

Vacation Bible School at Calvary Bible Church (1953)

MOMMY - A TRIBUTE

Hazel Marie (Arnold) Morgan

August 28, 1920 – June 21, 2009

As an adult I am aware that many of our attitudes and feelings develop when we are children. Certainly the behavior of parents contributes to the coloration of a child's world. I am convinced, however, that each human being is divinely endowed with a singular disposition at the moment God breathes life into the zygote. This disposition stands wholly apart from genetics and environment. The result is that, while a portion of behavior can be traced to lineage, there is much that is endemic to God's creative hand. In either case, parents are responsible for the cultivation of their children—the nurture and admonition of the Lord (Ephesians 6:4). This demands sacrifice and requires a careful balance of discipline and encouragement. God tells the caretakers of children to tenderly plant and water their seeds—this is how Mommy did it.

MOMMY LOVED - All of us, all of the time. She never once wished that her family was smaller or that she had greater freedom from responsibilities or that she did not have to face another day. I am positive of that, because I am seventy-seven years old, and for each and every one of my own children, it has daily been purest joy to have them and to sacrifice for them. I know exactly from where that attitude comes. She taught us that selflessness produces joy. She understood when Jesus said that to gain a greater life, it is necessary to lose a lesser one. His counsel has an immediate as well as eternal application.

MOMMY WORKED - every day, sunrise to sunset, and most days beyond. When I was in the early grades, I remember hearing early morning noises coming from the kitchen, long before daylight, as she made the wood fire in the cook stove, made cocoa from scratch, fried eggs and toasted bread, all before calling us to get ready for school. On especially bad weather winter mornings, she went to the barn and did the milking so that Daddy could start the tractor and drive Keith and me across the fields to Krick School, a one-room schoolhouse, which she, too, had attended years earlier.

Mommy believed that idleness was both laziness and "the Devil's workshop."

Regardless of the season, I have no recollection whatsoever of getting out of bed before she was up and about. She paid continual and strict attention to duty. During most of my years at home, she daily washed diapers and clothes, keeping a washboard by the side of our smokehouse where there was a hydrant, and Monday through Saturday, scrubbing clothes against that board. Cleanliness was an obsession. On more than one occasion I overheard neighbors comment that "You can eat off the floor in Hazels' house."

MOMMY COOKED - How God blessed us through her kitchen! We ate three cooked meals every day. Even on the summer Sundays when Daddy stopped at the country store in Maitland on

Mommy kept her garden as pristine as her house.

the way home from church in Lewistown and bought luncheon meat, Middleswarth potato chips, and Campbell's baked beans, she saw to it that there was fresh baked bread, pies, and cakes. When we had Sunday company, which was frequent, she fried chicken or ham to be served with mashed potatoes and gravy, creamed rice and home-baked beans, vegetables and fruit salads.

I enjoyed a special treat two or three days each week when she baked our bread. Mommy would save some dough, let it rise, and then fry a dumpling for me. I ate it hot with sugar and milk between meals.

Evenings, after her day of cleaning, washing, baking, and preparing meals (and often working in the fields or at the barn), she tended the garden. Our garden was large, and Mommy continuously weeded and watered. She picked the beans, cut the cabbage, husked the corn and dug the onions and potatoes. With bonnet and apron she withstood the onslaught of countless gnats and mosquitoes, the cries of children for something to eat, and the aches of mind and body.

There was always work to do. When the day wound down, she made snacks for hungry children, stoked the fire for the night, bathed little ones, and tucked them into bed after prayers were said. I have no memory of her going to bed while any member of her family was still up and about. Perhaps the most impressive product of her labor was simply the condition of our house. It was always clean. Polished clean. There was no dust on the top of Mommy's refrigerator.

MOMMY CRIED - Her life was flooded with both sunshine and rain. She cried over the simplest compliments. She cried when good things happened to others, and she cried with unadulterated joy when she counted her own blessings. She cried with friends and acquaintances when they shared their problems. She genuinely felt that the problems, burdens, and concerns of others were greater than her own. She was never too busy to listen when a visitor needed a moment of empathy. And her compassion did not stop with a willing ear. She fed them, wrote to them, and visited them.

With ready vulnerability, however, came other tears. Mommy was easily bruised. When a friend failed to speak or a neighbor failed to notice, she assumed culpability. She craved Daddy's affection and crumbled before his insensitivities. She acquiesced in order to mollify.

During my four years of college she phoned only once. In the spring of my junior year she called to tell me she was pregnant.[1] I was to be married that summer, and she was concerned I would be embarrassed to have a pregnant mother attend the wedding. She cried throughout our conversation, asking forgiveness for "letting me down." She called for a second reason as well: Daddy was upset at the pregnancy and was blaming her. She needed a consoling spirit.

Mommy's wounds festered when there were no apologies, no acknowledgments, no remedies. She craved reconciliation—immediate and genuine. Unresolved conflict produced stress that resulted in years of nerve medicines. The most severe source of her stress was her relationship with Daddy. He was moody, impatient, easily angered, and sometimes verbally abusive to both her and us children. Only once did I hear him apologize, and even then, it seemed disingenuous. Instead, after abusive, personal remarks steeped in self-pity, he petulantly stomped away, leaving everyone unsettled. Mommy would then spend the day on tenterhooks. Living resumed, but the cuts bled.

---

1. My beautiful sister Beth was born on October 28, 1964, and was a source of joy for both Mommy and Daddy the rest of their days.

Mommy prayed daily for each of us.
Left to right sitting: Bill, Beth, Mommy, Susie, RuthAnn – Back: Joe, Dave, Keith, and myself.

MOMMY PRAYED - Each school morning she stood in front of the kitchen door, where Keith and I waited, holding our brown bag lunches and books, as she asked God's care and blessing on us for the day. Her prayers were brief, primarily because we had to hurry to be in our seats before the school bell rang at nearby Krick School, or after we were in high school, because we had to catch the 6:45 am bus.

As children, she prayed with us at night after we climbed into bed. She repeated with us the lyrical supplication, "Now I lay me down to sleep, I pray the Lord my soul to keep. If I should die before I wake, I pray the Lord my soul to take." Even when we were older, she sometimes climbed the stairs, knocked on our bedroom door, and reminded us to say our prayers.

During our family devotional time, she never prayed for comfort or strength to see her through a difficult day, but instead she asked Providence to keep her from sin. She petitioned for financial relief, rain for crops, and safety for her family. She continually asked God to make plain His will for the lives of her children and to ensure their spiritual health.

Mommy had personal prayer time as part of her personal quiet time. She usually read from a published tract or devotional, and then, one by one, prayed through the prayer list she maintained on the note pages of her Bible. The list included family, friends, neighbors, and missionaries she had met through church.

Much later, after Daddy's death, as I stayed nights with her, we prayed together before retiring. In her loneliness for Daddy and her children, she refused to see her life as anything other than blessed. Every pain, every inconvenience, every complaint had the caveat, "God knows best."

Mommy was not without flaws. Sometimes she was difficult to please. I pulled weeds in her garden, satisfied that I had done a good job, then watched in dismay as she got to her knees and reweeded where I had been working.

When we killed, cleaned, and cut up chickens, she continually reminded me to "do a good job." I tried but never was able to satisfy her standards. I would remove every feather from a carcass, proudly lay it on the kitchen counter, and ask, "Is that good?"

"If you have to ask," she would say without looking at my work, "probably not." Then she would pick up the carcass and find a dozen feathers I had missed.

Seldom was her criticism verbal, but her look of disappointment was chastening. My rows of beans were seldom straight enough or deep enough or long enough. She reminded, "God watches everything we do."

Despite such idiosyncrasies, it was through her faithfulness and love, through the daily demonstration of her convictions, that she introduced us to her God whose love and steadfast faithfulness provides assurance that we will one day be reunited.

MOMMY'S MEMORIES

Sunday, May 3, 2009

Mommy was in Emmanuel Nursing Home in Northumberland, PA. I tried to visit every two weeks, spending Saturdays, usually arriving in mid-morning, updating family news, taking her to lunch as a means of getting away from the routine of

Emmanuel Nursing Home at Northumberland, PA

group-home life, returning to spend the afternoon, looking at old photographs, and watching Bill Gaither videos of gospel music (sometimes singing with the performers). In retrospect, the afternoons were a kind of worship as we reminisced, recalling God's blessings in our lives and claiming His promises of reunion with those now deceased. On my previous visit I had promised to return with pencil and paper, so I could make a permanent record of her days past, the culture and customs lost to time, and the names and places strange and removed from a second generation. Conscious that time with her was counted, not in months and years, but in days and hours, I wanted her to breathe life into the world of her childhood.

Her single room had a private bath, bed, small dining table with two chairs, a favorite gliding rocking chair, and a window that overlooked a small lawn and woods. The rocking chair sat beneath the window facing inward. It was a material and emotional attachment to an ordered past that had been ruptured, first by Daddy's death nine years earlier, and more recently by her move into the world of assisted living—a vestige of comfort amid transitory and insecure reality.

The lawn featured a bird feeder set back close to the building that permitted residents to pass time watching local aviary. Even on sunny days, the nursing home was a bleak reminder of finality. The home was a practical and necessary circumstance, but her sons and daughters did not escape the guilt that results when the dignity of so dear a parent is subjected to unsolicited dependency.

I arrived about 11:00 am, and an hour later the two of us drove to Selinsgrove where we ate lunch at a Kentucky Fried Chicken restaurant. She immensely enjoyed her buffet style meal but had piled too much on her plate. Her hunger sated, she fretted about what to do with the leftover portion. After considering both the uncouthness of returning uneaten food and the criminality of taking it with her, she took her plate and dilemma to the manager.

"Excuse me," she entreated. "I took too much and would like to pay for it."

The manager looked at the plate, confused by her request. "Didn't you already pay for it?" he asked.

"Yes, but I can't eat it, and I don't want to throw it away. I would like to pay for it."

Struck by her innocence, he stared in momentary paroxysm. Probity not only disarms, it imposes.

Momentarily incredulous that such virtue existed, he reached for the plate, set it atop the counter, placed the piece of chicken into a box, folded it closed, and returned it to her.

"What's your name," he requested.

"Hazel."

"Well, Hazel, take this home and enjoy it."

Thirty minutes later we arrived back at the Nursing Home. For the next three or four hours, she sat on a plain table chair facing me, re-

Mommy in her apartment at Emmanuel Nursing Home

calling her youth, her family, and some of the events that afforded special memories. I sat beneath the window in the glider rocker, asked questions, and took notes. I kept the material anticipating a second session when we could continue the interview. She began to fail shortly thereafter, however, and was not up to the clarity and concentration required. She died on June 21 at age 88.

> NOTE: I have tried to write this interview in Mommy's words, in her idiom. In the course of that afternoon, however, there were times when she unexpectedly changed topics, returning to something spoken earlier, or adding a comment somewhat out of context. As a result, I have taken license with the syntax. For those who never met her or heard her speak, the cadence of her speech was slow, thoughtful, with regular pauses.

Question: "Take me back to your girlhood and talk about your home. What was your father like as a dad? Your mother as a mom? Do you remember your grandparents?"

Mommy: "Pop's folks were farm people.[1] He grew up on the farm over by Emmet Hoffman.[2] I was little when Pop's dad died, so I didn't know him, but everyone said he was a hard worker. His name was Simon. He chewed tobacco, so they kept a spittoon next to his chair. They were nice people. They had a big family. Both my dad and mother's folks were farm people. They worked with horses.

"Mom's mother and dad lived on the Snook farm past Fern Knepp's farm.[3] I was very young when they died, too. They weren't rich, I guess, but they always had what they needed. Mom never talked much about it. Sometimes when we drove by their farm, she would show where they

---

1. While the reference to "farm people" was not pejorative, she was aware that farm people generally were not wealthy or sophisticated and lived lives of honest simplicity.
2. The Hoffman farm lay about four miles to the west of our farm on what is today Hoffman Road. Its terrain was similar to that of our own farm although it contained more woodland and slightly less tillable acreage.
3. The Snook farm was about three miles east of our farm. Today, it is the first farm on Fairview Road after passing the intersection with County Line Road. The Knepp Farm to which she referred lay at that intersection.

played or point out where her mother had a garden. Mom's dad died after he cut his hand and it became infected. Mom was next to the oldest, so she knew what it was to work in the fields. Mom had a picture of her dad and mother in her bedroom for years. Her dad had a moustache.

JAMES EDWARD SNOOK
SARAH GRACE (WILL) SNOOK
This picture of Mammie's parents hung on her bedroom wall for nearly fifty years.

"Pop's dad logged to make extra money. They had to get wood for winter, so he logged. Pop used to hitch his horses and go to the woods where they logged. Mom would pack his dinner, and he would return at dark. I guess they cut logs for fire and for building. He never talked much about it. It was hard work. Pop hauled logs for Mr. Paul Marshall to build the first funeral home in McClure. I was starting high school, so it would have been about 1934.

"When Pop came back at night, he watered and fed the horses before

THE FAMILY OF SIMON W. ARNOLD AND ANNIE RAGER ARNOLD:
Front Row, Left to Right, Bertha, Carrie, Annie, Simon, Charles, Anna, Hettie. Back Row, Emma, Henry, Rhetta, Delilah, Margaret, Samuel, Arthur, Effie. Beginning with Charles and moving counter-clockwise, the children are arranged by age.

supper, then went back to the barn before he went to bed, so he could curry them. I sat on a milk stool and watched. When he came home late, Mom and us girls milked. Mom stayed up late after Pop went to bed. I don't know if she couldn't sleep 'cause there was so much to do, or if she just couldn't sleep. When she finished, she folded her apron and went to bed. She always wore an apron. All the ladies did. Except for church, I don't remember her without her apron. I think she got up when Pop got up. We didn't sleep late. She always had supper ready and she always had meat. I guess I was like Mom. Mom made us stay at the table until he was finished. After supper us girls washed the dishes. Mom baked or cleaned after we went to bed. Winters we all stayed in the kitchen 'cause it was warm. She sometimes made taffy and let us pull it. We played outside till dark. Pop went to bed early. When I was little I climbed in beside him. Mom teased Pop about his snoring.

"I don't remember how old I was when Pop's dad died, but every Sunday we visited his mother. Her name was Annie. I think Pop was his mother's favorite because she always made a fuss over him. Pop would mow the yard or fix things for her.

"I don't remember Mom's mother and dad. I was just a baby, but Mom

Mommy and her sister Iva as high school farm girls about 1937

always spoke nice about them, and Mom's brothers and sisters were very nice people. When I was a girl we visited sometimes. We played with our cousins; school or dolls, you know, the things that kids play. Pop liked to visit on Sundays, but Bud (Mommy's brother) wanted the car a lot of times after he was in high school. When he didn't get it, he would sit behind the stove and pout. He got to go a lot of places with his friends, but Pop didn't say too much. He (Bud) thought he was big stuff. I don't remember Bud helping a lot with the milking. Mom helped, and she always washed the dippers and buckets, but I don't remember Bud doing much. I know he worked in the fields like the rest of us, but not much at the barn. Iva, she was always with Pappy in the fields. She drove the horses when we threshed and planted corn or anything. She was good at it. I worked in the fields too, but Iva worked a lot with Pop."

Question: "Can you recall something specific, a person or event that demonstrates your dad's personality?"

Mommy: "I don't think there was any one thing. Pop worked. He was restless when there was work to do. He didn't like us wasting time, playing when we were supposed to be working. He took us kids with him a lot. When we went to sales or to McClure, he bought candy for us. He liked peppermint sticks and would buy some in a paper bag and let us reach in the bag and choose. He was proud of his horses. When men came to visit on Sundays, they always ended up at the barn with the horses. I don't think he spanked us much. I can remember only once, when we were playing and upset the feedbags he had ready for the feed mill. I don't know if he spanked us or just said he was going to. We always minded him though. I didn't get into trouble. Beatty and I played together, and Iva, but Iva sometimes would do things. Sometimes we would tease Bud. We wrote his name in the chicken house with a girl's name one time and when he saw it, he was mad. Iva did it. We were playing, and Iva took a pencil Pop had laid on one of the window sills, and she wrote it. It was there for a long time. We played a lot up at the chicken house, in the entryway where the feed was. We would sit on the bags and play. Pop never said anything, but Mom wanted to know what we were doing.

"Pop and Mom loved each other. They didn't kiss or hug in front of us, but Pop always was nice to Mom. Sometimes, if he was upset, he would go to the barn, but Pop didn't get mad often. Mom would brush his suit before church and made certain we took water to him when he was in the fields. When he came back from McClure, he brought things for her. Pop liked hard candy or licorice or things like that. Mom tied hard candy in her handkerchief and carried it in her pocket. She always went with him when he went anywhere. Once, when he spent a day logging at McVeytown, Mom and us played a trick on him. It was Mom's idea. He came home. We were waiting to eat supper. He had walked from the main road, and we were hiding in the house: I think all of us were home. Mom had locked the doors as a joke and we hid and kept quiet. He walked around to both doors and couldn't get in. Finally, he opened the kitchen window that faced the barn and threw his lunch pail inside and started to climb through. We watched and then yelled, "Surprise!" He thought it was funny, and I remember him and Mom laughed, and we had a good time. We always looked forward to his getting home, and Mom wouldn't let us eat until he got to the table. When I was little, I always ran into his bedroom after he went to bed and kissed him good night.

"When we got older we had to work. We helped in the fields. Pop would get mad if we didn't do things right. He was particular. We didn't have a hayloader in those days, so I drove the horses and Beattie and Iva worked up on the wagon. Pop had to throw the hay up on the wagon and the girls built the load. If they didn't do it right, Pop yelled at us. He was always on my back for not keeping the horses in a straight line, or when we shocked oats or wheat, for not standing the shocks up straight and tying them so they didn't come loose. He had his way, and he wanted it done right. I guess I do the same.

"When I was little, Mom used to put me into the wagon box in my playpen. I would play while Mom and Pop husked the corn and threw it into the wagon. I remember freezing to death in the field above Sammy Hostetler's farm,[4] because it would get cold when the sun went down, and Pop always wanted to finish what he started. When I got older, I drove the horses. Pop would tell me when to go and when to stop. Mom carried a jar of water in the wagon box, and I could drink when I was thirsty. When we had to pee, we went off into the corn. Pop worked 'til after dark.[5]

"I was helping Daddy open the field one time, after Mom and Pop had moved, when Pastor Snyder and Hobe Sear stopped.[6] I had a corn chopper and was in my bandana. I was so embarrassed I didn't know what to do. They stayed for supper. I fried ham, and they made a fuss, but I still remember it. I don't know what they thought."

Question: "I am aware that there have been many changes to the farm. The farm on which you grew up is not exactly the same as the one I knew. How was it different?"

Mommy: "Well, we didn't have electricity like we do now, so we milked by hand. Iva and Beatty and me all knew what it was to milk. On

---

4. Sammy Hostetler and his family were Amish. Until Pappy and Mammie built their house in 1950-51, the Hostetlers were our closest neighbors, about a half-mile to the east. About the time I started first grade, they sold their farm to "Chip" Sheriff and moved to Belleville.

5. I have exactly the same memory of being in that same green wagon box in that same playpen and freezing while Daddy and Mommy husked corn in that same field.

6. They were men from Calvary Bible Church in Lewistown where we attended throughout the 1950s. Pastor Snyder was, of course, our preacher, and Hobe Searer was a deacon.

school days Mom helped Pop with the milking 'cause we didn't want to smell like the barn, and we had to be ready for the milkman or else we couldn't go to school. I don't remember when Pop bought the tractor. We had horses. Pop kept the horses in the pen where you first walk into the barn. I fed them, but I made Pop water them. I was always afraid to water the horses. Pop said to grab hold of their collar and lead them out to the trough, but I was afraid they would step on my feet.

"I guess another difference would have been that we used kerosene. In the evenings Pop used kerosene lamps in the barn. When we milked, we moved one of the lamps closer to the cow so we could see. I don't remember exactly, but I think there were three kerosene lamps in the barn. We didn't have light in the hay mow, so when we threw down hay it would be dark 'cause it was dangerous to have kerosene lamps around the hay.[7] Pop made us throw down hay while it was light, before we did the other work. He milked last 'cause there was light from the kerosene lamps.

Barn light was supplied by kerosene lamps.

"Before the silo was built, corn was shocked without tying the shock. We husked it and threw the ears into piles. Then, the ears were thrown into the wagon and taken to the cribs. After that, the corn stalks were cut and shocked. We cut a bunch of stalks and then picked up as many as we could get our arms around and propped them up against other stalks. The shocks were brought to the barn about once a month to be fed to the cows. After Pop bought the silo filler, we shredded corn fodder and blew it underneath the overshot. We didn't have a silo at that time, but Pop put one up right after. We got cracked corn for the peepies (baby chicks) when they got a little older, but I guess you did that, too. We bagged grain for feed for the cows and pigs just like you and Keith did. Pop emptied the cow feed into the feedbox, 'cause before the stanchions were put in, the cows or horses would get loose sometimes and tear open the bags. When we helped Pop with the barn work, it was our job to get the feed out of the feedbox and chop the cows.[8] After Daddy started working for Pop we got stanchions, and Daddy built a rack that we put the feed on. Pop always liked that because the feed-bags used to sit on the floor and draw damp.

"When you were boys there were two milk houses and two silos, but

---

7. Even the heated globes could set straw or hay afire.

8. "Chop" was a ground mixture of corn, wheat, oats and molasses

we had only one. The old milkhouse had a cement floor and a trough where milk cans could be lowered into the water. It was spring water so it was always pretty cold. Sometimes in summer, Pop would buy blocks of ice from the iceman and put them between the cans to keep the milk cold. Before the milkhouse was built, and even afterward for some years, we took the milk to the springhouse. Mom kept butter and cheese and other things in the springhouse. The men had built different levels in the springhouse so Mom could keep things cold. I don't remember how many cans were in the springhouse at one time but I would guess four. If we had a lot of snow there would be more cans 'cause the milk man couldn't get through, but normally there were about four. Sometimes when a cow was fresh, her milk wasn't good yet, and she wouldn't let her calf drink, so Pop mixed it with pig feed and slopped the pigs. Cows used to tramp the water shut around the springhouse, so Pop had to dig it out. He hooked up the one-bottom plow and made a ditch. He yelled at us when we played in the ditch, 'cause we would knock dirt in it. He said he didn't want to always keep plowin' it open. Later he built a fence around the springhouse.

Mommy and her sister Beatty. As a teenager Beatty dug the ditch that brought running water to the house.

"When we got water in the house, Beatty dug the ditch. She dug the ditch for the pipe, the whole way from the springhouse up to the cellar.[9] I guess we worked hard in those days. Mom always got on us about keeping the springhouse door closed, 'cause the horses would get in and make a mess. Pop didn't want us playing in the springhouse, but we would go down there sometimes and play. On hot days it was cool on the cement.

"The first pump we had in the milkhouse was a crank pump that turned in a circle. It was like the old gas pumps where the crank turned two or three times, and then you had to turn it backwards. We used it to water the horses and cows and wash the

---

9. My own estimate is that the springhouse was situated 120-150 feet below (south of) the house.

---

milk buckets, but Pop put in a new pump with a regular handle that went up and down 'cause it pumped more water faster. The horses used to push each other to get water first. The cows, too. My job was to fill the trough before the cows came and then keep water coming until they had enough. When Iva or Beatty would go down to the meadow and bring the cows, I would hurry to the milkhouse and start pumpin'. In the winter when the cows were in the barn, Pop let them out four at a time so they could drink. In the winter the milkhouse was cold, so I dressed warm when I drew water.

"When the milkman came, the milk had to be taken from the milk-house to his truck.[10] He would get Pop's wheelbarrow and take two cans at a time. He parked his truck out by that little grassy hill in front of the wagon shed. Park Coleman was our milkman. Iva and I rode to school with him. He came early to make his route, so we had to be ready. Our farm was one of his first stops. We rode with him while he made his other stops. It was about an hour before we would get to school. Each time he stopped to pick up a different farmer's milk, he would turn the truck off. We would get cold. We didn't like it when he would stand and talk. We wanted him to get back in the truck and start the motor. Pop and Mom knew Park and his family. In those days people knew each other. Once a month the (Park) Colemans, (John) Gosses, Arnolds, and (Walter) Wrights would get together and make ice cream, so Iva and me knew him real well. He was a tease. He used to tell us, "I'll go without you." Iva always took the door 'cause the heater was on that side. When he got in and out of the truck, the cold air would come in from his side. We wore dresses to school with nothing to cover our legs.

"Just like you kids, it was always us girls' job to get the cows. In the summer we didn't wear shoes except when we had to work in the fields or go to church or visit. Mom didn't like us goin' barefoot in someone's house. We went barefoot in the meadow to get the cows, and sometimes we stepped in the poop or stepped on thistles. I guess a lot of the things we did was the same as for you. We kept our shoes in the woodbox behind the stove in the kitchen. When we took off our shoes, we put them in the woodbox on top of the wood. Bud used to say he was going to throw our

---

10. Milk from the morning milking did not have to be cooled since it was immediately transported to the Dairymen's League Processing Plant at Beaver Springs. The previous evening's milk, however, had to be carried to the springhouse and set into the cold spring water. Thus, every morning the milkman had to retrieve the ten-gallon cans from both the milkhouse and the springhouse. After electricity was installed and an electric milk cooler was purchased, all the cans were kept in the milkhouse, and the springhouse fell into disuse.

shoes into the stove. I don't know the reason, but I was a little afraid of him sometimes. He could be mean.

"We didn't have a refrigerator. Two times a week, I think, the ice truck would come, and we would get two blocks of ice up in the woodshed. Mom would take the ice pick and break it in pieces and put pieces in the icebox. It would stay cold until he came again, but she used to yell to keep the door shut because it would melt, and we would have to throw things out. In the winter we had ice from the crick for ice cream,[11] but we didn't have ice water. When we wanted to keep something cold, we wrapped it in a towel. One time Mom told me to bring water to Pop and her over in the field next to Paul Wright's where they were husking corn. It was a hot day, and when it was time I got the water ready. We kept a mason jar in the springhouse and I went down and filled it. I couldn't find a towel, so I wrapped it in one of Mom's aprons, and I started off across the field. It was a long way across the fields, and when I got there, Pop told me to set the jar under a sheaf to keep it cool until they finished the shock they were working on. I dropped it and it broke. Pop didn't scold me, but Mom really let me have it.

"Mom always had to have something to drink, coffee or something. In the morning, first thing, Mom had to have her coffee."

Question: "What did your mother and dad do for relaxation? What were the "fun" things they did?"

Mommy: "When I was real little they had the Arnold reunion-picnic at our farm.[12] All Pop's family would come. We always looked forward to it. We had it right in the yard. They set up chairs and everyone had a good time. Pop was proud 'cause he was the oldest and his mom and dad were there, and he wanted them to see the farm. Everybody got along. In the evening, everybody had to get home to milk. They stopped having the reunion when I was in high school.

"We used to have the Samuel-Lawvers (Church) picnic at the farm.

---

11. This was our vernacular for "creek."

12. Pappy and Mammie bought the farm outright in the fall of 1923 after renting it for twelve years. In the early summer of 1924 my proud grandfather, wishing to show off his investment and express gratitude to his father and mother, invited his entire family, following church services, including spouses and children to a Sunday dinner at the farm. An unidentified local resident who owned a camera was asked to take some pictures. The photo on the following page is one of those snapshots. Mommy was 3 years old at the time. She is standing in the second row of the photograph.

THE EXTENDED FAMILY OF SIMON W. ARNOLD AND ANNIE RAGER ARNOLD
Left to Right: Russell Bickel, Iva Arnold, Danny Hassinger, Carrie Arnold Klingler, Ethyl Barnett, Marvin (Bud) Arnold, Dora Hassinger Boonie, Beatrice Arnold Boonie, Glen Arnold, Max Erb, Jim Bickel, Carmen Erb. Second row: Betty Knepp Baker and Rhett Arnold Knepp, Clyde David and Mag, Annie Bickel holding Kathryn Bickel Dubois, Annie Rager Arnold, Simon Arnold holding Loren Knepp, Miriam (Sissy) Arnold Adams and Mertie Snook Arnold, Hazel Arnold, Hettie Arnold Hassinger, Fred Arnold, Gerald Erb and Effie Erb. Back row: Henry Arnold, Pat Knepp, Art Knepp, Rueben (Ruby) Hassinger, Cluney Erb, Leroy David, Emma Arnold Wagner, Ira Bickel, Arthur Arnold, Bertha Arnold Cheslock, Samuel Arnold, Lydia Knepp, Charles Lester Arnold, Carrie Edna Snook Arnold.

After Daddy and I got married, Russell Riegel used to come down with his band and play in the old bandstand in Pappy's woods. The ladies made sandwiches and chicken and potato salad and a lot of food. Someone would bring candy for the kids, fudge or taffy or something. I don't know how many people came, but there were a lot. More from Samuels, I think.

"All of us went to the Bean Soup. We would see a lot of people we knew, and sometimes we would play with friends where Mom could see us.

"Mom liked to sew. She cut patches for Pop's pants or made new dresses for us. She and the ladies got together and made rugs. They would save rags and make beautiful rugs. In the winter, if it wasn't too cold, the women quilted. You can't quilt in the summer 'cause it gets too hot in the house. We had a quilt frame and Mom would set it up in the living room. We had our old wood stove in there, so it was warm. The ladies would walk to our house and then, at night, the men would pick them up. In the old days, if we had snow, they would hitch horses to the sleds and pick them up.

"After we got electricity, Pop liked to listen to *The Tom Mix Show*. He would stop his barn work if Tom Mix was on. In those days radio shows were 15 minutes. Daddy listened, too. On Sunday nights Pop liked westerns or Groucho Marx, and country music. He thought *Fibber McGee and Molly* was funny. Mom didn't listen. If we had the radio on while we were doing housework or making supper, we sometimes listened.[13]

"Pop and Mom liked to visit on Sunday afternoons: Mom's brothers and sisters or Pop's. We had cousins and played while the older ones talked or did things.

"We had fun. Pop liked to go to sales. He would talk to the men. I don't think he ever bought much. There wasn't a lot of money. After us kids were older, Mom would go with him, but she stayed in the car.

"Evenings, Pop liked to read the paper. He always sat in his rocking chair and read the paper. Mom read her Bible before she went to bed. She memorized verses. She told us kids hundreds of times *"Remember your Creator in the days of your youth, before the days of trouble come and the years approach when you will say, 'I find no pleasure in them.'"*[14] She didn't talk about the Bible like we do now, but she read it and kept after us.

"They didn't read books. After Bud got married, he used to bring papers and magazines for Pop to read, but I mostly remember him reading the paper. We got the *McClure Plain-Dealer* and there would be things in the paper and people we knew, so Pop liked to read that. They got TV after they moved, but Pop fell asleep early and didn't watch much. Mom had her programs – she watched *I Love Lucy, Beat the Clock,* and Groucho Marx on *You Bet Your Life.*

"Mom really missed Pop after he died. She always stayed at home. I used to go down and get her for supper. John and Nettie picked her up for church, but she didn't go out.[15] She really liked it when you kids went down. Before she died she went up to Iva's during the winters, but she wanted to

---

13. During the late 1940s and early 1950s, on afternoons when Mommy and Mammie worked in the kitchen, *Ma Perkins, Just Plain Bill, Backstage Wife, The Romance of Helen Trent, The Guiding Light,* and *Young Doctor Malone* played on our radio, but never did the ladies sit and listen. Nor did they ever discuss the programs. The Soap Operas seemed simply to provide a background diversion, or perhaps the housework, combined with radio signals that pulsated and faded, prevented their concentration.

14. Ecclesiastes 12:1

15. John and Nettie Goss were our neighbors. Their farm bordered our farm to the west.

be home."

Question: "Did you have any unusual experiences growing up? Experiences that other farm children your age did not have?"

Mommy: "When I was a little girl, Bud and Arvella had got married and they thought they couldn't have babies, so they took in a foster child. He must have been 4 or 5. His name was "Sonny." Arvella got sick, at least that's what they said. And Sonny came to live with us. We just loved him. So did Pop and Mom. It took about a year for Arvella to get better. While she was sick, Bud told Mom that Arvella was always after him to give Sonny back to the foster home, 'cause she couldn't handle the pressure of having a child in the house. When she was recovered Bud told Mom and Pop that he was giving Sonny back. All of us, including Mom and Pop, were heartbroken. Pop cried. We never saw him again."

Question: "Before you and Daddy married, what impression did you have of Daddy's family and home?"

Mommy: "Daddy's dad had a bad temper. I guess that's where the Morgan temper came from. His name was like Daddy's except it was William Cloyd. He went by the name "Cloyd." Daddy's Aunt Ethel had a bad temper, too. She was overweight and always in a bad mood. I was a little afraid of her. There was always a strain between Ethel and Daddy's father. They didn't get along. They had a brother, Lawrence. He was overweight, too.

Grandma and Irv at the Malta Home

"All Daddy's relatives called him "Jimmy." I first met Grandma at their house in Paintersville. It was the cleanest house I was ever in. I always cleaned before Grandma came to our house 'cause I didn't want her to think I was lazy. She always made everyone welcome and fed them. She was a great cook. Grandma worked at the shirt factory in Lewistown, but they had had tough times. After Daddy's father died, the Shawvers took them in 'cause there was no money. That's where Grandma met Irv. After Grandma and Irv got married, they would hold hands, but Dick and the others didn't like it, so they stopped. Some of Daddy's family never liked Irv. I always thought he was okay, except for one time he made a remark. He and I were alone in the kitchen, and he said he and I would make a "good pair." I didn't trust him after that, but I think he treated Grandma well. When Irv and Grandma got married, none of Grandma's kids went to the wedding."

Question: "I have never seen a wedding picture of you and Daddy. Didn't someone take a picture on the day you were married?"

Mommy: "We drove down to Beaver Springs, to Reverend Zechman's house, and got married there. I don't think anyone owned a camera. When we came back to the house Iva took pictures. I was wearing my graduation dress that Mammie made for me. It was very pretty, white with a colored print. Daddy thought I looked nice. I have a picture."

There was a small end table with side pockets and two shelves in the corner of her one-room apartment. On its bottom shelf, resting on a white doily, was her Bible and the most recent copy of Our Daily Bread, a monthly devotional booklet she read since its first publication in 1956. In one side pocket there were two magazines of word puzzles whose pages were littered with incomplete crosswords and eraser stains. On the top shelf a second doily supported a vase of artificial flowers. Beside the vase lay two pencils and an eraser. She arose and began shuffling through one of the side pockets. Finding several pictures, she came and bent beside me. The photographs held her as she fell silent, emotion choking her speech. The pictures had not discolored but remained clean and unwrinkled evidencing their import and care through nearly fifty years. She held one toward me. The glossy black and white print was of her high school glee club. She stood at the far right of row two, the altos, one of two dozen formally dressed graduates in abeyance. Her smile was genuine, proud, but lacked confidence, as though she was grateful to be included in the group. She placed a second photo in front of me.

On June 1, 1938, Mommy and Daddy drove to the preacher's house in Beaver Springs to be married. Afterward, her sister, Iva, snapped this wedding day photo.

"This is my dress. I wore it for graduation and for my wedding."

In the picture she and

Daddy are standing in the road that ran along the eastern boundary of the farm. Wishing an idyllic setting for the sake of memory, they had driven in Daddy's 1930 Ford coupe to this more secluded site where her sister, Iva, snapped several photos of the young couple. Daddy then took a picture of the sisters. Mommy returned to her chair opposite me, setting the wedding day pictures aside and picked up the glee club photo. Fingering it reflectively, she paused while her eyes teared. She spoke as though a painful revelation was being shared.

"I'm the only one left."

The moment deserved reverence. Long ago her life had been set in motion, animated and vital, sacred, as all lives are. Now it had come to the throes of loneliness, of separation, of a crumbling body and a weary spirit.

"Do you think we will know each other in Heaven?"

I knew she was thinking of Daddy, of her mother, of her brother and sisters, and of friends who had passed. Her pain begged to be assuaged with explanation simple and direct. Not possessing the skills that pare away complexity and present truth in clear and concise language, my penchant was to turn simplicity on its head and make the elementary complicated. In any case she sat in rapt concentration as I fumbled forward, the interview now a conversation.

"Mommy," I began, "Daddy and your friends have not died. Like you, they are living souls. They had a body that, like ours, grew older. Their bodies died. Your body and my body are going to die. But I am going to live forever and so are you. I don't like the thought of being separated from my body, and the parade of death frightens all of us, but separation means a new body, one without arthritis."

She looked down at her hands, the fingers twisted and bent out of all proportion, more resembling macabre claws than human appendages.

"You are wondering if we will recognize one another in Heaven. That is a complex question.

"When I was born you wondered what kind of person I would become. You fed me, bathed me, diapered me, comforted me and loved me. You knew my weight, habits, eye color, and other physical characteristics. You knew everything a person could know about another person, but you didn't know 'me' personally until I began to reveal myself through behavior and speech. The reason is quite simple. Even as a baby, 'I' was not just a body. My identity went beyond the way my body looked. There was a real 'me' inside that was more difficult to get to know. And the longer you knew 'me' and the more 'I' shared of myself, the more deeply your understanding and appreciation for me grew. The real 'I' was inside my body, that is, in some place greater than my body. The soul cannot be confined to a physical body. It has a mind that regulates the body through the use of the brain, but it is not a body, nor is it a brain. 'I' am a soul, and the soul does not die. In fact, if you think back to when you were a girl, the real 'you' has not changed very much. 'You' have learned things that we call wisdom, and 'you' have acquired self-restraint and an appreciation for God and His love, but the real 'you' has not changed much at all. Your body, however, has undergone profound change. It is not the same body 'you' had as a girl. It is your body, but it is not 'you.'"

Teary-eyed at first, she now sat passively, engrossed in thought. I realized that her question was more emotional than intellectual, but I knew no other way to assuage her concerns.

"Now, when 'you' go to Heaven, 'you' will not take your body along. 'You' will receive a new body. It may look altogether different. If the real 'you' had been just a body, then we might not recognize one another in Heaven. But the real 'you' is a soul that does not change essentially, so the people who knew the real 'you' will still know the real 'you.'

"My soul is 'I,' the 'I' who is going to Heaven, the 'I' for whom Jesus died. 'I' will not be some other person in Heaven. 'I' will be the same soul that you know in this life. The same is true for Daddy, your friends, and for all of your loved ones. We will know each other because our identity will be the same as it was in our former life, because the real 'me' was never a body."

"I just get scared sometimes," she whispered. "I've committed a lot of sins."

"Mommy," I pleaded, "If you think you've committed too many sins, you're telling God that His son's blood was not great enough. He died in vain."

"No, I didn't mean that," she apologized. "I just mean that I don't feel worthy."

"You're not," I emphasized, "none of us are. To be worthy means to be perfect, because that's what God requires. He is a Holy God. That's the reason God had to provide the sacrifice. The sacrifice had to be perfect, as Holy as God. In a way, God Himself had to die. The triune God is three persons, each equal in essence, so when Jesus went to the cross, God Himself died in our place so that we could be worthy.

"A long time ago, long before you and I came into this world, Eve had the same misgivings as you are feeling. She wondered if God's Word was reliable. Satan had persuaded her that God's warning about the penalty for sin was not true. In the same way, if we can't rely upon the promises that God has made, then we can't know for sure that we're going to Heaven. Just remember when doubts creep into our minds, it is Satan doing the talking. Romans 10:9 promises that '... *if you confess with your mouth that Jesus is Lord and believe in your heart that God raised Him from the dead, you will be saved.*'"

She did not immediately respond, so I continued, "You are saved and, although your body will stay behind, the real 'you' is going to Heaven to be with God, and the real 'you' will be recognized by both your Savior and your friends."

"That's a lot to think about," she reflected. She sat for several minutes, her hands folded, resting on the picture she held on her lap. Suddenly, conscious of the hour, she interrupted, "I know you have to go. Do you want something to eat first?"

"No," I assured, "I'll get something at home. I want to get on the road, so I don't have to drive after dark."

I always hated to leave her alone, and good-byes were becoming increasingly difficult. I searched for a less despairing exit.

"Is Susie going to stop in later today?" I asked.[16]

"She's coming to do my hair for church tomorrow."

"I'm glad you won't be alone."

"I'll be fine," she paused again. "I think I'll skip supper though. I have to sit in the seat they gave me, and I don't like to listen to Grace complain about her family. She gets on my nerves."

I later discovered that Grace, a recent addition to the assisted living quarters, was a rather fractious personality whose temperament threatened Mommy's accustomed complaisance.

"Do you want me to buy supper for you before I go?"

"No," she deferred, "I'll call Susie and have her bring a sandwich."

"Are you sure?"

---

16. My sister, Susie, who lived thirty miles away, with unparalleled magnanimity, visited nearly every day, tending to ordinary needs and providing emotional and psychological support.

"You go before it gets late. I'll be okay."

We hugged, and I promised to see her soon. Then I closed the door and started for my car.

Guilt enveloped me. I was leaving my mother alone in the impersonal and detached confines of an "old folks" home, aware that, although pragmatic demands seemed to permit no alternative, this was not God's intention for His creatures, either in Eden or at Emmanuel Nursing Home.

MOMMY'S MUSIC

The day after my mother died, my sister Susie asked me to compile a list of Mommy's favorite hymns to be shared as part of a memorial display at the funeral service.[1] As best as I could from memory, I began the list but soon realized there were far too many for such an occasion. I decided instead to list some that both of us enjoyed during the times we sang together.[2] She knew them all by heart and sang them repeatedly from the time she had become a Christian. It was a cathartic experience as the compilation transported me on the wings of sweetest nostalgia to days and nights long ago when she was my mother, and I had direct access to her love.

Mommy loved music. She sang in the kitchen while she baked and cooked, she sang in the cellar while she washed clothes, she sang on the porch swing while she podded peas or snapped string beans. On Sunday afternoons, after she took her nap, she tuned the radio to Charles Fuller's *Old Time Revival Hour* and sang along with the familiar words and melodies. When Calvary Bible Church, where we were members, announced that new hymnals were to be purchased, she asked to buy a discarded one. It remained at our piano until well after I left for college.

In the farthest recesses of our farm house attic, on a cool March afternoon when the annual spring house cleaning was in progress, exploring children discovered a long-abandoned acoustic guitar and were astonished to find it belonged to Mommy. She explained that shortly after their marriage, when Daddy played his own guitar regularly, the groom had bought a similar instrument for his bride. The gesture was replicated many years afterward when Daddy, who loved organ music, bought Mommy an electric model for the living room. She played both the piano and organ by ear and frequently during the evenings they were alone, sang and played his favorite hymns and choruses.

---

1. Mommy died at the hospice in Danville, PA, on June 23, 2009.

2. Among my favorite memories of singing with her are the times she abruptly stopped, raised her hand to silence me, and then sang alone. It was her way of correcting my wayward melody without directly criticizing me.

She loved singing Sunday mornings and evenings at church, and she especially enjoyed occasions of special music. One such occasion occurred on an August evening when I was about fourteen years old.

During most summers in the 1950s evangelical churches in the greater Lewistown area combined efforts and resources to sponsor revival services. One of the nearby rural hamlets made available a huge field or pasture where there was both ample parking and sufficient space to erect a large tent that could hold as many as 500-700 worshippers. Services were held for four or five consecutive evenings and featured a traveling evangelistic team that included a pianist and a vocalist. Daddy insisted that our entire family attend. He understood the importance of worship and the need to inculcate Biblical values into the lives of his family. He also appreciated the renewal that revival meetings brought into his own life. Annually, in the days immediately following the meetings, he recommitted his life to God's glory and attempted to adopt habits to that end. The emotional and some-times melodramatic displays of conversion and personal testimony during the services touched the core of his ethos. And, of course, the experience provided him fodder for our family devotions.

Mommy shared his enthusiasm and his values. The salvation of her family, her friends, and everyone who remained apart from a saving re-lationship with God dominated her thinking and behavior. It motivated her prayer life and was central to the songs and choruses she sang. On this August evening concern for loved ones inspired her to attend the re-vival services where she hoped her family and friends would accept Jesus as their Savior, and in addition, couched within this noble concern, she looked forward to the singing.

Daddy and Mommy both loved to sing old hymns and familiar choruses.

As a girl, she had sung alto in her high school glee club and once confided with sheepish pride that the school music advisor told her she had a "nice voice." Her favor-ite place, however, was anywhere there was found a piano or organ. She had taught herself to play, and, from my earliest years, I delighted in those evenings when she sat at the piano, in the far corner of our living room, and played and sang.

On coldest winter evenings, she made a fire in the living room stove and coaxed us to join her in singing while we huddled near the stove's warmth. It was there that I learned many of the grand hymns that have remained a treasure in my own life. Decades after she was grown older, and I returned to visit, rarely did an evening pass when she failed to ask if I would sing with her. On those occasions, I would stand or sit next to the organ in the living room and again sing those beloved hymns.[3]

We drove to the revival service that August evening in our Chevy pick-up truck, Keith, Billy, and I nestled in a blanket on the bed of the truck while our younger brothers and sisters squeezed into the cab with Mommy and Daddy. We kids detested the meetings. To compound the anguish of the long ride, the stifling heat, the hard-wooden seats, and

Summer revival services were usually held in an over-heated tent replete with mosquitoes and gnats.

the ninety-minute sermons, Daddy believed that arriving early was a virtue. We were always seated by 6:30 pm for a 7:00 pm meeting.

The program began with prayer and a salute to the area churches that sponsored the event. A local pastor introduced the evangelistic team after which the vocalist took his place at the pulpit and gave a testimony. By this time, we had been on the hard seats for fifty minutes. For most teenagers, singing full-throat in church is akin to torture. I had learned to modulate my voice just a few decibels below audibility, but Daddy's look askance let me know I was expected to put some effort into the singing.

Two choruses were sung. Then two hymns followed, each having a dozen verses. A prayer was offered, after which a love-offering was taken for the evangelistic team. Another hymn, a second prayer, and finally the

---

3. I have a most wonderful and related memory of my brother Joe playing his guitar and singing with us on the few occasions when we simultaneously returned to visit. It remains an irony that Daddy, who also loved the same music and had a pleasing voice, never sang with us as Mommy played. He would, however, fetch his guitar if Joe or I was playing ours, and join in playing and singing ballads and folk songs.

speaker approached the podium.

Waves of mid-afternoon heat, trapped within the tent folds, engulfed the assembly. Hundreds of ladies waved fans to cool their faces, men tugged at shirt collars which by now were damp with sweat. I could feel droplets of perspiration on my own brow and my T-shirt was sticking to the back of my chair. The torment to which we were being subjected had reached ninety minutes with no end in sight.

Before beginning his sermon, the evangelist announced there was to be a special recognition. The entire gathering was asked to stand. Chairs creaked, sighs echoed throughout the overheated tent, ladies laid aside their fans.

"Brothers and sisters," he invited, "I am asking everyone who came with your family tonight, everyone who is a father or mother, to remain standing with your children while the rest of you may be seated." A few dozen disappointed souls returned to their seats.

"Two or more children," he continued. If you came here tonight with two or more children, remain standing. Excitement rippled through the assembly. I began to feel uneasy in the same way one tenses when about to choose the short stick.

"And now, those of you who are a family of three or more children, ... three or more, ... please remain standing. The rest of you may be seated." Suddenly I felt the stares of strangers as our family continued standing for the review. Older ladies ogled and awed at the sight of our family of seven children, my mother holding a nine-month-old baby.[4]

"A family of six or more. ... Parents with four or more children. A family of six or more!" He paused, waiting.

I felt as though I was on parade. By now everyone realized the largest family was about to be identified. I prayed, "Please God, don't let it be our family." The speaker smiled a clandestine smile, delighting in my discomfort. He continued, "Five or more children. ... A family of seven or more. Has God blessed us with a family of seven?"

He paused again allowing the entire room to survey the curios still standing. "Isn't this wonderful." He effused, "no greater blessing on this earth than children."

The seconds wandered into minutes. "Continue standing," he directed. There was a long pause to heighten suspense. I was standing in the glare

---

4. Beth was born in 1964, seven years after these events.

of head lamps, an innocent fawn in the middle of the road. There was no escape.

"Six? Six or more children? ... Is there anyone with a family of six or more children?" I knew the end was near. In the vast arena there were now only two families standing. I feared the worst. What if we were called to the front? What if we were made to stand on the platform? What if the audience applauded? What if, after the service, teary-eyed ladies hugged me joyfully as though a poor orphan had found a home? I secretly vowed I would never again attend a revival service. I would walk on hot coals. I would feign death.

"Seven children or more! Do we have a family of nine?" The family of eight sat down. It had happened. I was frozen on the tracks with a great diesel bearing down on me. I was surrounded at the Alamo, defeated at Waterloo, vanquished at Armageddon. My life was ruined. I was a carica-ture—one of seven, one of Jim and Hazel's children, a member of the family on exhibit at the revival service.

The applause came—slowly at first, then a flood tide. The rows be-hind and before us extended hands of congratulations, a matronly wom-an caught me from behind, hugging her long, lost stray. A grandmother reached for the baby. Daddy and Mommy beamed.

When the ovation subsided, I sat—insensate and wretched. Napo-leon's retreat from Moscow. Humiliation and ignominy, survival.

How long I sat benumbed is difficult to recall, but my return to con-sciousness was occasioned when I realized that Mommy and Daddy and all my brothers and sisters were suddenly stepping out into the aisle and walk-ing toward the speaker's platform. Can cruelty beget further cruelty? Was there no end to suffering? Had God abdicated? This was the town square and I was entering the pillory. I looked straight ahead.

As we neared the platform, spontaneously, the congregants stood in joyous applause. The preacher lent a hand to Mommy as she mounted the step of the platform. He asked Mommy and Daddy to stand beside the lectern as he addressed his audience. "Thank you," he returned to the con-gregation, "you may be seated." Lingering at the microphone, but turning to face our family, he spoke to Daddy, "We have a gift for you and your family."

"Oh, no!" I thought. I remembered walking to the front of church during Vacation Bible School earlier that summer to accept a package simi-lar to the one that lay atop this speaker's stand. I had won a contest by turning pages more quickly than my peers to find Bible verses. Worse, I had been coerced to open the package in front of my jeering buddies. For a full minute I had stood in front of a hundred teenagers holding a pencil on which was inscribed "Luke 6:31: *Do unto others as you would have them do unto you.*" Mortification.

The preacher reached for the package and extended it to Mommy. He then shook Daddy's hand. Turning one final time to the assembly, he asked, "Would it please you to again recognize the Morgans? Let's give them one more round of applause."

A realization emerged. Some of my buddies and friends from high school were in the gallery ... misshapen souls who would fashion an embellished account of the evening for schoolmates the following morning—two or three snakes who were gleefully giggling over the prospects of tomorrow.

The remainder of the service lasted interminably. Perhaps the hour ran through the night. Regardless, I had been found out. The dark secret was divulged. I was part of a big family. An enormous family. Ignominy would trail me down the long corridor of time.

One phonograph record featured the gospel songs of George Beverly Shea.

The gift turned out to be two phonograph records of gospel music. Before climbing into bed that night, in the safety of my home, I read the jackets. Many of the songs were familiar. "Beyond the Sunset," "I've Got a Mansion," "Just a Closer Walk With Thee," "Some Golden Daybreak," "I Can't Feel at Home," and others made all of us anxious to listen to them. We could not, however, immediately play them. The turntable spun dutifully, but when the arm was lowered against the vinyl discs it produced no sound. Our cabinet record player was without a needle.

We waited until a Friday evening when Mommy and Daddy went to town and bought two phonograph needles.[5] Thereafter, the records were

---

5. Even though McClure was closer and had two general stores, a barbershop, a bank, two garages, a blacksmith shop, and a high school, it failed to qualify as a town. It remained, in our minds, a farm community; a sort of country village where familiar men and women closed shops at 5 pm, ate their suppers, and retired to front porches. "Went to town" was our expression for "went to Lewistown." There was romance in Lewistown. There, stores

played and replayed until we had memorized not just the words to the songs, but the order in which they were recorded. Mommy sang with those recordings for countless days. When a disc needed to be turned, she called for one of the small children who might be in the house, and they carefully flipped the record and played it *ad infinitum*. In fact, those recordings became so familiar that my brother Joe, more than fifty years later, sat with his guitar on the deck of his West Virginia home one cool, bright, autumn evening and was able to sing each song from memory.

There were few hymns she didn't like, but Mommy did resist singing choruses and contemporary songs that induced clapping and toe-tapping. As a Christian, she thought hymns and gospel music ought to produce reverence and worship. Despite that modest reticence, her love for gospel music was without qualification.

The funeral service was felicitous. Eulogy and sentiment were circumscribed with the restraint of simplicity. The list of favorite hymns was posted but adumbrated by dozens of effusive cards and nostalgic photographs. It mattered not. Mommy's legacy is not written in celebrated verse, nor is it chronicled by public photos and accolades. Rather, it is proclaimed in the lives of her children. Her commitment to her Lord and Savior, her work ethic, and her love for people all testify to the ethos of whom she was as a person and mother. And, of course, there is not a more fitting memorial than the love of music she inculcated into each of our lives.[6]

---

stayed open until 9 pm, restaurants served fancy dishes, and movies houses offered exciting entertainment.

6. Mommy's love and influence was multiplied by Daddy's zest for the same music. He kept a notebook of gospel songs in which he wrote annotations, and his enjoyment of hymns and traditional music, though less public, was as great as Mommy's. In fact, the songs listed in his notebook are much the same as those she loved.

FAMILY DEVOTIONS
<><><><><><><><><><><><><><><><><><><><><><><><><><><><><><>

During the early 1950s our family began attending Calvary Bible Church in Lewistown. It was there that Daddy became convicted of the need for daily family devotions. Concerned for the spiritual welfare of his children but lacking a frame of reference for methodology, he fell to pontificating Biblical exegesis each morning immediately following breakfast.

Breakfast was at seven and lasted until Mommy cleared dishes from the table to the kitchen sink. When she finished, each of us found our Bibles, gathered around Daddy, usually in the kitchen, and he began his discourse on that day's chapter from the King James Bible. A full chapter was read, regardless of its length, the interruptions of babies, or the exigency of bringing crops from the fields in the face of threatening weather. The ritual was solemn, regular, and compulsory. If a child complained of real or imaginary illness, he or she might be permitted to lie on the kitchen sofa or floor, but attendance was *de rigueur*.

Lamentably, for us children, the hour was tedium. There was no engagement, no discussion, and no inquiry. The exception might be a supporting remark from Mommy noting that Biblical lessons had practical applications, such as honoring parents, getting along with siblings, or not complaining about going to church. Daddy, however, was not accommodating, thus children endured most of these hours in peremptory reverence. Questions and comments were disruptive.

Dogma, even when garnished with good intention, is repugnant. That hour of family devotions was confinement – an hour of lead. We lingered in resignation after each breakfast for the call to assembly. As we sat beneath his sermonizing, our attention centered not upon the message, but upon the messenger. The moment smacked of the imperious—autocracy *sans affection*. Both the Scriptural passage and Daddy's tone were authoritative—God speaking through His written Word and Daddy's oratory. It was the concluding prayer, however, that seemed interminable, a mixture of confession, consecration, and petition, which encompassed both temporal and eternal concerns for each of us individually, as well as for the church and community generally. While missionaries in China sometimes absorbed his focus, he failed to notice the listlessness of disinterested children or their fatigue at prolonged inactivity. Mommy closed the hour with an endorsing "amen." Her pronouncement, like the exultation of breath after rising from submersion, announced our liberation.

Despite our displeasure, Daddy's protracted dissertations, and his petulant irritability, his struggle to build a moral foundation upon which we would survive both in this world and the next must be recognized and accorded some measure of virtue.

He set aside time for this daily devotional because he was convicted that it was beneficial and necessary to living a meaningful life. He also believed he must someday give an account of his fatherhood to a sovereign God, and, as such, his earthly responsibilities included the spiritual education and welfare of his children. The advantages were obvious. Each of us children became familiar with Biblical content and its application. Each of us was introduced to the person of Jesus and the gospel message. Each of us learned the value of organization, of punctual precise behavior, of

Daddy recognized God's handiwork in the beauty of our farm.

Daddy's many Bibles were filled with notes, observations, and emphases.

persistence and perseverance.

To us children his constraints seemed at times severe and lacking in the affection essential to teaching the love of a heavenly father for His earthly children, but Daddy believed strict discipline was both necessary and effective. And although our daily devotional seemed impersonal, fixed, and formal, his worship was genuine, and even on those days when he stumbled and fell to life's daily tensions and temptations, he continued to see a divine presence in the miracles and mysteries observed on our farm—the waving fields of grain, the sunrises and sunsets, the renewal of springtime rains, and he especially felt that presence in the hour he set aside each morning to inculcate Godly values into the lives of his family.

For my brothers and sisters who have made Christ Lord and Savior, we are wholly grateful for his commitment to begin each day with God's Word.

MEMORIES OF DADDY

PREFACE

Anything set to paper is autobiographical. The following recollections, comments, and illustrations of Daddy say much more about me than the impressions they form of my father. Thus, I fear this portrait is at times tendentious. As well, I am not only a father' son; I am a father. As such, I am much aware of similarities between Daddy and myself—similarities that make criticisms of him, even when accurate, rather hypocritical.

Egocentricity, in some form, characterizes all of us, and certainly there were times when Daddy was prone to self-absorption. Some people learn to develop behavior that mutes self-interest in favor of altruism and sacrifice. Others remain narcissistic. In either case, there is an inscrutability to personality and practice that evades logic and common sense and reminds us that the lens of perception suffers its own aberrations and limitations. With these self-admonitions in place, I offer these sketches.

DADDY: THE BARBER

D addy was neither stingy nor improvident, but he was practical. His shopping sprees took place in the Army-Navy Surplus Store or at Woolworth's 5 & 10 Cent Store. His shoes were resoled and repolished and went nicely with the one set of dress clothes he wore to church. His extravagance was a half-gallon of cherry vanilla ice cream for his family on hot summer nights, or the Sunday newspaper after church and noon dinner on the day of rest. His interest in the paper was centered on its full section of comics. Expedience dictated that he could not venture too far either left or right.

Our farm was nearly self-sufficient. Goods were provided in-house from the fields and meadows or by the chickens, pigs and cows, and services were supplied by Daddy himself, his family, and on occasion, by his neighbors. There were, however, exceptions. Sometimes our needs could be met only by the public sector. These were the times he typically turned to the "Montgomery Ward" or "Sears and Roebuck" catalogs.

One such exception arose in the mid-1950s when his three oldest boys entered their teens. Until then, whenever our hair began to grow over our ears, Daddy took us to Lester Bratton's Barber Shop in McClure. Lester charged only 25 cents per haircut and always added a generous massage of witch hazel, but we dreaded the exercise. Lester had a great ceiling fan in his shop whose blades turned more slowly than hot summer days. I think he used it to camouflage the 45 minutes he exhausted for each haircut. Only eternity was longer than Lester's haircuts.

It was silent in Lester's barber shop except for the droning noise of the fan and a small radio tuned just loud enough for Lester to hear the news. In those days I assumed that Saturday radios should broadcast baseball games or *Fibber McGee and Molly*, but Lester listened to the news, unequivocal

1954
Myself, Bill, and Keith

boredom for boys waiting for a haircut.

Three children and one adult times 45 minutes meant that we waited three hours for relief. Dusty copies of the month-old "Saturday Evening Post" or "Life" magazine offered no respite. Daddy's frugality wrestled with his patience. He did not complain to Lester, because Lester and his family attended our church. He did, however, vent his frustration to Mommy each time we returned home. "Lester Bratton," Daddy said, "is a poor excuse for a barber."

And then it happened. On one such Saturday he was registering his usual *a posteriori* complaint with Mommy when she suggested that Daddy cut our hair himself. The torturing of children in the market place was strictly forbidden, but in the recesses of country homes there was no restraint to cruelty.

Mommy announced that barbering tools could be ordered from the Sears and Roebuck Catalog. It lay atop the kitchen cabinet, well-worn from hours of paging, not from actual shopping, but from curiosity and entertainment. Daddy leafed through its contents until he came to the listing for weapons. An entire kit, complete with manually operated clippers, brush, comb and an extra blade, cost $6.95. In only ten months he would save a nickel, an incomprehensible bargain. He tore the order blank from the back of the catalog, wrote in pencil the seven identifying digits, folded it neatly, and along with a check for the amount, placed it into an envelope, licked it sealed, and carried it to the mailbox. The raised red flag on the mailbox both alerted the mailman to stop for the order and forewarned children that bad times approached.

In the more remote climes of Mifflin County, Pennsylvania, mail delivery traveled slowly in those days and was not altogether reliable; much of the time subject to weather, whim, and will. Exigency seemed foreign to postal workers who lived in small communities where technology could not yet compete with the instant communication of Aunt Sarah to the ladies at the quilting bee. The habits of country mailmen who made deliveries in second-hand cars might include skipping the eastern portion of a rural route on Wednesdays because there was a grange meeting that night. In fact, it was not unheard of for a long-awaited mail-order package to sit in the dusty bin of a postal office for weeks until a complaining patron stopped by and demanded a search. Thus, it was altogether possible that the prayers of small children could be answered, or at the least, be blessed by lengthy delay.

Sadly, such divine grace was not extended to the children of Jim Morgan on this occasion. The suspicious package had already been opened and rested atop the kitchen table when we arrived home from school a few cold, winter afternoons afterward. Daddy, with delicious anticipation, sat on a three-legged milking stool he had commandeered from the barn for the occasion. An insidious grin dominated his countenance as he imperiously directed me to change from my school clothes into something more suitable for an execution.

The operation began with a stool set atop a chair so that Daddy need not bend over, and his work could be more surgical. Next, a cape, fashioned by Mommy from an old tablecloth, was placed around our necks and tucked into our shirt collars. Daddy then wet our hair slightly, took his barber's comb and combed out the tangles. Breathing ceased. The impending storm neared, unavoidable and ominous. Daddy's meaty and calloused hands and fingers, fraught with discordant odors moved against the grimaces, squirms and jiggles of us children. He clutched the clippers and began moving up the side of the head, dangerously brushing the ears. He stepped back after each thrust to view the damage, tilting his head downward to permit his bifocals a close-up view. Then, the next foray, the clipper edges poking scalps or pinching the skin beneath tufts of hair. Each time we winced or flinched, he took it as a personal rebuke. We were biting the hand that fed us and casting a vote for Lester Bratton. Tension mounted as we anticipated his temper. Minutes turned into hours. Like a vise, his left hand gripped our heads. Intently, he drew close for inspection. His warm, stale breath could be felt on our cheeks. Only the mechanical clicking of the clippers broke the ominous silence. "I can't do this if you don't sit still," was always the warning. The clippers gored and scrapped. Victims longed for release.

The end came at a signal. Daddy took the brush and swept away loose hair announcing, "You're done." Air rushed out of lungs. Mommy intoned, "It looks good." The cloth was removed, and one at a time we stepped out into the fresh air to shake remaining hair from our clothes. Ahead might lay friendly giggles at school and church, but that small discomfort was more than compensated with the assurance of the six-week dispensation until the next massacre.

D addy's haircuts lasted for much of our growing up, but they finally came to an end one cold, winter Saturday with Billy in the torture chamber. Keith and I were finished and were standing on the short porch in front of our kitchen facing the barn. We were shaking out the cloths that we had worn for our haircuts and about to go back inside when Billy flinched in protest at the pinching clippers. Daddy had been nearing the precipice of his patience. Billy pushed him over the edge. Sardonically, Billy announced, "I think I'll go to Lester Bratton's."

Daddy said nothing. He didn't even put away the clippers and brush. He left that for Mommy. Instead, he brought his coat from behind the kitchen stove, pulled his cap to cover his ears, and went to the barn. He never again cut our hair.

But it was Daddy who had the final laugh. We had jumped from the frying pan back into the fire. Six weeks later we were watching the ceiling fan at Lester Bratton's Barber Shop.

DADDY: SCHOOL BOARD MEMBER

Daddy served as a Board of Education member for six years

Daddy's involvement with public education began in 1954. Decatur Township, where we lived, had for some years paid the necessary tuition and transportation expenses to permit students desiring high school diplomas to attend Lewistown High School. Previously, in 1951-52 the township had decided to take on the financial burden of replacing its six one-room schools with a regional elementary school. The new Decatur Elementary School was completed in time to accept students for the 1953-54 school year. Citizens of the township, long accustomed to the convenience of local one-room schools, complained of both the increase in taxes and logistical problems associated with student bus transportation. In the wake of this unrest, concern was compounded in 1954 when sending districts to Lewistown High School were notified there would be a tuition increase. The local Board of Education felt the ire of neighbors and began looking for solutions. A public meeting was held at the new school, and afterward, Lyman Guss, the Decatur board president, came to our house and asked Daddy to serve on a committee that was to investigate alternatives. He accepted a position on the committee.

Concurrently, the soon-to-be Chief Logan School District began building a new high school in Highland Park, a suburb of Lewistown, and its board, needing extra money, offered Decatur Township reduced tuition costs. The Decatur committee decided to submit the proposal to a referendum. It passed with the contingent compromise that students already enrolled in the Lewistown system would be grandfathered. Thus, by the fall of 1954, Decatur had become a sending district to the new Chief Logan High School. Daddy was instrumental in that change, his primary motivation being the reduced costs.

The entire matter was not settled, however. Being an agricultural community, many township residents were more interested in their sons and daughters receiving vocational training than an academic education. Unlike Lewistown, Chief Logan did not have a vocational facility. Children not yet enrolled at Lewistown were not grandfathered, thus, they were denied vocational schooling.

The Decatur committee on which Daddy had served was by now disbanded. Township residents who wanted their children to attend Lewistown's Vocational High School grew irritated. The debate heated. Mr. Guss remained the local board president. In the midst of the new controversy, again he came, with two fellow board members, to our house. The three men informed Daddy that a current member had decided not to seek re-election and pleaded with Daddy to run for the vacant position in the next election.

Daddy was proud, but never inflated or effusive, so he seldom talked about that upcoming election. I could tell, however, that he was anxious on election day when he drove to the "Election House" over by the now abandoned one-room Center School in order to cast his vote. An election officer drove to our house late that evening to inform him that he had won. In retrospect, his election was neither surprising nor curious. He knew he would win, because there was no opposition. Thus, he began serving in 1956 while Keith and I were in our eighth-grade year at Burnham School, a part of the Chief Logan district.

As a result of his attending the initial public meeting when Decatur Township decided it would not renew the Lewistown contract, Daddy had acquired a local reputation for "speaking up." When the new alliance with Chief Logan was formed, township residents were again grateful that he took a central role, insisting that children already attending Lewistown High School be permitted to finish there. Still, these new practices and policies introduced new problems and new complaints, especially regarding bus transportation. Parents became concerned with bus stop locations and earlier time constraints. Daddy again became a central figure.

One such case involved our neighbor, Ronnie Goss. He was a vocational student at Lewistown High School, and, as such, rode a bus designated for vocational students. The week before school began, he was informed that his bus stop would be at a crossroads more than two miles distant from his house. Walking two miles of country road in wintry weather is altogether different than hiking the plowed macadam of city streets. The thought of a son standing alone at a seldom traveled crossroad on a winter

CHIEF LOGAN SCHOOL DISTRICT BOARD OF EDUCATION
Daddy is in front row, second from the right. Lyman Guss is seated to his right.

morning, at the mercy of both the weather and the caprice of a bus driver, was upsetting to Ronnie's parents. His father, John, told Daddy of the dilemma. On the first morning of the scheduled bus stop, Daddy waited with Ronnie at the crossroads. When the driver arrived, Daddy ordered that Ronnie was forever afterward to be picked up at Joe McKinley's Store, a half-mile from the Goss house. Thus, Daddy was again a local hero for a time. Ironically, the issue regarding the bus stop was soon forgotten. In a few weeks Ronnie received his state driver's license and daily drove his father's pick-up truck to school.

I graduated from Chief Logan High school in Highland Park, PA in the late spring of 1960. That event was distinct for at least two reasons: my brother, Keith, the youngest member of the class, graduated with me, and Daddy, as president of the Decatur School Board, presented us with our diplomas. That evening was the culmination of his service on both the Decatur and Chief Logan Boards of Education. Never, thereafter, was he directly involved nor did he show as much interest in the machinations of education.

DADDY'S BASEBALL

I trust this observation is not that of a son romantically recalling his father's athletic interests and abilities and arbitrarily reconstructing his father from the fabric of imagination. Much of my life has been involved with athletics, especially baseball, and I have worked with all levels of proficiency, including the skills of professional athletes. I have especially committed much time to the study of biomechanics as they relate to athletic activity, so that my frame of reference stands on some objective ground. It is true that memory softens and embellishes, and I accept that small inaccuracies may be present, especially as they regard specific times and places, but I maintain that this is a clear recollection of Daddy as a baseball player and sports fan.

Daddy, the baseball player, is set against the backdrop of a forgotten time; a time before the advent of electronic communication and the demand for rapid motion. Country living during the 1920s and 1930s invites vignettes of hard labor coupled with bucolic innocence. It conjures a time when the pace of both baseball and rural living corresponded to phlegmatic summer evenings with back yard swings and picnic suppers. It is the tranquility that followed the Great War and the lull before the explosion of WWII. The game and the traditions Daddy knew were those established at the turn of the twentieth century when baseball peaked in its national appeal.

Daddy's baseball was the baseball of a very rural America. Sometimes the fields were flat meadows with stones or bags outlining bases. Other times, lots near town squares or bandstands were cleared and maintained for the sole purpose of weekend games. Seldom were there fences or baselines. Spectators stood along the margins or sprawled on cool grass growing beneath shady trees. Infrequently there was a covered grandstand where locals rooted for favorite sons, and old folks recalled the gallantries of an earlier time. The ball game was a social experience. Every hamlet had its own team. Girlfriends and wives comprised the galleries. Gloves and bats were communal. Balls were such a precious commodity that when they became frayed, tape was wrapped around the covers to assure longer life. Baseball shoes were non-existent, and uniforms were partial and various in their assortment. Despite this, many of the players were skilled and their competitive natures rivaled those of modern players.

D addy threw left-handed. He had what baseball people call a "stylish delivery." It began with the classic over-the-head windup of his time. His delivery was fluid and efficient and produced the illusion that the effort put into the throw was less than the velocity of the thrown object. In baseball parlance he was "sneaky fast." Until his late thirties his body was flexible, and his arm was loose. Coupled with his athletic balance, this permitted him to throw with unusual accuracy. In my early and mid-teens, he occasionally threw to me. I have vivid recollection of that "easy" motion and the liveliness of his pitches.

When I played high school baseball, older men frequently approached and asked if I was Jimmy Morgan's son. They recalled what a great pitcher he was and the wonderful control he possessed. Jim McNitt, fifteen years Daddy's senior, recalled the many times he had been Daddy's catcher on the area sandlots. He stressed that Daddy threw "smoke" and had a "drop" that "fell off the table." For a "change-of-pace," Daddy himself told me that he simply took "something off his fastball."

Only once did I hear him talk about his hitting. Curiously, Daddy hit right-handed. He choked-up on the bat handle as much as three inches, which revealed that he was not an accomplished hitter, but a batter who tried merely to make contact. As a result, he demonstrated no power and simply punched at the ball.

In the summer of 1950 Daddy played his final game. About 9 am on a Saturday morning two carloads of uniformed players pulled up in front of our house. Daddy was working in our wagon shed and came out to greet them. I was watching from the yard as the men pleaded with Daddy to go with them to a game. I learned afterward that they were his ex-teammates from McClure, and they had scheduled two games against the Rockview Penitentiary in Bellefonte. They had only one pitcher and needed Daddy's left arm. He had not played competitively for several years, but the enticement of competition and the warmth of camaraderie convinced him to go along. He stopped long enough in the house to get Mommy's approval, then grabbed a sweatshirt and his baseball glove and was off.

He did not return that day until after the barn work was finished and

ROCKVIEW PENITENTIARY
Daddy played his last baseball game in 1950. This 1956 aerial photograph shows baseball field (left of center) under repair and relocation.

darkness had descended. About 9 pm we heard a car stop by the mailbox in front of the house, and we knew he was home. Moments later, the front door opened. He came into the kitchen where we waited, tossed his glove behind our kitchen stove, and plopped down on the couch to remove his shoes. He complained to Mommy that he was "sore all over." She consoled that she had kept his supper warm and began setting a place for him at the table. His fatigue and soreness were obvious as he seated himself, but he ate as though he was famished. I watched with intrigue. I wanted him to share his adventure and detail the games' excitement, but I knew not to interrupt his meal. Mommy catered about him, exchanging pleasantries and ensuring he was contented. A second time he moaned of exhaustion and then asked if I had washed the milking machines. A short time later he went to bed.

His silence was not atypical. Daddy seldom talked about sports, at least not as frequently as I would have liked. Most of the time I initiated conversation, cautious that he was in a receptive mood. Whether it was his workload, financial concerns, the weight of raising a large family, or just his personal disposition, irascibility was part of the climate. When he did not respond, I knew to get on with my business.

As he grew older, however, he sometimes shared his baseball experiences. He spoke about those games at the penitentiary. He told of pitching the second game that day in 1950, throwing a shutout into the eighth inning when, suddenly, the "sky fell." He recalled for me sequences of pitches to particular hitters and spoke of the admiration his teammates displayed for him. At other times he told of occasions, when, as a young boy living at Paintersville, he and his brother Bill would walk a mile to a neighborhood ball field and spend hours throwing to each other, one stationed at home plate and the other in centerfield. He credited those sessions with producing his arm strength.

By the mid-1950s his body had surrendered suppleness for heavier muscles needed for farming. He still attended local games at Belltown and McClure, but the men who remembered Jimmy the athlete were gone, and thus began a gradual, complete withdrawal from baseball. His own boys were teenagers now, and sometimes he picked up a bat and hit fly balls to us or played "pass," his term for tossing back and forth in the yard. But mostly, baseball was forgotten. It was a game for leisure, and farm life afforded little leisure. My obsession with baseball remained his only link to the game of his past.

Although his passion for baseball was now distant, the memory of the part it had played in his youth produced a tolerance for my obsession. On a summer evening in 1956 a neighboring high school boy, Ronnie Goss, stopped by our farm to ask if Keith and I could play in a baseball game at Bannerville. I was in the barn helping Daddy with the milking. Keith was putting away a pump sprayer used to control the pervasive flies in the stables. I have seldom been so excited or so apprehensive when approaching Daddy. He did not permit us to play when there was work to do. Additionally, he seemed always to have a misanthropic perception of our neighbors' influence upon us children, as though they exuded a contaminating effect upon our character. With trepidation I relayed Ronnie's request. I think it took Daddy back to a similar time in his boyhood, because he relented, "Be back before dark."

That concession encouraged a continuum of requests in ensuing years: "Is it okay if I go out for the high school team?"; ... "Is it okay if I play American Legion baseball?"; ... "Is it okay if I play in the West Branch League with Paxtonville?" Paxtonville was thirty miles from the farm. Each time I asked permission to go, he begrudgingly yielded with the qualifier: "Make sure your work is done." Despite the acquiescence, his slow reluctance fostered high anxiety. Each day or evening of a scheduled game I had to make the same request. Each consent was granted with the bearing of a man who was being betrayed. It was accompanied with an emotional harangue that prevented my full enjoyment and precluded the relationship I would have liked. Sometimes, his perturbation left scars.

In the spring of 1960 I was chosen to receive the high school's Most Outstanding Baseball Player Award. The school athletic director called our home asking Daddy to guarantee that I would be at the banquet where the award would be presented on the following Thursday evening. It was assumed that proud parents would attend and maintain secrecy until the event.

It should have been an exciting time for a father. Daddy, however, answered the wall phone in our kitchen as

On Saturday evening, April 9, 1960, I received the high school's Outstanding Baseball Player Award.

though he was being inconvenienced, then turned to me. "You're supposed to be at the school cafeteria on Thursday night to get an award." There was no evidence of surprise or pride, just imposition. Thursday came. He did not go, nor did he ever ask to see the award.

He saw me play only once. I was a junior in high school when my Uncle Dick talked him into attending a spring game at Juniata Joint High School, located near McCallisterville where my Uncle Bill lived. It was a night game in early April and bitter cold. Still, I was excited. My father, who had never seen me play, was going to be watching.

I was the lead-off batter, and when the game began, neither Daddy nor my uncles had yet arrived. Daddy's track record for being on time to watch local baseball games was not good. On evenings when he took Keith and me to games, we regularly arrived in the middle of the second inning. Being late rankled me, but my greater irritation was his seeming lack of concern for punctuality. Before leaving the house, he might take a few minutes to browse the newspaper or listen to the radio. On this cold April night I was anxious for him to see me play.

Finally, near the end of the second inning, I saw a familiar car and watched Daddy and uncles Bill and Dick come from the parking lot, walk around behind the backstop, and take seats in the grandstand in back of first base. I feigned indifference, not acknowledging their arrival. Nevertheless, my consciousness was consumed by their presence. I led off the fourth inning with my team's first base hit. Bursting with the pride of youthful accomplishment and prepared to conquer any remaining worlds, I decided to steal second base on the second pitch. The first pitch to the next batter was a strike. I had already learned that many high school pitchers threw curve balls when they were ahead in the pitch count. A curve was an ideal pitch on which to steal a base. I returned to first base plotting my thievery when I saw Uncle Dick walking toward me at first base. Stopping within earshot, he announced that the three of them were leaving because it was "just too cold." I did not steal second base, and in the years that followed, Daddy never mentioned that game.

Daddy's efforts to please seemed always to miscarry. In the summer after graduation from high school, I was playing for Paxtonville. On July 4th the team was scheduled to play a doubleheader at Selinsgrove. I had no ride to the game and was preparing to walk four miles to the paved Route 522 from where I could hitch a ride. Independence Day was free from the daily rigors of farming, and probably Daddy would have liked to go fishing. Instead, he volunteered to drive me. I think his intentions were to drop me off at the paved road and return home, but when we reached Route 522, he pulled onto the highway and drove the entire thirty-five miles to Selingsgrove. Parking the car beyond the left field fence, he turned off the motor and said he would wait for me. I was overjoyed. On that afternoon I thought his magnanimity was without parallel. Finding a ride back to McClure and then home always involved the unwelcome imposition of begging. Some nights I hitchhiked. Once I was able to reach McClure, if necessary, I could walk the remaining seven miles. But now, I had a ride. Relief flooded over me. I wanted to tell him how much that meant, but the courage required to expose feelings to someone who had repeatedly wounded me, fled. I never told him.

When the first game ended, I headed toward the left field parking lot. I was excited. I had scored the game-winning hit. I wanted from him the recognition a boy needs from a father, and in turn, I wished him to know how grateful I was that he drove me to the game. His car was parked facing away from the baseball field. As I approached I heard him snoring and realized he had not watched the game. Disappointed, I fumbled to maintain equilibrium. I tapped on the front windshield. "Daddy," I hesitated, "The first game is over." He brought himself to full consciousness, sitting upright, absorbing what I had said. Then he stared in disbelief, not answering at first. As if trying to clarify his confusion, he incredulously asked, "First game?"

"First game?" he repeated. He did not look at me as his anger grew. "You didn't tell me there was a second game." My heart sank. I knew what lay in store. If I was to go home with him and skip the second game, my baseball manager, the man who usually gave me a ride to McClure, would be upset. If I stayed for the second game, I would have to find a ride home, and Daddy would be upset. It was a lose-lose situation. In reality, circumstances had already made my decision. Daddy was irritated that there was a second game, and his irascibility would last throughout the evening. I did not want to miss the game and ride 35 miles in strained silence with my father. Regardless, I attempted a compromise, "Maybe, Coach Rager will let me go early."

Daddy never negotiated. He declared, "Somebody has got to do the barn work." With that, he started the car motor and drove away.

Daddy's Baseball Tryout

Neither Daddy nor Mommy spent a lot of time in reverie or recalling the past. There was simply too much work to do, and much of it required full concentration. When family visited on Sundays men might rest against the barnyard gate, conversation drifting into the past, or on summer days, neighbors might lean on the fence railing that separated fields, chewing on stems of timothy, and recalling days of yesteryear, but only for a few minutes. There was always the prescience of work delayed and waiting. Men seldom sat, and they never visited one another by going into a house. Women, on the other hand, invited lady-friends to the kitchen. Visitors, however, were expected to pitch in and help snap beans or pod peas. Talk centered on the immediate: their men, their work, their children, the present.

There were times, however, when the slow pace of milking cows with machines or riding a wagon to and from the fields permitted reflection. Many times Daddy's retrospection was goaded by my curiosity surrounding the baseball of his youth. I wanted to know about his accomplishments and the excitement and aura of the game in days past. It was during one of these slow times that he first shared the account of his professional baseball tryout.

It was a winter evening when I was about fifteen years-old. I was standing at the far end of the cow stable waiting for him to finish the milking, so that I could begin bedding the stalls. I had heard of some of his exploits. Men at the feed mill or store, strangers at the McClure Bean Soup or Alfarata Fair, or neighbors had sometimes alluded to his baseball past, usually intimating that he had been a good player. Asked what those times had been like, he leaned against a stanchion and remembered.

Daddy's father died in January 1937. Afterward and until he moved to the farm, Daddy played baseball as much as was possible. The teams for whom he played were various and many times not associated with a particular league. Sometimes men from Alfarata and Paintersville banded together for games on weekends. Other times he was a rostered player for McClure, a team with a regular schedule. In brief, he played whenever opportunity was present.

The *McClure Plain Dealer*, our local bi-weekly newspaper, described local baseball during this time:

> "The West Branch League was formed in the year 1924 and has fielded teams from Sunbury, New Berlin, Middleburg, Selinsgrove, and other area towns. It became a highly regarded league and in the 1930s, drew crowds numbering over a thousand at a game. Sometimes, big names would be brought in for important games, such as the time around 1930, when opposing teams Middleburg and Beavertown brought in Lefty George from York and Harry Holsclaw from Williamsport to aid their teams in a double header. However, the local pitchers beat both "stars" from outside the area. From 1927 to 1930 the Tri-County League was formed and was made up of teams from the local towns. The league disbanded during the time of the Depression, but revived again with teams from Port Trevorton, Selinsgrove, Middleburg, Paxtonville, Beavertown, McClure, Bannerville, and others. Port Trevorton was a four-time winner of the league championship. The league was later moved farther south and eventually merged with the West Branch League."

One of the "big names" that was brought in on occasion was "Jimmy" Morgan. He was especially recruited during the times of fairs, reunions, and holidays by various competing teams. Such a holiday was the annual Bean Soup Festival at McClure.[1] Hundreds of patrons would gather at the local high school field to watch the locals battle archrival Middleburg. Daddy pitched some of those games for McClure. Afterward, everyone retired to the picnic grounds where the bean soup was served, and sideshows and rural exhibits entertained. It is noteworthy and historically accurate to conclude that the highlight of those celebrations was the baseball game. Local baseball was a significant part of local culture.

Against this backdrop Daddy was offered opportunity to tryout for a professional team. On a summer day in 1939 McClure played a Saturday game against nearby Bannerville. The Bannerville pitcher was Matt Chesney, who later owned a farm on the Old Stage Road several miles from our farm. He was regarded as the best pitcher in the area. The presence of a professional scout from the Washington Senators that day might be explained as coincidence, but the confrontation between Matt Chesney and Jimmy Morgan may have been of sufficient proportion to attract higher interest. Certainly, it adds to the romance of the story.

Both men performed well. After the game, the scout spoke first to Matt and then approached Daddy. The result was an invitation for both pitchers to tryout with Sunbury, a Class C minor league team in the Interstate League.[2] Excited, Matt and Daddy made plans to travel together the following week on an evening when the Sunbury Senators were playing a night game. In the ensuing days,

SUNBURY MEMORIAL STADIUM
The stadium where I watched my first professional game. (*photo courtesy of Ed Baker www.digitalballparks.com*)

1. See note 5 in chapter,"Pappy's Death."
2. Daddy's tryout opportunity took on special significance for me on a summer Saturday in 1955 when he and my Uncle Don took Keith and me to our first professional baseball game at Sunbury Memorial Stadium.

however, Daddy grew uncertain. In the end he did not go. Knowing him as I did, I suspect that a lack of confidence lay at the center of his decision. He suffered mightily from feelings of inferiority and the anxiety of unfamiliarity. He casually excused his behavior by saying, "I wouldn't have made it anyway," but there remained in him an unspoken and unfulfilled wonderment that surfaced whenever he recalled the day he was invited for a professional tryout.

Daddy, the Sports Fan

Daddy was not a serious sports fan, certainly not when measured against the passion with which I followed my favorite teams. His enjoyment resulted from playing, not watching. To be sure, as a teenager he had attended baseball games. He saw members of the Philadelphia Athletics and New York Yankees as they "barnstormed" through the area in the early 1930s. He was familiar with names like Lefty Grove, Jimmy Foxx, and Lou Gehrig, but could not recount their exploits. He had watched the House of David, a famous Jewish baseball team in 1934 with their visiting Negro star, Satchel Paige. He sometimes talked about these experiences, but only in general terms, and never with excitement or fervor. He did not listen to games on the radio or watch them on television. Before her death, my mother mentioned that after we children moved away, he sometimes watched a few innings, but usually fell asleep.

For the first four decades of his life, football did not compete favorably with baseball for public attention, so Daddy had only a cursory interest. It wasn't until Keith played high school football that he became curious enough to attend home games on a few Saturdays, and once drove to Hollidaysburg to watch a game. It wasn't that he became a fan of football, but simply enjoyed the opportunity to see Keith in uniform.[3] Daddy was not really interested in the game. It was never a topic of conversation, nor did he inquire which teams were playing or who was winning or losing when he found me listening to games on the radio.

An indication of football's cursory appeal occurred on the afternoon

---

3. The principle reason Daddy attended Keith's football games and later, Bill's basketball games, but not my baseball games was that baseball was played weekdays immediately after school, a time which conflicted with farm work. Saturday football games and evening basketball games seldom interfered with his work schedule.

of New Year's Day in 1954 when he sat in a rocking chair in front of our kitchen radio listening with me to the Cotton Bowl game. There was a dugout cellar in the hill above our house where we kept fall produce, such as potatoes, onions and apples, and during the early portion of that game, he sent me to the cellar to get some apples. By January the apples had mellowed, and many were spoiled, but I selected four or five good ones and returned to the kitchen. Daddy loved to snack on apples complimented by sharp cheddar cheese and saltine crackers. He sometimes bought five-pound waxed blocks of cheese from the Dairyman's League Milk Company, to whom we sold our milk. He ordered through our milkman and a few mornings afterward, the block was delivered to our milkhouse. On this January day Daddy sat in the rocking chair facing the radio, peeling apples with his pocketknife and eating the cheese and crackers. It was an exciting game, but by the start of the second quarter, he was spent and retired to his room for a nap.

In spite of this indifference, however, he delighted in throwing a football. On fall evenings, as we waited for milking to be completed, he would take time between changing the milk machines from cow to cow to step outside the barn and throw to Keith and me as we ran "pass-patterns" on the road that ran in front of our barn.

Curiously, Daddy seldom played baseball with Keith, Billy, or me. There were random occasions when we were in our pre-teens, usually on Sundays before our noon dinner, when he would appear in the yard with a bat and direct Keith and me to take positions in the field that ran east of our house. From the yard he would launch high, distant fly balls that seemed to ascend to unscalable heights and then return to earth with speed and suddenness that we were seldom able to calculate. Catching one of Daddy's fly balls was an accomplishment. The exercise lasted for a few minutes, then Mommy would call that dinner was ready. Those few minutes were unspoiled joy for me and hinted at the relationship we might have had, had not his temper so frequently alienated us.

In May of 1965 I graduated from college but remained on campus until September working for the food service manager and his catering firm. On a free day, two employees introduced me to golf, and a few days later, intrigued by its nuances, I packed a new set of second-hand clubs into my car and headed to the farm to practice. I was in the meadow on a summer afternoon when Daddy, fascinated by my ineptitude, decided he would try his hand. I handed him a fistful of tees, a half dozen golf balls and a club. It took but a few swings for him to become frustrated. Then, irritation gave way to anger. He completely missed two or three balls, dribbled a few more, and disgustedly walked away.

It remains for me the strangest of incongruities that a farmer whose very circumstances depended upon patience, should have, as his chief failing, impatience. Daddy regularly lost his temper. Sometimes he cursed and threw the objects of his aggravation, but usually, he stomped off leaving us in stupefied silence. Many times he went to the house where we would hear him railing to Mommy, and then, in a fit of fury, he would get into our Chevy pick-up and disappear.

When next I saw him on that summer day, it was evening, and he had taken some of my clubs and gone by himself to the meadow to practice. If he is to be condemned for impatience, he must be credited for persistence.

Over the next few years, on occasion, he would accompany me to the golf course located near the residence of his brother Bill. He would play a few holes, then exasperated, make his way back to the house. Ironically, years later he recalled these times in the fondest terms, as though his frustration and temper did not exist.

Daddy was, by nature, competitive, whether it involved the world of sports or the world of work. Sometimes he was unable to properly direct his intensity, but when husking corn, he was always the first to finish his row. When milking cows by hand, he was proud that he was faster than my grandfather. When I, in later years, worked with him at the cabinet factory in McClure, he always turned out the most finished cabinet pieces. His plowed rows were straighter, his loads of hay sturdier, and his early-rising earlier, but oft times his pride was excessive. Regardless, we, his sons and daughters, owe to him at least the acknowledgment that his competitive disposition has played an essential part in our achievements.

As inconstant and insensitive as he sometimes was, there were times when he demonstrated willing generosity and genuine love. In the late 1970s I was still playing and coaching sandlot ball. It was a most difficult time in my life because, in the aftermath of a broken marriage, my two children had been moved to Ohio. My need for them and my concern for their well-being resulted in driving from New Jersey to Ohio on as many weekends as possible. I was emotionally and physically fatigued.

On this particular Sunday, my new wife, Suzie, and I were returning from a visit to Ohio and decided to stop at my parents' house in Kreamer, PA. It was summertime and they asked us to stay for a few days. I told Daddy that I had to drive to New Jersey for a 6:00 pm baseball game because, as player-manager, the team was my responsibility. I had not given much time to my parents, and I knew they looked forward to my visits, so I promised I would drive back to Kreamer immediately after the game. Daddy made no response, but I knew he was concerned with my emotional and physical health. I ate something, said good-bye to Suzie and Mommy, and headed to my car. Closing the kitchen door behind me, I saw that he was already sitting in the driver's seat. "Come on," he said, "I might as well watch your ball game." He drove me to New Jersey while I slept, and it mattered not at all to me that he slept through both my game and our return trip.

DADDY'S READING

◇◇◇◇◇◇◇◇◇◇◇◇◇◇◇◇◇◇◇◇◇◇◇◇◇◇◇◇◇◇◇◇◇◇◇◇◇◇

Daddy loved to read, both fiction and non-fiction. He read the Danny Orlis series for teens that was mail-ordered for us kids from Theodore Epp's *Back to the Bible Radio Broadcast* from Lincoln, Nebraska, as well as novelettes from the Christian bookstore in Lewistown. The *Reader's Digest* was a favorite, as well as the Digest's abridged novels given to us by Uncle Paul and Aunt Ivy. From the time Daddy and his new bride began living with Mommy's parents in late 1939, until the older couple moved into their new home in 1950, Daddy read Pappy's subscription to *The Pennsylvania Farmer*, an esoteric monthly newspaper that tabulated grain prices and reported news within agriculture. He studied evangelist John R. Rice's fundamentalist Christian viewpoints and

The local bi-monthly *McClure Plain Dealer* and monthly *Pennsylvania Farmer* were among Pappy's favorite reading materials.

exegesis in *The Sword of the Lord*. He meditated over M. R. DeHaan's devotional series, *Our Daily Bread*. He took correspondence Bible courses, labored over Matthew Henry's volumes of Biblical commentary, and devoured Christian apocalyptic fiction, including Sydney Watson's chilling eschatological novel *In the Twinkling of an Eye*.

But mostly, Daddy read the Bible. He read it mornings and studied it nights. He kept a copy in the milk house, another in the garage, and several throughout the house. The ubiquitous presence of Daddy's Bibles was demonstrated for me four or five years after Daddy's death when I visited Daniel Yoder, the Amishman who had purchased our farm in the late '70s. He was walking from the barn toward the house as I was driving by one summer evening. I stopped my car and asked if I might take some pictures of the farm. I explained that I had grown up on his farm and I was nostalgic about the memories it held. I had never met Daniel, so I was astounded when he asked if I was Dennis. I said that I was. He asked if I would like to see his Bible. Puzzled, I patronizingly said, "Sure." He went into the house and returned with a Bible. He told me he had found it in the chicken house shortly after moving in, and that the names and birth dates of "Jim's children" were recorded inside the cover. He had been using that Bible to cross-reference his own German Bible, and in doing so, had memorized my brothers and sisters' names. He insisted that I take it, but I refused. Daddy would have been pleased that his testimony extended beyond the grave.

The Bible was, for Daddy, plainly the Word of God—its words were to be interpreted literally. As such, its weight and urgency inundated his thinking. His hermeneutics were conservative; his prejudice was the King James version; his theology was reformed; and his interpretation was Arminian. His Christianity was not the result of severe scholastic scrutiny, but was filtered through the undeniable doctrines of the Scriptures. It was an amalgam of Billy Graham, Bob Jones, and John R. Rice, and it was the strong current that influenced all of his other reading.

In the early 1950s Daddy packed Keith and me into our '46 pickup and drove us twenty miles to the Lewistown Public Library. He registered so that we could borrow books for two-week intervals. I do not remember with exactness any books he withdrew, but his reading interests never wandered far from Christian themes. In addition to indulging his own appetite for reading, I suspect he traveled those miles because he intuitively recognized the educational value of reading for Keith and me. Perhaps this is fantasy, because he never was interested in discussing any of our selections, but regardless, he must be credited with introducing us to the library at a time when libraries and even reading for pleasure were foreign to local custom.

Every Thursday the mailman placed a free copy of the *McClure Plain Dealer* in our mailbox. We read no daily newspaper, probably because it required a paid subscription or was not available in rural areas. Daily newspapers were traditionally sold only on newsstands or distributed by newsboys in more populated areas. In fairness to accuracy, Daddy was seldom interested in a broad spectrum of news, but he did enjoy reading news of local interest. I witnessed this in the mid 1950s when he built a meat display case that fit onto the bed of our Chevy pickup. On Thursdays we traveled to Lewistown with the pork, beef, and poultry that had been

The *McClure Plain Dealer* building and offices

slaughtered for the enterprise, and sold fresh meat, produce, and eggs from the back of the truck. Afterward he stopped on the corner where West Market Street emptied into the town square and treated himself to a copy of the local daily Lewistown *Sentinel*.

In 1976, after the farm was sold, Daddy and Mommy moved to Kreamer, a small Snyder County community, 30 miles east. The local newspaper was the *Sunbury Item* and Daddy bought a subscription. Thereafter, reading the local paper became a daily ritual.

Daddy's reading tastes did not tend toward the classics, but neither were they provincial. His curiosity and intellectual accomplishment far exceeded his eighth-grade education. He was proud of the Graduate Equivalency Diploma he earned in his early fifties (1969), and gave it prominent display above the desk in his bedroom. His lack of formal training may have motivated his continual reading and study. It also may have produced the inferiority he felt when engaging ministers, teachers, professionals, and frequently his college educated sons and daughters. While he hesitated to engage in

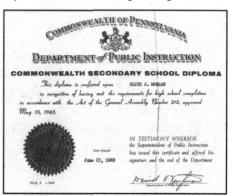

intellectual gymnastics outside his home (unless the topic was Scripture), he invested much time and thought into his arguments and rebuttals. His failing was not in the substance of his thought, but in his tendency to turn discussion into confrontation so that his ideas were too often lost in personality conflict. He became frustrated when he encountered disagreement, or when his point was lost in semantics or digression. The result was withdrawal and self-pity. Sadly, it precluded his realizing how proud his family was of his skills and intelligence, and how grateful we are that he introduced us to reading.

DADDY'S SENSE OF HUMOR
◇◇

D addy's legacy includes an appreciation for humor. In spite of financial struggles, marital tensions and other private and public frustrations, he enjoyed laughter. At picnics and holiday dinners with his brothers and sisters, he found comic relief in recalling incidents from childhood or observing the ironies of day to day living. Jokes heard on the radio or stories read in *The Readers' Digest* were repeated. Innuendo and understatement induced belly laughs, and self-effacement generated giggles.

As a storyteller, Daddy had a poor sense of timing and typically chortled through punch lines so that it was difficult to follow what he was saying. He told of softball games in the pasture when unsuspecting "city-dwellers" stepped in cow manure, and he cackled about the time the pastor decided to spend a day on the farm. The reverend arrived in work clothes and insisted on going to the field where he helped load bales of hay onto our wagon. "He lasted about an hour," Daddy snickered each time he recalled it for us. He borrowed jokes from the *Readers' Digest* or from copies of *The Saturday Evening Post* that his mother left with us when she visited, and when he was able to get a copy of the Sunday newspapers he delighted in reading the comics.

Psychologists maintain that a sense of humor is a strong indicator of intelligence. Whether or not it is true, Daddy demonstrated a quick and ready wit, a sense of irony, and an appreciation for the parodies and caricatures of burlesque.

Besides jokes and stories, he loved the situational comedies and slapstick humor found on radio. On weekends, Daddy gathered with us around the radio and laughed at the histrionics of *Groucho Marx, Burns and Allen, Fibber McGee and Molly*, and *The Great Gildersleeve*. He looked forward to weekly shows like *Amos and Andy, Our Miss Brooks, Jack Benny,* and *Abbott and Costello*. He placed an old plastic General Electric radio in the milk house where, at 6:00 am on weekday mornings, he tuned into the fifteen-minute *Bob and Ray Show*. On Sundays after arriving home from church, he sometimes listened to *Dagwood*, another fifteen-minute comedy. Humor was central to his notion of entertainment and would play a key part in our family's introduction to television.

In 1947 Daddy's brother, Dick, was discharged from the Navy after receiving training in the installation of television cables. He immediately  found a job in the growing industry, working for a company in Philadelphia, but, missing his family and the familiarity of home, he and his new wife soon moved back to Lewistown where he accepted a related job with a local cable network in its nascent stage of development. As such, he had access to television equipment, and, whether by hook or by crook, in 1951 he showed up at our house with a used eight-inch television set. When he discovered that we were able to receive snowy signals from WGAL in Lancaster, he left the set with us. One year later, a second channel, WFBG in Altoona, began broadcasting. The latter channel was unique in that it was affiliated with all four national networks: ABC, CBS, NBC, and Dumont. As a result we had access to a variety of programming.

RICHARD (DICK) MORGAN

On Saturday nights from 9:00-10:30 pm, NBC's *Show of Shows* was telecast. Daddy would leave the door of his bedroom open, make Mommy trade sides of the bed to improve his vantage, and watch through the open door into the living room where the TV faced opposite the bedroom. It required that he stayed awake beyond his 9:00 pm bedtime. From my upstairs bedroom I heard his laughter. Sometimes, if the show was bothering Mommy, he got out of bed and fell asleep on the living room sofa. He loved Sid Caesar and Imogene Coca, the lead comedians. On Sunday mornings at the barn, he would subject us to the routines he had watched the night before. He found especially funny the routine where Sid taught Imogene to drive a car.

On Sunday nights, he sometimes watched the *Colgate Comedy Hour,* the *Texaco Star Theatre,* or other variety shows. They featured more of Daddy's favorite comedians: Bob Hope, Red Skelton, Jimmy Durante, Martin and Lewis, Phil Silvers, Jackie Gleason, and Milton Berle.

While Uncle Dick's introduction of television into our home brought the pleasure of entertainment, Daddy soon experienced concomitant problems. His loss of sleep in order to watch late-night shows resulted in daytime fatigue and irascibility. Worse, he believed his children were spending too much time in front of the TV and were being exposed to undesirable programming. At first he limited the hours when we were permitted to turn on the set, but his regulations failed to address the inappropriate content. The amalgamation of cigarette and beer commercials, sexual innuendo, and the vulgarity of vernacular expressions posed a greater problem than he was able to control. On a Friday night in the winter of 1951 it came to a head.

Uncle Dick installed an 8-inch TV in our living room in 1951.

Our eight-inch set had become a local sensation, the only television in Decatur Township. Curiosity seekers and unfamiliar passers-by routinely stopped to ask if they could look at our TV in the same way a tourist might ask to see the bed in which George Washington slept. They were not interested in watching a program, but simply wanted to experience the sensation of seeing figures on a screen. Sometimes they stayed beyond their welcome, and frequently they intruded.

Among the most popular programs at the time was *Gillette's Cavalcade of Sports* on Friday nights which featured boxing matches from Madison Square Garden in New York. The fights lasted until 9:30 or 10:00 pm. Sometimes uninvited visitors stopped by on those Friday evenings, preventing us from going to bed at normal hours. A few brazenly brought snacks and drinks for themselves, insensitively leaving crumbs, wrappers, and bottles for Mommy to remove afterward. On some nights they used language that was forbidden in our home.

In the beginning Daddy, too, looked forward to the boxing matches and sometimes invited a friend or two to watch. However, the invasion of our privacy by complete strangers incensed him. The camel's back was about to break.

On the Friday evening in question, Daddy, Keith, and I had finished the barn work a bit later than usual. It was a cold night, and we were anticipating a warm house and a hot supper. Arriving at the house, we slipped out of our barn shoes and carried them to the summer porch where Mommy kept a large cardboard box for that purpose. Daddy was in his stockinged feet about to sit for supper when car lights shone through the kitchen window. There had been no invitations to watch the fights as both Daddy and Mommy were trying to eliminate intrusions into our home. Daddy was standing at the kitchen sink drying his hands. Irritated by what he suspected might be an unwanted caller, he asked, "Hazel, who is it?"

Peering from a window to stare at a visitor was unmannerly, but Mommy stole a glance and answered, "I don't know. Somebody in a truck."

We waited for the knock on the kitchen door. When Mommy opened it, three men were standing on the porch. Daddy recognized Bob Murray, operator of the feed mill in Beaver Springs where we had our cattle grain milled.

"Hi, Bob," he reluctantly greeted the miller.

The three visitors were awkward, imposition with restraint. "Jim, I hope we're not bothering you," Bob apologized, "this is my brother-in-law and a friend of his. We wondered if you would mind if we watched the fight?"

I knew Daddy was upset. He glanced at Mommy, and I think at that moment he made up his mind to get rid of our television. "We're eating supper," he explained. Cold incredulity crept into his voice, but he continued, "You can wait in the living room."

Momentarily I feared that the lack of cordiality, the trace of contempt in Daddy's response might cause a confrontation. He made no offer to turn on the TV or attend to any of the intruders' comforts. The three interlopers simply filed into the living room and took seats.

There was no door between the kitchen and living room, and while we ate our evening meal, we listened to their speculations about the upcoming fight. All three were pedestrian, oblivious to obtrusion, and insensible to impropriety. Daddy was silent, smoldering.

In retrospect I think Daddy's restraint that evening resulted from a personal, private struggle with his Christian testimony. He wanted to do the right thing, wanted to be Christ-like, but believed it pusillanimous to allow such an intrusion. Vitiated by the dilemma, he maintained a precarious equilibrium.

Minutes passed. Bob called from the living room, "Jim, do you mind if we smoke?"

The walls of Jericho were about to fall.

Mommy shook her head in disbelief as Daddy firmly rejoined, "Not in the house."

When he was embarrassed, frustrated, or humiliated, Daddy's explosions were sometimes delayed, but like the stretching of an over-inflated balloon, we knew he was on the verge of bursting, and when he burst, his vituperation would be fearsome.

Bob Murray was, in fact, a nice man. When we boys rode with Daddy to have grain ground at his mill, Bob let us watch the process through a dirt-stained window, the great cogs and grinders rumbling below the main floor, sending clouds of dust adrift throughout the mill. The noise was deafening and lent immense excitement to our day. We liked going to Bob Murray's Mill.

Daddy arose from his chair, his mission now clear. The enemy had fired the first shot, and he was free to counter. Standing in the doorway between the kitchen and living room, he announced, "Bob, you're going to have to leave. We don't want company tonight."

And that was all. The three men asked no questions, offered no apologies, but quietly surrendered and exited the kitchen door. We sat in stunned silence until their truck motor started and the vehicle backed out of our driveway and disappeared. Daddy retired to his bedroom. A small braided carpet that was used to seal the bottom of the kitchen door against the winter cold had been pushed to the side as the men left. Mommy put it back in place. We did not watch the fights.

When I was called downstairs the next morning to begin the barn work, I noticed at once that the TV was gone. Intuitively I knew its absence was permanent, and I was sufficiently familiar with Daddy's temperament not to ask questions.

The only eruption came at breakfast, but it more resembled a dying geyser than a violent, fulminating volcano. He announced firmly that Mommy and he had talked and were in agreement. The television was having a detrimental effect on our family. They were returning the set to Uncle Dick. While the edict was delivered matter-of-factly, and even though we children hated to see it go, we knew Daddy's word was final. There was no discussion.

I do not know when Daddy and Uncle Dick made the exchange, but television disappeared from our home for nearly fifteen years. I had graduated from college and was teaching school before it returned. Seldom home anymore, I cannot speak to Daddy's disposition nor to the habits a new TV may have reintroduced.

Ironically, the effect of its removal in 1951 was negligible. There was work to do, and any need for entertainment we might have experienced was supplied by books and radio. Novels and short stories were read and reread. Ball games, melodramas, and comedies were plentiful on AM radio stations, so instead of sitting in front of a snowy screen, we gathered nights around the radio and delighted in the more imaginative adventures of the older medium or sequestered ourselves with a book in the kitchen or bedroom. One might even conclude that we owe to Bob Murray and his companions a debt of gratitude.

DADDY'S DEATH
◇◇◇◇◇◇◇◇◇◇◇◇◇◇◇◇◇◇◇◇◇◇◇◇◇◇◇◇◇◇◇◇◇◇◇◇◇

Cloyd James "Jim" Morgan
February 12, 1917 – July 25, 2001

"For I have chosen him, that he may command his children and his household after him to keep the way of the LORD by doing righteousness and justice." (Genesis 18:19)

My sister Susie called at 3:06 pm on Wednesday, July 25, 2001, to tell me that Daddy had died. I had just finished spraying the grape vines at my home in New Jersey and had begun to change clothes. I had planned to go over to the Meadow Breeze recreation fields and play basketball with Cim, but for a few minutes reconsidered whether I should immediately leave to be with my mother. Concluding that time with a son is priority, he and I went to the park where we played for an hour or so before returning to the house. Suzie had packed clothes for me. I called a baseball client to cancel a pitching lesson for his son, postponed a doctor's appointment with Dr. Klein, my cardiologist, and phoned Jamie Lemp, whom I was tutoring in preparation for her freshman year of college. Sammy was not home. I knew she would want to be with me, so I wrote her a note explaining that I loved her, that it meant much to me that she cared as she did, and that Suzie would take her to Mammy's house the following day.[1] Keri helped load the car. His acts of kindness, as well as those of the other members of my family, brought tears as I drove, and the memories of their solicitude and sensitivity remain immeasurably precious. I also was aware that Cim and Keri were uncomfortable with the notion of the funeral. My dad had never bothered to form a relationship with my children, thus they felt no personal sense of loss. I understood their discomfort, and assured them that attendance would not be necessary.

I could recall vividly my maternal grandfather's funeral when I was fourteen. The circumstances were, for me, altogether different than the remoteness and unfamiliarity of my dad toward my children. I had been with Pappy every day of my life. The significance of his death was deeply personal. I had lost the closest of friends.

I left at 6:15 pm. My only regret was that I didn't take the time to write a special note for Suzie. I appreciated that this affected her too, and that she ought to be included. I was conscious of the need, but my mind would not compose anything of import, and I didn't like to drive after darkness, so I told her that I loved her, that I would be fine, and I left with that void.

Mommy and Daddy had driven to Lewisburg that morning for Daddy to see Dr. Ginsburg, his family doctor. He had confided to Mommy, "You have no idea how bad I feel."

When they returned home about noon, Mommy made lunch. Daddy then reclined in his chair for a nap. To keep the house quieted, Mommy went downstairs to play a computer game of solitaire. Some time passed, and sensing that Daddy had been too long asleep, she went to check and found him dead in his chair. She immediately called my sister. "Susie, come quick," she begged, "your dad is dead."

My sister Susie and her husband Ray lived within a few minutes traveling time from Mommy and Daddy's home. Susie had been sitting on her couch reading. She immediately put on her sneakers and drove the quarter mile to Daddy's house, numb from the initial shock.

---

1. "Mammy," in this case, refers to my mother. My children were taught to call her by that name, just as I had been taught to call my grandmother "Mammie." The difference in spelling is simply the way each lady signed her name.

Mommy was sitting outside on the porch swing and immediately recalled for Susie the morning's events. Susie asked, "How do you know he's dead?"

Mommy responded, "Come in and look at him."

Daddy was reclined with feet up and hands folded, but when Susie touched his face it was cold. Uncertain what to do, she called 911, informing the lady on the other end of the line, "My dad just died, and we don't know what to do." The lady said she would contact the proper authorities.

Suzie then turned to Mommy and suggested she return to the porch swing. Already emotionally broken, little good would result from remaining in the living room with Daddy's lifeless form. The house phone was installed in the laundry room, adjacent to the kitchen. Susie went back inside to call me. When I answered, her voice faltered, and she was unable to talk. After an untimely pause, I asked, "Which one?"

She asked if I could come home immediately. I hesitated momentarily, considering my personal and family obligations, but the tone of her voice countermanded my hesitancy. She pleaded, "I need you."

Susie then called their minister, Reverend Charles Cole, directing him to her own house. He was in his mid-fifties, knew Mommy well, and had been respected by Daddy for his evangelical, non-denominational teaching. Susie requested prayer as the minister promised that he would come immediately.

Susie then went to Daddy and kissed him, asking Mommy if she, too, wanted a final kiss. She did.

Daddy was proud of his craftsmanship.

I had anticipated this trip home for many years, knowing it would be difficult. Since leaving for college in the fall of 1961 my return visits had been to see Mommy and my younger brothers and sisters. Although I spent time with Daddy when I was there, our relationship was strained, awkward. His vagaries had become increasingly difficult, demanding exclusive attention, making it difficult to keep company with others. Like a child starved for attention, upon my arrival, he insisted that I go with him to his work shed, admire the pictures in his darkroom, or inspect his latest project. He continually pulled me away from the rest of the family, preoccupied with self-interests and unappreciative of others and their concerns. Though I had become an adult, I still feared the sulking and emotional outbursts that had characterized my boyhood.

Ironically, as difficult as Daddy had been, I already missed him. I considered the ways our family had been blessed through him: his demand that we work hard, the strong security of his presence, his insistence that we study Scripture, and his concern for our spiritual welfare. I recalled special gestures he had made singularly for me: riding along to Ohio to visit Timmy and Christy at a time when I was emotionally broken and distraught over being separated from them; paying for the gasoline at a time when my means precluded such a trip; giving me a ride to a ball game at Paxtonville when I would have had to walk or hitchhike; driving me to college through foreign and frightening towns and cities, over unchartered highways in a secondhand car that he had no money to repair if it failed.

I thought, as well, of his father, his early death, and Daddy's growing obsession in recent years for spiritual reassurance that they would one day be reunited. I thought of the financial and emotional struggles Daddy experienced as a boy and young man without a father. His loneliness had produced a palpable inferiority that was betrayed by his quick defensiveness. I thought of his brother Dick, who was so much like him in his irascibility and insecurity. I wondered if Dick would come to the funeral after vowing never to visit family members, because "they talk about me behind my back."

I wondered about my brother Keith. Daddy's greatest desire was to have his children accept Christ as their Savior and be assured of a heavenly reunion. Keith, however, reacting against the stern application of Christianity and sometime hypocrisy of Daddy's behavior, had rejected the gospel message. I prayed that God would use an earthly father's death to produce a son's eternal life.

W. CLOYD MORGAN'S FAMILY
My paternal grandfather with son Cloyd, daughter Helen, and his wife, Cora 1919. He died in the Cresson, PA Tuberculosis Sanatorium when Daddy was 19.

I speculated as to whom would deliver the eulogy. Over the years I had romanced the notion of speaking at my parents' funerals. I had even written a poem in anticipation of his death, but it was filled with self-serving emotion, and I had long since discarded it. I knew that I was not sufficiently strong or clever or articulate to share private sentiment at such a public occasion.

The paramedics were the first to arrive, parking at the bottom of the hill that sloped downward from the porch of the house. They questioned Susie regarding the circumstances of death. Bruce Hummel, the coroner, then arrived. He examined the body briefly, assured everyone that death was from natural causes, and walked outside to converse with the paramedics. In the midst of this activity, Susie called her husband Ray, who was at work in Lewisburg, 30 minutes distant, requesting that he come home.

Mr. Hummel politely asked that Susie and Mommy retire to the laundry room so as not to see the body removed. During this interim, Mommy cried quietly, plaintively repeating, "What am I gonna do?"

Mr. Hummel scheduled a time for the family to go to the mortuary in Selinsgrove and then left. Susie insisted that Mommy not remain alone in the house but stay overnight with her and Ray. Mommy resisted, but my sister was firm. She helped Mommy to the car she had parked on the grass in the front yard, anticipating that others would need the driveway space, and the two rode the quarter mile in silence. Ray arrived home shortly afterward.

Susie, Mommy, and Ray withdrew to the couple's living room where Mommy sat in a rocking chair and chronicled for Ray the morning's events. Pastor Cole and his wife Gloria then arrived. Susie remembered afterward that the pastor, conscious of Christian propriety, hugged her with one arm, then he and his wife entered the living room where Mommy retold her story. Pastor Cole probed for information that would make the funeral oratory personal and interesting. He took with him a wooden plaque on which Daddy had inscribed the Bible verse, "As for me and my house, we will serve the Lord." It was later used at the service. About an hour later the pastor and his wife left.

Before arriving at about 8:45 pm, I had telephoned Susie to ask whether I should come to hers or Mommy's house. She said Mommy wanted to sleep in her own bed, so she and Ray would take her to the house and wait for me there. When I pulled into the driveway, Mommy and Susie came outside to greet me. We hugged, and it was readily apparent that my sister was providing everything for which one could possibly ask at such a time: compassion, amity, and generosity. She, more than anyone, made the death pageant run smoothly. We ate something, and then Susie and Ray returned to their home.

Mommy and I were alone. We spoke of logistical concerns that needed attention, and I assured Mommy that she need not worry about such matters. I reminded her that Susie was a bastion of strength and was nearby. I promised that I would stay with her until everything was in order. As the hour grew late, Mommy said she was tired and thought she would be able to sleep (I found in the morning that she had), so we had prayer, and then I climbed into Daddy's bed and slept within the same sheets and blankets that had warmed him twenty-four hours earlier. The experiences of life are so terribly strange and wonderful that it is impossible to appreciate its nuances and depths. How wonderful it is to be at the mercy of God!

Suzie, Cim, and Sammy arrived early on Thursday morning, and even now I am reminded that life's meaningfulness is always linked to relationships. Suzie came because she knew this was difficult for me and understood that her comfort meant more than any other; Cim came because he is bound by character and experience to help when needed; and Sammy came because where the heart is fastened the heart must abide. Her devotion was further evidenced the following afternoon when Suzie and Cim returned to New Jersey to satisfy family obligations. Sammy insisted on staying. My mother and daughter much resemble William Wordsworth's Margaret of *The Ruined Cottage,* about whom he wrote:

> *Many a passenger*
> *Has blessed poor Margaret for her gentle looks*
> *When she upheld the cool refreshment drawn*

From that forsaken spring, and no one came
But he was welcome, no one went away
But that it seemed she loved him.

Earlier Thursday morning Mommy and I made a list of things to be done, however, it was not really necessary since Susie was so well organized. In the midst of notifying the minister, calling the newspapers, selecting the casket, and ordering the arrangements for services, she was remarkable. Her testimony was a blessing as she consoled and reassured Mommy. In addition she took upon herself much of the financial burden.

In the early afternoon Mommy, Susie, and I traveled to the mortuary to select a casket. I dreaded the walk through the aisles of caskets and hated the notion that I must select cold steel and concrete for my father, but God is faithful, and I was filled with His confidence that life is eternal. The remaining duties were performed, less with the regret of being separated than with the expectation of being reunited.

On Friday morning Susie, Sammy, and I drove with Mommy to Lewistown to select a tombstone that would mark both Daddy and Mommy's final resting place. She had rehearsed with Susie her desires for inscriptions and stones, and after arriving, she sat with the proprietor as he penciled the details: names of their eight children, a heart-shape bearing their wedding date, set between notations of their birth and death, and finally, one of Daddy's favorite scripture verses, Colossians 1:27, to be inscribed at the top of the stone.

"Christ in us, the hope of Glory."

With Mommy occupied, the three of us meandered through the aisles of stones, pensive, drawn to each other by circumstance, minds and hearts commiserative. About us, time went on. Cars out on the highway carried unsuspecting souls toward eternity. Birds, insensible to bereavement, sang their morning chorus. And my mother, in spite of the reconciliation and peace found in the promises of Jesus, suffered the loss of the union resulting from *"they shall become one flesh."* A part of herself was gone.

On the face of the memorial stone, Daddy asked for the inscription "Christ in us the hope of Glory" as a testimony to his confidence in our Savior.

On the back of the memorial stone, Mommy had inscribed the names of her children.

I do not remember Saturday clearly. I rode with Mommy and Sammy in a limousine to Samuel's Church where the burial service took place. I cried when the casket was lowered. I had not always been the son for whom every father wishes.

Among the memories of that Saturday two remain clearly embedded.

Ironically, both concern my mother. The first occurred after the graveside service was complete as friends and family began the slow procession away from Samuel's Church graveyard and toward the reception held at the Kreamer Fire Hall, 26 miles away. While the gathering dispersed, Mommy lingered by the casket in the reality that earthly closure was imminent. With this solemnity, most of my brothers and sisters remained nearby in polite civility, concerned for Mommy's equanimity, but deferent to the privacy of her final farewell. In the midst of that leaden circumstance, my sister Beth approached Mommy. She did not wish to disturb the sanctity of the moment, but she asked Mommy's approval to have her two small sons watch the lowering of the casket so they might see and remember. Mommy put aside her personal pain. Permitting the boys such an experience, she explained afterward, might underscore for them the reality of death and the need for a Savior. "Yes," she said, "it would be a good life-lesson; if it would cause one soul to be saved, it would be worth it." Her simplicity and humility touched deeply.

On the return from Samuel's Church to the reception hall, Mommy, Sammy, and I again rode in the white limousine furnished by the funeral home and driven by a family acquaintance, Roger Pheasant. Mommy talked of the friends who had come: the lady who had introduced herself to us at the gravesite had been a friend from childhood, the man in the wheelchair had been a schoolmate, the man in the blue suit who walked with a cane had once worked with Daddy. I reminded her of the consolation of eternal life, and she asked if I thought we would recognize one another in Glory. I assured her that identity is both logical and eternal. She asked if I would make certain that the Pastor and the pianist received the monetary gifts she had set aside. She asked if I thought it was a "nice" funeral.

The second memory took place at the reception hall. After I found seats at one of the long tables in the large assembly hall, Mommy excused herself to go freshen up in the ladies' room. She left Sammy and me to greet the friends who came to the table to introduce themselves. The line seemed endless, and I eagerly awaited Mommy's return so that she, too, might enjoy their love and concern.

I also visited with my brothers, sisters, Aunt Mary, and Uncle Don.[2]

---

2   It was an especially difficult time for my brother Bill, who had been struck with transverse myelitis, an inflammation of both sides of one section of his spinal cord, on Sunday,

When Pastor Cole rose to ask God's blessing on the meal, I was suddenly conscious that twenty minutes had elapsed and Mommy had not returned.

I was struck with the notion that she may have succumbed to private grief and secluded herself in the rest room. I asked Sammy to investigate. The rest room was empty. Anxiously we searched the assembly. She was not to be found. I inquired of several of her friends if they had seen her. They had not. Growing anxious, I looked for my sister, Susie, who was greeting arrivals at the building entrance. As though it were obvious to her, Susie asked if I had looked in the kitchen. I should have known. When memory shall have faded into shadow, the lingering image of Mommy will most probably be of her in the kitchen: cooking, sewing, ironing, washing, rocking a baby or small child.

She did not see me when I entered. She was standing over a steaming pot, ladling hot food into serving dishes that were then carried into the dining area. She was smiling and conversing with the ladies who had come to serve. I was struck with the irony that the hundreds who had come to serve her, were, instead, being served by her. Her *raison d'etre* had always been service, and now, in the midst of her greatest loss, comfort for her was still in servanthood. Hers was a beauty inscrutable in its simplicity and its sacrifice.

November 26, 2000. It damaged the insulating material that covers nerve cell fibers and for the next seventeen years left him paralyzed from the waist downward.

REFRESHMENTS ON THE FARM
◇◇

Growing up in rural America in the 1940s and 1950s I experienced firsthand the technological advance of moving from kerosene lamps to electric lights. Electricity brightened our world with instant, intense, and convenient methods of lighting, lessening Nature's grip on the length of a farmer's working day and the rigor required to "make hay while the sun shines." Electricity, in turn, introduced refrigerators and more choices in the varieties of foods and drinks available on the farm. Moving from an icebox to a refrigerator was a welcome and exciting revolution.

Until refrigeration became available in the late 1940s, the icebox extended the value of edibles for an extra day or two. Twice weekly an iceman, wearing a leather vest for protection from the cold and wet, delivered two fifty-pound blocks of ice to our wood house where Mommy or Mammie scored and broke off a block suitable to fit the ice compartment in the kitchen icebox. The ice blocks, however, melted rapidly and the storage space for food was insufficient for a large family. Fortunately, all dairy farms featured a springhouse, a small enclosed building where water was kept clean and protected from animals. Since the source was deep-earthed springs, the water was cold and provided refrigeration for the large quantities of milk transported to processing plants each morning. The springhouse was also used to preserve butter, cream, and other perishables.

On our farm at the far eastern end of Decatur Township, located on what has recently been named Decatur Road (still unpaved as of 2020), electricity also meant that the little whitewashed springhouse would no longer be used to cool food stores, and in fact, would no longer be trafficked by thirsty patrons who scooped dippers of cool water from the cement-bottomed trough. As the years passed and the flow of human activity waned, the building fell into disrepair. In its decline, curious boys sometimes left ajar its creaking door, inviting creatures from the surrounding marsh to residence. Frogs, mice, insects, and sometimes snakes became regular inhabitants as time grew still within its walls.

Years before the springhouse's abandonment, a ditch that extended from the springhouse to the cellar of the house had been dug. Plumbing was laid, a pump was installed, and cool water was pumped by a gasoline engine to kitchen and cellar faucets. The ditch spanned more than fifty yards and was dug entirely by Mommy's sister, Beatty, then a teenager. According to Mommy, the women wanted running water in the house so badly that Beatty propositioned her father—if he would buy the piping, she would dig the channel into which it could be laid. Afterward, clothing

Joe and Dave in doorway of springhouse. By the mid-1950s it was no longer essential to the farm.

was washed, meals were prepared, and, of course, water was drunk without a detour to the springhouse.

Cold running water soon became customary, but hot water remained a precious commodity. The ladies had to pour cold tap water into the belly of the wood stove or heat containers of water atop the stove. Thus, bathing involved the ordeal of heating water in quantity, then adding gallons of cold water as needed into the galvanized washtub which sat behind our kitchen wood stove and served as our bathtub.

Shortly after running water was introduced, Pappy installed pumps, and later, hydrants in the barn and chicken house. A few months later he added a third hydrant behind our woodshed where a source of water was needed for butchering, washing diapers and clothes, and feeding the young chickens that occupied the "peepie house."[1] Our spring-fed water supply was plentiful, pragmatic, nearly costless, and normally, our only beverage. With apology to the poet, Coleridge, it was "Water, water, everywhere….and all we had to drink."

Water was heated in the tank on the right side of the stove.

Actually, there were other beverages. Both my parents and grandparents were coffee drinkers, topping off meals with one or two cups.[2] Curi-

---

1. The "peepie house" was so named because it housed the young chicks, dubbed "peepies," which were recently removed from a brooding area.

2. When coffee was rationed during WWII, the adults drank Postum, a substitute made from roasted wheat bran, wheat, and molasses.

ously, however, coffee was not served between meals even when company was present. My brothers and sisters acquired coffee habits as adults, but while they lived on the farm caffeine was believed unhealthy for children, so we were not permitted indulgence.

Living on a dairy farm made milk readily available. At the same time, it was the primary source of revenue and was, therefore, used in moderation. Drinking quantities of milk meant a lesser paycheck. Although Mommy kept a Mason jar of milk in the ice box or refrigerator for breakfast cereal, and she utilized quantities in preparing meals, we did not usually drink milk at mealtimes.

There were two exceptions. One was milk for cocoa. Cocoa was as much a part of breakfast as the family devotions that followed. Each school day began when Mommy made fire in the stove, took a sauce pan ("dipper" in farm country) from the pantry, mixed Hershey's cocoa with sugar, salt, and water, brought it to a boil, added our raw milk, and heated it to taste. Hungry children then dipped toasted slices of home-made bread generously spread with home-churned butter, into the delicious drink.

The second exception took place on especially hot summer evenings. For several summers during the late 1940s my Uncle Don, whom everyone called Nipper, worked on the farm.[3] Eleven years older than I, he was like an older brother to us kids, and we really enjoyed him. He played in the hay mows with us, making tunnels, climbing the hay ladders, and hurling himself down into the loose hay. He told us scary stories at night, sang lyrical ditties, and provided us with lots of good times. Nipper's main legacy, however, resulted from nightly raids to the milkhouse.

After hot summer days in the fields or long hours sweating in overheated mows and dusty granaries, the notion of a cold drink at bedtime was bewitching. Nipper began inviting Keith and me to accompany him to the milkhouse. Borrowing a dipper and some glasses from Mommy's kitchen, he led the way as though we were on a secret mission. In the cool seclusion of those cement walls he introduced us to ice-cold milk.

The water in the milk cooler was mechanically agitated to prevent freezing. However, a thin sheet of ice usually formed overnight in the corners of the tank because the water temperature sometimes reached below 32 degrees. As a result of this refrigeration, the cement-block structure was

3. The nickname "Nipper" was coined years earlier when Uncle Don was a small boy. It had been the pet name of a wide-eyed, mischievous cartoon character who appeared daily in the Lewistown *Sentinel*, the local newspaper.

cooler than the other buildings and was a welcome retreat.

Once inside, we closed the door, which lent a clandestine air of excitement to our foray. Nipper then lifted the milk cooler lid, exposing the tops of the milk cans. With his bare hands he broke through the surface ice and reached for the handle of the nearest can. Pushing the ice aside he pulled the lid off the can, thrust the dipper down into the contents, and agitated the milk until the cream was homogenized.

Finally, he lifted the dipper and poured its contents into the glasses. We drank slowly as though the cold liquid was ambrosia. While we indulged, he would tell a story or recall an exciting adventure. He then refilled each glass. We leaned against the cement, listening and reveling in our escapade. Twenty minutes expended, we returned to the house. It was bedtime.

Daddy knew of our covert antics, and even participated a time or two, until he realized the bottom line on the monthly paycheck was affected. Appreciative of Nipper's gratuitous contribution to farm life, and not wishing to bruise his feelings, Daddy finally took Keith and me aside. On occasion, he decreed, we were welcome to trek to the milkhouse for an ice-cold glass of milk, but regular raids on his profits were, from that hour, *verboten*.

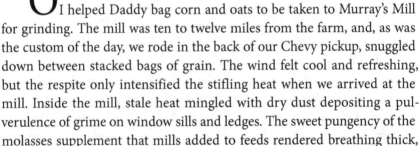

One hot August day when I was about eight years old, Keith and I helped Daddy bag corn and oats to be taken to Murray's Mill for grinding. The mill was ten to twelve miles from the farm, and, as was the custom of the day, we rode in the back of our Chevy pickup, snuggled down between stacked bags of grain. The wind felt cool and refreshing, but the respite only intensified the stifling heat when we arrived at the mill. Inside the mill, stale heat mingled with dry dust depositing a pulverulence of grime on window sills and ledges. The sweet pungency of the molasses supplement that mills added to feeds rendered breathing thick, viscid. Huge deafening grinders vibrated through the hardwood floor forcing workers to shout in conversation. Men dripped perspiration as they dumped grain into huge cogs or carried heavy sacks to and from unventilated granaries. A small closet adjacent to the hub of activity served as the office. The only accoutrements in the dingy room were an adding machine atop a dusty, wooden table that served as a desk, several shoe boxes filled with receipts and loose change, and a small fan whose switch was stuck in the "off" position. In the corner stood a soda cooler with "Coca Cola" emblazoned across its front. The cover had a hinge that ran along its center and allowed access to either of its sides, a style of machine that required patrons to reach down into icy water to make selections.

One of the attractions of Murray's Feed Mill was a bottle of "pop."

Daddy asked if we would like some "pop," the Decatur Township vernacular for carbonated drinks. We had seldom tasted pop, although we romanced the notion as a result of magazine and billboard advertisements. At Joe McKinley's store, where Daddy sometimes bought ice cream, I had once lifted the lid to his pop cooler and read the bottle tops, fantasizing about which flavor I might select if I had a nickel. I knew Daddy's favorite was 7-Up. Once or twice he bought pop for us, but it was an extravagance, and we knew better than to ask for something he could not afford.

A cold drink of any kind on this stultifying day was inviting, but I did not immediately respond to Daddy's offer. Something greater than thirst constrained. As an eight-year-old, I was not sufficiently sophisticated to fully appreciate the financial strains under which Daddy and Mommy struggled, but I was aware that money was a constant concern. I had frequently seen Daddy return a box of cereal or a bottle of catsup to a grocery store shelf when he realized he was short of cash. As a teen, I felt his humiliation when he had to ask cashiers to subtotal his purchases. On the occasions when I futilely searched through his wallet for a quarter to buy a rubber ball, Mommy matter-of-factly reminded me that he didn't have any money. Now, confronted with spending Daddy's money on a luxury, self-gratification wrestled with virtue, resulting in a kind of paralysis. It was the lady or the tiger.[4]

On this day, however, the crucible was removed when Daddy gave a quarter to Mr. Murray, asking for change. Mr. Murray fished through one of the shoe boxes atop the office table, dug out five nickels and handed them to Daddy. Then, with all the *noblesse oblige* a handful of nickels can command, Daddy lifted the cooler lid and invited us to reach for the nectar.

Cider was a regular drink, occasioned each fall after we sorted apples in our orchard. Medium and small varieties and those with

---

4. "The Lady or the Tiger" is a classic 19th century short story by Frank Stockton which posits the dilemma of choosing between two unpleasant options.

blemishes were set aside to be placed into burlap bags and transported to the cider press in Beaver Springs. Daddy and Pappy began the process by bringing the vinegar barrel up from the cellar in early September and placing it in an open area at the far end of the yard. Once there, Mammie cleaned the inside, removing the mother of vinegar left from last year's batch.[5] The plug was removed so that the barrel could dry in the warm sunshine, and a few weeks later Daddy held open burlap bags while Keith and I took apples from the piles in the orchard and deftly placed them into the sacks so they wouldn't bruise. Daddy then tied shut the eight or ten bags, loaded them onto the truck bed and departed for the cider press. When he returned the truck bed contained milk cans filled with cider. The clean vinegar barrel was then carried to an open area adjacent to the wood house, placed on wooden blocks, and the cider was emptied into it. For a week or ten days we were permitted the treat

Our vinegar barrel was seasoned and stored in the cellar.

of drinking the sweet cider. After that, a chemical change took place. The sweetness faded, and in its stead we tasted the pungent warmth of alcohol. Another ten days and the barrel, with its soured contents, was transported down into the cool cellar. In a short time the "mother" stopped working, and the resulting vinegar was used for cooking and medicinal purposes.

Changing technology brought variations to the process, especially after the milk-cooling machine arrived. The belly of the cooler was large enough to store gallons of cider for weeks or to keep watermelons cold for days. By the 1960s the use of cider vinegar for medicinal purposes vanished in the wake of miracle drugs, as it became cheaper to buy the small amounts of vinegar needed for cooking. By the 1970s the orchard itself had fallen into neglect and the blighted fruit was no longer useful.

July and August days were hot with dust, flies, and endless cycles of milking cows, cultivating corn, and weeding the garden. However, the fifty-pound blocks of ice that were delivered twice each week and stored in the wood house were too precious to be wasted on drinks. Farmers in fields or meadows or barns walked to the nearest springhouse or car-

---

5 "Mother of vinegar" is a stringy, mucilaginous substance consisting of various bacteria that cause fermentation when added to fruit juices.

ried mason jars filled with spring water to assuage their thirsts. Routinely, wives or daughters filled the jars from a spring-fed tap, wrapped them in towels, and sent them with one of the small children to wherever men were working. How good that water tasted!

Even after electricity arrived, we did not use ice in our drinks, principally because spring water was already cool. I never heard a farmer allude to an iced drink or a cold soda or beer. As a matter of fact, I never saw anyone drink beer until I was sixteen and playing baseball away from home.[6] There was never beer or soda in the farm refrigerator.

Root beer and orange extracts were sold by a traveling McNess Man.

Although commercial drinks were foreign, we tried our hand at domestic editions each summer. A traveling salesman (the "McNess Man") called in May or June. He brought his satchel of medicines, ointments, salves, and assorted household wares into our kitchen and presented a full display on the kitchen table. Protocol dictated that Mommy choose something. We were delighted when she selected root beer and orange extracts for drinks. Of course, there was no carbonation, but the sugary goodness of a flavored drink was a wonderful treat for us kids.

Just as our root beer and orangeade were seasonal, so was the sassafras tea we drank each spring. It had not yet been discovered that such plants might contain hallucinogens and be damaging to both humans and animals, thus, we dug the roots from fence rows, washed and scrubbed them free of soil, and boiled them to produce tea. The fragrance of sassafras is aromatic, and the sweetened drink is flavorful. An open pot of tea rested on the stove top for several days as Mommy simply added more

6. Between my junior and senior years of high school I played summer baseball in adult leagues. For an away game, six or eight men piled onto the bed of a truck and rode to the game. On the way home they sometimes stopped at a tavern and enjoyed a bottle of beer. The first time this happened I remained on the truck with the excuse that I wasn't thirsty. It was a ninety degree day, and we had just played a nine inning game on an all-dirt infield. My defense bore no credibility. Suspecting that I had never tasted beer, two or three of the still-uniformed players picked me up and carried me into the "beer joint" where they had already ordered a drink for me. I was about to have my first beer, they promised, whether I cooperated or not. They had a bit of fun at my expense for a few minutes, but when they realized my discomfort was genuine, they confessed the drink was ginger ale. I was teased about my drinking habit for years afterward.

water when the supply dwindled.

Tea was not a regular drink, but my maternal grandmother was a believer that catnip, spearmint, and blackberry teas were effective treatments for upset stomach, diarrhea, colds, and insomnia. There is nothing worse-tasting than a cup of unsweetened catnip tea. Many times, when a brother or sister was not feeling well, she designated me to walk to the woods and gather catnip or spearmint, or to the berry patch for blackberry leaves. If there was a chance I would be given a dose as well, I conveniently failed to find the plants.

Mothers believed unsweetened catnip tea was a panacea.

During cold winters, with a ready supply of both ice and cream, ice cream was common. It was one of those homemade products that years afterward holds a romantic appeal because it evokes a purer and less complicated time when food and drink was untainted by preservatives and other additives. Of course, the romance is usually illusory. When I am homesick for the farm, I am able to push aside the memories of long, hot, dusty days in the fields and mows, of cold winter days and nights at the barn, and of the tensions that were intrinsic to our home, and fantasize about homemade ice cream. Truth is, however, back then I complained homemade ice cream was runny, had lumps, and took forever to crank. I preferred the store-bought ice cream that Daddy sometimes brought home. The grass grows greener on the other side of the proverbial fence.

I also loved the chocolate milk shakes that my Aunt Mary bought for me when I visited Grandma Shawver. Mary lived in an apartment in Lewistown and spent much of her free time at her mother's house. After evening supper she sometimes walked with Keith and me across the Juniata River Bridge to the Royal Dairy, an ice cream store located a quarter mile away. We sat in quiet anticipation on the high bar stools waiting anxiously as she ordered a vanilla shake for Keith and a chocolate one for me. A soda jerk scooped dippers of hard ice cream into a metal shaker, added whole milk and syrup, attached the shaker to a mixer, poured the contents into tall cups, placed them in a white paper bag, and handed the precious package to Aunt Mary. We walked back to Grandma's house and feasted. A chocolate milk shake properly made is still my favorite drink.

It is true that the farm and my boyhood are gone. With them have disappeared many of the refreshments of an antique time: "raw" milk, homemade cider and root beer, and sassafras tea. As well, the McNess Man, the Royal Dairy, and the iceman are footnotes to history.

And of course, not all refreshments on the farm were beverages. Summer rains, warm spring mornings, snow-bound days playing in the mows and cribs, all revived the spirit and refreshed the soul. So too, did crispy apples and mellow pears picked from a tree on the way to the fields, wild fox grapes after frost, black cherries succulent and sweet, gobbled high-up, astride limbs and branches, and dewy-wet wild strawberries in the meadow at early sunrise on the way to fetch the cows to the barn. All these refreshed. All these spoke to the soul, of beauty, of life, of God. Spoke of something hopeful, something near, something fantastical, something real, but always, something refreshing.

SOFT-BOILED EGGS
∞∞∞∞∞∞∞∞∞∞∞∞∞∞∞∞∞∞∞∞∞∞∞∞∞∞∞∞∞∞

O n Wednesday, February 20, 1952, Daddy returned home in the evening after spending much of the day at the Lewistown Hospital where my beautiful sister, Susan Eileen Morgan, had made her entrance into the world. While Daddy attended Mommy at the hospital, Mammie came to our house, cooked meals, and took care of the housework. Pappy did the evening milking, fed and bedded the cattle, and waited in the house with us until Daddy returned. I was nine years old; Keith was eight; Billy was five; RuthAnn was a three-year-old toddler.

The sight of Daddy's car pulling into the driveway that night was exciting, for with it came the announcement that we had a second sister. It also signaled to grandparents that their babysitting obligations were finished for the day, and they could return to their own home. It was about seven o'clock.

Daddy had not eaten and indicated he was ravenous. Food was always plentiful but needed to be cooked. None of us had ever seen Daddy at the stove or sink, but the announcement of a new baby suffused something festive into the kitchen where we were gathered, and adventure was afoot as Daddy began setting pots, pans, and dishes atop the kitchen table. He announced that he was going to soft-boil half-a-dozen eggs for his supper and wanted to know if any of us were still hungry. Mammie had fed us earlier, but the thought of a bedtime snack tantalized, and we indicated that we wanted to join him.

Eggs gathered earlier that day sat in a basket at the top of the cellar stairs. Eventually they would be carried into the cool cellar, washed and graded, but on this evening they were easily accessed. Daddy selected a dozen from the basket, placed them into a pan, and brought them to the stove.

He took cereal bowls from the kitchen cupboard, a loaf of bread from the bread-box atop the counter, butter from the refrigerator, and forks and spoons from the cabinet drawer. We three boys sat at our places around the table, fascinated at the curious sight of Daddy cooking. RuthAnn, who had ceased to be the baby earlier in the day, waited in her chair, elevated on a Montgomery Ward Catalog.

Daddy recalled that his mother soft-boiled eggs for three minutes when he was a child. He decided she added vinegar to the water, but was uncertain of the amount. Regardless, he disappeared momentarily into the cellar where the vinegar barrel was stored, and soon returned with a glass half-filled with the sour liquid. He dumped the contents into the boiling water, and, satisfied with his preparations, began lowering the eggs into the steaming pot.

For good measure he allowed the eggs to boil an extra thirty seconds, then with a tablespoon lifted them one by one onto a dish towel he had laid on the table. When all twelve were accounted for, he carried them in the dish towel to the sink and rinsed them with cold water until they were sufficiently cool to the touch. Finally, he returned them to the table where he thanked God for the blessings of the day, picked up a knife and began cracking them open. When all twelve were cracked, he sat down, picked up a spoon, and scooped the contents of each egg into our bowls.

The ritual was to mash the eggs with a fork or spoon, apply salt and pepper, take a hearty slab of home-made bread, dip it into the bowl, and scoop the eggs onto its heavily buttered surface.

We ate with relish. Daddy talked contentedly of his boyhood, of his mother's cooking, of the bountiful provisions we enjoyed on the farm. Most of all, he raved about the delectable taste of the eggs he was eating. So delicious, in fact, that he volunteered he was going to cook some more. We were basking in his good humor, laughing at his stories, and strategically agreeing that he should boil more eggs for us as well, thus delaying bedtime.

Another dozen eggs plopped into the water, but appetites had been exaggerated and soon bellies were sated. The second batch of eggs congealed in our bowls as Daddy told of our new baby and the events of the day. We watched as he finished his meal and then carried our bowls from the table. The clock above the refrigerator said it was 9:00 pm, time to be in bed.

Normally, the entire family was asleep by such an hour, and although the arrival of our new sister had resulted in a delicious dispensation, we snapped to attention when Daddy told us to get to bed. As he picked up RuthAnn to carry her to the bedroom crib, he directed us boys to "go outside" if we needed to use the "potty."

He did not wash the dishes but piled them into the sink, informing us that Grandma would arrive early in the morning to stay with us and help Mommy when she returned home.

L ooking backward and reflecting, the events of that evening seem phantasmal and incongruous. Unlike so many other times when allowance had to be made for the caprice of his irritability and impatience, that evening provided a warm and wonderful memory of my father. When I left for college in the fall of 1961, I had been nineteen years on the farm. With almost no variation, each and every one of those days and years were spent with Daddy. From sunrise to sunset, through breakfast, dinner, and supper, whether in the fields or at the house and barn, we were together. The romance of that February night, however, remains singular, because it was the only night of my childhood when Daddy cooked supper and may explain the reason that I still love soft-boiled eggs.

THE OLD BRIDGE
◇◇◇◇◇◇◇◇◇◇◇◇◇◇◇◇◇◇◇◇◇◇◇◇◇◇◇◇◇◇◇◇◇◇◇◇

My brother Keith created this likeness of the farm. The old bridge is at the extreme left.
https://www.youtube.com/watch?v=O1FXkjwGuwM&t=27s

But often on this cottage do I muse
As on a picture, till my wiser mind
Sinks, yielding to the foolishness of grief.
"THE RUINED COTTAGE"
WILLIAM WORDSWORTH

Our house was built on a gentle slope that ran from a neighbor's fence-line two hundred yards to the north, down to a small eastward flowing creek fifty yards below the front porch. The barn lay sixty yards west. In the field between the house and the neighbor's fence was an orchard of some twenty trees, mostly apples, but containing varieties of pears and plums. An oak tree of majestic proportion stood in the fence-line, poised above the orchard as a silent sentinel overlooking both the house and the farm buildings.

Below the house and running parallel to the creek was a dirt road (now named Decatur Road) that ran eastward a half mile, past a neighbor's farm to where it intersected with Krick Road. A half-mile north on Krick Road sat the one-room Krick School which I attended during my first four grades.

To the west of the house, Decatur Road turned at a forty-five-degree angle southward where it crossed a one-lane cement bridge that routed traffic to the far side of the creek before turning parallel to the creek and running a half-mile up another slope past John Goss's farm and the final half-mile to Joe McKinley's general store where it intersected a paved roadway.

Decatur Road
Daddy taking the wagon to one of the fields with Dave and Beth riding in the bed. Mammie and Pappy's house is beyond the wooded area east of our house.

Decatur Road was a seldom travelled country road in every respect. It was baked dry and hard each summer by heat and drought, so that the mailman's car sent afternoon clouds of dust drifting across freshly scrubbed overalls and diapers hanging from clotheslines. Or it turned muddy and clay-slick in the spring when rains filled wagon wheel ruts turning them into brown pools. In a general sense it functioned as a conduit to schoolhouse, mill, and store, but in a more immediate and practical sense, led only to the labor of our fields. The notion that it connected to golden highways, that something more romantic and remote lay beyond the tedium and oppression of farm work, was a dim and distant nebula.

It was not the road, however, but the cement bridge just west of our house that held special interest for us children.[1] From the road above, we could lean over the bridge's concrete sides and contemplate the creek below. We enjoyed its solitude and were fascinated with the mysteries of its creatures. Its bottom was both an aquarium and a terrarium. During summer dry spells the stream shriveled to a rivulet. In contrast, spring rains sent pockets of water swelling beyond the shallow banks, piling against the bridge, and creating fiords through which pigs and children waded.

On lazy hot summer days, between "hoeing and haying," we sometimes stole noiselessly to the bridge to be alone or to investigate the shady

---

1   The bridge had been built by my maternal grandfather shortly after purchasing the farm in 1923. His initials were carved into the cement.

water below. Occasion-
ally, a piece of cord
string that had bound
a bag of chicken feed
was attached to the end
of a stick. A pin, bent
to form a hook, was
then tied to the string,
baited with bread and
lowered to a school of
unsuspecting minnows.
It was a respite under-
stood by labor.

A view of our house from the old bridge.

The creek had eccentricities. The eastern side of the bridge harbored
water skippers that could be observed miraculously walking on the water's surface, and snake doctors (dragon flies) could be detected lounging
mystically nearby, pricking childish imaginations with sinister warnings
that snakes were present. The banks along the stream were grassless, worn
bare by cows and horses as they stopped to drink or waded into the stream
to loiter in the cool water. Beyond the bridge the flow meandered circu-
itously for fifty yards past a springhouse and continued down through the
meadow. The surrounding earth was heavy with clay and much of the year
retained surface water from rains and the hidden springs that bubbled up
keeping the area around the bridge marshy wet.

Under the western side of the bridge lay an altogether different civilization. Schools of minnows lulled in pools, frogs sat on protruding rocks
poised to slide into obscure depths, and snakes lay in pregnant alarm. This
side was bounded by high grass and faced the adjacent pig lot. The banks
were seldom explored, because snakes hid in the morass, and an electri-
fied wire was strung from a charger installed inside the pig pen stretching
down to and under the bridge where it was connected to a similar wire
that ran the perimeter of the meadow. The electric shock that the charger
generated was strong enough to set on fire tall springtime grass that grew
shriveled and dried in the summer heat, and it was sufficiently mild to
permit pigs to lean against it as though it were an annoying but harmless
discomfort. It was on this side of the bridge that Daddy threw a memorable
tantrum one hot July afternoon in 1957.

Daddy, Keith, and I had spent the morning in one of the remote fields harvesting wheat. The binding and threshing of grain, even before McCormick's reaper revolutionized the process in 1831, required that the stalks had to be dry so that the grains could easily be separated from the straw and chaff. A farmer was seldom able to start such work until mid-morning as he had to wait for the sun to evaporate the morning moisture. On this day, however, a week-long heat wave had set early morning temperatures in the upper 80s and enabled us to begin by eight o'clock.

Combined with the earlier barn work, we had already spent six hours in the sweltering heat when, at noon, Mommy called us to dinner by waving a towel from the front yard. We eagerly responded, quickly unhitching the combine, one of us driving the tractor while the others found a fender seat or jumped aboard the tractor hitch, opening the throttle, and dashing to the house. We were hungry.

All farm meals were copious: breakfast, dinner, and supper. The modern mid-day "lunch" of sandwich and soup, or worse, salad and soup, was foreign to families who labored manually from sunrise to sunset. On this day we would spend another six hours at farm work before retiring. Bodies needed replenishment.

The dinner table was opulent with slabs of ham, crispy pieces of fried chicken, or a roast of pork or beef. Mashed potatoes and gravy, noodles swimming in milk and butter, or deep dishes of creamed rice waited in steaming bowls. Buttered peas, carrots, green and yellow string beans, lima beans, or combinations rested in serving dishes. A tray laden with raw scallions, radishes, lettuces, dandelion greens, and beets, all fresh from the morning garden, served as a center piece. Thick slices of crusty home-made bread were stacked on a dinner plate, while pies, cakes, and cookies waited on the sideboard.

Meals were eaten with little talk. Daddy thanked God for His blessings and entreated His guidance, but casual conversation wilted under the constant exigency not to waste time. Children said "please" when requesting vittles, but the tinkling of glasses and the scrapping of silverware on plates dominated the sounds of dinner.

Halfway through each meal, Daddy outlined our post-meal assignments. Between forkfuls of food, he directed, "I hooked the hay rake to the big tractor. Keith, you can begin raking that alfalfa in the field above the meadow."

The strategies that went into each boy's assignment were never explained, but early on, I concluded that mine involved a need for greater attention to detail. "Dennis, I put the cultivators on the little tractor. You can get started as soon as you finish eating." The job was not difficult but required constant concentration so the blades of the cultivators did not dislodge stalks of young corn.

"Billy, you come with me. We have to bag grain for chicken feed."

Sometimes, sensing our despair over the long hours ahead, he positioned light at the end of our tunnel. "When we get the rest of the wheat in the granary, we're gonna take a day and go fishin."

Daddy loved to go fishing, but he never enjoyed the actual fishing. He romanced the picnic lunch that accompanied such forays, delighted in the preparations, and loved the treks to the mountains, but the patience to sit or stand beside a river or stream while waiting for a fish to respond to his favorite lure was beyond his reserve.

We boys ate quickly. An afternoon of labor lay before us, but Daddy habitually lingered over his second cup of coffee, and those fifteen minutes provided free time. He never required that we begin work until he was ready to do the same.

Billy, Keith, and I finished our wedges of raspberry pie and were excused to our interlude. Billy and I began playing "pepper" (a baseball game) in the yard while waiting for Daddy's call to return us to the fields.

Meantime, Keith wandered down toward the meadow to investigate the world below the bridge. Carefully he stole to its cement side, peering down into the stony bottoms of the shaded pools. The head of a snake protruded above the water. As was custom, he noiselessly withdrew from the bridge, then ran toward the house to get the .22 caliber rifle that was kept in Mommy and Daddy's bedroom. Daddy, finished with his meal, stepped out onto the porch. He was about to muster us into work detail, when seeing Keith with the gun, asked, "Wher'er you going?"

Keith offered, "I saw a snake."

The old bridge where Decatur Road turned west.

Snakes, from their initial appearance in the Garden of Eden to the present, have been held in lowest esteem. The stealth exhibited by that first serpent has been transferred to every succeeding creature that crawls or slithers on its reptilian belly. To farm boys in Decatur Township, snakes were personifications of evil and had to be summarily executed.

From our ball field in the yard Billy and I listened to the exchange, saw Daddy take the gun, and at once joined the excitement. Intrigue was in full flower when we reached the road in front of the bridge. Daddy was acknowledged to be an expert marksman. Neighbors sought him to do the shooting when butchering beeves or hogs, and we boys had seen his steady hand, from a standing position, kill rats and other vermin.

Cradling the gun in his right hand, he began cir- cling away from the bridge and down toward the bank of

The .22 caliber rifle that Daddy accidentally held against the electric wire.

the creek. Stepping into the high grass that grew alongside he cautiously screened himself from the snake. Stealthily he moved forward with gun at the ready. In his concentration, however, he failed to remember the elec- tric wire. With slow deliberation he brought the snake into the gun's sights when the barrel of the rifle touched the charged wire.

Daddy's reaction was both seismic and illogical, as befitted a man of ill humor. At first he recoiled at the shock, his senses momentarily stunned, then without warning, he savagely flung the gun in the direction of the pig pen as though the gun were to blame. Scrambling up the grass bank away from the scene of the crime, he stood for a moment reclaiming his equilib- rium, his anger mounting. Then just as suddenly, he picked up a length of two-by-four that was propping closed the door of the adjacent wagon shed a few yards away, returned to the creek and, with a single blow, snapped the diabolical electric wire. It was a fit of fury, void of reason, behavior so eccentric that it warranted neither explanation or response.

We stood fixed, staring at each other, until he angrily turned and strode to where the tractor waited for its afternoon detail. It was our signal to follow, to get back to work. I picked up the gun, emptied the cartridges into my pocket, and told Billy to put it away. Hurriedly Keith and I climbed aboard the tractor and, with Daddy driving, headed back to the wheat field. No one spoke.

For the next four hours we harvested the grain. The bridge and the snake were forgotten. Daddy's temper passed, dissolving in the heat of the day as the harvesting demanded his concentration. Our discomfiture with his volatility, however, remained permanent.

Daddy's tantrum on that summer afternoon contradicted reason, but he grew in later years to laugh at what he had done. He delighted when one of his sons retold the old story, giggling at himself, grateful that his boys enjoyed the humor.

The old bridge and the farm are gone. Gone, too, is the boyish world of innocence and wonder that existed beneath that old bridge. In its place is only memory: of days and nights when time was slow and summer afternoons when boys witnessed the mysterious behavior of their father from the side of the old bridge.

THE OUTHOUSE
◇◇◇

Recording memories of an outhouse requires an explanation. It is not my desire to elicit sympathy nor to idealize simplicity nor to draw attention to the graphic that prompts the following description, but simply to accurately recall a part of my life.

Our outhouse was a small, white-washed shed hidden away from the center of routine and daily activity, beyond the perimeter of wood house, smokehouse, and garden, sufficiently distant for privacy and sufficiently near for convenience. The exterior was weather-beaten pine boards with a tin roof, a door that opened from the right, and a step fashioned from a large stone that permitted easy entrance.

By the mid-fifties the outhouse was no longer a convenience.

The interior consisted of a boarded floor, two platformed "seats," one on the right for adults and a second smaller "hole" for children, both facing a hinged door with a cabin hook. Not insulated, the contraction and expansion of the wooden structure caused by weather created numerous cracks and crannies that, during daylight hours, permitted light to stream into the otherwise unlighted interior. At night the interior was illumined by ambient moonlight or a portable candle or flashlight.

After using the facility, hands had to be washed. In the wintertime, adults and children alike came to the house and used water from the kitchen sink faucet. All other times of the year washing was done at the hydrant behind the wood house, where Mommy kept a basin and a bar of lye soap.

Periodically my father and grandfather combined efforts to lift the housing off the base, move it to an temporary adjacent site, remove the sewage from the substructure, and then reassemble the building. The cleaning was neither repugnant nor gallant, but unremarkable and necessary. Dignity is not found in the task performed but in the character of the performer. The virtue of mundane labor is seldom celebrated.

While using the outhouse was routine, circumstances were singular and private. In most cases the accoutrements included a multi-paged catalog or, during times of scarcity, corn cobs or husks. Summertime accessories might also consist of a flyswatter as a defense against flies, bees and spiders. When small children used the facility, an adult or older child accompanied him or her, making certain that the toddler did not "fall through the hole."

In the wintertime, the elements presented themselves: icy wind whipping through the cracks sometimes accompanied by snow showers across bare legs. In the summertime the tin roof funneled heat into the interior resulting in temperatures that produced immediate perspiration, or, during rain storms, amid a concord of drums overhead, the sheeted rain attacked the secluded fortress from all sides sending a refreshing mist through dozens of breaches.

When visitors, accustomed to the chrome and porcelain of indoor facilities, were forced to use the outhouse, they generally concealed their revulsion, but sometimes friends excused themselves and left early so they could arrive home before suffering indiscretion. Thus, convenience was defined by available alternative.

The notion of an outhouse providing convenience has long since been lost in the elegance of recent decades. Primitive man must have appreciated the old advantages: protection from weather, dignity of concealment, and even retreat into solitude. The modern experience, however, contravened such perspective.

Modernity introduced itself to rustic America with a slow progression of events. First, the local house of worship or some public gathering place introduced an out-of-the-way room that provided privacy with a flush, hygiene with running water, and floral fragrance with a decorative decanter. Next, the newest innovation was found in the homes of relatives who lived in "towns." Finally, in the late 1950s the revolution reached the agrarian culture who for centuries had toileted in outhouses or discreetly utilized secluded corners of barns, fields, and woods. Subsequently, those who had gazed through the window of progress no longer regarded an outhouse on a freezing January night as a convenience.

The indoor convenience came to our house in 1957. By that time, many of our neighbors, including Pappy and Mammie, had already in-

The farmhouse in the early 1960s. To the right are the wood house, the smokehouse, and the outhouse.

stalled indoor facilities. Although Daddy never felt compelled to "keep up with the Jones's," he detested unrefinement. That fall he excavated a large basin in the yard outside the living room, and before Christmas a septic tank was lowered into the cavity. Pipes conducting any discharge were laid, a leech field was seeded with crushed stone, covered with sod, and grass seed was sown to conceal the septic. Inside the house a portion of the living room was partitioned, and Daddy and Pappy put into place the components that permitted us to compete with fashionable folks. By winter, most of our family had dispensed with the notion that the sound of a flushing toilet was a public announcement of private doings. Bed pans disappeared, shaving moved behind a closed door, and brushing teeth became a regularity.

My first shave took place that same year within the seclusion of the new facility. Daddy attached a medicine cabinet to the wall directly above the porcelain sink, and I found a space into which I shoved a Gillette Safety Razor, a dispenser of Gillette Blue Blades, a can of Rise Shaving Cream, and a styptic pencil. At first, this ritual of manhood seemed romantic, but within a few shaves, the ordeal took on tones of masochism. It was impossible to use the razor without

Gillette called this sadistic weapon a "safety" razor.

nicking and cutting my face. In fact, compounded by the pimples of teen-age acne, the result resembled mutilation. Salvation came in the form of the styptic pencil.

Styptic is an agent that works by contracting tissues to seal injured blood vessels. As an astringent, it promotes a burning sensation. This dis-comfort was, however, negligible compared to the indignity suffered at school or church where teenage girls snickered at the dozens of bloody wounds. Worse, feeble attempts to explain away the cuts induced belly-laughs from my friends. I claimed to have been attacked by Sasquatch, to have had a mild case of small pox, and I once insisted that I had fallen into a patch of Canadian thistles. Fortunately, I soon began to see the lighter side. And, after a while, I learned to apply a sufficient quantity of Clearasil to hide the blotches.

Looking backward can be dangerous, producing a kind of paralysis that idealizes the past and prevents objective scrutiny, thus leaving a kind of hermetic seal against realism and truth. The outhouse and the rural America in which I spent my boyhood are extinct. On the other hand, past experience opens the mind to appreciations and understandings that inculcate hope and create the romance which looks through the eyes of imagination and faith to the future. I shall always be grateful to God for my past, and to the people and places He elected to bring about my life's events and experiences. One of those experiences was growing up in rural Pennsylvania, in Mifflin County, in Decatur Township, on a dairy farm in the middle of the 20th century, with parents and grandparents, brothers and sisters, and aunts and uncles who, despite the flaws that are endemic to human beings everywhere, loved life and one another. And of course, I am thankful that I can look backward, not in gratitude that modern conve-nience has shuttled the outhouse into oblivion, but that I grew up in a time when country folk were gratified to have an outhouse.

OMEGA
◇◇◇◇◇◇◇◇◇◇◇◇◇

TO MY FAMILY

"Father, I will that they also, whom thou hast given me, be with me where I am; that they may behold my glory, which thou hast given me: for thou lovedst me before the foundation of the world." (John 17:24)

My body has grown old. I will soon experience death. But there is wonderful news—life does not end. The Word of God provides assurance that life is everlasting, not in posterity, but in the eternal present; not in sons and daughters, but in the permanence of the soul. His resurrection empirically substantiates Jesus's promise that life is eternal.

My body will most certainly cease to exist, but my body is not "I." Adam was the first person to have a body. Adam's body came into being when God formed it from the dust of the ground, but Adam did not become a living creature until God breathed into Adam's nostrils the breath of life. (Genesis 2:7) Adam then became a living soul. When Adam died, only his body passed away. The soul of Adam never died. He lives forever. Adam accepted God's promise that a Savior would one day pay the penalty for Adam's sins so that Adam could enjoy God eternally.

In the very same way God took seed from my parents, fashioned my body, and breathed life into me so that I, too, became a living soul, just like Adam. And, like the soul of Adam, my soul is eternal. Jesus defeated sin and death when He arose from the grave. I have accepted the same promise that Adam accepted. I have confessed that I have committed terrible sins. I have acknowledged that I have no righteousness to offer God that would make me worthy to go to Heaven. I have simply claimed God's gracious gift of forgiveness and eternal life. In fact, Jesus tells me that He personally is going to take me with Him when I die:

"And if I go and prepare a place for you, I will come again and will take you to myself, that where I am you may be also." (John 14:3)

Thus, my sorrow at leaving you is directed only to the space between being with you in this immediate place and being with you in the next place. I do not like the thought of being without you, even for a short time, but God has recognized the pain of separation and has promised to never leave my side while I wait for you in the next place, and He has promised to never leave you while you remain in this place. Thus, I am confident of our reunion and the restoration of our love.

"It is the Lord who goes before (me). He will be with (me); he will not leave (me) or forsake (me)." (Deut. 31:8)

For those of you who choose to read some or all of these pages, I want more than anything to spend eternity with you. I have made daily supplication for your eternal life for many years. God has shown many times that He is willing to do everything within the bounds of His sovereignty to save the people He has created. He cannot, however, force anyone to love Him. The decision as to where you will spend eternal life is laid at your feet. Thus, I plead with you to make Jesus your Savior and Lord. Of course, it is not possible to make Him one without the other. Therefore, read His words, study His life, walk in His ways.

"... if you confess with your mouth that Jesus is Lord and believe in your heart that God raised him from the dead, you will be saved. For with the heart one believes and is justified, and with the mouth one confesses and is saved."
(Romans 10:9,10)

"See, I have set before you today life and good, death and evil. If you obey the commandments of the Lord your God that I command you today, by loving the Lord your God, by walking in his ways, and by keeping his commandments and his statutes and his rules, then you shall live and multiply, and the Lord your God will bless you in the land that you are entering to take possession of it. But if your heart turns away, and you will not hear, but are drawn away to worship other gods and serve them, I declare to you today,

that you shall surely perish. You shall not live long in the land that you are going over the Jordan to enter and possess. I call heaven and earth to witness against you today, that I have set before you life and death, blessing and curse. Therefore choose life, that you and your offspring may live, loving the Lord your God, obeying his voice and holding fast to him, for he is your life and length of days, that you may dwell in the land that the Lord swore to your fathers, to Abraham, to Isaac, and to Jacob, to give them."
Deuteronomy 30:15-20

Just as my days on this earth have been numbered, you too will grow old and pass from this temporary abode to one that is eternal. Every death provides evidence that material things such as our bodies are not lasting, and at the same time, Jesus's victory over death provides verification that He loves us and wishes us to have eternal life. Please, please, get to know Him. I want desperately to spend eternity with you.

"... I know whom I have believed, and am persuaded that He is able to keep that which I have committed unto Him against that day."
(II Tim. 1:12)

BOOKS THAT IMPACTED MY LIFE
◇◇◇

NOTE: To compile such a list without mentioning the works of Plato, Aristotle, Dante, Milton, any of the great playwrights, or a host of other literary figures, suggests, perhaps, a shallow and cursory appreciation of literature. I choose, rather, to be grateful for the richness any and all of these have contributed to my understanding of, affection for, and worship of the Greatest Artist.

1. **BIBLE**
    I sometimes am overwhelmed with the notion that, through literature and the other arts, I have access to many of the greatest minds God has created. It is impossible to be passive with such access to truth, love, and beauty. And yet, these sixty-six books of Scripture transport the soul beyond art, to an epistemology that provides a personal relationship with the greatest mind of all, the Creator of minds and the source of beauty, love, and truth. Within the words of this text are found God's Holy Words explaining and illustrating life's origin, morality, purpose, and destiny.

2. **Complete Poems of Emily Dickinson**
    Shelley lost his equilibrium at the sight of a sunset at sea; Dickinson's poetry is a breathless transport to the same beauty.

3. **Lyrical Ballads of Wordsworth and Coleridge**
    Great music need not be confined to instruments. These poems are the music of language.

4. **Poetry of Tennyson**
    I hope to see Lord Alfred "face to face when I, too, have crost the bar."

5. **Complete Works of G.K. Chesterton**
    Orthodoxy, *Heretics*, and *The Everlasting Man* should be required

reading for all breathing souls.

6.   **Complete Works of C.S. Lewis**
Lewis' defense of Christianity and its application remains unparalleled in its simplicity and clarity.

7.   *The Sound and the Fury* - **William Faulkner**
Faulkner's four narratives demonstrate the need for a Savior in the face of human depravity, but they also celebrate the dignity and worth of individual humanity. Faulkner's metaphor corresponds so closely to reality that it must be termed Great Art.

8.   *Look Homeward, Angel* – **Thomas Wolfe**
This is poetry disguised as prose. It is also the autobiography of every soul who has ever been in search of "a stone, a leaf, a door" that will provide meaning to life.

9.   *The Brothers Karamazov* – **Fyodor Dostoyevsky**
Three world views and their consequences illustrated in one work.

10.   *Trilogy* – **Francis Schaeffer**
Christians ought to have an intellectual understanding of culture. Schaeffer wrote the textbook.

11.   **Complete Poems of A.E. Housman**
He gave pen to our deepest despair.

12.   *Can Man Live Without God?* – **Ravi Zacharias**
His five-fold system for testing truth claims is an indispensable aid to the study of metaphysics. As well, any of his other materials contribute mightily to Christian apologetics and evangelism. It is impossible to estimate the impact his ministry has had on my life.

13.   **The Works of William Lane Craig**
"Reasonable Faith" may be the most thorough treatment of Christian apologetics in print. Craig's studies on time, philosophy, epistemology, cosmology, Naturalism, and his lectures and debates with leading secularists have become Christian classics.

14. **The Works of Alfred Edersheim**
Indispensable to understanding historical Judaism as it applies to the Scriptures.

15. **The Works of J.P. Moreland**
Scaling the Secular City, Love Your God With All Your Mind, Philosophical Foundations for a Christian World View, The Soul, and the *Blackwell Companion to Natural Theology* are among the best theological, philosophical, and metaphysical studies to date.

16. **The Plays of Eugene O'Neill**
A Long Day's Journey Into Night, A Moon For the Misbegotten, The Iceman Cometh, Beyond the Horizon, etc. are vivid illustrations of the means and ends of secularism.

17. *The Consequences of Ideas* **- R.C. Sproul**
This condensation of the world's greatest philosophers and their ideologies was motivational in my reading and study, and provoked a better understanding of the forces that have shaped history.

18. **The Poetry of Henry Wadsworth Longfellow**
"Paul Revere's Ride," "The Wreck of the Hesperus," "A Psalm of Life," "The Village Blacksmith," and "Curfew" were my earliest introduction to the beauty of lyrical verse.

19. **The Works of Norman L. Geisler**
Big Book of Christian Apologetics, and *Systematic Theology* are exhaustive resources for Evangelical Christians.

20. **The Works of William Shakespeare**
If quotable lines are any indicator of a work's literary quality, Shakespeare's stature among other English authors is obvious.

POETRY
◇◇◇◇◇◇◇◇◇◇◇◇◇

The portion of my verse found on these pages was written during a dark time when the despondencies of life seemed to be swallowing up its enchantments. As a result, it is tinged with a melancholy coloration. Fortunately, a beneficent God did not surrender me to myself. His love overcame my resistance, and I came to rest in the promises of my Savior and the assurance provided by His resurrection.

This verse — and nothing else beside
Nothing else - except one tear
The pulse was all a'tremble here
Till breathing was denied

1

I stand upon your grave tonight,
'Tis cold where you are lying;
But colder far, the hours are
In vales where I am dying.

2

Truth?... I don't know.
I have suspicions though —
I've seen its shadow on the grass
Where regularly minutes pass —
And gravéd flowers grow.

3

If you should come
And breath be gone —
Start not!
Time but kept the promise
Your memory forgot.

4

On a silent, snowy morning
Beyond the fields of play,
In a little silver casket
A faded flower lay.

Her simple hands were folded
The customs all in place.
The fastened smile, the settled brow
The ringlets trimmed with lace.

But no one quite remembered
The color or the face;
The fragrance or the fashion
Of warmer, sweeter days.

The gold had gone to Glory,
The pink had gone Below,
The life had gone forever
To a little mounded row —

And left — a lonely garden;
Not of bloom nor breath;
But in a heart as 'reft as mine, —
The spectre, — whitest Death.

5

What joy!
Awakened to surprise!
Lonely daisies for the sun
At dawn may half surmise.

6

He told you quiet stories
He spun an hour's lace
He lit you pretty candles
To light a darkened place.

He made your day a'merry
He sang you songs of glee
He made a verse of anguish
And then he let you be.

7

The prison hath its charm,
And rhymes their reason be;
But desolate the garden
Where Fancy waved to me.

8

Children at the House of Death
Start not nor show surprise;
They analyze the edifice
With calm, acceptant eyes.

'Tis rather like the House of Life
Where children-life began;
Save that the silence everywhere
Stills bird and beast and man.

9

To Nancy on Her 16th Birthday

Sixteen —
That unchartered route,
A simple mile from play.
But go —
Uncertainty be worse than doom,
And unsuspecting pass the turn
Where birthdays all must come.

10

The road runs on in moonlight,
The stranger stops for breath.
The night invites the silence,
The Country here is Death.

The doors remain unopened,
The windows ever closed,
The lamps are years unlighted,
The tenants here reposed.

The lawn sometimes a'mounded,
The stranger stoops at one;
The petal pressed in darkness,
The love and loving done.

The question yet unanswered,
The stranger yet alone;
The citizens oblivious
Content to stay at home.

11

If you should come, don't knock!
That small alarm suspends the life
That waits within the lock.

12

When a boy
I died;
A numbing time.
(Though pain requites
A greater self.
Since,
Am lonely.
This new death,
Vaster,
I shan't endure.

13

A little boy, the while at play,
A cemetery stole away.
The little life, the flesh and bone;
Was fitted for a field of stone.

14

There's laughter in the kitchen
And boys and girls at play,
And a stranger at the window
To steal the life away.

15

A little boy —
Three years old —
Died tonight.
I loved him.
A snowman remains.

Frosty death creeps on icy feet.
The cold blast stings.
Chilled blood thicks a slacken vein.
Glacial eyes stare.
And the night falls.

Time
Walks on barren streets.
Omniscient skies stare
Cold... dark...
Forgotten.

The hill is unclimbed.
The motion undone.
The passion unfelt.
The kiss chills
On lifeless lips.

A little boy —
Three years old —
Died tonight.
I loved him.
A snowman remains.

16

A form within a narrow way;
On shadowed, shapeless time.
Its penciled denotations
Marked with catalectic line.

And drawn a tiny diagram
That runs from space to space,
Of circles all in circles,
And each unique in place.

The other side is penmanship,
But language not of man.
To ascertain as literate
Though not to understand.

I brought it to analysis;
Opine to honest men —
Consistency interpret
In the fire of acumen.

But mind cannot interpret
And heart is all afraid
To wonder at the mighty form
And face that God has made.

This overt demonstration
Of Absolute unknown;
Reduction being physical,
Truth's textbook far from home.

17

Tomorrow will not come,
Though clocks will turn their time.
A lover's eye shot dead tonight
Tomorrows that were mine.

I sit in shrouded silence
And bitterly have cried.
The gold went all a'tumble
Tonight when Fancy died.

18

To say goodbye — that final time,
Some sudden scalding morn;
Such anguish grip the marble stair
That ever man was born.

19

Expectancy luxuriates each drop of vintage time.
The appetite anticipant lends colour to the wine.

20

I cannot stay — the grave insist
This carrion be gone.
These gentle screams no more disturb
That quiet clamor, Dawn.

Bedecked in fiendish splendor,
The deadly suitor comes —
Without the trumped announcement
Or bloody beat of drums.

The children go on playing —
And never turn aside —
To see the steady ambush —
And shadow of the bride.

The day will turn from mourning
And night and time be still,
But I had hope of living —
And now I never will.

21

By a dark grave — over a last, slow horizon
Grows a fairest pink flower.
But the steep and the climb lock its fragrance
While time passes on constant feet.

22

Violent bursts of energy,
In meadows,
Some call Daisy.

In fields less distant,
A fairer storm,
Nameless, ... Love.

23

Another night — another day
And where will poets be?
The saffron season left at home,
Respectability.

24

Night nears —
Eternal night.
I have climbed a thousand hills,
Borne countless days
Now color fades —

Romance,
The wonder of unseen beauty,
The unfulfilled desire of tomorrow
Is lost.
Night nears.

25

For want of love the coffins close;
Oblique runs tangent to the truth
And tongues stoop low to prose.

26

Warm —
Where spirits meet —
Between flesh
And eternity.

27

(Even in laughter the heart may ache, and the end of joy is grief. Proverbs 14:13)

Detachment
That other armor —
For crueler blows.

Applause withheld,
The wounded soul —
Withdraws — topples —
Prepares a firmer hold.

Fixed its public hurt,
Bleeds —
In hidden places.

28

O! That tongue might utter
What the heart would speak.

29

How lonely —
The shadow of yesterday.

30

Of late, I note, the window dark,
A specter at the door.
Familiar friends withdrawn from play
And Fancy comes no more.

Time - more cumbersome and slow,
Now knits a broken brow;
That other country came to call,
The one that knocks so loud.

He set at every step, a tear;
At door, unsteady stride.
He stole address from porch and left
Eternity inside.

31

I'm told of Kings and Princes,
'Fore such as time began,
Would condescend estates of gold
For little fellowman.

With quietest decorum
And manner all serene;
A touch of regal kindness
Midst royal mystery.

And then for untold century
Such stately care desist;
The bead of anguish on the brow,
The eye a teary mist.

The realms fantastic were forgot;
Their magic here was done;
The cold without, decay within,
The golden courses run.

Yet sometimes in the silence
Startled still to see
A Princess in the house next door
In regal reverie.

32

To Emily Dickinson
(After visiting her home in Amherst)

Enamored so of thee,
I crossed the White Abode
And tip toed to your chamber
Entranced to find you home.

You sat me at your table;
I drank the honey cup.
I ate the manna from your hand,
Gratuitously loved.

Lips that kiss the misty morn;
Enjoin the vale to prayer,
Bestow on me impassioned kiss
And label it — Affair.

33

Sunday — that shadow time,
More cumbersome and slow;
Where anguish stalks the quiet zone
Within the chamber, woe.

34

The flower long has finished
Its flowers' pretty toil,
And living gone to dying;
The corn and kernel spoil.

'Tis now a time of winter;
The wood and hill be bare,
The snow to come a'calling
And mourning everywhere.

The earth will lose her stillness,
The silence be forgot;
The summer it will come again,
But time and I will not.

35

Where heart stoops and voice betrays
Where word and gift despair,
In the unsecond pause of time —
Touch — softest touch — embraces life
Enshrouded in the weight of eternity.

36

A lover's time has come and gone.
And now, the ring and rose
But only sting the memory
With tears and sighs and prose.

The years continue one by one
To move beyond the light,
But I caress the ring and rose
In silence and in night.

37

A crystal moment;
The looking-glass of man's hour existence.
The blithe animal motion of youth
Against the shadow of approaching darkness,
And time reduced to a crystal moment.

Discontent;
Everlasting discontent.
And a fleeting, whispering smile
In a crystal moment.

38

Tis the nearness
   Not the distance
That multiplies the pain
   Of loving you.

39

I send this simple letter
Where letters never come,
Beyond the mind and mantle,
For there the mail is done.

But love outrun this postman,
And heart leap off the page —
My life must beat its bloody pulse,
This anguish to assuage.

40

The heart — convey its sweet
Would cross the silent sea
Share the swell — distended
Where arms may never be.

But equilibrium — be lost
In quiet — and in doom.
The sea contain such peril
Beyond the bow — Presume.

So find a safer — love you —
A dark — more subtle wound —
The fleeting smile — the frenzy,
And exit from the room.

41

When but a boy, I studied graves
And wept for those grown old.
How feeble is the whitened limb —
How atrophied and cold.

How sorry must the wizened be
To silently behold —
The beauty and the blossom fled -—
The glory and the gold.

I, now, no boy, consider graves
As older now I must.
I wonder not how old men feel
When drawing nigh to dust,

But cry for those tomorrow
Whose matter and whose might,
Is spent in blinded vanity
Ignoring pitted night.

42

To run beyond the gauntlet —
The other side of now —
Without the limitation —
Providence allow.

43

Twas never told this fellow
What some were luck to find;
That drink and dance and daring
Restore the human kind.

That folly heals the cancer
That burrows at the soul,
That madness numbs the canker
That turns the clay a'cold.

44

O Christ! What narrow margin
Where agony must come.
The breast contains such swelling
Before the heart is done.

The day becomes a requiem —
The night becomes a tomb —
The life becomes a shadow —
Before the prophet — Doom.

Yet, You in loving sapience
Did take the nail — for me.
Twas I was resurrected
At awful Calvary!

45

How lovely lies the summer green,
How deep the sky and blue.
And I will walk the flowered field,
And I will taste the dew.

And I will bid the town a'day,
And at the jest will smile —
And friend with friend the sport will play,
And merry all the while.

And I will write a simple verse
Tonight when dark is come,
To lay beside my chalky corpse —
The affectation done.

46

It is the "quick" that I love. —
O! to restore the quick to lost men —
But that is Poetry.

OBSERVATIONS
◇◇◇◇◇◇◇◇◇◇◇◇◇◇◇◇◇◇◇◇◇◇◇◇◇◇◇◇◇◇◇◇

1
Beauty

> "Worship is the submission of all of our nature to God.
> It is the quickening of conscience by His holiness, nourish-
> ment of mind by His truth, purifying of imagination by His
> beauty, opening of the heart to His love, and submission of
> will to his purpose. And all this gathered up in adoration is
> the greatest of human expressions of which we are capable."
>
> SIR WILLIAM TEMPLE

God's beauty stands apart from human perception because it is an objective beauty. In his dialogue, *Euthyphro*, Plato asks if the gods are pious because their behavior conforms to piety, or if their behavior establishes the standard for piety. Aquinas answered that conundrum by reasoning that God is not revealed by an extrinsic standard, but by His intrinsic character and personality. Thus, God is not only beautiful (and just and loving), but He is Beauty (and Justice and Love). Beauty (and justice and love) is an inherent reality of His ontological being.

In the same manner, God is not beautiful because His behavior conforms to an external standard of beauty (as in Plato's forms), but because He is Beauty. Beauty is an objective reality inherent in God's infinite person.

This begs the question, Is the sunset beautiful if no one sees it? Is beauty in the eye of the beholder, or is beauty a reality that exists extrinsic to human experience? Does beauty depend upon observation? The Christian philosopher, George Berkeley (1685-1753), attempted to answer this when he agreed with the Empiricists that observation is necessary, but, since God is omnipresent and omniscient, it is not possible for anything to occur without His observation.

This answer is vital to Sir William Temple's concept of purification.

Either the imagination is effected by an ontological reality (a real observation) or else the transcendent relationship is mystical. Either there is a real measuring stick or it is imaginary.

The recognition of beauty, of course, depends upon the existence of design, an eponym for God. Chaos is antithetical to God and can never be objectively beautiful. Thus, the naturalist must provide a constructed sense of beauty, one that can have only relative significance. Since beauty lies in the recognition of design, it follows that the Christian is able to find beauty in each and every Christian experience (including suffering). This is an important part of the purification process since the contemplation of and faith in God's purpose permits us to look beyond present difficulty and live without regret or bitterness.

As the imagination draws us near to God, it is quickened, both by what is and what can be. It is presented with infinite beauty and wonder - infinite dimension. In contrast, the secular imagination must regard only a finite, existential possibility. Not only do Christians have access to objective, infinite Beauty, but God permits us to view that Beauty in the glory of personal performance.

Human determination of what is beautiful begins, not at the point of expression, but at the point of perspective. A point of view must be formed and defended before art can be justified. That is, a life united with God is transformed to recognize the divine intervention that is immanent in every person, place and thing. The secular view of beauty, however, is limited to existential reality and defined by utility. Since truth is exclusive, only one "weltanschauung" can be true.

The Christian perspective of beauty imposes strict boundaries. Beauty is evocative in that it causes a response of delight; however, the pleasure cannot stand alone. There must be an affirmation of intellectual, emotional, spiritual, and physical value within the worldview. As Christians, we worship God in the beauty of His holiness (I Chronicles 16:29). This means that our perception of Beauty has parameters. Beauty is not purely evocative, but has intellectual substance and moral restraint.

Keats was very much correct when he penned, "Beauty is Truth, Truth Beauty." However, there is a third component; God's Love enables Beauty to be recognized and Truth to be comprehended. All of this is completed in the Person of Jesus Christ: the physical, the spiritual, the emotional, and the intellectual. Once this truth has been revealed, then it is incumbent upon both the artist and the percipient to operate within that worldview.

The Genesis description of Sarai, Rebekah, and Rachel alleges that they were beautiful women. I may suppose that the beauty to which these verses allude is a physical beauty, because Abram reacted to the probability that men would "see" his wife. If so, their beauty was relative to perception and had, as its foundation, the base desires of perception. If, however, their beauty transcended the physical, then, a sense of purpose, of design, must necessarily have been present in the perception. No physical thing has an explanation for itself within itself.

Since God is not a physical being, and Beauty is frequently a descriptor of God, it follows that God's Beauty is of a different nature. Again, I Chronicles 16:29 (KJV) places God's Beauty within His Holiness. If God is Beauty, in the manner that God is Justice, then Beauty has no ontology of itself, but is inherent in the person of God. Psalm 50:2 supports such a notion.

While God's Beauty is absolute, the varying degrees of beauty appreciation that exist existentially must be accounted for. Here, the eye of the beholder comes into play. For the Christian, the process of sanctification in both the artist and the percipient produces an ever-refining point of view as to what is more or less beautiful. Age, experience, intelligence, and other factors effect perception. It may be said that all of God's creatures are beautiful in that they contain the stamp of a Creator whose essence is Beauty. And, to the degree that Creation (including Creatures) maintains and reflects God's image, it can be termed beautiful. Each and all of these account for the reasons that human beings sense varying degrees of beauty.

2

Spinoza's *Necessary Being* is necessary because, without an uncaused cause, being would have to exist prior to itself, and, thus, existence could not be explained.

3

"The truth shall make you free." John 8

After sinning, I can be free from its emotional and psychological web because I can be forgiven. Christ looses me from these entanglements if I permit. However, I am not free from the natural consequences.

4

The desire for human autonomy leads egocentrically from trusting a sovereign God and having an active personal relationship with Christ to deism; from deism to transcendentalism; from transcendentalism to atheism (egoism). It moves from a concern for eternal life to a concern for temporal existence.

5

Naturalism cannot sufficiently explain death.

6

Ivan Karamazov (*The Brothers Karamazov*, Dostoyevsky) points out that love becomes more difficult as the object of love moves from an abstraction to a personal relationship. If so, God's love for me transcends credibility.

7

In the province of pure selflessness, joy exceeds pleasure.

8

Confession is difficult where there is no reciprocity. When empathy or love is not returned, groveling and humiliation result. This is the shortcoming of the earthly priesthood where understanding and compassion are limited and often absent. Herein lies the miracle of the cross, where omniscience extends unconditional love.

9

In *Mere Christianity* C.S. Lewis contends that a universal sense of fairness exists, thus, there is a universal notion of good behavior, of doing the right thing, of virtue. Virtue results from choosing to do that which is good (or fair), namely that which corresponds to God's desires, in whom fairness and goodness is defined. Virtue, factored to the small, is simply behaving in a manner that accords with God's desires for a personal, eternal relationship of romance, truth, and love.

In contrast, Mortimer Adler, in *Six Great Ideas*, defines good as desiring that which is truly needed (truth, love, beauty, justice, equality, and liberty). This differs from Christian virtue, which results when self-desire yields to God's purpose. Adler, an atheist when he wrote his book, was unable to attach his virtues to an ultimate purpose. He recognized absolute virtues but failed to identify their source.

10

A child seldom accepts what a parent says when parental behavior runs counter to the admonition. Rationalization of such behavior by a parent stultifies and confuses children. Children may seldom hear what you say, but they always see what you do.

11

Rene Descartes attempted to begin his quest for certainty by discarding presuppositions, relying wholly on reason. However, reason cannot exist without assumptions. Those assumptions include the notion that truth exists, that right reason exists, and that the mind is capable of right reasoning. Each of these ultimately begs a First Cause. Friedrich von Hügel, stated that causality in both the physical and the metaphysical world begins, "God is previous."

12

Great art transports the percipient to an appreciation that is both emotional and intellectual. The emotion that art engenders, however, must be grounded in reason, else art transports on a rudderless ship. Untamed emotion, coupled with natural instincts, inevitably results in shipwreck. Spiritual health requires that emotions be directed toward an objective which transcends self-indulgence. Art for art's sake, or beauty resting only in the eye of the beholder, denies objective truth, that is, a *raison d'etre*. Without objective truth, art transports on a ship lacking an ultimate destination. The percipient must then construct existential value, if, in fact, living only for the moment can be termed valuable.

13

No two lives are the same. Thus, loneliness is intrinsic to the human condition. None can walk in the place of another. Human empathy stops short at the point where experience is singular. It is true that human understanding and appreciation are vital to human relationships, and that some are more able to empathize than others, however, no two lives are the same.

Twenty odd years ago I was separated from my two small children. It was a painful time. I doubt that even death brings greater anguish than I felt over that loss. Weeks afterward I was one evening in the company of a friend who had earlier suffered a similar experience. I longed for commiseration; a kindred spirit with whom I could find understanding and healing. As I spoke of my anguish, and shared my most intimate feelings, an insidious realization came. My friend was not as sensitive as I had hoped. In fact, his concern seemed riveted on his own life, and I concluded that his willingness to listen was a contrivance that would obligate me to hear his tribulation. I left feeling doubly wounded.

The early twentieth century American writer, Sherwood Anderson, gave a superb illustration of this in his novel, *Winesburg, Ohio*. Enoch Robinson, a young man from Winesburg takes an apartment in New York city and enrolls in art school. His passion for art results in many lonely hours of painting and studying.

As weeks turn to months Enoch feels a growing need to share his passion. He invites other artists to visit, but grows frustrated as he discovers that their responses to his paintings fail to touch the essence of his spirit. His loneliness is intensified.

Finally, he meets a young woman, and in the tenderness of their relationship, he tells her of his art. Enoch explains, "I began to tell her ... about everything that meant anything to me... I talked and talked and then, all of a sudden, things went to smash. A look came into her eyes and I knew she did understand....I was furious. I couldn't stand it. I wanted her to understand but, I....couldn't let her understand. I felt that then she would know everything, that I would be submerged, drowned out, you see. That's how it is. I don't know why."

Enoch's encounter reveals what all of us have found repeatedly to be true. As children, we trusted that parents fully knew us. Adolescence revealed otherwise. As we grew into adulthood, we assumed that some golden girl or boy would provide the perfect compliment to our lives. Experience again has revealed otherwise.

Herein lies a most wonderful irony; the singularity that provokes human loneliness also provides each of us with individual identity. Through individual difference, God has made each of us irreplaceable. Each of us is special in His sight. We are each, singular, and that provides us with a unique and special identity. Conversely, since we are unique, we cannot find the empathy we seek in another human being. Thus, the empathy for which we look can be found only in God who has shared each and all of our experiences.

14

The Reign of Terror in France in 1793 should have been a final indictment of reason as a savior.

15

Genesis 1:27

"Made in the image of God" means mankind has been given the ability to love. This love is sacrificial and exists apart from reciprocity. The source of such love is God who loves unconditionally. Having received this gift, mankind struggles in its exercise and fails to experience its fullness. Jesus was aware of human depravity and warned that mankind should "Love God with total being, and love one another," but added the qualifier "as self is loved." Loving self, then, means that man loving God is not the same as God loving man. Mankind cannot love selflessly as God is able, but rather God has recognized that human depravity precludes the purity of God's love. God's agape love for mankind exists (a) prior to man's ability to reciprocate, and (b) in spite of man's inability to reciprocate. The hell that awaits those who reject God's love is a condition where the "image of God" is no longer able to exercise love. Thus, is introduced the horror of never again being loved or being able to love.

16

Memory and recognition are wholly dependent upon the presence of design. First, something must exist in order for identification to take place. Second, the organization or arrangement of that something must have as its property, that which is constant and can be repeatedly observed. Third, that something must conform unfailingly to previous identification.

Identification of randomness (chaos) is a contradiction. Identifying randomness (chaos) is really an admission that design is absent. Thus, even the suggestion of randomness (chaos) is a confirmation of design.

17

God must be presented in relational terms, not just propositional ones.

18

"Faces"

SARA TEASDALE

People that I meet and pass
In the city's broken roar,
Faces that I lose so soon
And have never found before,
Do you know how much you tell
In the meeting of our eyes,
How ashamed I am, and sad
To have pierced your poor disguise?
Secrets rushing without sound
Crying from your hiding places —
Let me go, I cannot bear
The sorrow of the passing faces.
— People in the restless street,
Can it be, oh can it be
In the meeting of our eyes
That you know as much of me?

Paul tells in I Corinthians 2:11 that we cannot know each other exhaustively, because we cannot know each other's thoughts, desires, sensations, or beliefs unless: (a) the other person chooses to reveal such information, and (b) we have a mind and spirit capable of and willing to receive such information. Thus, we have but snapshots of even our closest loved ones. Why then are we not, ourselves, more transparent, since falsity and concealment result in alienation and loneliness?

19

There is a disturbing practice found in much modern fiction and poetry. It is the notion that expression need not be restrained by rules. As a result of the loosening of structure, both verse forms and narratives have become complicated by irregular rhythms and stream-of-consciousness. In addition, the naturalism which has colored much of the philosophy of modern art produces art forms that do not communicate, but leave meaningfulness to the reader. Suddenly the reader is confronted with literature which has no inherent meaning and writers who follow no rules. However, neither new complexity nor new philosophy needs to have a negative impact on art. Truth is not always simple, nor is communication always simplistic. Problems arise, not when literature becomes complex in its expression, but when the truth expressed is treated as modern or antiquated.

20

Logic requires being and is a contingency of being, but not all beings are logical. Most of the biological world exists apart from a sense of the logical. The existence of logic, however, demands that a non-contingent being exists, or else contingency would have to beget contingency. Whatever or whoever this non-contingent being is, the logic inherent in its being has been visited upon the contingent beings who are logical.

21

There exists a contention that men and women with advanced degrees merit a kind of reverence, and their assertions cannot be challenged by the less formally educated because the latter have not proven Pythagoras' equation. The molecular chemist can well explain the chemistry of bread, but something of admiration must be reserved for the baker. All scholarship benefits from professional criticism and laboratory verification, but it also benefits from the richness of personal experience. It is not only snobbery, but a kind of self-immolation to assert that formal epistemologies are open only to the university professor. The man who forged the steel, planted the potatoes, and dug the well has, too, a mind capable of perception. His practical experience both augments and argues his reason.

22

Government is most effective when the people seek its favor, not when it compels the people to satisfy its demands.

23

The condition of the human heart argues against a strong central government.

24

Proselytization is preferable to coercion.

25

For every action there is a Divine reaction.

26

In the midst of crises people turn to tradition and familiarity.

27

There is no objective certainty within epistemology excepting analytic propositions. Neither reason, nor empirical science rise above probabilities. Beliefs reside within probabilities. As Christians, we believe that God gave us objective truth in the form of revelation. However, material proof of this reality relies upon reason and empirical science, neither of which can be reduced to pure mathematics, the only science that deals with certainty. All physical laws (i.e. the laws of causality and non-contradiction), point to a transcendent source for their truth, but actual material demonstration is not possible. Simply, metaphysical reality transcends cognitive learning and the laws of reason and relies upon revelation for both instantiation and substantiation. Thus, we believe not only that truth exists, but that material evidence confirms something beyond the materials. That same process is an apologetic that God exists. Kant reasoned that empirical evidence reveals that which we can know, not what may really exist, but he also maintained that the empirical evidence argued for something beyond the empirical. This is the beauty of God's placing us in a sphere of probability. It allows Him to reveal that which we are able to know and that which He wishes us to know while providing us the opportunity to seek knowledge and experience the wonder of learning, and all the while, shielding us from that which is beyond our ken.

28

Argument is an assertion that reason is universally valid and truth is absolute.

29

Schopenhauer accepted Kant's explanation of reality but concluded that the noumenal could not consist of things in the plural, because for different things to exist there has to be differentiation. Differentiation can only take place in a condition where there is time and space, thus reality, in a noumenal sense, does not exist. Ultimately, this ends in Eastern philosophy's concept of monism. Schopenhauer believed that the empirical world was without meaning or purpose, and was ultimately, in itself, nothing at all. He believed that we should not be taken in by it, that we should hold it of no concern, and not let ourselves become involved in its ways. All this is astonishingly similar to Buddhist teachings that worldliness must be repudiated by being true to ourselves. Animal nature particularly symbolized worldly conditions for Schopenhauer. He was disgusted that "nature red in tooth and claw" was reality. He saw the human world rife with violence and injustice. He concluded that life is a meaningless tragedy ending in death. Individuals spend their lives as slaves to desires that offer no satisfaction. This extreme pessimism became a major influence for the art of Tolstoy, Turgenev, Chekhov, Maupassant, Maugham, Zola, Proust, Hardy, Conrad, Mann, Byron, Housman, Shaw, Beckett, Eliot, O'Neill, Joyce, Faulkner, etc. In addition, Marx, Nietzsche, Freud, Jung, Wittgenstein and Popper acknowledged Schopenhauer's influence on their thinking.

30

When adventure or suspicion invites the youth beyond the familiar, he will soon discover that the God of yon country also dwelt at his doorstep.

31

A state or agency cannot work for my happiness or health while divesting me of choices. Ironically, states and agencies were formed for the very purpose of providing choices.

32

"Now the Lord Is the Spirit, and where the Spirit of the Lord is, there is freedom." II Corinthians 3:17

God does not want adherence to the letter of the law, but obedience to the spirit of the Law (Jeremiah 7:21-23) (Matthew 22:21). There is no liberty under the "letter of the law" if the "spirit of the law" is neglected. It is true that man lives with desire and passion and is needful of checks and balances, but Jesus was emphasizing the spirit of the law when He condensed Levitical laws into two commands: love God, and treat neighbors as you treat yourself. (Psalm 51:17).

33

It is ironical that the incarnate Jesus, who is critical to Christianity, is never described physically in the Scriptures.

34

D. A. Carson suggests that modernity began in 1637 with Descartes' *Discourse on Method*. *"Cogito ergo sum"* (I think, therefore, I am) is fundamentally different from, "God is, therefore, I am." The former gave rise to modern reason and skepticism by creating a disjunction between the subject and all objects, including God.

35

Natural law itself confirms the existence of a power beyond itself, because natural law is not a cause. Miracles further confirm the existence of that power as the suspension of natural law points to an even higher law.

36

Reason appears to be a tool given by God to men who have need of testing reality. Reason confirms God, but does not prove Him. It is the great irony of the Enlightenment that reason confirms revelation, the very phenomenon that much Enlightenment philosophy meant to dispel.

37

When I suffer doubt and suspend faith, it is because my relationship with God has fallen solely to emotion as a cause rather than as an effect. God provides reason, not only for empirical study, but for faith.

38

Since the body is comprised of many independent systems that cannot operate unless all parts are fully developed, it demonstrates that systems cannot arise in their own time, i.e. a cell cannot give rise to a system, and a system cannot generate a body. This reality contradicts the Darwinistic theory of the origin of life.

39

Deconstructionism argues that there can be no specific meaning in a word and that only the writer-speaker can know the intended meaning. It is a kind of decentering. It moves focus from the text to the reader. Modernity earlier removed it from the author to the text.

Constructionism and deconstructionism are similar in that both reject objective truth. Constructionism can be understood as an existential phenomenon while deconstructionism is simply relativity. The former constructs meaning *ex nihilo*, while the latter drifts irrevocably *ad nihilo*.

40

The most accurate interpretation of truth is, at best, limited. That which I see does not always reveal that which I do not see. That reason could be left handed, sobers.

41

God is eternal and exists outside the constraints of time. Thus, it seems logical to conclude that God's decision-making does not involve or require time. Predestination must then be understood in the absence of time, not ahead of time. This confuses human intellect, which requires time to reason. Divine intelligence is omniscient and may exist in the eternal "now." This permits the assertion that God knows (present tense) outside of time what will happen, but precludes the contention that God foreknew (past tense) in time what would happen. This truth leaves mankind with the inscrutable paradox that God did not take time to elect, a conundrum beyond human ken.

42

When education emphasizes knowledge rather than character, knowledge loses its value and education loses its virtue.

43

Explaining election outside the constraints of time dispels the discordant notion that God is arbitrary. Simply, God loves, not because he weighs options, but because His love is immanent. Might this not be an explanation for election? That is, election flows out of who God is rather than what God does. Divine personality has ordained that human understanding of election be limited to our willingness to accept in totality and appreciate in part God's affirmation to Moses, "I AM WHO I AM."

44

Aristotle's Syllogism

Actuality must precede potentiality. Thus, Being must precede becoming. Thus, Being precedes becoming by logical necessity. This forms the root for the notion that God is a logically necessary being.

45

Buddha taught that one who seeks enlightenment must look inside himself for answers. This is accomplished through meditation. This principle, however, forms a contradiction. If enlightenment comes only from within, listening to the teaching of Buddha is pointless.

46

It is unspeakable comfort for Christians that their relationships never end. Thank you, Lord.

47

God does not move from place to place. He is omnipresent. That is, He is.

48

Choose friends who will stretch you. They must be of integrity and purpose. Granville Sharpe, John Newton, Edmund Burke, William Pitt, William Cowper, William Wilberforce, George Whitfield and John Thornton were friends.

49

Depersonalizing God in the form of idols places God "in time" and locates Him. This, in turn, removes one or more of the attributes of God: omniscience, omnipotence, and omnipresence. Each of these attributes inevitably necessitates the other two.

50

Will Durant is never so wrong as when he states on page 337 of Volume II, *The Story of Civilization*, "Since the organization of a religious group presumes a common and stable creed, every religion sooner or later comes into opposition with that fluent and changeful current of secular thought that we confidently call the progress of knowledge."

If Christianity is true, then knowledge is limited to the discovery of reality. The propositional and experiential truths of reality do not change. Since secular thought is never moored to transcendent, unchanging truths, it can never be termed "progressive." Progress connotes movement toward something fixed, immutable. Momentary progress in the direction of a momentary goal identifies a relative objective and divorces it from the ethos of

Christianity. If the goal is not fixed, there is no way of identifying progress.

51

The reason Jesus spoke in parables is answered in Matthew 13:10. First, He answered that revelation is only given to those who believe. This confirms that Christians have special understanding. But something equally great must not be missed here. Good analogy moves instruction to the field of common experience. Speaking in an unknown language or sharing a foreign experience precludes communication. Since there is no perfect analogy, the revelation given to believers fills the vacuum that analogy cannot completely fill.

Part of the wonder of God's Word is that Jesus anticipated language differences and communication needs and provided means that resolve the problems of idioms.

52

Socrates failed to understand the human condition when he said, "Without proper knowledge right action is impossible; with proper knowledge right action is inevitable." He also stated, "Men never do that which they know to be wrong, that is, unwise or injurious to themselves. The highest good is happiness, the highest means to it is knowledge or intelligence." This defines evil as the lack of knowledge and explains the Greek emphasis on the academy.

53

God has no potential because a simple being is actual. That is, God is not just; rather He is Justice. He does not have knowledge of the Truth; rather He is Truth.

54

Reason, when applied to understanding God, can result in reductionism. How miserable is the man who is able to explain Divinity.

55

Jonathan Edwards' analogy of the cycles of history to a wheel is superb: he likens these cycles to a wheel turning in a familiar path but never treading on the same track.

56

The details of the ceremonial observance of Passover defy contention that the Exodus did not occur.

57

Romans 8:29,30; John 10:26; John 11:25,26

God chose to love and to permit persons created in His image to have limited choice. It, of course, follows that permission can be granted only by a being whose power exceeds that of the licensee. Therefore, a created being can never have the same autonomy as that of the Creator. The granting of choice permits virtue, but it also opens the door to vice. If this condition is to have ultimate significance, disobedience must result in death. Without hell, heaven has no meaning.

58

Kant's categorical imperative recognizes that, for life to have meaning, justice must exist in a final and perfect form. Justice presupposes ethics, an ethical standard, and a judge who is omniscient and almighty. Only God qualifies for the post. Further, justice presupposes duty, evil, and penalty. Simply, God is necessary for life to be meaningful.

59

God does not arbitrate, neither is He arbitrary. Thus, election cannot be whim.

60

Art, by its nature, attempts to communicate. To the degree that it is good art, it conveys truth. Truth, by definition, is permanent and unifying. Interpretation is limited to the boundaries imposed by truth. To make any concession is to deny the possibility of perversity and misinterpretation. The "eye of the beholder" cannot be the basis for determining beauty, and interpretation cannot be the basis for determining truth.

61

The act of worship is the recognition of holiness, the submission to holiness, and the desire to experience holiness. If God loves us, then he desires that we, too, be holy. Thus, if God is holy, it follows that He desires our worship, because worshipping God ultimately results in our becoming part of God's holiness.

62

While discussing the spiritual joy embodied in art and its forms, a friend remarked, "Fiction, too, can produce joy." The reference was to sustaining joy, not sensual pleasure. He ought to have added, however, "But only if the fiction is not fictitious."

63

The sustaining pleasure of poetry or music, or any of the arts, is not sensual, even though the ear is quickened and the eye is brightened. A verse of babble, though it is alliterative, does not captivate the soul. Only when the senses inform the mind that truth is beauty is the soul elevated. Beauty rests in the recognition of truth: the truth that life is meaningful, that it has design, that it transcends the moment. The beauty resulting from this recognition dances before the mind's eye and ear as sound and sense confirm the meaningfulness of living, and pleasure is lifted soulward toward life's satisfying and complete experience.

64

Postmodernism, in spite of its denial that objective truth exists, relies upon objectivity to argue its point. Questioning the historical accuracy of either text or writer on the basis of voice rather than the actuality of the past, still demands reason, and reason both demands logic and assumes objective truth. Thus, it is illogical to make history contingent upon perspective, because the very argument supporting such a position purports to be objective. Nowhere is this contradiction more blatant than in Carroll Smith-Rosenberg's *Hearing Women's Words: a Feminist Reconstruction of History*, in the chapter "Disorderly Conduct: Visions of Gender in Victorian America." (128) Arguing that the perspectives of women have been excluded in nearly all traditional studies is much different than claiming that previous perceptions are inaccurate. She writes, "We struggled to master the skills necessary to reconstruct women's past." (128) She is not speaking of reconstruction as invention or fiction, but correction of the fallacious and misidentified. Therefore, when error is discovered, either by feminists or traditional scholarship, the error itself argues for objectivity.

As Gertrude Himmelfarb indicates in "Postmodernist History and the Flight from Fact" in her *On Looking Into the Abyss,* "It is agreed that objectifying history is impossible due to "the fallibility and deficiency of the historical record on which it is based; the fallibility and selectivity inherent in writing history; and the fallibility and subjectivity of the historian." (290) However, all historical study is an attempt to identify that which is actual (in Himmelfarb's word: fixed) and to apply identification and discovery to actual living. This requires objective detachment on the part of the historian rather than political immersion, for 'beauty in the eye of the beholder' produces an egocentricity that denies social need. T. S. Eliot stated, "The Progress of an artist is a continual self-sacrifice, a continual extinction of personality." (291)

65

The inability to know God exhaustively was perhaps demonstrated by conditions in the Garden of Eden. Adam and Eve ate food, apparently for reasons other than survival, since death had not yet been introduced. There is no earthly frame of reference for this condition. In fact, Jesus, Himself, following His resurrection, ate food that could not have had any relationship to His survival, because He had overcome death.

Since eating earthly food suggests a need to survive, it is fascinating to presume that a heavenly diet might be an experience that awaits God's eternal community where eternal life is inherent; that the joys of earth may be maintained and even heightened when a full relationship with the Creator is restored. The act of tasting food raises similar questions regarding the other senses.

To be able to personally converse with one other person and to make sense of what he or she says, the singular sound of his or her voice must be filtered from all other sounds. When I hear multiple conversations in a room while someone is speaking personally to me, it is required that I filter out the other sounds to make sense of the personal conversation.

If we are to commune with God and one another in His heaven; if we are to fellowship using our senses, it seems necessary that it take place on a personal level and that ambient distractions are filtered. Otherwise, meaningful personal communication is precluded. Surely, God provides earthly experiences that foreshadow heavenly ones, especially to demonstrate that heavenly relationships will continue to be personal, and that there will continue to be personal communions that embrace and celebrate.

Even so, this type of hearing must be very unlike God's hearing. He hears every sound simultaneously, but does so in a manner that maintains each as singular. Thus, He speaks personally to many simultaneously, and He listens personally to many simultaneously. A portion of the Creator's greatness lies in the irony that His omnipresence is intimate.

It is an exceedingly great comfort in our relationship with Him to know that we cannot exhaust His mystery or His love.

66

In the middle of the 19th century, Christians were condemned for trying to legislate an absolute morality. Now that we are a more secular society, political interest groups are trying to legislate a relative morality.

67

Pragmatism, Art And Education

Words demand definition. Communication is contingent upon mutual understanding. When differing contexts utilize similar terms, clarification is requisite. For example, pragmatism holds a far different meaning within the philosophy of Naturalism than within that of Christendom.

It is altogether logical that Naturalism defines pragmatism to be that which lends comfort and sustains survival. The Naturalist must, by definition, live in an existential world. His concern must necessarily be immediate. His efforts, because death is extinction, are either pitched toward comfort or the elimination of distress. His art, thus, is an expression that either produces sensual pleasures or suggests means of eliminating discomfort. Evidence can be found in contemporary art and entertainment. Much of music, art, and literature are centered on either self-gratification or nihilism. Pornography is made natural rather than deviant; ethics are situational rather than ordered; and drugs are recreational rather than medicinal. In a Naturalistic world, art need not communicate in a social or cultural sense, but can exist as art for art's sake, a psychological emancipation for the artist.

Within this framework a pragmatic education is simply vocational preparation with comfort as its goal. Since reality is reduced to materials, emphasis is on the acquisition of material comforts. Schools encourage students to get grades that will enable them to attend a superior university. In turn the superior university degree will permit a superior wage that will, in turn, permit a comfortable lifestyle.

Christianity, however, looks beyond immediacy and identifies prag-matism within transcendent reality. That is, survival in the present world is not critical because life is unending. Art, in this sense, cannot exist for its own sake, because it represents something beyond itself—truths and persons that are eternal.

68

No one has ever been able to say precisely what he or she intended to say, not with the tone, nor with the expression desired. The spirit, the logos, is never communicated in pure essence. Enter Jesus, who reveals Himself to us through His Word and His creation. As we study His Word and cre-ation, communication with Him gradually becomes more precise as the person of the Holy Spirit, who indwells us, enlightens and informs, and, in fact, speaks for us and gives vocabulary and expression to our desires and needs. In this way we come to know, not just the spirit of the Law, but the person of the Law. Communication, at this point, is able to reach the core of a relationship. Matthew Arnold wrote the following verse commenting on the joy found in a special human relationship. How much more when it is applied to our relationship with God:

> Only—but this is rare—
> When a belovèd hand is laid in ours,
> When, jaded with the rush and glare
> Of the interminable hours,
> Our eyes can in another's eyes read clear,
> When our world-deafen'd ear
> Is by the tones of a loved voice caress'd—
> A bolt is shot back somewhere in our breast,
> And a lost pulse of feeling stirs again.
> The eye sinks inward, and the heart lies plain,
> And what we mean, we say, and what we would, we know.
> A man becomes aware of his life's flow,
> And hears its winding murmur; and he sees
> The meadows where it glides, the sun, the breeze.
>
> And there arrives a lull in the hot race
> Wherein he doth for ever chase
> The flying and elusive shadow, Rest.

An air of coolness plays upon his face,
And an unwonted calm pervades his breast.
And then he thinks he knows
The hills where his life rose,
And the Sea where it goes.

THE BURIED LIFE
MATTHEW ARNOLD

69

Modern Christian culture, feeling a need to be politically correct, supports "traditional" values. Unfortunately, tradition relies not upon Truth, but precedent. Practice ought never to be established solely upon tradition. Consider the legal profession which attempts to establish the letter of the law as a foundation for truth. It divorces the spirit of the law from a transcendent foundation, and argues, not about the logos, but about detail and uses precedence (tradition) as its base. The Spirit of transcendent law is a person who can be known, and thus, the Spirit of His law can be learned from His Word.

70

Christianity admits to mystery, but not to contradiction. A lack of knowledge in the face of observation always produces mystery. Ironically, it is the earmark of knowing God that the more and better we know Him, the greater His mystery. The closer we approach infinitude and perfection, the greater our awareness of His magnitude and our limitation. This ought to result in reverence and humility.

71

For life to have meaning something must be defined as valuable. This cannot be done without at least two realities: God and immortality. Without eternal life, there cannot be ultimate value, and without judgment ultimate value cannot be actualized. This necessitates an eternal judge who is holy, omniscient, and omnipotent, because justice requires absolute objectivity, complete knowledge, and sovereign power.

72

Like the genius of any great artist, the inspiration of Scripture provokes a source of endless reflection. Did Paul wrestle with which "verb" to use? Might a better verb have been utilized? Or was Paul conscious that every word which came to mind resulted from God's voice so that he (Paul) made no decisions of vocabulary? If so, the role of Paul's education is called into question.

The historical record seems to place much import on Paul's classical education. The same can be applied to Moses, David, Solomon, and Luke. As well, Jewish tradition suggests that High Priests and Judges were formally educated. Prophets were so familiar with the Jewish Canon that they might be credited with law degrees. The conclusion seems to be that God carefully prepares His servants for His work.

Paul's materials are replete with his classical education and experience. The words he chose required study in a cognitive sense, and the artistry of his materials in both their logical consistency and compositional clarity provokes a beauty that transcends both random selection and rote reproduction. It seems logical to conclude that God carefully chooses His artists, and that Scripture, in fact, is the work of The Great Artist. Thus, the verbs are precise.

73
Happiness begins with gratitude and culminates in humility.

74
For the Calvinist, human desire is intrinsically evil because the effect of original sin has resulted both in a fallen will and a separation from the source of goodness. The fallen will does not desire God, but seeks egocentric gratification. Doing "good" is to behave within the framework of God's nature and desire, because God's nature is both the source of goodness and the standard by which goodness is defined. To be alienated from God is to operate under the directive of a fallen will. Thus, a fallen soul cannot do good, i.e. cannot please God, because the first impulse is self-gratification directed by an egocentric will. Real good results when behavior conforms to the will of that which is goodness, namely God. Apart from this relationship, acts of kindness and sacrifice can only be motivated by an existential morality built entirely upon human desire.

75
The beauty of a tree may be termed "sublime," "divine," "glorious," "heavenly," even "sacred," but its beauty can never be quantified. Genuine beauty transcends material form. The tree in its wholeness suggests some-

thing more than trunk, branches, and leaves. This something moves the observer to a spiritual dimension, to something pure, some notion of the ideal. The tree must be taken in its wholeness for its beauty to be meaningful. The parts ennoble the whole, but the leaf does not enlarge itself. In this sense the whole always transcends the parts. It is the notion of transcendence that provides beauty, for within this lies not transitory but ultimate, eternal beauty. Likewise, the concept of beauty, without unifying transcendence, is reduced to a celebration of sheer pragmatic materialism. Beauty at this level is but an existential construct and is ultimately reduced to the sensual.

Thus, beauty lies not in component parts but in unity. In an age of specialization, this relationship is often lost as emphasis moves from the garden to the science lab, and scholarship becomes mathematics without music. The disciplines are alienated from each other, transcendent meaning is removed, and learning is reduced to measurements. In a secular world, the final interests are mathematics and sensuality, relationships are replaced with war and isolation, and the memorialized dead are remembered with facts rather than poetry. Beauty becomes simply that which provides indulgence. The tree can only be regarded as "sublime," "divine," or "glorious," when the observer recognizes the transcendent reality beyond its material form.

76

If God's law flows from God's personality, then God's law existed eternally. The presentation of this law to Moses formalized man's sinful condition and provided a comprehensive set of rules by which man could live both eternally and existentially. (God had already identified right and wrong in the Garden, and He had earlier clarified to Abraham the way of salvation). The need for a hiatus between presentation of the law through Adam and formalization of the law through Moses is understood in analogy. Consciousness and understanding develop throughout childhood years, but responsible behavior depends upon a greater maturity. The injustice of Egypt and the trials of the Wilderness demonstrated the need for civil and spiritual laws that permitted a people to live in unity. Mosaic Law did not produce new law, but it presented old law in a new context.

77

When, following the Enlightenment, universities began rejecting revelation as an epistemology, the way was opened for liberal theologians to challenge mainstream Christianity. Unable to subject revelation to scientific testing, the God of Christianity became impersonal (Deism), the divinity of Jesus was renounced, and miracles came to be regarded as fictitious or illusory. Prior to this shift, the revealed Word of God stood preeminent to both reason and empiricism. Moral awareness resulted from religious knowledge through special revelation. Thus for a time, the most knowledgeable were believed to be the most pious. After Enlightenment philosophy took root, knowledge became morally neutral so that the more educated were believed the more able to form and regulate rules and ethics of behavior. Thus, the scientific method provided a ready and credible epistemology for secularism.

78

The observation of truth from a singular perspective cannot render a complete objective account of reality. Rather, information from multiple perspectives permits a more plausible substantiation and minimizes misconception. The application of this concept to truth identification suggests that affirmation from a second source or from multiple sources is essential to truth claims.

Two additional conclusions may be drawn from this demonstration: first, that any perspective is limited, and second, that conscious distortion of reality is mutually harmful. My value to fellowmen is that I have been given a unique and essential perspective to reality. My obligation is that I must attempt clarification of that perspective without bias or egocentricity. In short, my value is in discovering and objectifying truth, and my obligation is in demonstrating and sharing that truth.

79

Perhaps the simplest explanation for the relationship between truth, love, and beauty lies within the reality that love is beautiful only if it is true. That is, there is no beauty unless the proposition "I love you" contains truth. Each of these properties is personified in God's attributes. He cannot be other than who He is; therefore, the three attributes cannot be separated. That is, God cannot be truthful and unloving, or loving and unbeautiful, or beautiful and untruthful.

80

God is the source of all propositional truth. The statement, "I like eggs for breakfast" is true; however, it is not a propositional statement. It is an experiential statement. Truth, as a philosophical-theological category, is a metaphysical concept and does not rely upon human experience. Just as God is a Necessary Being, so truth and all of God's attributes necessarily exist. In this sense His attributes are analogous to a triangle. Neither God nor a triangle can be otherwise.

81

The Christian philosopher, Alvin Plantinga, argues that Naturalism entails the tenet that behavior causes belief, because unguided natural selection chooses not what is true or right, but what is most adaptive. If so, Darwinism must treat beliefs as bio-chemical products, invisible in the natural selection process, and merely the result of chance.

82

In *Meditations,* Rene Descartes argues that it is impossible that anything can create something greater than itself out of its own resources. If Descartes is right, then the Darwinian argument for survival of the fittest dissolves.

83

The process of thinking appears to demand freedom of the will regardless of whether the thought is moral or immoral. Conceding that all thinking human beings rise above conditioned responses, and that moral decisions depend upon free will, it may then be argued that where thinking exists free will is required. Thinking cannot logically conjoin total determinism. It is true that Romans 8 affirms determinism at some level for all humans. This paradox suggests that human beings experience limited free will, the exercise of which rests within divine parameters. The coalescence of these inscrutable contrarieties, perhaps, is evidence of and explained only by Divine personality.

84

Love has its ontology in the person of God. Thus, love predates creation.

Love, by its nature, requires an object. Thus, two or more beings are necessary for love to exist.

Thus, there had to be multiple persons prior to creation. The theological assertion that God is love could not be true without the Trinitarian relationship described in Christian Scripture.

85

Teaching religion in the public square when the public square is subsidized by the government violates the constitution, because it permits the state to impose itself and its religion upon citizens. But what becomes of religious instruction when the private sector is operated by the state, such as may be found in government sponsored housing projects? On January 3, 1922, Lenin banned the teaching of religion to children in the private home. His, of course, was a totalitarian regime imposed upon a communist state. Could not, however, a constitutional government, having control of the private sector, issue the same mandate?

This will happen when a people has ceded its liberty, not to government, but to self-indulgence.

86

Religion loses its significance when it loses epistemological credibility. If, however, religion reveals truth, it must not be banned from the public forum of ideas, for its absence removes the signpost on which is written the significance of epistemology.

87

Probability may only be applied to possibility.

88

Perception requires that a perceived object is so ordered that it has an identifiable intelligent arrangement. Likewise, the percipient requires intelligence to identify the object. Thus, both the percipient and the object of perception involve intelligence. This poses an obstacle for the naturalist: intelligence involves information, and information requires both an informer and a medium. One cannot exist without the other. Intelligence cannot evolve as a product of the Darwinian process because both its arrangement and the arranger must be simultaneously present. It is tantamount to irreducible complexity as described in Michael Behe's *Darwin's Black Box*. Intelligence exists in the same way that love exists. There must concurrently be a lover and an object of love.

89

For the Christian, existential doubts regarding God's existence are remedied with reading, research, and reflection. A few hours of Bible study contemplating and confirming the death and resurrection of Jesus should reposition the feet upon substantial ground.

90

There is no new information. The first law of thermodynamics, which applies to the physical world, may be applied here to metaphysical reality. Information can neither be created nor destroyed. The learning process is simply to discover what already exists. Marvelously, for those who love learning, the author of information is Himself an inexhaustible supply of learning and promises an eternity of delight as we abide in Him.

91

Immanuel Kant, in his *Critique of Pure Reason*, alleges that God cannot be known. He contends that to know something with certainty, reason and empirical science must be able to demonstrate it. Kant considers revelation as a third kind of epistemology, but rejects it outright because it cannot be verified by scientific methodology. Revelation, for him, was not a demonstrable epistemology.

Thus, for Kant to know God would require that science and/or reason be able to prove His ontology. However, neither method is equipped to validate transcendent or immaterial being. Empirical science runs aground because it is limited to physical reality, and reason is impotent to explain the miraculous.

It is important to note that Kant never argues that God does not exist. In fact, he asserts in *Critique of Practical Reason* that there are categorical imperatives (moral duties that transcend human imperatives) necessary for living. He only introduces the dilemma that there is no epistemological access to God, because epistemology is limited to science and reason.

Herein lies an irony. Kant's syllogism that we cannot know God depends upon knowledge which transcends science and reason. Further, his attempt to present a logical, coherent discourse relies upon his belief in the laws of logic, laws whose existence cannot be established by either reason or science.

Kant's error is not trivial, but his failure to investigate fully the empirical history of Jesus Christ, who claimed to be God incarnate, and to overlook God's revelation in the documented history of the Old Testament, is egregious. If Jesus was an historical reality, and if God performed observable wonders, then science and reason can be employed to satisfy at least some of His claims, especially those surrounding His resurrection.

If the claim of Jesus that He was God is validated by His resurrection, then God satisfied man's epistemological dilemma by providing reasonable and empirical proof that, not only does God exist, but that He can be known personally in the being of Jesus.

92

There is no greater irony or madness than finding delight in God's non-existence.

93

Imagination is the best transportation.

94

Before reason can be utilized, it must be assumed that it is functional. It is with this faith that reason is first employed. Thus, it is the irony of ironies to attempt to jettison faith with the employment of reason.

95

As do many others, Bart Ehrman, the skeptic from the University of North Carolina, contends that he was once a Christian. Such a claim introduces a conundrum. Since being a Christian necessarily involves having a personal relationship with Jesus, Bart cannot argue that Jesus did not exist or that Jesus is not divine. First, it is obviously foolish to claim that someone known personally does not exist. Bart might claim to have hallucinated or dreamt, but he cannot rationally maintain that he had, for that interval, a genuine relationship with Jesus. Second, if Bart knew Jesus personally and knew that Jesus was not divine, why did Bart worship a man who was a pretense? Logic refutes the claim of anyone who insists that he or she was once a Christian, but came to realize either that Jesus was not God or that Jesus never existed.

96

Secularism argues against any ultimate hope and attempts to find pleasure in the moment, but it is a preposterous deception and perversion to assert pleasure can be experienced in the face of ultimate hopelessness. It is the reason that Eugene O'Neill, the American playwright, stated that the best possible condition was to be stupified by drink or drugs and to die in that stupifaction, oblivious to ultimate despair.

97

Solomon stated correctly in Ecclesiastes that "All is vanity." However, vanity does not preclude virtue. My every impulse begins with vanity, but God can, by His grace, use a surrendered vanity and assimilate my narrow self into His unbounded kingdom. Thus, my life is His continuing miracle as He turns into gold my life of straw.

98

"There is nothing so annoying as a good example!"

MARK TWAIN

The person who refuses to cheat or lie, who looks us in the face is never popular because his/her virtue reveals our sinful state. Sadly, it is this sinful condition that inhibits us from appreciating and accepting God's special revelation. Renouncing pride, false as it is, leaves us naked before both God and fellowmen. Accepting Christ and His personal revelation demands that we accept God's sovereignty and admit our ineptitude. We then can participate in the glorious epistemology that results from God directly revealing to us His word, His world, and His Self.

99

God is a person, and, as such, can only be known "personally." That is, general revelation permits us to know about Him, but special revelation provides a full relationship. We may speculate that eternal communion with the triune God will be a learning experience and process, because, in the analogies he has provided for us (i.e. marriage, etc.) there is the suggestion that we continually grow. Scripture tells us that eternal living will be experiential, thus, we will be constantly growing. Knowledge of God transcends space and time, so that when we learn (appreciate) more of His attributes and more recognize His Glory and more realize His love from unbridled motive, we will find our experience in a dimension not explicable to a mind and soul that is now limited to a corporal frame.

100

If the Genesis account is true in any literal sense, then God breathed into Adam the breath of life. That is, Adam's body, which is mentioned first, was inanimate. When God imparted soul-life to the body, it became animate. This lends credence to the substance-dualist theory that states the soul is an ontological reality, different from the brain, but dependent upon the brain to carry out some of its functions. At death, the soul departs and the body becomes inanimate. Thus God, through the soul, animates the body.

101

Pain is evidence that something matters.

102

God displays His revelation in a variety of forms that include music, art, and propositions. Music and art rely upon the imagination to communicate truths, but truths stated propositionally rely principally upon verbal language and reason.

If Scripture is inspired, then the language of Scripture is affected by inspiration. God's revelation utilizes various forms of communication and takes into account human epistemological limitations, but reason demands that truth is stated in verbal propositions. Thus, verbal language is a necessary property of God's inspired Word. Scripture is, therefore, displayed in language rather than in music or in art because reason must be employed. It is the rudder that steers the ship. Reason is a property of God, just as goodness, love, and beauty are properties. God is the logos, the Word, the truth.

God is the source of truth and communicates His truths through both imagination and reason, but reason, in the form of propositional truth, places necessary limitations on imagination and its forms.

103

The laws of Causality may move us toward determined ends, but the Law of Non-Contradiction requires conscious behavior. Information accumulated by the senses is nothing more than stimuli recorded in the brain. Meaning and the application of meaning are mind tasks not brain tasks and involve something greater than the chemical materials comprising the brain.

104

The laws of logic and the laws of physics are absolute, determined laws. They introduce inevitable ends. They may, in fact, provide an explanation for predestination, election, and the mysteries of Divine personality. The paradox lies in the reality that while this determinism moves us toward Divinity's ultimate purpose, the application of knowledge requires freedom so that predestined activity is altogether compatible with free activity.

105

If we are moral beings, it follows that God has given us the freedom to make choices since choice lies at the very heart of morality.

106

Getting to know a person requires revelation, that is, it requires that the person reveals himself/herself. Empirical science and reason permit us to know about someone. They tell where a person is, how tall he is, how many arms he is holding up. They may be able to tell if he is angry, compassionate, cold, or wet. But they do not permit us to know what he is thinking, why he feels shame or guilt, or what he believes. If the soul is a reality, then a person is an embodied soul or, in the case of God, an unembodied mind. To know someone beyond physical recognition requires that souls communicate, and since the essential person is not material, this must be done by revelation. If Naturalistic conclusions regarding cognitive learning are applied to persons, then the soul does not exist and a person's spiritual qualities are simply products of the brain. Thus, we can only know about each other. If Kant was right that God cannot be known, because He is noumenal, the same must be applied to the soul. We cannot know one another, because Kant recognized only two epistemologies (Reason and empirical science), and neither is able to deal with the soul. Person to person communication requires revelation on the part of at least one person.

107

Descartes's *Discourse on the Method of Rightly Conducting One's Reason, and Seeking Truth in the Sciences* compels the conclusion that plausibility, not certainty, must be the end of argument. Descartes's accepted that the only trustworthy reality that consciousness establishes is that mind exists, though it may exist only within a "vat of

chemicals." This produced an unwieldy skepticism that made function impossible. Thus, when he analyzed epistemology, he accepted
the intuitive knowledge that he existed, but dismissed reason as unre-
liable, because the data being processed by reason was the product of
the senses and could not be attached to certainty. Further, his rejection of reason was contradicted when he used reason as the basis for
his conclusions. His repudiation of sensation is intriguing, because it
was impossible for his experiment to be conducted without the use
of his senses. In order to eat, bathe, dress, visit neighbors, etc., it was
obviously necessary to trust his senses of seeing, hearing, smelling,
touching, and tasting.

108

Jesus said to him, "Why do you call me good? No one is good except
God alone." (Mark 10:18)

If God is the Good Himself, then the Good is not an abstraction but a
person of substance embodied in Jesus Christ. Just as the nature of water is
to be discovered in the water, not in our conception of water, so Goodness
is to be experienced in a personal relationship with God, not in an intellectual understanding of the abstraction.

"Can I claim… that if it is good to admire or love x, that is because x
resembles God in a certain way? I do mean to claim that." (Robert Mer-
rihew Adams, *Finite and Infinite Goods*)

109

Much of education comes in the form of another man's perspective.
His interpretation of reality informs our own. His conclusions reveal our
ideas to be either gold or dross. Discover where he is right. Discover where
he is wrong. But, above all, value his criticism.

110

The Age of Reason was a direct product of the Protestant Reformation.
Rome had long dictated her dogma to an illiterate and uninformed popu-
lace. Gutenberg and Luther changed that. Luther stated he could not accept
the tenets of Rome unless they complied with reason and the Scriptures.
The appeal of Protestantism was that it provided individual liberty to think
and act. In fact, it paved the way for the American Experiment.

Lamentably, it also paved the way for an emphasis on self-reliance and transcendentalism. In a fallen world such liberty fathered rebellion on the earth and in the heavens, against both civil and transcendent law.

The American Revolution was the child of the Protestant Reformation, as was the French Revolution. In spite of human depravity and its perversions, inquiry, criticism, and scholarship owe much to Luther's rebellion because it underscored the human right to determine as an individual what Scripture and reason affirm as truth.

111

The church was never designed to be a physical institution (Matthew 18:20: *Wherever two or more are gathered in my name*), but it was from inception an invisible body whose sole head was the risen Christ. Therefore, it logically follows that a political-religious magistrate has no office within a spiritual institution other than shepherding since Christ is the lone intercessor-governor. Christ alone provides the benefits of membership.

Ephesians 4 demands unity within the church (body of Christ). The divorce between Roman Catholicism and the Reformed faiths can be explained as an attempt to establish the church as a physical institution. This may have resulted from doctrinal misunderstanding, but more probably from private and tendentious interpretation.

112

The imprint of an immaterial being on a material world must have empirical residue or else the existence of the immaterial being may logically be doubted.

113

Deductive logic equips reason with empirical evidence for inductive application.

114

Neo-Darwinists claim that living systems give the appearance of having been designed. Nevertheless, they regard that appearance as entirely illusory. This presents a contradiction in practice. If it is true that the appearance is illusory then it follows that observation is not trustworthy. Experiencing the mirage of a pool of water in the middle of a highway is, in fact, illusory. It differs, however, from the appearance of design in living systems because it can be tested and proven a mirage. In real life, however, scientists rely upon the reality of the design in order to practice science, asking that their observations be accepted as truth. Thus, Neo-Darwinists, by their practice, contradict their philosophy.

115

If sensory perception can be altogether explained by Darwinism (which it has not yet done), reason posits a more difficult and complex phenomenon. From where comes the ability to compare, contrast, assimilate, apply, criticize, love, hate, enjoin, abstain, etc.? If these are brain-states only, where is the physical location of love, hate? In addition, blind, indifferent chance must be ruled out as a facilitator, because both love and hate have defined patterns.

Beyond perception and reason, a third dimension, consciousness, presents an even greater difficulty for the Darwinian model. And, if consciousness can be reduced to the physical operation of a material brain, it remains that an explanation for cognition must be linked to the same brain. Certainly, perception depends upon reason for application, and reason requires consciousness; however, even consciousness fails to explain self-consciousness, 3rd person awareness, or the reason something that has not yet happened will please, anger, placate, or frustrate.

116

Christian testimonies are most effective when Christians are being the best they can be—as lawyers, athletes, students, parents, etc. Christians should be motivated to be the best, because the Christian life is a form of worship.

117

Darwinists have sold the world a bill of goods including the notion that the brain is a repository for knowledge and a neuro-electrical system that determines intelligence. The theory is a product of a materialistic world-view. If it is so that the brain contains the bio-chemical apparatus that produces thought and records knowledge, then the death of the brain makes both personal knowledge and personal intelligence temporal. Such a claim is antithetical to Christianity. With that perspective, when Jesus, on the cross, promised the thief next to him "Today you shall be with me in Paradise," Jesus was well aware that the thief's brain would, in a few hours, be both non-functional and non-existent.

Thus, it follows, if Christianity is true, and if the thief went to be with Jesus after his physical death, then, either the thief's identity was something more than brain matter or the thief's identity was lost. The fact is, however, that Jesus spoke to a being whose identity was inextricably bound to a personal pronoun. "'You' shall be with me in Paradise." Thus, identity could not cease. This, deductively, leaves one option – there is something beyond the material brain that is the seat of knowledge and the conductor of intelligence.

A relationship with God demands that essence not be limited to materials, because God is not material. As He is a person, so is a human being a person. Personal identity transcends a material brain and body. Clearly, Jesus taught that a human person is an embodied soul, that the soul has compartments, and that the compartments are eternal. One of those divisions is the mind, a non-material essence that sets apart human kind from other forms of life, because the mind is stamped with the "image of God."

118

Imagination, as a human property, is a faculty that operates outside of reality, a gift of God, no doubt, but one limited to anticipation and theory. Imagination does not reveal. It evidences a lack of knowledge and an unwillingness to accept circumstance. It does not exist as a divine property, because God is omniscient, that is, God knows all propositional truths. There is nothing about which He can imagine.

119

The question whether to attend a Christian or secular school entertains issues of free thought and free inquiry. Secularism assumes that an institution can present information void of religious bias, moral coloration or intentionality, and that, in doing so, students can be open-minded and able to choose behavior most advantageous for both themselves and their fellowmen. Such a position presumes that a student can determine for himself how knowledge is meaningful, where and when it is best applied, and what its ends should be. It further maintains that information can be presented with neutrality, and that the recipient is capable of assigning relevance to the information. It does not explain from where the moral framework comes that permits the student to differentiate between good and evil, virtue and vice.

Christianity teaches that the heart is deceitful and desperately wicked, and its first impulse is egocentric. Thus, from this point of view, until moral restraint is imposed, selfish behavior is the norm. Further, the moral register that identifies good and evil has been supplied by a transcendent God who has personally entered human history and provided explanation and guidance. Christian educators argue that this register is a necessary filter through which knowledge must be disseminated and by which the parameters of free thought and moral choice must be exercised.

Secular humanism disagrees, arguing that history is replete with demonstrations of social and scientific benefits and improvements made without reference to religion or to religion's god. However, free choice without the imposition of moral parameters begs a myriad of questions: What is obscenity? What is virtue? How should conflict be resolved? Is there never a need for indoctrination? Can freedom exist without parameters? What provides the rudder for this ship at sea?

A Christian education begs questions as well. Should students be taught what to think as well as how to think? If education requires a moral filter and if morality is dependent upon transcendent law, then education requires religious instruction. Is this not a type of indoctrination? When does a child become capable of distinguishing truth? If it is by degree, is there a time when a student is fully capable of apprehending knowledge objectively?

120

If Kant is correct that there is a moral law written within, then' conscience finds its directives within the concept "made in the image of God." Conscience may be divinely programmed, but it is a divine guide only so long as it is in communion with a divine source.

121

"At the sound of the trump the dead in Christ will rise." I Corinthians 15:52

This will be a bodily resurrection. Jesus's resurrection is the prototype, confirmed in several New Testament books by different writers.

A bodily resurrection seems necessarily to involve a new creation. (1) Since the elements comprising DNA acids, molecules, cells, tissues, etc., decompose at death and return to elements, there would have to be a regrouping of the specific atoms of the particular elements that composed the original body if it is to be restored. However, the cells that form any organic material are continually dying and being replaced so that it cannot be stated that any particular cell comprises any particular body for the lifetime of that body. (2) Regrouping seems impossible because the atoms that once were a part of A's body, through the cycles of life and death, ultimately are recycled through the bodies of innumerable later generations of plants and animals. Thus, using any particular atom of any particular element to reconstitute A's body at the resurrection of the saints would require that it not be a part of any organic thing.

When Christ raises me with an eternal body, that body must be fashioned ex nihilo, because the original elements are: (a) imperfect, (b) functioning as another person's body, or (c) in a non-human state. Without an ex nihilo rebirth the materials that will comprise my heavenly body will have to come from existing organic human, plant, and animal bodies, or, from inorganic material. A miracle similar to the one Christ experienced in His resurrection will perfect my eternal body.

122

Reason, unlike material organisms, cannot be explained by particle physics. Something latent that cannot be material had to exist from the beginning, or else metaphysical realities, such as reason, would have had to evolve as organisms reached certain levels of complexity. There is neither evidence nor explanation for this.

123

Too much of the time the Christian community is convinced that secular sources have reliable data which undermines and even disproves the Biblical account of reality. It is not so and underscores the need for Christians to be familiar with the Bible, history, and science. There is much difference in secular and Christian interpretations of reality, but no actual empirical data contradicts the Christian world-view. In fact, there are many scientists, both secular and Christian, who are convinced that the secular naturalistic model fails because it relies upon chance as the apparatus that determines survival. Such a mechanism removes intentionality, free will, and reason and eliminates morality. It also throws into question whether any conclusions are reliable since they are the product of chance.

"When we go back far enough, to the origin of life—of self-replicating systems capable of supporting evolution by natural selection—those actually engaged in research in the subject recognize that they are very far from even formulating a viable explanatory hypothesis of the traditional materialist kind. Yet they assume that there must be such an explanation, since life cannot have arisen purely by chance." ...

"In fact, that assumption may be based on a confusion. In an important 2013 paper, MIT atheist Roger White (admits) that the search for an explanation of the origin of life in terms of the nonpurposive principles of physics and chemistry—an explanation that will reveal that the origin of life is not merely a matter of chance but something to be expected, or at least not surprising—is probably motivated by the sense that life can't be a matter of chance because it looks so much as though it is the product of intentional design. But the hypothesis of intentional design is ruled out as unscientific. So it seems natural to conclude that the only way left for life not to be a matter of chance is for it somehow to be made likely by physical law. But as White points out, this inference is illegitimate. Here is what he says: "The line of reasoning ... is something like the following. That molecular replicating systems appear to be designed by an agent is sufficient to convince us that they didn't arise by chance. But in scientific reasoning, non-intentional explanations are to be preferred, if possible, to intentional ones—hence the motivation to find a non-intentional explanation of life. (Thomas Nagel, *Mind and Cosmos*)

124

Feelings, properly experienced, are the product of propositional truths. Otherwise, feelings result from mere sensation and lack the control of reason.

125

Ultimately there can be only one source of authority. If one universal "ought" exists, then God is a necessary being.

126

God's Word should control the lives of His people. When the Holy Spirit vivifies the human conscience through knowledge of Scripture and/or personal revelation, gratitude impels the Christian to live within a sphere where choice is ceded to a Holy God whose decisions and desires are entirely benefitting.

Human response to this vivification cannot be explained within human agency. That is, the embracement of this gift cannot be explained within human disposition, because all human disposition is egocentric. Rather, human election to espouse God's will depends upon a transcendency that employs metaphysical laws of an entirely spiritual nature.

In the opposing sphere, free will is, perhaps, the capacity to reject that which is wholly determined by spiritual realities. That capacity may be limited to non-Christians. For the Christian, free will is yielded to the determinism of a transcendent determiner.

127

If truth, by its very nature, must necessarily be couched in propositions, then language becomes the nexus of salvation. Further, reference to the Word in John 1:1 is amplified. If thought is the father of proposition, and thought relies upon language for the formation and exercise of its propositions, then the greatest potential for clarity, accuracy, and eloquence lies with the linguist most capable, most skilled, and most artistic.

Deductively, the inability to facilitate language restricts both the expression and understanding of truth. Thus, it behoves Christians to study language, its grammar, its syntax, and its poetry, in order to become the most effective witness of God's image: His mind, His word, His truth.

128

"God shows his love for us in that while we were still sinners, Christ died for us." (Romans 5:8)

This verse, along with Ephesians 5:33 and I Peter 3, puts to rest the notion that love and respect must be earned. Rather, it is part of the greatest commandment: "You shall love the Lord your God with all your heart and with all your soul and with all your mind. And a second is like it: You shall love your neighbor as yourself." (Matthew 22:37-39)

Human beings are created "in the image of God." As such, they are intrinsically valuable and should be loved and respected.

129

Cognitive learning is two-headed. That is, it requires both deductive and inductive experience. A child learns to avoid touching a hot object. The learning experience is deductive. Afterward, he avoids a similar experience. The avoidance is an inductive application. He may, through inadvertence or coercion, repeat the touch, but what he has learned permits him to avoid choosing the hot object a second time. Thus, cognitive learning has no application unless choice exists.

130

Scripture tells that God is three unembodied persons, capable of both creation and incarnation. Further, Scripture assures that God created embodied human beings and endowed them with God likenesses. Properties stamped upon these creatures existed in the First Cause, and since God is necessarily immaterial, eternal, immutable, etc., the images stamped upon human beings were not physical. Rather, God's image is displayed in consciousness, emotion, thought, belief, desire, will, etc.

One of the emotions inherent in His image is agape love. God gifted His human creatures with the capacity to love as He loves; agape love, a love that is sacrificial and benefitting to others. Amongst all God's creatures, agape loving is unique to human beings. Of course, both human and non-human creatures can experience friendship, sex, and loyalty, but only agape love is part of the endowment that sets human beings apart from other creatures. Through common grace God has given each human being a taste of heaven, namely, the capacity to love holiness, truth, beauty, and goodness. In other words, human beings have the capacity to love God and His attributes. These attributes exist nowhere apart from God and flow only through human beings made in His image.

In addition, these attributes are dynamic, functioning things, flowing moment by moment from the common grace of a loving God. If human beings were to be separated from the source of love, then holiness, truth, beauty, and goodness would disappear. The result would be complete depravity: holiness replaced by evil, truth by perversion, beauty by deformity, and goodness by malevolence. The result would be the hell described in

Scripture. It is a most wonderful irony that God's command to love Him and the human beings He has created results, not in the hell of self-servitude, but in the liberty of love.

131

It is nearly impossible, if, in fact, it is not altogether impossible, to offer homiletic advice, or suggest moral direction, or post warnings of discretion, without recognizing transcendent duty. It is either, "Because I said so," or "because He said so." The first is mortal construct; the second immortal charge.

132

The authority of the Roman Church finds its basis both in the Scriptures and in the Canon of its traditions. The Church cannot claim that the Canon and Scripture have separate authors because that would involve two Gods, a contradiction in terms. Further, they are forced to argue that there are no contradictions between the two sources. Although Ephesians 2:8,9; Romans 4:5; I Timothy 2:5; Revelation 22:18,19 seem clearly to be contradictions, they have been rationalized in tomes of canon that Ockham's razor can no longer penetrate.

The Council of Trent recognized these contradictions and reacted accordingly, mandating that the interpretation of Scripture had been heretofore completed by the clergy, and it was hereafter anathema for criticism or change. Thus, the Council made correction of error impossible, but in so doing saved Roman Catholicism from the Protestant Reformation.

133

Taking another's time is abusive unless it contributes to his welfare. Not being on time violates the second commandment: love your neighbor as you love yourself.

134

Propositional statements must be about something. That is, something had to exist prior to the logical statement about it. The logic may be aboriginal, but the statement cannot be. If God's rules are aboriginal, then they had to exist prior to being stated.

135

Since truth exists, it follows that God necessarily exists. This conclusion is unavoidable because there are only two possibilities for the authorship of truth: God and man. It cannot be man because it removes a universal application. Therefore, if anything is true, God necessarily exists.

136

Laws are descriptions of phenomena. The phenomena are active, alive. If laws make God necessary, then the activity ascribed to them is God actively, second by second, at work.

137

The Law of Causality is demonstrable and overwhelming evidence that there is intentionality to life. This argues against accidental genesis and forms a compelling apologetic for the reality of God and immortality.

138

Every normal human being experiences the presence of oughts: his sense of justice tells him he ought to practice fairness; his guilt tells him that evil exists and he ought to abstain from its practice; his fear of rejection declares that he ought to treat his fellowman as he wishes to be treated. Immanuel Kant stated that, if justice exists, it must exist in the omniscient consciousness of an almighty transcendent being in the hereafter, because it is obviously absent in this life. He would have agreed with the Christian explanation. God said, "Let us make man in our own image." The image includes the duty to be obedient to Holiness.

Conversely, if God does not exist, these psychological reactions to realities must be explained some other way. Rousseau believed the oughts are constructs instilled by society to suppress the individual. Freud decided they are crutches devised in our youth to provide a heavenly security blanket. Darwin suggested they are chemical reactions in the brain attributed to the effects of an evolving material process. For all three, oughts are relative, evolving through the Darwinian mechanism of natural selection and driven by chance, an instrument incapable of reason. Ironically, each had to borrow the Judeo-Christian concept of absolute morality in order to establish an ethic that would explain personal and social oughts. This creates the contradiction that the only way to free mankind from the repressive oughts of an absolute morality is to establish another absolute ought.

139

In a pluralistic world freedom is desirable only if objective goodness exists. Jesus said as much in the Golden Rule (Matthew 7:12). Without virtue freedom becomes anarchy.

140

FINAL OBSERVATION

Please, please, study God's Word. There is no other resource so important that provides so clear an explanation of the Gospel message. Find out from God Himself how to be saved from the curse of sin. Neither materials, nor popularity, nor education can save. Neither personal philosophy, nor worldly wisdom, nor the church has saving power.

Logic reveals that there can be only one ultimate truth, only one ultimate authority. That authority is God, and God's explanation for getting to Heaven is, of course, found in His Word. Ephesians 2:8,9 and Romans 4:5 clearly states works will fall short. Romans 3:10-12 warns that we cannot, through our own efforts, please God who is Holy. It is God's grace supplied at Calvary that alone buys us entrance to eternal communion with God and one another. Please, please I want more than anything to spend eternity with you.

Printed in the United States
By Bookmasters